The Covenant of Peace

The Covenant of Peace

A Liberation Prayer Book

by The Free Church of Berkeley

Compiled by

John Pairman Brown

and

Richard L. York

Morehouse-Barlow Co.
New York

Preface

A traditional formula determines what the prayer
book of any community should contain: *lex orandi
lex credendi*, the rule of faith is the rule of
prayer. The only standard of our prayer book must
be the standard of our commitment. As the bleeding
witnesses to peace and liberation multiply, we feel
an overwhelming urgency once again, for our time,
to put together texts that will point a wandering
Church back toward its Pole Star. We can't help it
if the message we're committed to is the two-edged
sword of the God who is a consuming fire. We are
in conscience bound to warn users that they are
playing with fire; but also that in the end we will
all, whether by a decisive act or by repeated inde-
cision, fall into the hands of the living God.

This is a prayer book for all those groups, in America and elsewhere, committed by their Gospel and the
needs of the planet to the struggle for peace, justice, and environmental renewal. It has been prepared by one of those groups, the Free Church of
Berkeley, in large part out of words we heard on the
street. Men who are neither hot not cold sometimes
ask us, "Are you a Christian group or another radical political group?" We are unwilling to say
that we are the Church as distinguished from the
struggle; we are unwilling to say that we are another political group. One purpose of this book is
to challenge the legitimacy of that question.

The Church of all our groups is one with no national
headquarters, budget, or membership rolls; it is a
movement inside the Churches and inside something
where the Spirit first stirred in our decades--the
Movement. The existing structure to which both of
us in the Free Church happen to sit lightly is the
Episcopal Church. This Liberation Prayer Book ob-
viously stands in some relation to the work of
Thomas Cranmer. In *The Living Church* of 2 June
1968, one of us (Jock Brown) criticized the attempts
of the Episcopal Church to update Cranmer. At that
time we were challenged to do better; here, with
complicated emotions, is our response.

Like Cranmer, we are living in an age of revolution.
He came down on the side of encapsulating the Church
into a hierarchic, mercantile society. We have

thrown in our lot on the side (which we believe to be the side of the prophets and Gospel) of supporting and humanizing the revolution. We are not concerned to argue here whether expensive church edifices should stand and be filled on Sundays with affluent worshippers. We are very much concerned, so long as the edifices and worshippers exist, to offer them a specimen of what they ought to be doing and saying.

Cranmer had the supreme advantage of living when the English tongue came to full maturity--partly of course as a result of the Reformation, which he helped to build. Still he went wrong in two ways (much more so his bowdlerizers after him): he did not print the right selection of biblical texts in his book and he interpreted wrongly the ones he did print. As a result, his effort to free the English church from an authoritarian religious hierarchy ended in putting the church to work for an authoritarian secular government; he had only exchanged one false master for another. Two excuses can be made for him. First, biblical scholarship had not opened to him the true historical figure of Jesus or the prophets; second, he was too remote to hear the contemporary people's reformation, which did grasp those figures through insight into its own world. Neither excuse is available to people who want to go on using Cranmer's work today.

The understanding of the Bible, of history, and of the current crisis which we presuppose has been stated in his own way by Jock Brown in *The Liberated Zone: A Guide to Christian Resistance* (John Knox Press, 1969). Its working out in an actual youth congregation has been the twenty-four hour job of Dick York for the past three and one-half years. The network of Movement churches--also supported mostly by young people--that have sprung up across the country like mushrooms after rain is recorded in the quarterly issues of *Win With Love: A Directory of the Liberated Church in America* (Free Church Publications, Box 9177, Berkeley, California 94709).

Our revision of liturgical tradition begins with the title. The second half of our Bible calls itself a "New Covenant," a phrase taken from Jeremiah by Paul, and applied to the worship of his scattered communities. But what makes the covenant new is the fact that it carries personal fulfilment, social liberation, and environmental renewal. And so *Ezekiel* 34:25 announces it as a "covenant of peace,"

berith shalom. Our decision to enter the covenant
is an act of "choosing life" rather than death
(*Deuteronomy* 30:19), a phrase which George Wald
has bound on us all. That choice is made possible
when the Power of history at the right time breaks
through our stubbornness and puts the spirit of the
Liberator in our hearts, saying "Abba Father" (*Galatians* 4:6). This book is built around those three
texts.

"From the masses to the masses." We have used that
maxim from the *Little Red Book* of Mao Tze Tung in
putting together this handbook for the Green Revolution. In all important respects it is user-developed from inside the Movement. Nearly everything
has been tried and revised in the Free Church of
Berkeley; much of the material records oral improvisation from our people. Our rubrics are not
legislation but description of what actually has
been done. Throughout we have done our best to find
out what people wanted to have said, we have tried
to root it in its proper tradition, and then we
have given it back to them again. We should like
our work to be judged on our success in that
enterprise alone.

What we could not improve on in the tradition, we
kept: the canticle of Francis, Cranmer's formulas
for marrying and burying. But as we studied the
tradition we became more critical of it. Thus we
dropped the *Te deum* and greatly modified the *Gloria
in excelsis,* for these are acclamations of an emperor (Roman and Byzantine, respectively) who hardly
differs from other holders of secular power. We
replaced them with compositions that define how the
Liberator is different from other claimants. Our
version of the *Abba Father* is that reconstructed by
Günther Schwartz (in *New Testament Studies* XV
[1968/69], 233-247) as it probably existed before
Matthew the liturgical compiler went to work on it.

In our collaboration each has done his own job.
The dramatic structures, the choice of services provided, the range of idioms, come from Dick's needs
in a street ministry. The choice of biblical passages, the new versions, and the final compilation,
have been Jock's work. This book includes an anthology of the biblical passages that are of central
importance to us; its index allows it to serve also
as psalter and lectionary. Our translations use
liturgical freedom in very different degrees, from

highly literal versions to modernized paraphrase; they are not specimens of another whole-Bible translation. We have tried only to use words which communicate the desired sense to our actual audiences. Thus the two groups of words, both in Greek and Hebrew, usually translated *Lord* and *Savior* mostly come out *Liberator*.

We intend our book as both celebration and education. We have aimed at putting the right words together into that right order whose highest name is Poetry; use will determine where we have succeeded. We have tried to avoid celebrating the wrong things, like Cranmer, or (worse) celebrating nothing at all, like group-sensitivity liturgies on the one hand and the COCU liturgy on the other. We are celebrating the freedom won by our struggle for global justice in community, and brought in by the Liberator. So we also wish to be as informational and didactic as a newspaper from Viet Nam or the Black Panthers. Several texts give a rundown of cosmic and planetary history. Our Pentecostal theme, and our hope for use in the Third World, are symbolized by certain words in foreign tongues,with translation: *Salaam, Miru, Hòa Bình*.

We hardly know where to begin or end general acknowledgements. Ed Kelley gave us the publisher's invitation we were waiting for. Tony Morlet got us the bread to write on. Bob Castle's litanies have been on our mind. Bits of these liturgies have been publicized by Bob Haskell, Tom Pike, Al Thomas, Stephen Snyder, Massimo Theodori, John Robinson, the Nine for Peace, and the Hawaii Resistance. Mike Itkin has done us the flattery of ripping off the bulk of these materials and reworking them for his own community. We would never have thought of guerrilla liturgy if Abbie Hoffman had not been himself. As Viv Broughton's CHURCH in London has evolved in parallel with the Free Church, we have borrowed liturgy back and forth. Special thanks, for benefits recorded only by the Operator of the universal Switchboard, is due to Greg Mack, Glee Bishop, Mike Baxter, Phyllis and Otto Smith, Carl Bangs, Joe McCarty, Gail Braunstein, Janie Dickinson Allen, Emily, Melinda, and the thirty thousand people who marched on Memorial Day, 1969. From another point of view, without the work of Lyndon Johnson, Dean Rusk, William Westmoreland, Richard Nixon, McGeorge Bundy, Melvin Laird, John Mitchell, Spiro Agnew, Richard

Daley, Charles Hitch, Edward Teller, Ronald Reagan,
Frank Madigan, and their associates, this book
would not have been needed in the first place.

We have not written a weekly office or lections for
a Sunday cycle. For we are still a Movement, called
into getting ourselves together from time to time,
in the style of prophetic confrontation. Our book
takes the form in which it was shaped by History.
But in another book we do hope to print suitable
day-by-day readings for our whole Calendar.

The Calendar. The general plan arose spontaneously
when we two were driving with Tom Hayes to Port
Chicago; Jim Kennedy has contributed many revolutionary dates. We wish to record our rejection of
any Perpetual Calendar which would rationalize the
date of Easter or put patriotic holidays on long
weekends; the sun, moon, and history all have their
own integrity. More than half the dates are occupied by persons or events that call for celebration;
they are printed in Roman type, with those that are
major in Berkeley capitalized. Around them are
political commemorations, printed in italics. Since
politics is the realm of the ambiguous, these events
call for a mixture of celebration and penitence,
which we let each user determine for himself. All
our commemorations are arranged for liturgical convenience; where our date does not coincide exactly
with the historical or traditional date of the event
celebrated, we have tried, with as much accuracy as
possible, to indicate the original date in paren-
theses.

The Litany. This is the oldest element in the liturgy; it has passed through at least a dozen states.
Our scrapbook shows it as first used in a solidarity
event for the Berrigans on 15 June 1968. It works
as a whole public service in its own right; also
each section is recommended for use by itself elsewhere.

The *Prayers* and *Celebrations* provide a topical substitute for a yearly cycle of collects.

Entering the Covenant. At the Free Church we have
never yet gotten ourselves together enough to covenant; but we do use most of the texts here some-
how or other. We offer the form to our more advanced sister communities across the country. The
November Fifth Statement is our current working
confession.

The Book of Changes. Cranmer, assuming a passive,
illiterate peasantry, begins each office with the
priest telling the people why they are there. Our
materials, being user-developed, mostly begin with
the people telling the minister why they are there.
The understanding of the life-cycle is that worked
out by Jock in *Planet on Strike* (Seabury Press,
1970). The participants are supposed to have this
book in their hands.

1. The form for *receiving a baby into the covenant*
came from the impromptu blessing of new hippy babies
on Telegraph Avenue.

2. *Going through the waters* is our normal adult
baptismal form, first used on 11 November 1968; it
is now combined with an Easter Eve liturgy.

3. The *wedding celebration* pages are likely to wear
out first. The vows are a distillation from hun-
dreds of couple-written services at which Dick has
officiated; they also incorporate a suggestion
from Michael Allen.

4. The form of *commissioning for ministry* has the
texts which Jock preached from at Dick's ordination.
We take it for granted that any ordinations henceforth will be wholly ecumenical; so this form is an
outline to be filled in by negotiation among the
churches taking part.

5. The form for *visiting prisoners* is an expanded
text for what we have long been doing. We prescribe
the Kiss of Peace with a *shall* because some jails
are uptight about it and we want to provide the
visitor with some leverage on the warden.

6. The *memorial of the dead* expands Joe Hill's saying: "Don't mourn, organize."

The *Freedom Meal* is a revision of the tattered mim-
eographed sheets which have already gone around the
world; we are moved at the response found by these
words--not ours but the people's. The *Shalom* theme
comes from David Kirk. The nucleus of the Affirmations, a chain of Movement slogans or bumper stick-
ers, was first used before two thousand screaming
kids on 4 July 1968. We trust communities of the
Spirit to improvise inside the framework we pro-
vide--or outside it.

The *Disarmed Forces Prayer Book* was compiled in
consultation with Joe Sonntag and his colleagues
at the Pacific Counselling Service; it rests on a

large base of contact with GI's on duty. Thanks to
Tim Parkinson in *Green Flag* for the refrain "Count
me out"; to Joan Baez Harris and the War Resisters
League; and to the Order of Saint Maximilian.

The *Medical Cadre Manual* has been done up for the
use of our own medical cadre working with Mike Baxter; it represents the needs of the Medical Committee for Human Rights and other allied groups.

The *Guerrilla Liturgies* are designed for outdoor
or cathedral use with a bullhorn or loudspeaker before a hostile or uninstructed crowd. A cadre of
three or four with prayer books is enough to organize the people's responses. Each liturgy is in
three parts: a preparation at the staging area; a
liturgy in procession; and a prophetic action or
takeover. Especially in the third part, what we
provide is resource material for the leader to select from on the spot, in the street, in temples
filled with money changers, at headquarters of piggery. Sometimes you will want to proceed directly
to the action before you split or get busted; at
other times you will want to claim sanctuary and
filibuster praying-in until reinforcements arrive.
If there is time for guerrilla theater, each text
has an interlude that takes up hostile criticism
by a straight man who stands for the congregation.

These liturgies have been designed in a general way
around the Church and national calendar. But the
Catholic scheme of a seasonal cycle of observances
has been modified here into a topical cycle of confrontation. Incarnation, penitence, lament, resurrection, and earth rebirth have been put back into
history.

1. The *lament for victims and executioners* is a
much modified Good Friday liturgy. The Reproaches
in this form were first used at Cobo Hall in Detroit during the National Council of Churches tri-
ennial (December 1969), just after censorship of
the Song My atrocity had been pierced. We owe the
broken pot to Rosemary Ruether.

2. *Burn out the mark of the Beast* is a generalized
Ash Wednesday text, with borrowings from *A Solemn
Rite for the Public Burning of Draft Cards,* printed
by the Davis (California) Resistance. We owe special thanks to Dan Berrigan, fugitive and prisoner
for the Liberator, for permission to use his beautiful meditation, here slightly cut. This liturgy was

used on Ash Wednesday 1969 outside the Federal
Building in San Francisco (where the fountains a
little later turned to blood), and in 1970 at the
consecration of Oakland Army Base Chapel to Saint
Maximilian.

3.   Successive stages of the *Decontamination* liturgy were used in exorcising the Pentagon on 21 October 1967; at the University of California in Berkeley and the Graduate Theological Union on 11 April
1969; at the Oakland Conference Against Facism; at
the National Council of Churches in Detroit; and at
Saint Maximilian's Chapel, Presidio of San Francisco,
on 6 March 1970. It now includes a Palm Sunday (or
Advent) procession. More often the litany response
has been "Power to the people; out demons out."

4.   The *Sanctuary of peace* is a new Christmas service; its nucleus was the conversion of the General
Convention of the Episcopal Church into an AWOL
sanctuary at South Bend in August 1969. We are in-
debted to Raymond Jennings for letting us adapt his
translation from Kanzō Uchimura.

5.   *Earth Rebirth* evolved from the consecration of
People's Park on 11 May 1969; it was used in the
Berkeley festival of 18 January 1970, and we know
that a lot of copies have gone out. It is super-
ficially syncretistic for wide coalition with ecol-
ogy activists. Thanks to Viv Broughton for "How
shall we sing the Lord's song"; to Gary Snyder for
"earth household"; to various straight sources for
well-known slogans; to Incredible String Band for
the Benediction; and to Smokey the Bear for kind
permission to reproduce his Sutra free forever.

We have tried here to present nothing but the biblical testimony and we ask Bible churches to take
our work seriously. Each item carries a clear witness against militarism, exploitation, and pollu-
tion--in a word, Sin. Each is designed to strike
a clear note of that revolutionary nonviolence,
whether in personal crisis or social confrontation,
which *is* our Good News. We hope to have found the
narrow way between sectarian withdrawal and harm-
less generalities. We offer our book as a service
to the movement for revolutionary change outside
and inside the Church. We want very much to hear
from critics, and under the Gospel will do our
best to satisfy them in any future edition. Our

farthest hope is that some materials here will one day become a genuine bond of unity for the New Church constantly in birth: that this book will actually become that Covenant of Peace it calls itself.

John Pairman Brown

Richard L. York

Witness day of Jeffrey, Allison, Sandy Lee, and William

Year of our Liberator 1970

Year not-too-many before Peace and Liberation

Contents

Preface   5

The Covenant of Peace

    Calendar   19

    Litany   31

    Liberation Prayers   37

    Entering the Covenant   51

        The November Fifth Statement   58

A Book of Changes

    1. Receiving a Baby into the Covenant   61

    2. Going through the Waters   67

    3. The Celebration of a Wedding   86

    4. Commission for Ministry   95

    5. A Form for Visiting Prisoners   101

    6. Memorial of the Dead   110

The Freedom Meal   121

The Disarmed Forces Prayer Book   129

    Medical Cadre Manual   138

Guerrilla Liturgies

    1. A Lament for Victims
       and Executioners   141

    2. Burn Out the Mark of the Beast   157

    3. Decontamination: The Advent
       of the Liberator   166

    4. The Sanctuary of Peace   181

    5. Earth Rebirth   191

Index of Biblical Lections   203

The Covenant of Peace

Calendar

JANUARY

1	A	THE NAMING OF JESUS; *Emancipation Proclamation* (1863); *New Year's Day*
2	b	
3	c	
4	d	Albert Camus, man of goodwill (1960)
5	e	
6	f	EPIPHANY
7	g	
8	A	Giotto di Bondone, painter and follower of Francis (1337)
9	b	Galileo Galilei, observer of the creation (1642)
10	c	
11	d	
12	e	
13	f	THREE PEACEMAKERS: Menno Simons (1559), George Fox (1691), Ammon Hennacy (1970)
14	g	
15	A	*Birthday of Martin Luther King, Jr.* (1929)
16	b	
17	c	Antony, hermit in Egypt (356)
18	d	
19	e	Jan Palach, resister in flames, Prague (1969)
20	f	
21	g	
22	A	
23	b	
24	c	
25	d	The conversion of Paul
26	e	Polycarp, martyr of Smyrna (156)
27	f	
28	g	Fyodor Dostoyevsky, student of humanity (1881)
29	A	
30	b	GANDHI THE MAHATMA, apostle of nonviolence (1948)
31	c	

FEBRUARY

1	d	IGNATIUS OF ANTIOCH, visionary and martyr (about 115); *First sit-ins, Greensboro, N.C.* (1960)
2	e	The Presentation of Jesus
3	f	Ansgarius, apostle of Scandinavia (865)
4	g	
5	A	
6	b	
7	c	
8	d	Student martyrs of Orangeburg, S.C. (1968)
9	e	
10	f	Caedmon, first poet of England (about 680; moved from 11 February)
11	g	ABRAHAM JOHN MUSTE, peacemaker and organizer (1967)
12	A	*Birthday of Abraham Lincoln* (1809)
13	b	Innocents of Dresden (1945)
14	c	*Valentine's Day*
15	d	CAMILLO TORRES, revolutionary and priest in Bolivia (1966)
16	e	
17	f	
18	g	Martin Luther, reformer (1546)
19	A	Michelangelo Buonarroti, artist of humanity (1564; moved from 18 February)
20	b	Frederick Douglass, black liberator (1895); *Chicago Conspiracy sentenced* (1970)
21	c	*Murder of Malcolm X* (1965)
22	d	*Birthday of George Washington*, general in First American Revolution (1732)
23	e	
24	f	
25	g	
26	A	
27	b	
28	c	
29	—	

MARCH

```
 1  d
 2  e
 3  f   JOHN WESLEY (1791) and CHARLES WESLEY (29
        March 1788), street ministers
 4  g
 5  A   Boston Massacre (1770)
 6  b
 7  c   Perpetua, Felicity, and their companions,
        martyrs in Carthage (202)
 8  d   Thomas Aquinas, student of natural order
        (1274)
 9  e
10  f   Harriet Tubman, black liberator (1913)
11  g   James Reeb, martyr in Selma (1965)
12  A   MAXIMILIAN, draft resister (295)
13  b   Gregory, bishop of Rome and musician (604;
        moved from 12 March)
14  c   Karl Marx, prophet of justice (1883)
15  d   JOHNNY APPLESEED (John Chapman), planter of
        Eden (1845; date uncertain)
16  e   INNOCENTS OF SONG MY (My Lai; 1968)
17  f   Patrick, apostle of Ireland (461)
18  g
19  A   Joachim of Flores, visionary of the future
        (1202)
```

spring equinox

```
20  b   Isaac Newton, searcher into the creation
        (1727)
21  c   Innocents of Sharpeville, South Africa
        (1960)
22  d   D.C. Nine destroy Dow Chemical office
        (1969)
```

```
23  e   Nikolai Berdyayev, Christian ideologist
        (1948)
24  f   Selma march ends (1965); Viola Liuzzo shot
        (25 March 1965)
25  g   The Annunciation to Mary; Death of Ishi,
        last native American (1916)
26  A   Ludwig van Beethoven, visionary (1827);
        Walt Whitman, poet (1892)
27  b   Alice Herz, witness in flames (1965)
28  c   Uchimura Kanzō, founder of "No-Church" re-
        form in Japan (1930); Roger Williams,
        seeker (March or April 1684)
29  d
30  e   Jesus the runaway (12)
31  f   John Donne, priest and poet (1631)
```

APRIL

1   g   *Feast of Fools*
2   A   John Frederick Denison Maurice (1 April 1872) and Eugene Victor Debs (1 April 1925), socialists
3   b
4   c   MARTIN LUTHER KING, JR., peacemaker and martyr (1968)
5   d   *Boston Massacre* (1770)
6   e   *Oakland police shoot down Bobby Hutton* (1968)
7   f   El Greco (Domenico Theotocopoli), visionary (1614)
8   g   GAUTAMA THE BUDDHA, mask of Christ
9   A   DIETRICH BONHOEFFER, revolutionary (1945); Innocents of Deir Yassin, Palestine (1948)
10   b   PIERRE TEILHARD DE CHARDIN, voyager in time (1955)
11   c   Antonio Ruíz de Montoya, organizer in Paraguay (1653); Emilio Zapata, agrarian reformer in Mexico (10 April 1919)
12   d
13   e   Innocents of Jallianwalla Bagh, India (1919)
14   f   Justin, martyr in Rome (about 167)
15   g   Damien (Joseph de Venster), priest and leper (1889); *Peace Mobilization* (1967)
16   A   Benedict Joseph Labré, priest and panhandler (1783)
17   b   Francisco Jose de Goya y Lucientes, artist and war protester (1828)
18   c   Albert Einstein, cosmologist (1955)
19   d   Charles Robert Darwin, historian of life (1882)
20   e   *Warsaw ghetto revolt* (began 19 April 1943); *Massacre of Ludlow, Col., miners* (1914)
21   f   Peter Abelard (1142) and Heloise (1163), lovers
22   g   Thomas Cranmer, liturgist and martyr (1556; moved from 21 April)
23   A
24   b   Genocide of the Armenians (1915)
25   c   Mark, evangelist
26   d   *Black Manifesto promulgated* (1969)
27   e   Innocents of Guernica (1937)
28   f   Sundar Singh the Sadhu, disappeared on mission in Tibet (April 1929)
29   g   *Columbia University student revolt* (1968); Hernan Mery, agrarian reformer in Chile (1970)
30   A   Catherine of Siena, visionary and social worker (1380)

MAY

1	b	Joseph the worker; *International Workers' Day*
2	c	Leonardo da Vinci, universal man (1519)
3	d	William Shakespeare (23 April 1616 O.S.)
4	e	Monica, mother (387)
5	f	Student martyrs of Kent, Ohio (4 May 1970)
6	g	Henry David Thoreau, hermit and war resister (1862)
7	A	*Vietnamese victory at Dien Bien Phu* (1954)
8	b	Revelations to Dame Julian of Norwich (1373)
9	c	
10	d	
11	e	Cyril (869) and Methodius (885), apostles of Russia
12	f	*Ghetto massacre in Augusta* (1970)
13	g	
14	A	*Destruction of People's Park, Berkeley, Calif., begun* (1969)
15	b	Aristide Peter Maurin, Catholic worker (1949)
16	c	Student martyrs of Jackson (15 May 1970)
17	d	*Catonsville Nine burn draft files with napalm* (1969)
18	e	
19	f	JAMES RECTOR, martyr for ecology, Berkeley, Calif. (1969)
20	g	Alcuin, liturgist (804)
21	A	
22	b	
23	c	Girolamo Savonarola, reformer (1498)
24	d	Nicolaus Copernicus, astronomer (1543)
25	e	*Chicago Fifteen burn draft files* (1969)
26	f	Antonio Henrique Pereira Netto, apostle to youth and martyr in Recife (1969)
27	g	Bede, historian (735)
28	A	
29	b	Boris Pasternak, poet (30 April 1960)
30	c	*Massacre of steel workers, Chicago* (1937)
31	d	Signing of the Barmen Declaration (1934)

JUNE

1	e	
2	f	Martyrs of Lyons (177)
3	g	POPE JOHN XXIII, apostle of unity (1963)
4	A	
5	b	*Assassination of Robert Fitzgerald Kennedy* (1968)
6	c	
7	d	
8	e	
9	f	Columba of Iona, holy man (597); *First English Prayer Book* (10 June 1549)
10	g	Innocents of Lidice (1942); THICH QUANG DUC, resister in flames (11 June 1963)
11	A	Saint-Denis, first gothic church, dedicated in Paris (1144)
12	b	Medgar W. Evers, martyr in Mississippi (1963)
13	c	*Peasants' Revolt led by John Ball, London* (1381)
14	d	
15	e	*Magna Carta signed* (1215)
16	f	
17	g	
18	A	Denmark Vesey, black liberator (1822)
19	b	

summer solstice

20	c	
21	d	James Chaney, Andrew Goodman, Michael Schwerner, martyrs in Mississippi (1964)
22	e	Alban, martyr of Britain (304)

23	f	
24	g	Birth of John the Baptizer
25	A	
26	b	
27	c	*International Workers of the World founded* (1905)
28	d	
29	e	Peter and Paul, apostles in Rome (about 67)
30	f	

JULY

1	g	
2	A	Visitation of Mary
3	b	*Algerian independence* (1962)
4	c	*U.S. National Liberation Day* (1775; holiday)
5	d	
6	e	Jan Hus, reformer and martyr in Prague (1415)
7	f	William Faulkner (6 July 1962)
8	g	
9	A	
10	b	
11	c	Benedict of Monte Cassino, monk (about 540)
12	d	*Newark ghetto revolt* (1967)
13	e	
14	f	*Capture of the Bastille* (1789)
15	g	*Nine for Peace resign from U.S. Armed Forces, San Francisco* (1968)
16	A	Meister Eckhart, mystic (1328; date unknown)
17	b	
18	c	
19	d	
20	e	*First Moon landing* (1969)
21	f	Albert John Luthuli, peacemaker in Africa (1967)
22	g	Mary Magdalen, harlot
23	A	
24	b	Thomas à Kempis, mystic (1471)
25	c	James, apostle; Walter Rauschenbusch, activist (1918)
26	d	*Cuban Revolution* (1953)
27	e	
28	f	Johann Sebastian Bach (1750)
29	g	Mary and Martha of Bethany
30	A	William Penn, peacemaker (1718)
31	b	Joseph of Arimathea

AUGUST

1	c	Ignatius Loyola, organizer (1556; moved from 31 July)
2	d	
3	e	
4	f	Jean Vianney of Ars, pastor (1859); Anne Frank arrested (1944)
5	g	
6	A	TRANSFIGURATION OF JESUS; HOLY INNOCENTS OF HIROSHIMA (1945)
7	b	
8	c	
9	d	FRANZ JAEGERSTAETTER, draft resister in Austria (1943); Innocents of Nagasaki (1945)
10	e	
11	f	*Watts ghetto revolt* (1965)
12	g	WILLIAM BLAKE, visionary (1827); Clare of Assisi, abbess (1253)
13	A	Florence Nightingale, nurse (1910)
14	b	Maximilian Kolbe, O.F.M., of Poland, volunteer substitute victim (1941)
15	c	MARY
16	d	
17	e	
18	f	Benjamin Bufano, peace sculptor (1970)
19	g	Blaise Pascal, confessor (1662)
20	A	Jonathan Daniels, martyr of Selma, Ala. (1965); *First blacks landed at Jamestown, Va., as slaves* (1619)
21	b	Bernard of Clairvaux, visionary (1153; moved from 20 August)
22	c	
23	d	Execution of Nicola Sacco and Bartolomeo Vanzetti (1927)
24	e	Simone Weil, mystic (1943)
25	f	
26	g	Women's suffrage granted (1920)
27	A	William Edward Burghardt DuBois, black liberator (1963)
28	b	Augustine of Hippo, ideologist (430)
29	c	*Freedom March on Washington* (28 August 1963)
30	d	Ruben Salazar, Chicano peace martyr (29 August 1970)
31	e	John Bunyan, tinker and visionary (1688)

SEPTEMBER

1	f	Gregorio Alipay, reformer in the Philippines (1940)
2	g	James Albert Pike, innovator (1969)
3	A	*Death of Ho Chi Minh* (1969)
4	b	Albert Schweitzer, physician (1965)
5	c	
6	d	
7	e	
8	f	Birth of Mary
9	g	
10	A	
11	b	
12	c	
13	d	
14	e	THE HOLY CROSS; SIMON OF CYRENE, inductee; INNOCENTS OF BIRMINGHAM, ALA. (15 September 1963)
15	f	Dante Alighieri, visionary (14 September 1321)
16	g	*Mexican Independence* (1810)
17	A	
18	b	Dag Hammarskjöld, peacemaker (1961)
19	c	
20	d	*Delano farm workers begin strike* (1965)

autumn equinox

21	e	Matthew, evangelist
22	f	*Nuremberg war-crime verdicts* (1946)
23	g	Sigmund Freud, physician of souls (1939)

24	A	*Milwaukee Fourteen destroy draft files* (1968)
25	b	
26	c	
27	d	
28	e	Louis Pasteur, physician (1895)
29	f	Michael and all angels
30	g	*First use of anesthetics* (1846)

OCTOBER

1   A   *Chinese revolution* (1949)
2   b   Student martyrs of Tlateloco, Mex. (1968)
3   c   Woody Guthrie, singer (1967); *Fort Hood Three resign from U.S. Army* (1967)
4   d   FRANCIS OF ASSISI (1226)
5   e   Teresa of Avila, visionary (1582; moved from 4 October)
6   f   William Tyndale, translator (1536)
7   g   John Woolman (1772) and Jose Clemente Orozco (1949), artists and liberators
8   A
9   b   *Murder of Ernesto Che Guevara* (1968)
10   c
11   d
12   e   *Circle of the Earth joined* (1492)
13   f
14   g   *Presidio Twenty-seven resist murder, San Francisco* (1968)
15   A   *David Miller first to burn draft card* (1965)
16   b   Hugh Latimer and Nicholas Ridley, martyrs (1555)
17   c   *John Brown begins black liberation at Harper's Ferry* (16 October 1859)
18   d   Luke, historian and physician
19   e   Nikos Kazantzakis, prophet (18 October 1957)
20   f
21   g   *Exorcism of the Pentagon* (1967)
22   A   James, brother of Jesus, Jewish Christian
23   b   Paul Cézanne (1906)
24   c   *United Nations Charter in effect* (1945)
25   d
26   e
27   f   Miguel Servetus, physician and martyr (1553); Holy Innocents of the Wars of Religion
28   g
29   A   Marcellus, military resister (298); Clarence Jordan, translator in Georgia (1969)
30   b   David Darst, witness by fire (1969)
31   c   NINETY-FIVE THESES POSTED BY LUTHER (1517); *Halloween*

NOVEMBER

1	d	ALL SAINTS
2	e	ALL SOULS; NORMAN MORRISON, confessor in flames (1965)
3	f	
4	g	Søren Kierkegaard, lover of truth (1855)
5	A	
6	b	*Russian Revolution* (24-25 October 1917 O.S.)
7	c	
8	d	John Milton, poet (1674)
9	e	Martin of Tours, pacifist (397; moved from 8 November)
10	f	Roger LaPorte, witness in flames (1965)
11	g	*Execution of Haymarket defendants* (1887)
12	A	
13	b	
14	c	Innocents of Coventry (1940)
15	d	Amos Comenius, educator (1670); *Anti-war mobilization* (1969)
16	e	
17	f	
18	g	
19	A	Murder of Joe Hill in Utah (1915)
20	b	Leo Tolstoy (7 November 1910 O.S.)
21	c	
22	d	*Assassination of John Fitzgerald Kennedy* (1963)
23	e	
24	f	
25	g	Isaac Watts, musician (1748)
26	A	
27	b	
28	c	
29	d	
30	e	Andrew, apostle

DECEMBER

1	f	Charles Foucauld, apostle of Algeria (1916); *International Prisoners for Peace Day; Rosa Parks keeps bus seat, Montgomery, Ala.* (1955)
2	g	*Sproul Hall sit-in, Berkeley* (1964)
3	A	Francis Xavier, apostle of the Orient (1552)
4	b	Clement of Alexandria, pacifist (about 210); *Massacre of Chicago Panthers* (1969)
5	c	Wolfgang Amadeus Mozart (1791)
6	d	
7	e	
8	f	
9	g	
10	A	Karl Barth and Thomas Merton, confessors (1968)
11	b	
12	c	
13	d	
14	e	John of the Cross, mystic (1591)
15	f	*Bill of Rights adopted* (1791); Sitting Bull, red liberator (1890)
16	g	*Boston Tea Party destroys private property* (1773)
17	A	*First air flight* (1903)
18	b	*Nonviolent sit-in, Oakland, Calif., Induction Center* (1967)
19	c	
20	d	

winter solstice

21	e	Thomas, apostle
22	f	
23	g	---
24	A	John Muir, naturalist (1914)
25	b	CHRISTMAS
26	c	Stephen and other victims of lynching; Joseph L. Hromádka, socialist (1969)
27	d	JOHN, apostle and visionary
28	e	HOLY INNOCENTS OF JERUSALEM, AUSSCHWITZ, AND TOKYO; INNOCENTS OF WOUNDED KNEE, S.D. (29 December 1890)
29	f	John Wyclif, reformer (1384; moved from 28 December)
30	g	
31	A	

The Covenant of Peace

Litany

I. THE OPENING OF PERCEPTION

Our fingers, eyes, ears, nose, tongue, all windows
     of perception, open our senses to sink us in
     the glory of the world: Open our senses.
Birds and bats, moths and bees, and all fliers;
     fish and dolphins who travel the whale's
     road; all animals that share our being: Open
     our senses. *And so on.*
Flowers and green things, redwood trees and all
     forests, mantle of the living globe:
Folded mountains and the sand of the shore, rocks
     and all hard things:
All bridges and temples stepping on the hills:
Salmon-filled rivers and lakes, waters of life:
Unaltering Sea, the wave of drowning and mother of
     us all:
Earthquake and volcano, uneasy continents, and
     wandering icecap:
Wind and clouds, thunderstorm and snow and rain,
     breath of this jewel earth:
Moon and all planets, clocks of the darkness:
O Sun, our Sun, source of life and watcher of our
     days:
Stars in your imagined constellations, companions
     of shepherd and sailor:
Milky Way and the ten thousand cubed galaxies:
Protons and electrons, all units of existence, who
     alone know your own names:
Cosmos of space and time, island in the sea of
     nonbeing:
Universal consciousness, everywhere potential
     since actual in us:
O Power behind space and time, Fountain of matter
     and energy, Organizer of change and revolu-
     tion: Open our senses.
Open our senses, God of nature and history, so
     that we may serve our neighbor in love, free
     from all dangers and compulsions: Open our
     senses.

II. PRAYER FOR DELIVERANCE

From napalm and fallout, from shrapnel, gas, and
     bullet, from poison, torture, and mutilation:
     Good Lord, deliver us.

From prison and detention camps, from conscription
    and from unjust sentences: **Good Lord, deliv-
    er us.** *And so on.*
From rats and bedbugs, from crowding and eviction,
    from hunger and unemployment:
From neglect by parents, from neglect by children,
    from neglect by callous institutions:
From cancer and stroke, from ulcers, madness, and
    senility:
From starvation and epidemic, from overcrowding of
    the planet, from pollution of the soil, the
    air, and the waters:
From poverty and disease, from segregation and
    prejudice, from harassment, discrimination,
    and brutality:
From racism and affluence; from the concentration
    of power in the hands of ignorant, threat-
    ened, or hasty men:
From propaganda, fads, frivolity, and untruthful-
    ness:
From arrogance and unfeeling, narrowness and mean-
    ness, from stupidity and pretence:
From boredom, apathy, and fatigue, from lack of
    conviction, from fear, self-satisfaction, and
    timidity:
From retribution at the hands of our victims, from
    the consequences of our own folly:
From resignation and despair, from cynicism and
    manipulation:

Through all unmerited suffering, our own and
    others':
Through the unending cry of all peoples for jus-
    tice and freedom:
Through all concern and wonder, love and crea-
    tivity:
In our strength and weakness, in occasional suc-
    cess and eventual failure:
In aloneness and community, in the days of our ac-
    tion and the time of our dying:
By the needs of mankind and of the earth, and not
    by our own merits or deserving: **Good Lord,
    deliver us.**
Deliver us, Good Lord, open our eyes and unstop
    our ears, so that we may see the figures of
    the saints and hear their witness: **Good
    Lord, deliver us.**

III. INVOCATION OF THE SAINTS

Bridegroom of poverty, our brother Francis, fol-
lower of Jesus and friend of the creation:
Stand here beside us.

Apostle of nonviolence, Gandhi the Mahatma, re-
proach to the churches: **Stand here beside
us.** *And so on.*

Good Pope John, friend of the poor, who longed for
the unity of all people:

Peacemaker in America, Abraham J. Muste, father of
activists:

Peacemakers in the world, Dag Hammarskjöld, Albert
John Luthuli, and all your brothers, called
children of God:

Mask of the Christ, Gautama the Buddha, fountain
of compassion:

Harriet Tubman, Frederick Douglass, John Woolman,
Eugene Debs, and all freedom fighters:

Madman in America, Johnny Appleseed, planter of
Eden:

Inductee of Africa, Simon of Cyrene, who carried
the cross of your Liberator:

Visionary and apostle, John of Patmos, resister to
the World Beast:

Visionaries and poets, Caedmon, Dante, William
Blake, John Bunyan, Isaac Watts, pilgrims of
the inner light:

Faithful harlot, Mary Magdalen, first witness of
new life:

Priest and panhandler, Benedict Joseph Labré, fool
for Christ:

You who speak the soul's language, Johann Sebas-
tian Bach, Wolfgang Amadeus Mozart, Ludwig
van Beethoven, and all your brothers:

Students of the earth, Charles Darwin and Pierre
Teilhard de Chardin, voyagers in the past and
in the future:

Children of the synagogue, Albert Einstein, Karl
Marx, and Sigmund Freud, divers in the sea of
humanity:

Vanguard for the Liberator, John the baptizer, who
condemned the crimes of princes:

Witnesses in England, John and Charles Wesley,
street ministers:

Reformers and leaders of protest, Amos of Tekoa,
Paul of Tarsus, Jan Hus, Martin Luther,
Uchimura Kanzō, and all your companions:

Explorers in the Gospel, Menno Simons and George
Fox, generals in the warfare of the Lamb:

Free men in chains, Maximilian and Franz Jaeger-
    staetter, draft resisters:
Confessor in Africa, Augustine of Hippo, city-
    planner for God's people:
Confessor in Russia, Tovarisch Boris Pasternak,
    poet of reconciliation:
Confessors in America, Henry David Thoreau and
    Thomas Merton, hermits and resisters:
Confessors in flames, Norman Morrison, Alice
    Hertz, Roger LaPorte, David Darst, Jan
    Palach, Thich Quang Duc, and all your com-
    panions, immolated for the sake of peace:

Innocents of Guernica, Sharpeville, and Birming-
    ham, all victims of lynching, in your unde-
    served deaths:
Innocents of Coventry, Dresden, Tokyo, and all
    victims of bombing, caught up in a sea of
    fire:
Innocents of Hiroshima and Nagasaki, pierced by
    needles of flame:
Innocents of Ausschwitz, Dachau, and all concen-
    tration camps, in your despair and dying:
Innocents of Biafra and Armenia, Albigenses and
    kulaks, all unpopular objects of genocide:
Innocents of Wounded Knee, Deir Yassin, and Song
    My, God's wheat ground in the mill of war:

Martyrs of Africa: Perpetua, mother; Felicity,
    slave; and your companions:
Martyrs and confessors, Polycarp, Ignatius, and
    Justin, who refused the incense to Caesar:
Martyr in Berkeley, James Rector, witness to green
    revolution:
Martyrs in the streets of the South, Jonathan
    Daniels, James Reeb, Medgar Evers, Michael
    Schwerner, Viola Liuzzo, and all your com-
    panions:
Martyr in Athens, Socrates the hippy, Christian
    before Christ:
Martyr in England, John Ball, priest and revolu-
    tionary:
Martyr in Colombia, Camillo Torres, priest and
    revolutionary:
Martyr in Germany, Dietrich Bonhoeffer, confessor
    and revolutionary:
Martyrs of Orangeburg, Kent State, Augusta, and
    Jackson, witnesses to youth revolution:
Martyr in America, Martin Luther King, organizer
    for peace and justice:

Unwed mother, blessed Mary, wellspring of our
      liberation:
Our hero and leader, Jesus the manual laborer,
      root of our dignity:
Our hero and leader, Jesus the prophet, who re-
      sisted the Establishment:
Our hero and leader, Jesus the Liberator, a king
      because first a servant:
Our hero and leader, Jesus the poet, who laid down
      a new form of speech: **Stand here beside us.**
Our hero and leader, Jesus the Son of God, bright
      cornerstone of our unity in a new Spirit:
      Stand here beside us.

IV. INTERCESSIONS

For the poor and hungry, migrant workers and
      hoboes, outcast and unemployed: **We call on
      the Spirit.**
For street and ghetto people, for unmarried moth-
      ers and children unwanted in their homes: **We
      call on the Spirit.** *And so on.*
For the wounded, for prisoners and exiles, for all
      persecuted because of conscience or resist-
      ance:
For the sick and suffering in mind or body, for
      alcoholics, for those spaced out on drugs or
      fear:
For the mortgaged and manipulated, fearful of
      crime and competition, pawns in a game of the
      affluent:
For prostitutes; for policemen, jailers, and sol-
      diers; for all prisoners of a degrading
      system:

For uptight authorities and officials, that they
      may listen to the voice of the different and
      weak:
For oppressors, exploiters, and imperialists, that
      they may be confused and disarmed by love:
For the masters of war *(especially N, N, and N),*
      that they may be given a new transplant of
      flesh in place of their heart of stone:
For all whom we fear, resent, or cannot love; for
      the unlovable:

For those who are dying and have died, in bitter-
      ness or tranquility:
For doctors, nurses, and social workers, for min-
      isters to the poor:
For organizers, students, and writers, all who
      raise the cry for justice:

For all who are close to us, here and in every
      place:
For the reconciliation of mankind through the non-
      violent revolution:
For the established churches, that they may be
      humbled, reformed, and united:
For the global movement of peace and liberation,
      the church of Jesus incognito:
For reformers and prophets, preachers and poets,
      that God may raise them up where they are
      least deserved and most needed:

That all couples may realize their union with the
      universal flow of love:
That our tables may be spread with the natural
      fruits of the earth, that our grandchildren
      may inherit a restored planet:
That all persons in their work may express ancient
      wisdom through the child's vision:
That each one who enters our house may receive the
      hospitality due to the Christ whom he bears:

In thankfulness for all who have turned from ex-
      ploitation to the Way:
In thankfulness for all who have been freed from
      prison, poverty, illness, or fear:

Here whenever possible the people make free inter-
cessions and thanksgivings.
For all those things we are not wise enough to ask
      for ourselves: We call on the Spirit.
We call on the Spirit to bind us in solidarity
      with all who are using their lives to resist
      evil and affirm community: We call on the
      Spirit.

Liberation Prayers

(Arranged alphabetically by catchword)

For American Indians
O Great Spirit, you that watch the fall of every
sparrow, restore to the true inhabitants of this
land their own forests and prairies. By their
voice teach all pilgrims and sojourners on this
continent the secrets of its life; let us learn
that it is not our property but yours.

For Animals
O Spirit of change, you who made mankind bud out
from the world-tree of life, bless our brothers of
other language. Do not let us in our thoughtless-
ness harm them or the wild world we share; have us
live together in sympathy, by the example of
Francis the friend of all.

For Black people
Jesus our Liberator, you were a black man in
Galilee. Stand beside all black people today in
their struggle for liberation; let them become
your hands and your voice to bring all people
knowledge of your Way.

For Broken families
Our Liberator, you knew the pain of an uncompre-
hending family. Take up all broken families in
your arms; break the chain of misunderstanding and
provocation. Teach parents and children gentleness; bring the alienated together by building
them into your new community.

For Casualties
Jesus our Brother, you also at the end despaired
of the Father; raise up all who have fallen casualty through sickness, anxiety, bitterness, or
fear, just as you did in your lifetime on earth;
and unite them with us in one movement.

For Church leaders
Our Liberator, smile with pity and sorrow on those
who are called leaders in your Church. Call their
administrative procedures into question; give reality to the words they daily repeat. If they cannot build for peace, justice, or conservation, let
them at least not support war, oppression, pollution. If they cannot embrace your poverty, let

them at least not embrace the world's affluence.
Raise up beside them prophets and ministers of
your way, and so call your church back to yourself.

For the Churches
Our Liberator, you make the message of your peace
known in many ways; set fire to all the churches
where it is spoken ignorantly, partially, coldly,
perversely, falsely; let their tinder blaze up
into your truth.

For Clergy and Sisters rejected by their churches
Our Liberator, you told us that your followers
would be expelled from the houses of God and investigated by synods. Walk beside each of our
brothers and sisters who have been penalized for
their faithfulness. Take their suffering up into
your suffering, make your victory their victory;
build the casualty-rolls into your new community.

For the Coming of the Liberator
Jesus, you came before when expected, and unexpectedly; in every age you have brought your Way
to men's hearts, not through official channels,
but through your own channels. Today, come in the
right way for you to come, and give us eyes to
recognize it. Maranatha, come quickly, our
Liberator.

For Confidence
O Truth of all being, from time to time we see a
hint of your reliability. Extend those times to
all our time, make our confidence in your faithfulness the root of all our being, so that we can
say Yes to life; through the Liberator who is the
living evidence for our faith.

For the Convention of a church
Spirit of our Liberator, you presided over the
councils of the apostles, even when unworthy or
shortsighted. Move the hearts of all here assembled, so that our sole agenda will be to turn
back the breaking wave of violence; let us act to
liberate the poor, to restore the natural order,
to break the weapons of militarism. Teach us that
renewal begins with the house of God; smash racism,
war, exploitation, in our hearts; set our own
house in order.

For the Conversion of ourselves
Our Father, our hearts are transparent to you; you
understand the excuses, delays, rationalizations,
that we put between ourselves and the next step.
Sweep away that spiderweb. Do not let any doubt

shadow our certainty of the one thing necessary.
Resolve all complications in the simplicity of becoming ourselves, so that we may be agents of your
love and fellow-soldiers with the Liberator in
your battle.

For Courage
Our Liberator, we do not ask that our fear should
be taken away from us, but we do turn it over to
you. Let it be your business. Turn our own actions back over to us, and we for our part will
make them our business.

For the Courts
Our God, with you is the book of justice, in you
is no violence at all. Overshadow each court of
this world which claims to do your justice. Expose its hypocrisies, halt its harassments, break
through its tunnel vision. And let all its seeds
of justice bear true fruit, for our peace and
liberation.

For Defense against demonic powers
O God our only Strength, surround us with the defense of commitment, and put into our hands the
weapons of truth and nonviolence, so that we may
not succumb to the World Pig, but stand beside
Jesus our hero and leader.

For Directors of corporations
O Director of the universe, examine with care the
accounts of all who claim to be agents in your administration; let the voice of the poor and oppressed be heard in their boardrooms; touch their
hearts with doubt and uncertainty; distribute
their accumulations; halt their manufacture of
poison and death; show them how their task may be
turned over to all whose hands do the world's
work.

For the Dying and dead
O Fountain of life, you allowed Jesus your son to
be taken over by death; lift in your hands our
brother [*sister*] now leaving this common life, and
unite *his* dying with the Liberator, so that *he* may
also be raised up by your spirit in the community
of love.

For Engineers and scientists
O God of truth, you have showed to students the
hidden things of your creation. Let them swear by
your faithfulness never again to destroy man or
nature by their knowledge; let them no longer accept the wages of death from the prince of death.

For Families
God, it is your way to build great things out of
small. Maintain each family against all suspi-
cions and anxieties, so that it may become an example and a building-block in the home of us all,
that new mankind which you are bringing in through
Jesus our Liberator.

For Farmworkers, foresters, biologists
Jesus our brother, you appeared first in your new
life to a woman of the street as a Gardener. You
are the true Adam; walk always with men and women
who are doing the work of Adam, planting the garden of this planet; liberate them from all oppression, help us all learn their secrets.

For Hope
You who are our Future, show us your hand in the
still undetermined events to come. Help us work
with the hope that our work makes a difference;
help us rest in the assurance that we are not in-
dispensable; help us die in solidarity with our
brothers and sisters of all times, and especially
with our elder brother the Liberator.

For Housing
God, you are our home in the Age to come. Turn
your pity towards the homeless of this Age: the
exploited, the unwanted children, the evicted,
hoboes, vagrants. Turn your indignation towards
all heartless institutions and landlords that have
kept them so. With your bulldozer, level the
world ghetto; build the new Jerusalem on this
green and pleasant earth.

For Justice in the economic system
O you who are all our wealth: break down every
concentration of money, overthrow every industry
that pollutes the earth, give all men and women a
creative job for their hands and a true share of
the common wealth.

For Love
God, we recognize you as author of change; we are
ready to spend our time where you command. For
your part, show yourself to us as the Unchange-
able. Hold us fast to our friends and lovers,
give us time to spend with them, which is also
your time. Let our love be the strength and the
model for our struggle.

For Media people
O Power of being, you made the Liberator the word
and image of yourself. Let all who work with

words and pictures hold up everything they touch
to his example; let them enrich not themselves but
your people; give them strength and will to expose
every system of violence and to advance your
peace and liberation.

For Meetings
Our Father, you are known to us through the words
and needs of our brothers. Speak to us in this
meeting, so that our brothers may be helped and
your revolution of love pushed forward, through
Jesus our Liberator who never showed himself hard
of hearing.

For all in Mental confusion
Jesus our brother, take up in your hands all whose
inner self has been broken by a violent age. Let
them find good friends and relatives, quiet and
greenness and running water. And smash the world
of meaninglessness that has smashed them; bring in
everywhere the things that make for our peace.

For the Military
Jesus our only leader, go and speak to the Generals and Admirals. Tear down the pictures of yourself they have hung on their walls, put a worm in
their apple, wormwood in their highballs. Infect
their minds with knowledge of what they have done;
find a useful vocation they can retire to. And
break the chain of command; let them have no suc-
cessors, let their in-baskets be filled with
cobwebs.

For the Ministry
O Well of our peace, you told our Brother to pass
by the great ones of the world, and to call the
poor as his organizers. Let many men and women
hear the cry for justice raised by the victims of
force or neglect on every continent. Let them
serve the fallen and strengthen the struggling,
with commitment and joy, to their life's end.

For National Liberation Movements
O God of justice, let all who struggle for national liberation establish their own culture,
sitting unafraid under their vine and figtree.
Make their revolutions humanized and democratic.
At your right time turn them from all violence
or dictatorship; make them true spokesmen for justice in the World Revolution of peace and freedom
which you have begun.

For the Old
Our Father, we pray for our fathers and mothers,
who will see only by hope and trust the new thing
you are doing. Let them live with their grandchildren, let them not be pensioned away by their
sons and daughters to die. Help them understand
that their strange children are bone of their
bone, flesh of their flesh; that the catechism
they taught in their churches is being worked out
in the streets.

For Peace and Freedom
O God, the source of change, break all chains,
stop all wars, and end the hate which causes both,
so that your people may live with peace and freedom in Jesus our Liberator.

For the Planet
Architect of the worlds, you put man and woman in
the garden to keep it; show us the true harmony
between ourselves and the earth, between green
things and animals, air and water. And give us
the secrets of knowledge and will, to restore all
damage done to the planet by our ignorance or
malice, and to let all living things have the
freedom which is proper for them.

For the Police
You who have given laws to man and all creation,
supervise all those who profess to be maintaining
law. Raise up protest whenever their law becomes
a new lawlessness. Remind them that they are
servants, not masters, of the people. Help them
to neither use nor carry the weapons which our
Liberator renounced. And give them dignity to reject the role of rich man's pawn in oppressing
those poor for whom our Brother died.

For Politicians
O Light of truth, shine on all those whose profession is named compromise and show them those
things which cannot be negotiated; in the spirit
of the one who is our way, our truth, and our
life.

For the Poor
Our Liberator, you called the poor blessed, for
you became one of them. Let them realize their
blessedness as the vocation to struggle for justice and freedom on the planet which your Father
gave us all.

For the President of the United States
O God our only strength, look with indignation and
pity on *N.*, the President of these United States.
Break down the fence around his White House; let
him hear the voice of a colored nation, of a colored world. Inspire him with distrust of his ad-
visers. Repeat daily in his ears the words of his
childhood preacher, that men do not gather grapes
from thorns, nor figs from thistles. Teach him
that peace is not built by killing, nor justice by
repression. Make him the servant and not the ex-
ploiter of his people, after the example of Jesus,
his Liberator and ours.

For Prisoners
Jesus our brother, victim of brutality and political prisoner, be with all our brothers and sisters
unjustly jailed. Give them the strength to do
what must be done without useless anger and bitterness; soften the hearts of their guards with
pity or at least justice; and speed up your promised coming to open all prison gates and set captives free.

For any Project
O everlasting Word, who at the beginning shaped
all worlds, put your spirit into the fingers and
brains of those who have begun this project; let
them push past midpoint fatigue to the end; remove
all obstacles not of their own making, so that we
all may share with you in the work of creation.

For Purity of air and water
O Power of being, you have spread an envelope of
clean water and air around this sapphire earth.
Break every chimney, rust every pipe which deliv-
ers poison into your living world; teach our
brothers and sisters to live invisible on the only
planet they will be given.

For a Remnant of God's people
O Rock of Israel, you promised salvation for those
who endure harassment. In time of testing let
your people not return evil for evil; by your gentleness keep the fabric of this earth from irre-
versible harm; and in the end lead a remnant out
into your Liberated Zone, for the sake of the one
who stayed steadfast in trials, Jesus our
Liberator.

For other Religions
O Power of Being, you nowhere leave yourself without a witness. Let us learn truth from all men,

by whatever name they call it. Let Mammon and
Beelzebul be unmasked, whenever they come to us in
the name of the Liberator; and let his incognito
be removed, whenever he comes to us once again
under a new name, as he did also at first.

For Reparations
Our only true Judge, you who delay condemnation
and love gentleness, help us turn from our complicity in racism; break the chain of our guilt; let
us hear both the patience and the anger of the
victims; help us to take their side, and to bring
with us reparations for our sin and the sin of our
fathers; for the sake of that homeless brother who
was wounded for our offenses, Jesus the Liberator.

For the Revolution
O God whose Name is revolution, cut our ties with
all that is wrong and dying; help us to carry out,
not our revolution, but yours. Do not let us continue in the old way of murder, but direct us onto
the new Way of love, which we learn from the
spirit of our brother the Liberator.

For the Rich
O Power to whom all things are possible, we do not
know whether you can bring a camel through the eye
of a needle. Let our rich brothers and sisters
not trespass forever on your gentleness and for-
bearance; let them rather hear the word to the
rich young ruler, and give it all away; may their
reward be in the future and not in the past.

For Rights everywhere
O Power of being, your love is the only law; in
you is no injustice at all. Hold up every legal
system, every court and administrator, to the
plumbline of your impartiality. Smash all dis-
crimination, use our hands and voices to build a
world of equal rights for all.

For a Runaway
Father of all the unwanted, take under your care
each one who for a time has no family in the
world. Soften the heart of *his* parents, make possible *his* return if that is your desiring, for the
sake of Jesus the teenager who ran away to be
about your business.

For Scholars
Spirit of truth, through our fault the powers of
darkness have obscured the truth of the Gospel by
a false learning. Raise up true scholars to con-
found its pretensions and to light a true beacon;

let them point to the unschooled poor who do your
work by the Liberator living in them.

For Schools and seminaries
Fountain of wisdom, have you not put springs of
knowledge into men's hearts and into books? Let
our schools reject all subservience to oppression;
let them stop at no truth short of the truth of
liberation; let them find nothing good enough but
your goodness.

For Simplicity of life
Jesus, without self-punishment you reduced your
needs to a minimum; your message was short; you
did not travel far nor live long. Give us a share
of your simplicity and truthfulness, so that our
success may be of the same kind as your success,
and our failure measured by your failure.

For Strength in troubles
O Judge of history, you have let troubles surround
us; we are tired, in pain, near despair. Send
your Spirit to each one of us, and underneath our
fatigue put an energy from outside us. Hold us
fast in the love of the brotherhood, remembering
that everything we suffer has already been suffered by the Liberator.

For the Threatened
We pray for all those so burdened with a sense of
mediocrity or guilt that they cannot let go of
supposed securities, for fear that justice will
strip them naked. God, give them other ground to
stand on. Show them that to renounce complicity
is the beginning of true security in the brotherhood of the Liberator.

For Travelers, hitch-hikers, drivers
God, in every age you send men and women from
their homeland like Abraham to build a new community in a distant country. Watch over those who
go out on trip. Do not let them fall into sickness or the hands of the violent, and each night
find them a meal and lodging for the sake of the
Son of Man who had no place to lay his head.

For a Trial
O Judge of the Ages, hold up the standard of your
truth to those who in this place are called agents
of your justice, so that they may speak not what
is conventional but what is right, remembering the
unjust condemnation, long ago and yesterday, of
their Liberator.

For the Unemployed
Jesus the manual laborer, stand beside those whom
oppression has deprived of useful work; turn their
hands to your work. Care for their needs, for
their wives and children; and do not let them be
muzzled by welfare. Redouble their cry for justice; build a true society on the solid base of
their indignation.

For Union organizers
O Source of change, you called Moses your first
prophet as an organizer of the exploited, the
leader of a general strike. Give all union organizers his commitment and power; by their work
break down every system of injustice and oppression, build a human society on this garden planet.

For Unity of people
O God of life, you who have made men and women of
one stock and one family, turn our eyes from out-
ward differences to the common humanity and let us
embrace, as children of one house, through the
Brother of us all.

For the Unity of the Church
O Fountain of unity, build all humankind into a
new creation around your Son, the true Adam. Do
not let administrative schemes deceive the simple.
Raise up everywhere people's organizers, who will
unite your church in order to do your desiring:
the works of freedom, conservation, and peace.

For Victims
Our Liberator, that Power which we do not understand has brought many persons (and especially *N.*)
into union with your suffering. Raise up cham-
pions for their cause. Do not leave them as victims long; and while they are such, give them your
confidence and a foretaste of the new life.

For the Vision of God
Bright Sun of all the worlds, you have made the
fullness of all the universe your splendor. Bring
us to such simplicity that our eyes can see the
Day of your liberation in every day, through the
one whose face reflects the knowledge of that
glory, Jesus our brother.

For the Vocation of everyone
Our God, you are no respecter of persons; all work
is your work, no man's is more important than another's. As our Brother learned in the carpenter's shop the whole task of liberation, so may

each of us bring to his task the whole person he
must become.

For White people
O God of history, you are taking this planet from
the white people who have long usurped it, and
giving it to others. Turn the children of the
colonialist to their brothers; let them bring with
them their treasures of science and art. Together
let them build one family without exploitation on
one living planet.

For our Work in the revolutionary Church
God, you make all things work together for good
among those who love you; help us build each word
and action into a consistent program of change,
looking forward to the coming New Age of cooperation among all in the Liberator.

For the Young
O God, in you is every future; stand beside the
young people in whom our future lies. Help them
avoid the mistakes of their parents; renew in them
all truths which their parents once affirmed.
Make them cells of a more just society, builders
of a restored planet.

For Liberation
Our Father, the Prince of this world had shut us
up very tight in his castle Despair; now the Liberator with the weapon of his Spirit has broken
down its walls, and we learn a new song of
freedom.

For a Safe Return
O Power of history, you exiled your people in
Babylon and brought the Liberator down to Egypt;
you have brought us home from the discomfort and
dangers of exile; we trust you also at the end to
anchor humankind, and the whole universe, in the
destination of their hoping.

For the Creation
Creator, you who have filled the universe with
splendor, even as we struggle against the powers
of darkness we celebrate your magnificence; we
make our road of combat part of the desired goal
and we salute you as our final Goal.

For Nature and History
Fountain of life, we praise you for the excellence
of the planet where we labor, for the lives and
works of our brothers and sisters in the past, for
touching our hearts to see both. Do not let us be
satisfied with less than whole commitment; let us
be your agents in life and liberation.

For a Saint
O Source of life, you pour humankind into many
shapes; we thank you for the example and witness
of your servant *N.*; help us take on the form of
humanity that our time and place call for, in the
strength of that Brother who is the perfect man.

For our Food
O King of the Ages, blessed are you who bring the
grain out of the earth and make the sap rise in
the vine. We praise you in these your gifts, we
ask that the hungry never be turned away from our
door, through that Liberator who declared all food
sacred and who never ceases offering us the bread
of life.

For Childbirth
Father of all living, we thank you that your
daughter *N.* has safely brought a child into the

world of light; watch over them both and, by your
Spirit, have the child brought up in the presence
of Jesus the Liberator.

For Harvest
Source of life, we praise you that once again in
its season the land has given its increase and
your people are fed in joyfulness; may the earth
never grow less green, and may all mankind ever
rejoice in your liberation.

Entering the Covenant

A form for the mutual compact of a group which may not yet have called or commissioned a minister; and where some may not yet have gone through the waters, or may have doubts about their baptism as infants.

SALUTATIONS

Leader and People:
It is time for us to wake up from sleep;
   Our freedom is nearer than when we believed.
                    [*Romans* 13:11]
See, now is the proper time;
   Today is the day of liberation.
                 [*2 Corinthians* 6:2]
You are the light of the world;
   A city set on a hill cannot be hidden.
                  [*Matthew* 5:14]
God has made with us a covenant of peace;
   He sends down the rain in its season.

He has broken the bars of our yoke;
   And freed us from the hand of our oppressors.
               [*Ezekiel* 34:25-27]
He removes bow and sword, and war from the land;
   He makes us lie down in safety.
                  [*Hosea* 2:18]
The habitation of God is with men;
   He lives with them and they are his people.
               [*Revelation* 21:3]
Change your heart and turn back;
   The fulfillment of time has arrived.
         [*Acts* 3:19; *Galatians* 4:4]
Be confident in the good news;
   The Liberated Zone is at hand.

                    [*Mark* 1:15]

THE PROMISE OF THE COVENANT

Leader: Friends, we are here as a group because we have tried and failed to make a life for ourselves individually. But a seed has been sown in the world, and each of us is aware of its germination in his heart. Today we want to throw off complicity with an old order of violence and to bind ourselves together in a new compact, so clearly that not the simplest person will doubt for an instant where we stand. We know that by ourselves we lack the insight and the will to do

this. So let us hear the old promise of a covenant freely made available to men and women, whose
terms are not arbitrary but the laws of the universe, offering that peace which the world cannot
give.

Assistant: See, the days are coming, says the
Power of history, that I will seal a new covenant
with the house of Israel. It will not be like the
covenant which I sealed with their fathers, on the
day when I took them by the hand to lead them out
of Egypt, the land of exploitation; for they rejected that covenant, even though I was their husband. For this is the covenant I will seal with
the house of Israel after those days: I will put
my law in their midst and write it on their
hearts; I shall be their God and they will be my
people. No more will a man teach his neighbor or
his brother, saying, "Know God"; for they will all
know me, from the least to the greatest. I will
pardon their crime and remember their complicity
no more.   [*Jeremiah* 31:31-34]

The Threefold Rule

Leader: Friends, let us hear from the prophet
that Way of justice which is the first rule of the
covenant.

Assistant: Is not this the fasting that I have
approved, says the Power of history:
>   To break the chains of injustice,
>   To cut the straps of the yoke,
>   To release the oppressed into freedom,
>   And to throw off every yoke;
>   To share your bread with the hungry,
>   And bring the landless poor into
>   your household;
>   When you see the naked, to cover him,
>   Not hiding away from your own flesh?
                              [*Isaiah* 58:6-7]

Leader: Let us next hear from the book of Moses
the permanent task laid on man and woman, to plant
the garden of this living planet.

Assistant: Then God took man and put him in the
paradise of Eden, to cultivate it and tend it.
And God blessed them and said to them, "Be fruit-
ful and increase, spread over the earth and regu-
late it; assume leadership over the fish of the
sea, the birds of the air, and every animal that
moves on the earth."   [*Genesis* 2:15; 1:28]

Leader: Friends, the good news we bear is that
Jesus is the agent of the new covenant. In him,
we who are called will receive our promised inheritance. Let us then finally open our ears to
the new Way of Love laid down for us by our
brother the Liberator.

Assistant:
> You shall love your enemies,
>> Do good to all who hate you,
>
> Bless those who denounce you,
>> Pray for those who harass you.
>
> If someone hits your right cheek,
>> Turn him the other also;
>
> If someone takes away your coat,
>> Give him your shirt also.
>
> Give to everyone who demands;
>> Do not ask to have back what is seized.
>
> And as you wish people would treat you,
>> You treat them just that same way.
>
> Your reward will be great,
>> For you will be children of the Highest,
>
> Who raises his sun on the evil and good,
>> And rains on the just and unjust;
>
> So you shall be merciful,
>> Just as your Father is merciful.
>>> [*Luke* 6:27-31, 35-36; *Matthew* 5:45]

LIBERATION FROM COMPLICITY

The following Statement of Complicity *is either
read by the people along with the leader, or repeated after him line by line.*

> We confess that we are accomplices
>> With the demonic powers of violence.
>
> We grow rich by daily oppression;
>> We sleep in beds of racism.
>
> We take pride in freedom and justice,
>> And we invent new slavery.
>
> We say that our goal is peace,
>> And invent new instruments of war.
>
> We live off the fat of the land,
>> And we poison it for our children.
>
> We say that we love our neighbor,
>> And we try to breed him off the earth.
>
> We cry out against exploitation,
>> And exploit each other and ourselves.
>
> And so we are accomplices
>> In the crime of burnt bodies;
>> Burnt ghettoes;
>> Burnt earth;
>> Burnt freedom.

We are accomplices by our violence,
    By our violence,
    By our most grievous violence,
  In turning our faces away
    And in doing nothing.

Leader and People:
    Kyrie eleison. Kyrie eleison.
    Lord have mercy upon us. Lord have mercy
        upon us.
    Christe eleison. Christe eleison.
    Christ have mercy upon us. Christ have
        mercy upon us.
    Kyrie eleison. Kyrie eleison.
    Lord have mercy upon us. Lord have mercy
        upon us.

Leader: The Power that lighted the stars, that
puts down oppressors and lifts up the poor from
the dust, can also transform our twisted and broken lives. For the door of our freedom opens by
itself for all that knock; whoever is in Jesus
our Liberator has become a new being. And so,
may he who provides us with bread from the earth,
air to breathe, and fire to purify rottenness, now
also in his great waters drown our old self, and
give us a fresh start through this community of
love. Amen; so may it be.

Psalm 111

I celebrate God with my whole heart
    In the community of those who love
            justice.
Great are the events he brings,
    To be studied by all who delight in him.
Splendor and beauty is his work;
    His justice stands forever.
He sets up a memorial of his marvels;
    Loving and gentle is our God.
He gives food to those who honor him;
    He always remembers his covenant.
He shows his people the power of his works
    By giving them the inheritance of the
            violent.
The works of his hands are certain and just;
    All his demands are true;
They are fixed for ever and ever,
    They are done in truth and confidence.
He sent liberation to his people;
    To eternity he upholds his covenant.
Blessed and holy is his being;
    His fear is the summit of wisdom.

A true mind is theirs who do his will;
His praise will stand forever.

MAKING THE COVENANT

Here a representative of the community reads their covenant statement; see the specimen appended.

Leader: Brothers and sisters, are you determined in your minds, without any reservation, to carry out the provisions of this covenant for the time provided?

Then each in turn, ending with the leader, expresses in his own words his adherence to the covenant.

Leader: Are you prepared, for that purpose, to study the Holy Scriptures, and the natural laws of society and this planet, building into your lives whatever new truths may come from that study?

People: We are prepared to do so.

Leader: Friends, it is a narrow door of service and commitment that we are entering today: more than an hour of ceremony, more than a summer of community organizing. For while there is a lower class, we are in it; while there is a soul in prison we are not free; while the earth is polluted we are unclean; wherever bombs fall, our wholeness is wounded. And if we claim to be perfect in knowledge or action, we deceive ourselves and injure our brother. Let us then always have in mind the story of the two men, which our Liberator taught us.

Assistant: Two men went into the sanctuary to pray, a clergyman and a sheriff. The clergyman stood up and prayed thus to himself: "God, I thank you that I am not like other men, exploiters, unjust, or unfaithful, such as this sheriff. I fast twice in the week, I give ten percent of all my income to charity." But the sheriff stood far off, not daring to lift his eyes to the sky, and struck his breast, saying: "God be gentle with me, a guilty man." I tell you, the second man went back to his house liberated, but not the first. For everyone who lifts himself up is put down; but the person who puts himself down is lifted up.   [*Luke* 18:9-14]

Leader: But we have been told, and believe, that the full commitment of the Liberator makes up for our failure in commitment: the news of his life is the power of God for liberation to everyone who trusts it [*Romans* 1:16]. Are you ready at this time to make that act of trust?

People: We are ready, in the strength of the Liberator.

Leader: Look then, sky and earth witness this day, that there have been set in front of us good and evil, blessing and curse, life and death. Which will you choose?

All: We choose life, that we and our children may live.   [*Deuteronomy* 30:19]

Leader: The covenant of peace is sealed; for God at his right time has sent the Spirit of the Liberator into our hearts, crying out:

[*Galatians* 4:6]

All:
        Abba, Father:
        Blessed be your working;
          Soon be your appearing;
            Done be your desiring.
        Our bread provide us;
          Our debts forgive us;
            From trials free us.

Then all present sign the document of the Covenant.

THE NEW UNITY

Leader: Brothers and sisters, we who have taken on the covenant of peace are no longer strangers, but fellow-citizens with the saints and residents in God's household, at one with the apostles and prophets. The cornerstone of our community is Jesus the Liberator, in whom we are becoming a living temple, a forest cathedral, of the Spirit. Let us then take to our heart the life of the original Church as Luke describes it.

Assistant: So all who accepted Peter's word went through the waters. They committed themselves to the teaching and community of the apostles, to the breaking of bread and prayers. And every person was afraid, for many great acts were done by the apostles. And all those who believed lived together and had all things common; they sold their possessions and property, and distributed them to all, as any one happened to have need. Daily they attended the Temple together; and house by house they broke bread and ate in gladness and joyfulness of heart, praising God and maintaining goodwill to all the people. And God added liberated

persons day by day to their number.
[*Acts* 2:41-47]

Here follow the Affirmations God is not dead
etc. from p. 123.
Then the Intercessions from the Litany (p. 35), or
in some other form.

Leader: This is my command, that you should love
each other as I loved you. No one has greater
love than this: to lay down his life for his
friends. You are my friends, if you do what I
command. And my yoke is easy and my burden light.
Peace I leave to you, my peace I give to you; not
as the world gives, do I give to you. Shalom.
[*John* 15:12-14; *Matthew* 11:30; *John* 14:27]

Here follows the Kiss of Peace.

Assistant:
    I your God love justice;
        I hate robbery and oppression.
    I give you your reward in truth;
        I seal with you a covenant of my Age.
    Your children are known among the peoples,
        Your descendants in the heart of all
                nations;
    All who see them will agree:
        They are a people that God has blessed.
[*Isaiah* 61.8-9]

BENEDICTUS

    Blessed is the God of Israel,
        For he has visited and ransomed his
                people;
    And lifted up a horn of liberation for us
        In the house of David his servant.
    As he promised by the mouth of his holy
                prophets
        Who have been since the start of his Age:
    Liberation from our enemies
        And from the hand of all that hate us,
    Showing gentleness to our forefathers
        And remembering his holy covenant,
    The promise he made to Abraham our father;
        That we, rescued from fear of our
                enemies,
    Should serve with holiness and justice
        All of our days in his presence.
[*Luke* 1:67-75]

Leader: Thus says the Alpha and the Omega, the
first and the last, the beginning and the end: I
was dead, and see, I am living in the Age to come;
I will give everyone that is victorious to eat
from the tree of life in the paradise of God.

[*Revelation* 22:13, 1:18, 2:7]

Specimen of a local covenant:

THE NOVEMBER FIFTH STATEMENT

Adopted by the staff of the Berkeley Free Church,
5 November 1969

The Free Church of Berkeley is a community within
the revolutionary Movement which relates to the
radical tradition of Jesus, the Prophets, and the
Church of Liberation.

> I will make for them a covenant on that day
> with the wild animals, with the birds of the
> air, and with the creeping things of the earth.
> [*Hosea* 2:18]

We recognize the Spirit of God at work in the
movement of our brothers and sisters for the restoration and preservation of the ecological balance of our planet. We believe that uncontrolled
production and consumption constitute violence
against ecological law and order. We admit our
complicity, individually and collectively, in the
pollution of our environment by chemicals and radiation, in the exploitation of natural resources
and wilderness, in the horror of overpopulation.
Therefore we dedicate ourselves to working toward
a life-style which holds a viable ecological order
as a sacred and revolutionary priority.

I will break bow, sword, and battle out of the
land, and allow them to sleep in safety.
[*Hosea* 2:18] I will make with them a covenant
of peace . . . and they will know that I am the
Power of history, when I break the bars of
their yoke and liberate them from the hand of
their oppressors. [*Ezekiel* 34:25-27]

We recognize the Spirit of God in the movement for
peace and liberation throughout the world. We
join in the struggle for the liberation of oppressed peoples (the poor, the Third World, racial
minorities, women, and youth) from exploitation
and racism at home and from imperialism abroad.
We dedicate ourselves to serve the victims of
force and oppression, avoiding the trap of the
colonialist mission in perpetuating a corrupt system, and recognizing that the highest form of
service is organizing the oppressed for resistance. We will struggle for the establishment of
social and political structures which are just,
humane, and participatory. We will resist institutions of war, conscription, racism, imperialism,
and injustice, and shall attempt to offer an alternative through the life of joy and suffering in
our voluntary community of brothers and sisters.

I will marry you to myself for ever, marry
you with integrity and justice, with tenderness and love. [*Hosea* 2:19]

We recognize the Spirit of God at work in the
struggle of our time toward sexual intimacy, vocational creativity, psychic integrity, and interpersonal sensitivity. We resist those institutions of our society which dehumanize and destroy
real interpersonal relations. We accept the imperative to develop attitudes and life-styles that
are personally and communally liberating and non-
exploitative. In celebration we will be freed to
work toward the ecological and social revolutions.

A Book of Changes

1. Receiving a Baby into the Covenant

Including the form for adoption of a child

The act of going through the waters implies that an individual is able to answer for himself or herself. By the present form a baby is brought into the covenant of peace in the fullest way that something can be done for one person by others.

PSALM 139

O Power of being, you have searched me out;
    You see my thoughts from far away.
You surround my path and my bed.
    And have knowledge of all my ways.
Before a word is on my tongue,
    My God, you know it perfectly.
You encounter me in front and behind;
    You lay your hand upon me.
The marvel of your knowledge is beyond me;
    It is too high for me to reach.
For you shaped all my parts;
    You formed me in my mother's womb.
I will praise your works;
    For I was wonderfully made.
You knew my life altogether,
    My substance was not hidden from you,
When I was being made in secret,
    Fashioned in the depths of the earth.
Your eyes saw my unformed shape;
    In your book my members were written,
And all the days that were made for me,
    Before they had yet come to being.

Minister: We celebrate you, our Father, master of sky and earth, that you hid these things from the wise and learned, and revealed them to babies. Yes, our Father, for this was your joyful will.
                        [Luke 10:21]

THE PRESENTATION

Here the mother, holding her child, prays in her own words or as follows.

Mother: Fountain of all life, I thank you because you have entrusted me with a share in your work of creation, and given me a child for the covenant of your peace. Like Hannah I have brought *him* [*her*] to your congregation; and I pray that *he* may live all *his* life in this community, through Jesus our Liberator who was once a child.

All: Amen; so may it be.

Or if the baby is adopted, the mother can say:

Maker of all life, another has given birth, and I have been entrusted with the child that was born. I bring *him* [*her*] as my own child into the presence of this congregation; and I pray that *he* may live all *his* life in the covenant of your peace; through Jesus our Liberator who also found a new mother in the community of love.

Father: Friends, we have read in the book of Luke how the child of Mary, eight days after his birth, was given his name of JESUS and taken to the Temple to be brought into the covenant; there he was blessed by Symeon and Anna. So likewise we have brought this child of our bodies [or, this child whom we have taken as our child] to the present company. Here we will renew our own commitments, name this child and enroll him in this community, and begin his education in it.

Reader: They brought him children so that he could lay his hands on them; and his Disciples criticized them. But when Jesus saw this he was very angry, and said to them, "Allow children to come to me, do not prevent them; for to such belongs the liberated zone. Truly I tell you, unless a person receives God's liberation like a child, he will never enter it." Then he took them up in his arms, put his hands on them, and blessed them.   [*Mark* 10:13-17]

LITANY

O Child, our promised Prince of Peace: **Accept your own children.**

O Child praised by shepherds and their animals: **Accept your own children.** *And so on.*

O Child honored by kings of the earth:

O Child given the name JESUS of liberation:

O Child, carrier of the world's spirit:

O Child, born in the city of royalty:

O Child, taxed by a foreign oppressor:

O Child, presented in God's temple:

O Child acclaimed by Symeon the prophet:
O Child, a displaced person for the covenant's
    sake:
O Child, in whose place the innocents were
    murdered:
O child apprenticed to the manual laborer: **Accept
    your own children.**
O Child, a runaway for your father's business:
    Accept your own children.

THE PROMISES

Minister: Let us all at this time renew the promises which we once made in the presence of this
community.

*Here the Minister and People repeat the six ques-
tions from the form of going through the waters
(pp. 73-74).*

Minister (to the parents): Brother and sister, we
have just reaffirmed our own commitments. Are you
determined to bring this child up in a household
where those convictions are living, while also
letting *him* [*her*] have *his* own integrity; and at
the right time help *him* to a free act of going
through the waters?

*Here the parents express their willingness in
their own words.*

Minister (to the godparents): Do you undertake
full responsibility for the care and education of
this child if its parents should be taken from
this community, as if it were your child?

Godparents: **This child is flesh of our flesh.**

THE COVENANT

Minister: Let us hear from the prophet Hosea
God's promises of hope in the covenant of peace,
which this child is about to enter.

Reader: On that day I will seal for you a covenant with the wild animals, with the birds of the
sky and the beasts of the earth. I will break the
bow and sword, and remove war out of the land; and
I will make you lie down in safety. I will marry
you to me forever, marry you in justice and integrity, in love and gentleness; I will marry you to
me in steadfastness, and you will know that I am
God.   [*Hosea* 2:18-20]

Minister: Sky and earth witness to us that God
has set before us today good and evil, blessing
and curse, life and death. Which will you choose?

All: We choose life, that we and our children may
live.

Here follow the Affirmations God is not dead *etc.
from p. 123.*

RECEIVING THE CHILD

Then the father and mother say together:

> This child of our flesh has found a new
>   family;
> We name *him* [*her*] N.;
> We entrust *him* [*her*] to you our brothers and
>   sisters.

Or if the child is adopted they say:

> We take this child as flesh of our flesh;
> We name *him* [*her*] N.;
> We entrust *him* [*her*] to you our brothers and
>   sisters.

*Then the Minister enters the child's name in the
book of the community, saying:*

Blessed are all those whose names are written in
the Lamb's book of life. As this child sees the
faces of its family on earth, so may its guardians
beyond space and time see the face of our one
Father.

All: Abba, Father:
            Blessed be your working;
                Soon be your appearing;
                    Done be your desiring.
            Our bread provide us;
                Our debts forgive us;
                    From trials free us.

Reader: All those who are led by the spirit of
God are children of God. For you did not receive
a spirit of slavery in fear, but a spirit of adoption, in which we cry out, Abba, Father. The
Spirit itself witnesses together with our spirit
that we are children of God; and if children, then
also heirs; heirs of God and joint heirs with the
Liberator. With him we suffer together so that we
may live together with him in splendor.

                        [*Romans* 8:14-17]

Minister: Whoever wishes to be first among us,
must be last of all and a servant of all. For the

Liberator took up children in his arms, saying: "Whoever receives such a child in my name receives me; and whoever receives me, receives not me but the one who sent me." Shalom, brothers and sisters, sons and daughters, the covenant of peace be upon you all, Shalom.

Then follows the Kiss of Peace, begun by the parents kissing the child.

PSALM 23

My shepherd is the God of creation;
    There is nothing I lack.
He lets me lie down in high pastures;
    He guides me to the water of peace.
He opens my life in liberty
    To walk in the ways of justice.
Although I go through death valley
    I am not afraid of wickedness;
For you are walking beside me,
    The way of my leader guides me.
You set a table before me
    In the face of all my oppressors;
My brow is bright with the olive,
    My cup is filled overflowing.
Joy and gentleness follow me
    All the days of my life;
I make my home in God's keeping
    Until the end of all days.

Then the Minister marks a cross with oil on the child's forehead, saying:

May the Father send guardians to watch over you at night, and to be your shade by day.

Then the parents give the child the Bible (or the New Testament or Psalms) and also the prayer-book of the community, saying:

Take the words we live by; we set your feet in no other way than the one we ourselves have chosen.

MAGNIFICAT

My heart praises the Power of being,
    My life leaps up in my Liberator.
For he saw the oppression of his servant;
    Every age will now hail me as happy.
That Energy has dealt with me nobly;
    Blessed is the name of his being.
His sympathy spreads on all ages
    Of those who are fearful before him.

He has done a new thing with his arm,
 And scattered the arrogant in their
   schemes.
' He has pulled down the powerful from their
   seats
 And raised up the wretched of the earth.
He has filled the hungry with his food,
 And turned the wealthy away.
He has restored his servant Israel,
 Remembering his constant kindness,
As he promised to our fathers, to Abraham
 And his offspring until the new Age.
        [*Luke* 1:46-55]

Minister:
 God bless you and watch over you;
  God shine his face on you and love you;
   God lift up his face to you, and set
    his peace among you.
        [*Numbers* 6:24-26]

2. Going through the Waters

This form, the act of permanent adult commitment to the new Way, is an adaptation of the old Roman Easter Eve liturgy and baptism. It is set in the context of the Freedom Meal, and should only be shortened in prisons, in sickness, or other emergency. If possible it should be a Vigil service and ideally it will be scheduled for the Eve of Easter or Pentecost; but any baptism is of itself a festival of the Resurrection.

THE NEW FIRE

Outside the room new fire is struck.

Minister: O Light beyond all worlds, in the beginning you organized the primeval darkness into our universe; let this new fire signal for us the great work by which you placed Jesus our Liberator in the center of history, a man transparent to your illumination, so that the spirit of his new life may shine in our community of love.

People: Amen; so may it be.

A taper is lit, and the procession enters the darkened room, while three times is said:

Minister: The light of liberation.

People: Thanks be to God.

Reader: Rejoice now, you army of Powers beyond space and time, your Captain of humility is at hand; blow the trumpet of freedom for the servant King who conquers by love. Let the stars of morning shout as they did at the first moment of creation, for our Brother is making a new sky, a new earth. Sing with joy, forests and oceans, mountains and grainfields; for your mother the Earth has passed out of eclipse by demonic powers into the noontide Sun of justice, who restores her for all creatures that live on her. And gather together here, you whole cloud of witnesses in the liberated community of love, and fill our halls in the glory of the Illuminator.

Here the Candle and other lights are lit.

Reader and People:
> Peace be with you all.
> And with you, our brother.

Lift up your hearts.
    We lift them up to our Liberator.
Let us celebrate the Power of being.
    It is good and right for us to do so.

Reader: It is right that here and now we should
thank you, O Power of history, through Jesus our
Liberator, the true Adam, who was executed by the
oppressor and lives in us with triumph; he is the
Lamb sacrificed at the Passover feast, in whom
death has died. In this night you led our fathers
out of the house of exploitation, passing through
the great waters on dry land; in this night those
who walk the new Way pass out from the valley of
darkness into the clear light of your Liberated
Zone; in this night our Brother breaks the chains
of our hell of separation, and builds us into the
society of mankind. To free an unfaithful servant
you gave up a loyal son; O fortunate guilt of man,
that warranted such liberation!

Therefore, O Father of lights, accept this candle,
that it may burn continually to push back the
frontiers of darkness. May the Morningstar who
knows no setting, when he comes in splendor to
consummate his work, find it still burning, and us
his brothers still working by its light. Amen; so
may it be.

THE SIX PROPHECIES OF THE WATERS

*Then a spokesman for those who wish to go through
the waters says:*

Friends, we are here at this time as refugees from
the occupied territory of exploitation; we wish to
enter the liberated zone of your fellowship.

Minister: Brothers and sisters, you are welcome.
You know and we know that no person can enter new
life except through the purification of death to
the old way. Let us then be quiet and hear the
promise of the waters.

Reader: Hear the first prophecy, the bounding of
the great deep, from the book of Job.
    Where were you when I compacted the earth?
        Speak if you have such knowledge.
    Who (if you know) set its dimensions?
        Who put his yardstick against it?
    What did its foundations rest on,
        Who laid its cornerstone,
    When the stars of dawn sang together
        And the sons of God called out in joy?

And who fenced the sea with gates,
    When it broke out from the womb,
When I made the clouds its clothing,
    And wrapped it in the dark storm,
And planted a boundary for it,
    And set up its gates with their bar,
And said, "So far you may come, and no
        further;
    The pride of your waves is here broken"?
                              [*Job* 38:4-11]

People:
    When he fixed the sky, Wisdom was there;
        When he drew a circle on the face of the
            deep.   [*Proverbs* 8:27]

Reader: Hear the second prophecy of the rainbow,
from the book of Moses.

And God said, "This is the symbol of the Constitution which I am making between myself, and you,
and every living creature that is with you, for
all the generations of time. I am setting my bow
in the stormcloud, and it will be a symbol of the
constitution between me and the earth. Whenever
I bring the stormcloud over the earth and the bow
appears in the cloud, I will remember the constitution between me and you and all living creatures, every kind of animal. The waters will
never again become a flood to destroy all flesh.
When the bow is in the stormcloud, I will see it
and remember the everlasting constitution between
God and every living creature, every animal on
earth."   [*Genesis* 9:12-16]

People: For all the days of the earth, sowing and
harvest, heat and cold, summer and winter, day and
night shall not cease.   [*Genesis* 8:22]

Reader: Hear the third prophecy, how a new people
was born by going through the great waters, from
the book of Moses.

Then Moses stretched out his hand over the sea,
and God pushed the sea back by the strong wind of
his breath from the east, all the night long. He
made the sea dry land, and the water was divided.
And the children of Israel went into the middle of
the sea on dry ground; the waters were a wall for
them on the right and on the left. And the
Egyptians were pursuing and came in after them,
all Pharaoh's horse and chariots and cavalry, into
the middle of the sea. And in the morning watch

God looked down on the army of Egypt from the pillar of fire and cloud; and he held up the army of
Egypt by muddying their chariot wheels so that
they were too heavy to roll. And Egypt said, "Let
me run away from the face of Israel; for God is
fighting on their side against Egypt."

Then God said to Moses, "Stretch out your hand
over the sea, and the water will come back over
Egypt, over his chariots and cavalry." And Moses
stretched out his hand over the sea, and the sea
returned at daybreak to its usual place, and the
Egyptians rushed into it. So God wiped out the
Egyptians in the middle of the sea. The water returned and covered the chariots, the cavalry, and
all Pharaoh's army that went after them into the
sea; not one of them remained. But the children
of Israel walked on dry ground in the middle of
the sea, and the water was a wall for them on the
right hand and on the left.   [*Exodus* 14:21-29]

People:
    I will sing to the Power beyond armies,
      For he has utterly triumphed;
    The horses and the chariots
      He has thrown into the sea;
    They were covered up by the floods,
      They went down in the deep like a stone.
                   [*Exodus* 15:1, 10]

Reader: Hear the fourth prophecy of God's victory
over the dark powers of the deep, from the book of
Isaiah.
    Wake up, wake up, get dressed with strength,
      O Arm of the Power beyond all hosts;
    Wake up as in the ancient days,
      The generations of the ages.
    Was it not you that cut up the Beast,
      That wounded the great monster?
    Was it not you that dried up the sea,
      The water of the great deep,
    That made the abyss of the sea a road
      For the liberated to go through on?
    All those ransomed by God will return,
      And come to Zion with singing;
    The happiness of the Age to come
      Shall rest as a crown on their heads;
    Gladness and joy are given to them,
      Mourning and tears are abolished.
                [*Isaiah* 51:9-11]

People:

> He has drawn a circle on the face of the
>   waters,
>   At the horizon of light and darkness;
> The pillars of sky are shaking
>   And cower at his demands.
> With his power he stilled the sea,
>   By his knowledge he smashed the World
>   Beast.
> By the wind of his breath the sky grew fair,
>   His hand impaled the Pig retreating.
>   [*Job* 26:10-13]

Reader: Hear the fifth prophecy of drowning and
rebirth, from the book of Jonah.

> I called out of my distress
>   To the Power of being, and he heard me;
> From inside the belly of the prison
>   I cried and you heard my voice.
> For you threw me in the heart of the sea.
>   I was surrounded by the flood;
> All your waves and breakers
>   Have passed over my head.
> The waters shut in over my life,
>   The deep was on every side of me,
> Weeds were wrapped around my head
>   At the roots of the mountains.
> I went down to the land
>   Where gates shut against me forever,
> But you brought me up living from that death,
>   O God my liberator.   [*Jonah* 2:2-6]

People:

> Out of the depths I cried to you, my God;
>   O Liberator, hear my voice;
> May your ears consider well
>   The voice of my complaining. [*Psalm* 130:1]

Reader: Hear how Jesus our brother went down into
the great waters, from the book of Mark.

The beginning of the message of Jesus the Liberator, as it stands written in the prophets: "See,
I send my messenger before your face, he will prepare your way"; "A voice of one crying, in the
desert prepare God's way, make his paths
straight." John the baptizer was in the desert
proclaiming passage through the waters as a fresh
start for liberation from crimes. The whole land
of Judea went out to him, and all the people of
Jerusalem. They went through the waters at his
hands in the Jordan river, admitting their crimes.
John's clothing was of camel hair, with a leather

belt around his waist; he ate locusts and wild
honey. And in his announcement he said: "One
stronger that I am is coming after me, whose sandals I could not stoop down and unloose. I make
you pass through water; he will make you pass
through the holy Spirit." In those days there
came Jesus from Nazareth of Galilee and went
through the waters in Jordan at John's hands. And
just as he was coming out of the water, he saw
the sky split and the spirit coming down on him
like a dove. And there was a voice from the sky,
"You are my beloved son, in you I am well
pleased."   [*Mark* 1:1-11]

People: I have waters I must go through; I am uneasy until it is finished.   [*Luke* 12:50]

THE RULES OF THE NEW WAY

*Here are read the three Rules of the new way from
the form of entering the covenant (pp. 52-53).*

THE LITANY

Reader: And Cain said to Abel his brother, "Let
us go out to the desert." And when they were in
the desert, Cain rose up against Abel his brother
and murdered him. And God said to Cain, "Where is
Abel your brother?" And he said, "I do not know;
am I my brother's keeper?" And God said, "What
have you done? The voice of your brother's blood
is crying to me from the ground. And now you are
cursed on account of the ground, which opened its
mouth to receive your brother's blood from your
hand. When you work the ground, it will no longer
yield you its strength; you will be a fugitive and
a wanderer on the earth."   [*Genesis* 4:8-12]

Reader and People:
    Whose blood is this on my hands? **Wash off
      your brother's blood.**
    Whose sweat has built my affluence? **Wash off
      your brother's blood.** *And so on.*
    What burned flesh is in my nostrils?
    My finger has pressed the bomb-release.
    My hand has voted the war-lever.
    My ears are deaf to the beggar.
    My eyes have turned away from the wounded.
    My key has locked out the poor.
    My axe is sticky from the redwoods.
    My voice is hoarse from lying.
    My loins have subdued the slavegirl.
    I put death in my children's milk.
    I programmed the death-computer.

I made my lover a stranger.
I breathe the poison of my inventions.
I do not know my brother.
Am I my brother's keeper? Wash off your
    brother's blood.
What blood is this on my hands? Wash off
    your brother's blood.

THE QUESTIONS

Minister: Brothers and sisters, you have heard
the rule of justice from the book of the Prophets,
and Jesus' rule of love from the Gospel. Are you
committed from now on to walk by those rules in
your dealings with other people?

Candidates: Yes, I am committed to serve and liberate the oppressed and to love my enemies.

Minister: You have also heard the rule of our
common life on this earth from the book of Moses.
Will you undertake to help limit the numbers of
the human race and to maintain the order of the
planet?

Candidates: I take on the task of Adam, to build
the paradise of Eden.

Minister: Are you ready at this time to break off
your ties with all that destroys God's created orders, both of nature and society?

Candidates: I renounce cooperation with every
system of violence and oppression.

Minister: Are you convinced that Jesus our Brother, through the new Way of revolutionary nonviolence which he teaches and illustrates, is our
only salvation from disorder, guilt, and meaninglessness?

Candidates: I trust in Jesus as my only Liberator.

Minister: Are you ready to follow his way in joy
and sorrow, in comfort and deprivation, in life
and death; and in solidarity with the Church, of
which the fellowship assembled here is part?

Candidates: I will follow his Way wherever it
leads; his Way is peace, peace is his Way.

Minister: In the spirit of this community, will
you constantly renew the promises you make here
and the life you receive here; and work consistently for renewal of the planet, of society, of
our own freedom, teaching and organizing to your
life's end?

Candidates: I join the revolutions of justice and love.

ACCEPTING THE COVENANT

Minister: Friends, you have heard how in the beginning the Power beyond nature and history
brought this earth into existence from the ocean
of nonbeing; how he has again and again kept the
family of mankind from being swallowed up by the
floods of the Beast; and how at the right time of
history he brought Jesus our brother through the
water of Jordan and the greater waters of death as
the firstborn of the new Age. Some of you may
have been brought to the waters as babies by social convention, or as adults without any clear
understanding. Now you have considered the radical change laid on us by the sacred books, and demanded by the needs of the earth, of the poor, of
our own souls. Are you then prepared, for what is
truly the first and last time, to make a fresh
start, accepting the death and life, the suffering and promise, of the waters?

*Here each candidate in turn expresses in his own
words his readiness to go through the waters.*

Minister: Brothers and sisters, we welcome you as
fellow-soldiers in the warfare of the Lamb. Our
leader said that if his kingdom were of this
world, his servants would fight; but his kingdom
is not of this world. And although we live in
this world, we are not fighting a worldly war,
for the weapons of our warfare are not of this
world, and therefore have power to destroy the
fortress of the dark powers [*2 Corinthians* 10:3].
For our strength is made perfect in weakness. Will
you accept induction into this army and no other,
at whatever cost?

Candidates: I accept induction into his army and
no other, at whatever cost.

Minister: See, sky and earth witness to us, that
God has set before us this day good and evil,
blessing and curse, life and death. Which will
you choose?

Candidates: I choose life, that I and my children
may live.

Minister: Hear from our brothers and sisters the
affirmations of our commitment.

75

Then are recited the Affirmations God is not dead *etc. from p. 123.*

The Blessing of the Waters

Minister: Lift up your hearts.

People: We lift them up to the Liberator.

Minister: Let us celebrate the Power of Being.

People: It is good and right for us to do so.

Minister: It is right that we should praise you, O Energy of creation, because by your wisdom humankind was born from the womb of the waters, and each passes back into them; but still, at every threat to our continuance, new communities of hope have emerged from a passage through the great seas. And so, may all who, trusting in you, pass through these waters be washed clean from their brother's blood and embrace him in peace; may they strip off complicity for guilt and put on the white clothing of justice; may the old man of aloofness be drowned and a new man of solidarity be raised up. By your life-giving spirit, O God, which at the beginning hovered over the deep, bless these waters as the means of our union with Jesus our Brother, the vanguard of your new creation. Amen; so may it be.

Then the candidates one by one pass through the waters according to local custom, while over each is said:

Minister: In the name of Jesus our Liberator, may the Power of Being bring you through the great waters of death into the new community of his Spirit.

The Clothing and Anointing

Then the candidates are dressed in white clothing, while is said:

Minister: As our Brother, after he first took on the necessity of suffering, was seen by his friends transfigured in light, so may you take this white clothing as a symbol that you are united with the splendor of his commitment.

And after all are so dressed:

Minister: Who are these dressed in white clothing, and where have they come from?

People: These are ones who have come out from great oppression; they have washed their clothing

and made it white in the blood of the Lamb.
[*Revelation* 7:13-14]

*Then each candidate is anointed on the forehead,
while is said:*

Minister: As prophets, priests, and kings were
once anointed for their office; since you have
shared the death of Jesus our brother, may you
also share the new life of his anointing, whom we
recognize as our only prophet, our only priest,
our only king.

Reader: Hear how the Liberator was anointed for
death and for life with the best gifts of the creation, by a woman from among the oppressed.

One of the clergymen asked Jesus to eat with him;
and he came into the house of the clergyman and
took his place. Now a harlot of that city, when
she learned that he was at the clergyman's table,
took an alabaster jar of ointment. She stood at
his feet weeping, and with her tears she began to
wash his feet. Then she dried them with the hair
of her head, and kissed his feet, and rubbed them
with the ointment.   [*Luke* 7:36-38]

THE SIX PROPHECIES OF THE SPIRIT

Spokesman for the new members: Friends, we thank
you for taking us in from out of Babylon the
great. But many of our brothers and sisters are
still lost in the City of destruction; go out and
help them also.

Minister: We welcome you, our brothers and sisters, into the community of love. But neither you
nor we have power to go out into the doomed
streets and speak the word of life unless the sea-
breeze of the Spirit is blowing through us. So
let us again be quiet and listen for the voice of
the west wind of life and change.

Reader: Hear the first prophecy of the Spirit,
how man and woman received the breath of life,
from the book of Moses.

In the day when God made earth and sky, there was
at first no wild plant on the earth, no wild herb
had yet grown; for God had not brought rain on the
earth, and there was no human being to work the
ground. But then a flood rose up from the earth,
and watered all the face of the ground. And God
shaped mankind of clay from the ground, and
breathed a living spirit into his nostrils; so man

became a living creature. And God had planted a
garden in Eden (that is, "Delight") from of old;
and there he set the human beings he had shaped.
And God brought out of the ground every tree beautiful to see or good to eat, the trees of life;
and in the middle of the garden, the tree of
knowledge of good and evil.   [*Genesis* 2:4-9]

People:
> He gives us a new heart,
> He puts a new spirit in us;
> He takes the stone heart out of our flesh,
> And gives us a heart of flesh.
> [*Ezekiel* 36:26]

Reader: Hear the second prophecy of the Spirit,
how men became deaf to each other, from the book
of Moses.

And the whole earth had one tongue and few words.
And as they wandered from the east, they found a
valley in the plain of Shinar, and settled there.
And each one said to his neighbor, "Come, let us
make bricks and bake them." They had bricks for
stone, and asphalt for mortar. And they said,
"Come, let us build ourselves a city, and a tower
with its head in the sky; let us make ourselves a
memorial, so that we shall not be scattered on the
face of all the earth." And God came down to see
the city and the tower that the sons of man had
built. And God said, "See, they are one people,
and they have all one tongue. This is only the
beginning of what they will do; now nothing they
plan to do will be walled off from them. Come,
let us go down and confuse their tongues there, so
that a man will not hear his neighbor's tongue."
And God scattered them from there over the face of
all the earth, and they stopped building the city.
[*Genesis* 11:1-8]

People:
> He gives us a new heart,
> He puts a new spirit in us;
> He takes the stone heart out of our flesh,
> And gives us a heart of flesh.

Reader: Hear the third prophecy of the Spirit,
the vision of an age of alienation, from the book
of Ezekiel.

The hand of God was on me; and he brought me in
the spirit of God and set me in the middle of a
desert full of bones. And he led me around
through them; there were very many of them in the

desert, and they were very dry. And he said to
me, "Son of man, will these bones live?" And I
said to him, "Lord, you are the one that knows."
And he said to me, "Prophesy to these bones, and
say to them, You dry bones, hear the word of God:
See, I am bringing breath into you, and you will
live. I will lay tendons on you, and draw flesh
over you, and put skin on you, and give you breath
for you to live; so you will know that I am God."

And I prophesied as I was told; and when I prophesied, there was a noise of rattling, as bone came
together with bone. And I looked, and saw tendons
on them, and flesh on them, and skin over it; but
they had no breath. Then he said to me, "Prophesy
to the Spirit; prophesy, son of man, and say to
the Spirit, Thus says God: Come from the four
winds, O Spirit, and breathe upon these corpses,
so that they may live." And I prophesied as he
told me; and the breath came into them, and they
came to life, and they stood on their feet, a very
great army.   [*Ezekiel* 37:1-10]

People:
     He gives us a new heart,
       He puts a new spirit in us;
     He takes the stone heart out of our flesh,
       And gives us a heart of flesh.

Reader: Hear the fourth prophecy of the Spirit, a
vision of the Liberator, from the book of Isaiah.
     The Spirit of God is upon me,
       Because God has anointed me;
     He sent me to tell the oppressed good news,
       To restore the broken-hearted;
     To announce liberation to the captives
       And daylight for all those imprisoned;
     To proclaim the year of God's pity,
       A day of vengeance for our God;
     To comfort all those who mourn,
       To give them the oil of gladness.
     So that men will build up the ancient ruins
       And repair the desolate cities.
                [*Isaiah* 61:1-4]

People: He gives us a new heart,
       He puts a new spirit in us;
     He takes the stone heart out of our flesh,
       And gives us a heart of flesh.

Reader: Hear the fifth prophecy of the gifts of the Spirit, from the letter of Paul to the Corinthians.

We speak wisdom among the fully committed. Not a wisdom of this age, nor of the demonic rulers of this age, doomed to destruction; but the wisdom of God hidden in secret, which he set up before time and space to honor us. None of the magistrates of this age recognize it; for if they had recognized it, they would not have executed the Liberator of splendor. It is written, "No eye has seen, no ear has heard, no heart has imagined, what things God has prepared for those who love him." These things God has uncovered to us through the Spirit; the Spirit searches out all things, even the abysses of God. No one knows a man's affairs except his spirit inside him; so no one knows God's affairs except the Spirit of God. And we have not received the spirit of the world but the spirit of God, so that we should know the free gifts made by God to us; which we do not speak in words taught by human wisdom, but in words taught by the Spirit.
[*1 Corinthians* 2:6-13]

People:
       He gives us a new heart,
         He puts a new spirit in us;
       He takes the stone heart out of our flesh,
         And gives us a heart of flesh.

Reader: When the Fiftieth day after the Passover, which is Pentecost, arrived, they were all together in one place. And there came suddenly from the sky the sound of a strong steady wind which filled the whole house where they were sitting. And there appeared to them tongues of fire, distributed and resting on each of them. And they were all filled with the sacred Spirit, and they began to speak in other tongues, just as the Spirit put in their mouths. Now there were staying at Jerusalem Jews and religious men from every nation under the sky; and when the sound was heard, a crowd of them gathered and was astonished, because each one heard them speaking in his own language. They were carried out of themselves in wonder, saying: "Are not all these who are speaking Galilaeans? How is it that each of us hears them speaking in his own language, that he was brought up in? Parthians and Medes and Elamites, inhabitants of Mesopotamia, of Armenia and Cappadocia, Pontus and Asia, Phrygia and

Pamphylia, Egypt and the districts of Libya near
Cyrene; Romans in residence, Jews and converts,
Cretans and Arabs; we hear them speaking in our
own tongues the great actions of God."

[*Acts* 2:1-11]

People:
>He gives us a new heart,
>>He puts a new spirit in us;
>He takes the stone heart out of our flesh,
>>And gives us a heart of flesh.

THE GIFT OF THE SPIRIT

Minister: Brothers and sisters, after the new
thing has been born, it must still be given the
breath of life. You have heard how again and
again in the past the spirit has been transmitted;
will you here and now receive it in your hearts?

Candidates: I open my body as a temple of the
Spirit.

Minister: Will you bring the same Spirit to your
own household, helping the young to desire the
things done here, so that your family may be an
example and nucleus for the larger community of
love?

Candidates: I will help build the lives around me
into the new City.

Minister: As the Artisan of nature designed the
galaxies and earth with his fingers, will you make
your vocation and job transparent to his Spirit?

Candidates: In my work I stand beside my Brother
the carpenter.

Minister: As he was content to be the servant of
all, will you in his spirit always take thought
for the poor, the suffering, the oppressed?

Candidates: I will be union spokesman and waiter
at table.

Minister: When your own hour of casualty comes,
will you with confidence rely on the same spirit
of ministry in this brotherhood?

Candidates: In strength and in weakness I trust
in the spirit of life.

Minister and People:
>Be all of one mind in the Spirit. We are all
>of one mind in the Spirit.

Through the love of the Fountain of life:
   We are all of one mind in the Spirit.
   And so on.
Through Jesus our brother's fidelity:
Through the hope of his people in every age:
In prosperity and in harassment:
In our families and our aloneness:
In our suffering and celebration:
At the day of death, in the years of living:
In solidarity with God's whole people: We
   are all of one mind in the Spirit.
In unity with all the creation: We are all
   of one mind in the Spirit.

Then the Candidates kneel down before the Minister and his colleagues, who lay hands on their heads, saying:

In the name of Jesus our Liberator, may the healing Spirit of God rest upon you; the spirit of wisdom and understanding, the spirit of counsel and strength, the spirit of gentleness and the love of God, in this reconciled community of friends.

Then likewise the Ministers kneel down and receive the spirit from the new members; and so throughout the congregation. The Kiss of Peace follows, while the Minister says:
Shalom, my brothers and sisters, the peace of our Liberator be with you. Shalom.

Minister: The covenant of peace has been sealed; for God has sent the spirit of repentance into your hearts, crying out:

All:

    Abba, Father:
    Blessed be your working;
     Soon be your appearing;
      Done be your desiring;
    Our bread provide us;
     Our debts forgive us;
      From trials' free us.

CANTICLE

And after this I will pour out
   The breath of my spirit on all flesh.
Your sons and daughters will prophesy,
   Your old men will dream dreams,
Your young men will see visions;
   On your servants I will pour out my spirit.
               [*Joel* 2:28-29]

AT THE FREEDOM MEAL

Then begins the Litany of the Saints (p. 33), during which the Ministers can leave the room and return in celebration vestments. Immediately afterwards follows the Gloria in Excelsis (p. 122), during which bells are rung.

Minister: Let us hear that Word from which, we believe, there is fresh light yet to break.

THE EPISTLE

All of us who went through the waters to Jesus our Liberator, went through them to his death. For we were buried with him through our immersion into his death so that, just as he was awakened from the dead by the splendor of the Father, we also might walk in new life. For if we have been grafted onto the manner of his death, so shall we also be with his rising. We are aware that our old self was executed along with him, so that our complicity with evil might be destroyed, for us to serve evil no longer. And if we have died with him, we trust that we will also live with him. For we know that, after the Liberator was waked up from among the dead, he will not die again; death has no more control over him. He died to evil once and for all; he now lives to God. So we must think of ourselves as dead to evil, and alive to God in Jesus the Liberator.   [*Romans* 6:3-11]

PSALM 98

Sing a new song to the Power of history,
    For he has done wonderful things;
His right hand and his holy arm
    Have carried off liberation.
He has made his victory known,
    To all races he showed his justice;
He remembered his mercy and truth
    To all the house of Israel;
And all the continents of the earth
    Have seen the liberation of our God.
Sing to him, the whole world;
    Rejoice, cry out and praise.
Praise him with every music,
    With music and voice of melody,
With trumpets and sound of horns
    Be happy before the King of power.
Let the sea in its fulness thunder,
    The globe and its inhabitants;
Let the rivers clap their hands,
    Let the mountains laugh together,

Before the Power of history
  Who comes to judge the earth;
He will judge the globe in fairness.
  And all the races with equity.

THE GOSPEL

Now two of them on that day were walking to a village named Emmaus about sixty miles from Jerusalem, and discussing together all these things that
had happened. And while they were talking, Jesus
himself drew near and began walking with them; but
their eyes were kept from recognizing him. He
said to them, "What words were you exchanging in
your journey?" They stood still, discouraged.
One of them named Cleopas answered: "You have
been staying in Jerusalem, and do not know the
events that have happened there in these days?"
He said, "What events?"

They said, "The affair of Jesus the Nazarene, a
prophet powerful in action and word, in the sight
of God and all the people--how the chief priests
and magistrates turned him over for a death sentence and executed him. But we were hoping that
it was he who would liberate Israel. Furthermore,
this is the third day since it happened. And some
women of our number have given us an astonishing
report; they were at the grave early in the morning and did not find his body; but told us they
had seen a vision of Messengers, who said he was
alive. Some of us went to the grave, and found it
as the women reported; him they did not see."

He said to them: "You fools and slow of heart to
trust all that the prophets said; did not the Liberator have to endure these things before entering
his splendor?" Then starting with Moses and all
the prophets he explained to them the things
about himself in all the Books.

They came near the village they were going to, and
he appeared to be journeying farther. But they
urged him, saying, "Stay with us, for it is near
evening and the day is almost done." So he came
in and stayed with them. And when he joined them
at table, he took the loaf, gave thanks, broke it,
and divided it among them. Then their eyes were
opened, and they recognized him; but he no longer
was seen by them.

They said to each other, "Did not our hearts burn
in us, when he was talking to us on the road, at
the way he opened the Books to us?" And they got

up at that very hour and went back to Jerusalem,
and found the Eleven and their companions assembled and reporting: "The Liberator has really
been raised up; he appeared to Simon." They in
turn told what had happened on the road, and how
he had been made known to them in the breaking of
the loaf.   [*Luke* 24:13-35]

THE PRAYER

Minister: O Power of the universe, we ask that,
as the Liberator has broken a new way through the
gates of death to your light, so we, turned by him
from the darkness of guilt, may walk into the city
of justice and peace, through his loving spirit in
the community of life. Amen; so may it be.

*The Affirmations are not said again; in their
place can be sung:*

THE WAR IS OVER

Tune: "Victory," Palestrina 1588 (*The Hymnal 1940*,
no. 91; 8 8 8, with Alleluias)

1   The war is over, and a zone
    Of liberation here has grown
    Where life returning cracked the stone;
        Alleluia.

2   The dark exploiters had their day;
    See how their violent powers decay!
    Our Guide has marked a better way; Alleluia.

3   The sap above begins to flow;
    The axe lies rusting far below;
    The winds of future landward blow; Alleluia.

4   The Sun of Justice lights the east,
    And breaks the handcuffs of the Beast,
    While humankind sits down at feast; Alleluia.

5   On green sierras near the sky
    He wipes the tear from every eye;
    Oppressor Death begins to die; Alleluia.

6   He put himself in others' care;
    The Dark Lord found no foothold there.
    His laurel wreath we all may wear; Alleluia.

7   The people's armies of the night
    In every land move towards the light;
    At dawn they reach their City bright;
        Alleluia.

8   The Swimmer rises from the wave
    To crush the Crab that digs our grave.
    Come quickly Jesus, strong to save!
        Alleluia.

9   Our guilt no longer fears the tomb.
    The landless poor have found a home.
    Our Brother tastes the honeycomb; Alleluia.

    Alleluia; Alleluia; Alleluia.

For the Offertory canticle is sung:

    Jesus our Lamb is sacrificed;
        Therefore let us keep his feast
    Not with the old leaven of violence,
        But with the new bread of plainness and
            truth.   [*1 Corinthians* 5:7-8]

    For now the Liberator is awaked from the
        dead,
        The vanguard of all who sleep;
    For since by a man came death,
        By a man comes rising from the dead.
                        [*1 Corinthians* 15:20-21]

    We have died, and our life is hidden
        With the Liberator in God;
    And when Jesus our life appears,
        We also will appear with him in splendor.
                        [*Colossians* 3:3-4]

For the Dismissal is said:

Reader:
    Go in peace and love.
        Go out into Babylon and bring them in.
    Keep the faith, baby:
        You are the Liberated Zone.

3. The Celebration of a Wedding

*The service as printed is complete in itself; by
the addition of items in square brackets, it is
set in the context of the Freedom Meal, with the
engagement taking the place of the penitential
section, and the marriage proper becoming the
conclusion of the offertory.*

AT THE PROCESSION

Until the first breath of day
   And the retreat of shadows
I go up to the mountain of myrrh,
   To the hillside of frankincense.
You are wholly fair, my love;
   There is no defect to be found in you.
Come with me from Lebanon, my bride,
   Depart from the head of Hermon;
Away from the dens of lions,
   Down from the mountains of leopards.
You have made off with my heart, my sister,
   My bride, made off with my heart;
By a single look of your eyes,
   By one jewel of your necklace.
Sweet as the bees' comb are your lips;
   Honey and milk are on your tongue.
And your garments in their perfuming
   Are as the smell of Lebanon.
A garden enclosed is my sister, my bride,
   A garden enclosed, a fountain sealed.
Your buds are a paradise of pomegranates
   And all spice: henna with nard,
Saffron, calamus, cinnamon,
   With every tree of frankincense,
Myrr and wood of aloes,
   With all the chiefest of balsams.
A fountain of many gardens,
   A great spring of living water,
     And streams flowing from Lebanon.
               [Song of Solomon 4:8-15]

*[If the Freedom Meal follows, the minister reads
Francis' prayer for peace, p. 121.]*

THE GREETINGS

Minister: Shalom, my brother and sister, the
covenant of peace be upon you, Shalom.

Couple and Others: And peace be with you, our
brother, Shalom.

Minister: For the Liberator himself is our peace;

People: He breaks down all walls of hatred.
[*Ephesians* 2:14]

Minister: And we have been betrothed to him

People: As a faultless bride to her husband.
[*2 Corinthians* 11:2]

THE LITANY FOR A WEDDING

(Replacing the Invocation of the Saints)

Minister and People:
Blessed is the Fountain of all the worlds:
Blessed is he whose name is Love.
Blessed is he that established the light of
the Sun: Blessed is he whose name is
Love. *And so on.*
Blessed is he that compacted the earth:
Blessed is he that filled up the great sea:
Blessed is he that brings down the rainfall
of life:
Blessed is he that raised cedars from the
ground:
Blessed is he that makes grain sing in the
field:
Blessed is he that makes our heart glad with
the sap of the vine:
Blessed is he that made birds and insects,
deer and all living things:
Blessed is he that formed man and woman after
his own image:
Blessed is he that makes the womb swell with
new life:
Blessed is he that puts his own creativity
in our fingers:
Blessed is he that raised up Jesus as our example and Liberator:
Blessed is he that surrounds us with the pillars of his saints:
Blessed is he that makes the nations live in
peace:
Blessed is he that forgets not love in the
grave of our death: Blessed is he whose
name is Love.
Blessed is he whose splendor is the universe:
Blessed is he whose name is Love.

THE DEMANDS OF THE LIBERATOR

*The three rules of the new Way are replaced by the
following:*

Reader: Hear the light burden laid on us by Jesus our Liberator. The first demand is this: "Listen, Israel, our God is one; and you shall love our God with all your heart and soul and mind and strength." And the second is like it: "You shall love your neighbor as yourself." No other demand is greater than these.

[*Mark* 12:29-31; *Matthew* 22:38]

The Engagement

This replaces the entire penitential section of the Freedom Meal. First the couple address the congregation as follows:

Man: Friends, after thought and prayer I have come here today, with the intention of taking the hand of *N.* in marriage. I ask your approval; and I call on our brother here, as your representative, to witness our promises.

Woman: Friends, after thought and prayer I have come here today, with the desire to offer my hand to *N.* in marriage. I ask your approval; and I call on our brother here, as your representative, to witness our promises.

Then the minister says to the couple:

My brother and sister, today you are to accept from each other the joyful burden of that love in which the worlds were made. As Isaac our fore-father went a long journey to his homeland, and there found the fair Rebeccah he was in search of, so you two have found each other. Our Liberator offered up all for this beloved community here assembled, with which he is one flesh. Likewise I ask you today, in its presence, if you are prepared to do the same.

Then the minister says to the woman:

N., will you take this man to your wedded husband? Will you love him, comfort him, honor and keep him in sickness and in health; and, forsaking all others, keep only to him, so long as you both shall live? I will.

Likewise to the man:

N., will you take this woman to your wedded wife? Will you love her, comfort her, honor and keep her in sickness and in health; and, forsaking all others, keep only to her, so long as you both shall live? I will.

*Then the woman speaks to the man as follows, or in
words of the couple's own choosing:*

I, *N.*, promise that I will strengthen and support
you, *N.*, by sharing my joys and fears; and at the
same time, in patience and trust, give you room to
grow, and freedom to be your own self.

*And likewise the man to the woman, in the same
words. Then the minister says to the couple
together:*

N. and *N.*, will you take pains not to burden the
earth with the number of your children; but to
make your family a nucleus for a more just and
happier society, helping build this planet into
the garden it was meant to be? **We will.**

*Then the woman either is given away or steps for-
ward with the man.*

Reaffirming the Covenant

Minister: My brother and sister, let us listen to
the joyful promise made by the Power of Being.

Reader:
"For the mountains may be removed
    And the hills may be shaken,
  But my love shall not be removed,
    And the covenant of my peace shall not
        be shaken,"
says the God who has felt sympathy for you.
[Isaiah 54:10]

Minister to all: Friends, today these two join
our community in a new relationship. So let us
once again reaffirm that covenant by whose assurance we live. For see, God calls sky and earth to
witness that he has set before us this day good
and evil, blessing and curse, life and death.
Which will you choose?

People: **We choose life, that we and our children
may live.**

[*The Gloria in excelsis can be said here or
omitted.*]

Minister: Let us hear that word from which, we
believe, there is fresh light yet to break.

Lesson

Reader: And God said, "It is not right for a man
to be by himself; I will make him a partner suitable for him." And God shaped from clay every

wild animal, and every bird of the air. He
brought them to man to see what he would call
them; and whatever man called each creature, that
was its name. So man gave names to all the animals, and to all the birds of the air, and to every creature of the wilderness; but for man no
suitable partner was found. Then God brought un-
consciousness upon man, and he slept; and he took
one of his ribs, and brought flesh back over its
place. And God built the rib he had taken from
man into woman, and brought her to man. And man
said, "This time it is bone of my bone and flesh
of my flesh; she will be called woman, because
she was taken from man." Therefore a man leaves
his father and mother and embraces his wife, and
they become one flesh. And the two of them, the
man and his wife, were naked and not ashamed.

[*Genesis* 2:18-25]

Psalm 128

Happy are all that stand in awe of God,
   Who walk in his ways;
You will eat the produce of your hands,
   You are happy and joyful.
Your wife is a fruiting vine
   On the walls of your house;
Your children are slips of olive
   All around your table.
So shall the man be blessed
   That stands in awe of God.
God will so bless you from Zion,
   You will see Jerusalem happy all your
     days;
You will see your children's children,
   And Israel in peace. Shalom.

The Gospel

On the third day there was a wedding in Cana of
Galilee. The mother of Jesus was there, and Jesus
and his followers were invited to the wedding.
Now when the wine ran out, the mother of Jesus
told him, "They do not have any wine." Jesus told
her, "What is that to you or me, lady? My hour is
not yet at hand." But his mother told the servants, "Do whatever he tells you." Now there were
six water jars lying there, each holding two or
three gallons. Jesus told them, "Fill the jars
with water," and they filled them to the brim.
Then he told them, "Now draw off from the jars,
and take it to the master of ceremonies"; and they
took it. Now when the master of ceremonies tasted

the water which had become wine, and did not know
where it came from (only the servants who drew off
the water knew), he called the bridegroom and said
to him: "Everybody brings out the best wine at
the beginning, and then the poorer wine when people are drunk; but you have kept the best wine until now." Jesus did this as the beginning of his
signs in Cana of Galilee, and thus showed his
splendor; and his followers had confidence in him.
[*John* 2:1-11]

THE PRAYER

Minister: O Fountain of love, make the hearts of
this man and this woman firm, so that they can
carry out joyfully the things they have today
promised; for the sake of the one who has set us
the precedent of his own love, Jesus our Liberator. Amen; so may it be.

The Affirmations can be replaced by the following

CANTICLE

All of you that went through the waters
    Have clothed yourselves in the Liberator.
In him there is neither Jew nor Greek,
    No oppressed or oppressor,
Nor any male or female;
    In Jesus you are all made one.
[*Galatians* 3:27-28]

Here if desired can come a short sermon.

*The Freedom Meal intercessions can be replaced by
the following*

INTERCESSIONS

For *N.* and *N.*, now to be married in the sight of
    God and in the presence of this community: We
    call on the Spirit.
For the happiness of couples everywhere: We call
    on the Spirit. *And so on.*
For the poor; for prostitutes, unmarried mothers,
    orphans; for all the unloved and unwanted:
For doctors, nurses, and social workers; for all
    ministers to the oppressed:
For the peace of the world, for an end to all war:
For the whole creation; for animals without voice,
    that we may become their voice:
For children and grandparents, that they may enjoy
    love in a family:
For every person in his vocation, that each may
    remain faithful to his best vision:

That the Christ incognito may never be turned from
   our door: **We call on the Spirit.**
We call on the Spirit to bind us in solidarity
   with all here and elsewhere, living and dead,
   who build their lives into the golden circle of
   love: **We call on the Spirit.**

*[If the Freedom Meal follows, the Offering is be-
gun by the Minister saying:*

And I saw the holy city, new Jerusalem, coming
down out of the sky from God, made ready like a
bride adorned for her husband. *[Revelation 21:26]*

The Presentation is the usual one on p. 125.]

The Marriage

*The man takes the woman by her right hand and says
as follows:*

> I *N*. take you *N*. to my wedded wife,
>   To have and to hold,
> From this day forward,
>   For better, for worse,
> For richer, for poorer,
>   In sickness and in health,
> To love and to cherish,
>   Until death do us part,
> As the first man took his wife Eve
>   In the paradise of Eden.

Likewise the woman:

> I *N*, take you *N*. to my wedded husband,
>   To have and to hold,
> From this day forward,
>   For better, for worse,
> For richer, for poorer,
>   In sickness and in health,
> To love and to cherish,
>   Till death do us part,
> As the first woman took her husband Adam
>   In the paradise of Eden.

*Then the minister blesses the ring or rings,
saying:*

As *these rings have [this ring has]* neither beginning nor end, and *lose [loses]* neither luster nor
substance, so may the Wellspring of love maintain
these two persons constant and joyful in the community of peace, through our Brother who gave himself for it.

*Then the man puts the ring on the woman's finger,
saying:*

```
With this ring I marry you,
    With my body I honor you,
        With all I have I present you.
```

And the woman likewise, if she has a ring.

Minister: Once again the covenant of peace has been sealed; for God who marries us to himself in love has sent the Spirit of the Liberator into our hearts, crying:

All:

```
            Abba, Father:
            Blessed be your working;
                Soon be your appearing;
                    Done be your desiring.
            Our bread provide us;
                Our debts forgive us;
                    From trials free us.
```

Minister: Let us pray for peace among men. O Power of history, let the home of these two, as of couples everywhere, become a city set on a hill, a sanctuary of peace; by their work and play may people learn love and not war, sitting unafraid under their vine and figtree; through the Liberator who blessed peacemakers as your children. Amen; so may it be.

Let us pray for peace in the natural order. O bright Sun of creation, let the joyful union of this couple (if your desire is such) overflow into the birth of children, not too many for the planet to bear, who will carry on in their generation the renewal of society and nature; so that in your right time the wolf may lie down with the lamb and the paradise of Eden be restored; through the bond of our unity, Jesus the true Adam. Amen; so may it be.

Then the Minister joins their right hands, saying:

Those whom God has joined together let not man put asunder.

Then he says to the people:

Friends, you have heard what things *N.* and *N.* have promised, and watched their exchange of rings; on your behalf I declare that they are man and wife, in the name of the Fountain of love who has filled this community with the spirit of Jesus the Liberator.

Then follows the Kiss of Peace, begun by the couple, during which is said:

My beloved is mine and I am his,
 He feeds his flock among the lilies.
Come quickly my love like a gazelle
 Or a stag on the mountains of spices.
The bed underneath us is green,
  The beams of our house are of cedar.
    [*Song of Solomon* 2:16, 8:14, 1:17]

[*If the Freedom Meal is to be celebrated, the Sursum corda is then said. The* Abba Father *need not be repeated. The Blessing and Dismissal are replaced by the following.*]

Minister: May the Power behind space and time bless you, and unite you with his own Name of love, to take your intended place in the unrolling of his will; through the spirit of our Brother who gave us the true picture of humankind. Amen; so may it be.

At the Departure

Rise up my love with me,
 My fair one, and come away;
For see, the winter is past;
 The rain is over and gone;
The crocus appears on the earth,
 The time of singing is near,
And the voice of the turtledove
 Is heard in our land.
    [*Song of Solomon* 2:10-12]

4. Commission for Ministry

An outline of commissioning for any office of min-istry in the community. It is set in the context of the Freedom Meal, in which the three Rules and the form of Liberation from Complicity can be omitted.

THE PROPHECY

Son of Man, speak to the children of your people and say to them: If I bring the sword on a coun-try, and the people of the country take a man of their own and make him their watchman, and he sees the sword coming against the country, and blows the trumpet and warns the people; then if someone hears the voice of the trumpet and does not take warning, and the sword comes and takes him away, his blood is on his own head. He heard the voice of the trumpet, he did not take warning, his blood is on himself; for if he had taken warning, he would have saved his life. But if the watchman sees the sword coming and does not blow the trum-pet, and the people are not warned, and the sword comes and takes away any one of them; that man is taken away in his complicity, and his blood I will require at the hand of the watchman.

Son of Man, I have made you a watchman for the house of Israel; whatever thing you hear from my mouth, you are to warn them from me. If I say to the criminal, "O criminal, you will certainly die," and you do not speak out to warn the crimi-nal to turn from his way, the criminal will die in his complicity, and I will require his blood from your hand. But if you warn the criminal to turn from his way, and he does not turn from his way, he dies in his complicity, and you have saved your life.   [*Ezekiel* 33:2-9]

CANTICLE

Have the way of life among you
    Which was also in Jesus our Liberator;
Although in the form of God,
    He did not set his heart on that equality,
But he made himself empty,
    Taking the form of a slave.
And receiving the nature of a man,
    He accepted humiliation,

And became obedient to death,
    Even the death of the cross.
And so God raised him high,
    And gave him a name over all names;
So that to the name of Jesus
    Every knee should bow down,
Of creatures above, on earth, and below,
    And every tongue should agree
That Jesus is leader and liberator
    In the splendor of God the Father.

[Philippians 2:5-11]

THE GOSPEL

The rulers of nations exercise authority over
them, and their influential men are called Bene-
factors. It is not to be like this among you.
Rather, let the greater one among you become as
the less, and the leader as the servant. For
which is greater, one who sits at table or one who
serves him? Is it not the one who sits at table?
And am I among you as the one who serves. You are
the ones who have stayed with me during my trials.
And I make a covenant with you as my Father made a
covenant with me, that you should eat and drink at
my table in my liberated zone, and sit on thrones
judging the twelve tribes of Israel.

[Luke 22:25-30]

*Here follows an address on the character of
ministry.*

THE PRESENTATIONS

*A statement of the candidate's calling is read by
an elected representative of the community where
he or she is to minister. Then a statement of the
candidate's suitability is read by a minister recognized both by him and by the community, in ac-
cordance with the covenant of the community.*

THE QUESTIONS

Presiding Minister: Friends, you have heard that
this our *brother* has been called to the office of
------ by the representatives of this community.
And you have heard testimony to *his* qualifications
by these others who have already been called and
commissioned for such a ministry. We now wish to
hear from our brother himself, in his own words,
how he understands this task, so that we will have
good grounds to believe he will prove serviceable
to his people, and not himself fall casualty.

My brother, you are being called to serve others

in the way of a waiter at table, which our Liberator defines as the truest work of a human being.
It was indeed said of Jesus our Brother, Others he
saved, himself he cannot save; and all here present stand ready to hold up your hand if you fall
casualty. Still, what you are being commissioned
for is to hold up the hand of others. Do you then
feel that you and your family are solid and stable
enough in your individual commitments, in your
personal relations, so that with a quiet mind you
can take on the burden of helping others, day in
and day out? Also, as our Liberator and his Apostles often had no place to lay their head, you are
not guaranteed money or support, even from an affluent society, for a work which means building a
different society on new foundations. Few if any
of those you see here are wealthy. Do you then
have a useful vocation by which you can support
yourself in this work if other support fails? And
are you settled in your mind to go on in this work
without bitterness or resentment, if necessary at
your own expense?

You must understand clearly from our sacred writ-
ings the tasks of a minister. First of all, because he is a fellow-servant with the Liberator,
the minister is a watchman, as we heard from the
prophet Ezekiel. The minister, through his study
of the sacred Books, of the lives of the saints,
of the news, of men's hearts, is given the spirit
of prophecy, to see how the crimes of a nation are
bringing the sword upon it. Are you then prepared
with Amos, Jeremiah, and all the prophets, to condemn when necessary the complicity of rulers,
priests, the rich, judges, the exploiters of man
or nature in an oppressive system; and to work for
change in it? Are you willing to share the poverty or harassment of the victims, and to take
your chance on joining them in prison?

Second, the minister of Jesus is a herald: he announces the Liberated Zone where men and women,
society and nature are starting to become themselves. Can you testify with conviction that his
liberation is already at work in yourself? Are
you prepared to let the Spirit build the community
of love around your work, according to God's style
rather then your style? Have you determined to
help recall the Churches of Jesus to their original charter, supporting everything true in them,
rejecting or reforming everything corrupt in them?
Will you take on the burden of poetry, delivering

your message in such language that it can be heard
by your audience?

Third and most important, the minister of the Liberator is above all a servant, as we heard from
Luke; that is what his title means. Whatever his
faults in vision or weaknesses in organization, he
can always take the side of the oppressed, binding
up their wounds, making their suffering his suffering. Are you prepared to do this, becoming, so
far as lies in you, a spokesman for all those who
have no other spokesman?

These tasks are simple to state, difficult to
carry out. But carrying them out is made a little
easier if you hold fast to simplicity of statement. So finally we wish to hear your assurance
that you will not obscure the real nature of your
work by compromise, mystification, double speaking, hidden agenda. Will you be a person who, so
far as possible, holds nothing in reserve, keeps
nothing secret but the confidences of others, permits himself no unexplained absences or unavail-
ability, and has no ambition but usefulness; so
that the simplest man or woman will not for an instant hesitate to trust you, because he can see
instantly what you stand for, and see that you are
one who trusts in a Power greater than us all?

*Then the candidate, in his own words, as simply
and directly as possible, reads or speaks a statement of where he stands in answer to these
questions.*

Minister: Are you prepared to bring your whole
life under the guidance of the Spirit, as known to
us in the Bible, in the lives of the Saints, and
in our own history through the Providence of God?
I am prepared to.

Will you use the worship and covenant of this community as your constant guides to the working of
the Spirit; and at the same time hold them up to
the plumb-line he has given us? Yes, I will do
so.

Have you determined to trust that Jesus our
Brother, by his example, teaching, and work, is
Christ and Lord--that is, Liberator of man and of
all creation? I have so determined.

May the Fountain of strength who has brought you
to this commitment today keep you in it all your
days. Amen; so may it be.

Here follow the Affirmations God is not dead,
etc. from p. 123.

LITANY

Come quickly Jesus the helper of all mankind:
  Come quickly our helper.
Come quickly, you that make broken bodies and
  lives whole again: Come quickly our helper.
  And so on.
You that pronounced the blessedness of the poor
  and suffering:
You that bring in the liberated zone to all
  nations:
You that were fearless to denounce the crimes of
  the powerful:
You that observe the lilies of the wild and the
  sparrow's fall:
You that in your coming bring in the paradise of
  Eden:
You that love children, join the marriage feast
  and mourn the dead:
You that call sinners of the people, and sinners
  against the people, into one community:
You that took on our guilt, so that we could take
  on your wholeness:
You that throw out the demonic powers from our
  living:
You that led the march of protest to the Temple of
  God:
You that passed through the dark waters, and were
  anointed with the Spirit:
You that were lifted up in transfiguration and in
  brutality:
You that broke the evil powers by offering yourself to them:
You that refresh all people with the bread of life
  and the sap of the vine: Come quickly our
  helper.
Come quickly, our helper, and pour out your spirit
  on all called to be your fellow-servants: Come
  quickly our helper.

THE COMMISSIONING

Minister: O Spirit of God's breath, Spirit of the
Liberator's life; this community is dead unless
you are the atmosphere it breathes. Come and fulfill the dream of your saints that a new society
will rise out of the ruins of the old. As you
have always in the past come on those who trusted
you, today fill this one who asks only to do your
work in your strength. Through *him,* and *his*

brothers and sisters everywhere, may the golden
ring of our fellowship become one and the same
with the sphere of this planet, so that all created life will exist together in love and peace.

*Then the ministers, and other representatives of
the community, lay hands on the candidate's head,
while is said:*

May the Power of Being make you a faithful servant
of his covenant of peace, in the office of ------,
not by the letter of human institutions, but by
the Spirit of life; through Jesus our Brother and
Liberator, who was among us as a servant and gave
his life for the people.

*Then the newly commissioned minister is given the
Bible, while is said:*

Receive the word of life; put no other book above
this or beside this; let all your words be spoken,
all your actions done, in its spirit.

*Then any other appropriate instruments or symbols
of office are given. The new minister is in-
stalled in his office by a representative of the
community. The papers are signed. Then the presiding minister, assisted by his new colleague,
continues the Freedom Meal, starting at the Offering. The Beatitudes are replaced with a blessing
of the new minister:*

May your mouth speak the word of justice in and
out of season; may you plant the peace garden of
this earth wherever your feet stand; may your eyes
always be turned towards the poor and exploited,
your hands be quick to lift them; and may the
Spirit of God accompany you, so that at the Liberator's coming you will hear the word spoken to a
faithful servant: Since you did it for the least
of these my brothers, you did it for me.

5. A Form for Visiting Prisoners

This form is not suitable for a prison-appointed chaplain making official visits. It assumes a fellowship between prisoner and visitor; that is, it is intended primarily for political prisoners, in the broad sense. Prayers especially for military prisoners are found on pp. 129-137.

Visitor:
> Lift up your heads, you gates;
>> Open up, you everlasting doors;
>>> For the King of splendor to come in.
> Who is this King of splendor?
>> Our God strong and mighty,
>>> The God beyond all armies.
> Lift up your heads, you gates;
>> Open up, you everlasting doors;
>>> For the King of splendor to come in.
> Who is this king of splendor?
>> The God of all true armies,
>>> He is the King of splendor.
>>>> *[Psalm 24:7-10]*

Grace be to you and peace from Jesus our Liberator, the first political prisoner.

READINGS

(1) From the prison diaries of Dietrich Bonhoeffer.

Nothing can make up for the absence of someone whom we love, and it would be wrong to try and find a substitute; we must simply hold out and see it through. That sounds very hard at first, but at the same time it is a great consolation; for the gap, as long as it remains unfilled, preserves the bonds between us. It is nonsense to say that God fills the gap; he does not fill it, but on the contrary, he keeps it empty and so helps us to keep alive our former communion with each other, even at the cost of pain.

The dearer and richer our memories, the more difficult the separation. But gratitude changes the pangs of memory into a tranquil joy. The beauties of the past are borne, not as a thorn in the flesh, but as a precious gift in themselves. We must take care not to wallow in our memories or hand ourselves over to them, just as we do not gaze all the time at a valuable present, but only

at special times, and apart from these keep it
simply as a hidden treasure that is ours for certain. In this way the past gives us lasting joy
and strength.

Times of separation are not a total loss or un-
profitable for our companionship, or at any rate
they need not be so. In spite of all the difficulties that they bring, they can be the means of
strengthening fellowship quite remarkably.

I have learned here especially that the facts can
always be mastered, and that difficulties are mag-
nified out of all proportion simply by fear and
anxiety. From the moment we wake until we fall
asleep we must commend other people wholly and un-
reservedly to God and leave them in his hands, and
transform our anxiety for them into prayers on
their behalf.

What times these are! What memories for the years
to come! What matters is that we should direct
these memories, as it 'were, into the right spiritual channels, and so make them harder, clearer,
and more defiant, which is a good thing. There is
no place for sentimentality on a day like this.
If in the middle of an air raid God sends out the
gospel call to his kingdom in baptism, it will be
quite clear what that kingdom is and what it
means. It is a kingdom stronger than war and danger, a kingdom of power and authority, signifying
eternal terror and judgment to some, and eternal
joy and justice to others, not a kingdom of the
heart, but one as wide as the earth, not transi-
tory but eternal, a kingdom that makes a way for
itself and summons men to itself to prepare its
way, a kingdom for which it is worth while to risk
our lives.

*(2) From the acts of Saint Perpetua, Carthage,
A.D. 203.*

During those few days we were baptized, and the
Holy Spirit told me to make no other request after
going through the waters than for bodily endurance. A few days later we were lodged in prison,
and I was in great fear, because I had never known
such darkness. A day of horror; terrible heat,
due to all the crowds; brutality by the soldiers.
On top of all I was tormented there by anxiety for
my baby. Then those blessed deacons who were min-
istering to us paid for us to be removed for a few
hours to a better part of the prison and refresh

ourselves. Then my baby was brought to me, and I
suckled him, for he was already faint for lack of
food. I spoke anxiously to my mother on his behalf, and strengthened my brother, and commended
my son to their charge. I was wasting away because I saw them wasting away for my sake. Such
anxieties I suffered for many days. Then I got
permission for my baby to stay in the prison with
me, and I at once recovered my health, and was relieved of my trouble and anxiety for my baby. My
prison suddenly became a palace to me, and I would
rather have been there than anywhere else.

(3) From the journals of George Fox.

One time in this jail there came a soldier to us;
and whilst one of our Friends was admonishing of
him and exhorting him to sobriety, I saw him begin
to draw his sword. Whereupon I stepped to him and
told him what a shame it was to offer to draw his
sword upon an unarmed man, and him a prisoner; and
how unfit and unworthy he was to carry such a weapon; and that if he should have drawn it upon some
men, they would have taken his sword from him and
have broken it to pieces. So he was ashamed, and
went his way; and the Lord's power sustained us.

At a later time I had a fit of sickness, which
brought me very low and weak in my body; and I
continued so a pretty while, insomuch that some
Friends began to doubt of my recovery. I seemed
to myself to be among the graves and dead corpses;
yet the invisible power did secretly support me,
and conveyed refreshing strength into me, even
when I was so weak that I was almost speechless.
One night, as I was lying awake upon my bed in the
glory of the Lord which was over all, it was said
unto me that the Lord had a great deal more work
for me to do for him before he took me to himself.

Endeavors were used to get me released, at least
for a time, till I was grown stronger; but the way
of effecting it proved difficult and tedious; for
the King was not willing to release me by any
other way than a pardon, being told he could not
legally do it; and I was not willing to be released by a pardon, which he would readily have
given me, because I did not look upon that way as
agreeable with the innocency of my cause.

(4) From the Acts of the Apostles, 12:6-11.

Now when Herod was about to bring Peter out for
execution, on that very night he was sleeping

between two soldiers, bound with two chains, and sentries in front of the door were guarding the prison. Then a Messenger of God stood there, and a light shone in the cell; he tapped Peter on the side and woke him up, saying, "Get up quickly." And the Messenger said to him, "Put on your clothes and your sandals"; and he did so. And he said to him, "Wrap your coat around you and follow me." And he went out, following him; he did not realize that what the messenger was doing was real, but thought he was dreaming. After they had passed the first and second guards, they came to the iron gate leading into the city; it opened for them by itself. They went out and walked for a block, and then suddenly the Messenger left him. Then Peter came to himself and said, "Now I know truly that the Lord has sent his Messenger and has saved me from the hand of Herod and from the ex- pectation of the people."

(5) From Paul's second letter to the Corinthians, 11:23-31.

Are all those others ministers of the Liberator? Though I speak like a fanatic, I say that I am more so. I have had more labors, more imprison- ments, been often beaten, often in deaths. Five times I received from the Jews forty lashes save one; three times I was beaten with clubs; once I was stoned; three times I was shipwrecked; I drifted at sea for a night and a day; constantly on journeys, in danger from rivers, in danger from highwaymen, in danger from my own people, in dan- ger from foreigners, danger in the city, danger in the desert, danger at sea, danger among false brothers; in work and hardship, often sleepless, in hunger and thirst, in cold and nakedness; and beside these outer things, my daily companion-- anxiety for all the churches. Who is sick, and I am not sick? Who falls casualty and I am not angry? If I must boast, I will boast of my weak- ness. God the father of Jesus our Liberator, blessed for all the Ages, knows that I am not lying.

PSALM 142

I raise my voice to my God,
    With my voice I ask for his gentleness;
I pour out my trouble before him,
    In his presence I make my complaint.
When my spirit sinks low,
    It is you that know my way.

For on the path where I walk
    They have hidden a trap for me;
I look to the right hand and watch,
    And there is none to take notice;
All refuge has gone away from me,
    No man looks after my life.
My God, you alone are my fortress,
    My share in the land of the living;
Pay attention to my cry,
    For I have been brought very low.
Save me from those who harass me,
    Because they are too strong for me;
Bring me safe out of prison,
    So that I can give thanks to your Name.
Then just men will surround me,
    And you will deal fairly with me.

Visitor: The golden circle of mankind cannot be broken by any enemy, but only by ourselves. Once again, in spite of all difficulties, the community of love has been restored even in this place. Others have perhaps offended against that community more than we. Still I know for myself that I have been at fault; and if you feel the same, I invite you to confess after me.

My brother, I confess in the sight of God, in your presence, and to our brothers and sisters everywhere, that in my thoughts and words and actions I have broken the fellowship of our community, broken the image of God in myself.

> [In particular, I have neglected the poor and
>   oppressed by . . .
> I have myself exploited the poor by . . .
> I have exploited the natural environment
>   by . . .
> I have exploited my brothers and sisters
>   by . . .
> I have wasted my own abilities by . . .]

I am willing to do reparation; I ask forgiveness from God, and pardon from you, my brother, and from all my brothers and sisters present and absent.

Then the prisoner can make the same confession as appropriate.

Visitor: God has laid two ways before us, of death and of life; since we have chosen life, he is faithful to maintain his covenant. All breaks in the community of love have been made whole by

Jesus our Liberator, who is the ground of all
unity. Amen; so may it be.

All:

> Abba, Father:
> Blessed be your working;
> > Soon be your appearing;
> > > Done be your desiring.
> Our bread provide us;
> > Our debts forgive us;
> > > From trials free us.

Prisoner: Jesus came to Nazareth, where he had
been brought up. And on the sabbath, according
to his custom, he went into the synagogue, and
stood up to read. There was given him the book of
the prophet Isaiah; and, unrolling the book, he
found the place where it is written:

> The Spirit of God is upon me,
> > He has anointed me with oil.
> He has sent me to tell the poor good news;
> > To heal the broken in heart;
> To proclaim release to the captives,
> > An opening of eyes to the blind;
> To set the oppressed at liberty;
> > To announce God's year of justice.

Then he rolled back the book, and gave it to the
attendant, and sat down; and the eyes of all those
in the synagogue were fastened on him. And his
first words to them were: "Today this writing is
fulfilled in your ears."   [*Luke* 4:16-21]

LITANY OF JESUS THE LIBERATOR

Jesus the first political prisoner, visit all
   political prisoners: Hear us our brother.
Jesus who stole from the grainfields: Hear
   us our brother. *And so on.*
Jesus who stayed with prostitutes:
Jesus who lived with revolutionaries:
Jesus who called the tax-collectors:
Jesus who slept with the poor:
Jesus who proclaims release to the captives:
Jesus who sets the oppressed at liberty:

In our need of bread and meat, clothes and
   medicines, books and paper:
In all times of heat and cold, loneliness
   and harassment:
When we are brutalized or neglected, insulted or threatened:
In our temptations to counter-brutality,
   counter-violence:

For all prisoners weaker than ourselves,
    whose needs are greater than ours:
For all jailers and wardens, especially *N.*
    and *N.*, that humanity may win out over
    routine:
For all judges, officers, governors, and
    presidents, that for their hearts of
    stone they may be given hearts of flesh:
For all those sick, persecuted, poor, dying,
    inside and outside, that you may be with
    them to the end:
For women prisoners, for juveniles, for
    mental patients:
For our family and friends (especially *N.*),
    that they may receive their needs and not
    lose confidence in your way:
For a speedy reform of the courts and prison
    systems everywhere:
For an opening of gates, for recovery of
    sight to the blind:
For liberation of all oppressed, for help to
    the victims of violence:
For an end to war and exploitation, here and
    in every land which you liberated by your
    blood:

[*Here can follow free intercessions.*]

In solidarity with draft resisters, Maxi-
    milian, Franz Jaegerstaetter, David
    Darst, Thich Quang Duc, Jan Palach,
    Norman Morrison, and all their brothers:
In solidarity with all executed for your
    sake: Polycarp, Ignatius, Perpetua and
    Felicity, Justin, and all their brothers:
In solidarity with all murdered for resist-
    ance: Camillo Torres, Joe Hill, Sacco
    and Vanzetti, Martin Luther King, James
    Rector and all their brothers:
In solidarity with all unjustly imprisoned
    for your name's sake: Paul of Tarsus,
    George Fox, Gandhi the Mahatma, Abraham J.
    Muste, John Bunyan, Dietrich Bonhoeffer
    and all their brothers:
By your unjust arrest and trial, imprisonment
    and beating:
By your undeserved death, by your permanent
    life in our community: **Hear us our
    brother.**
Hear us, Jesus our brother, and by your name
    of Liberator be with us always: **Hear us
    our brother.**

Psalm 40:1-3

I waited patiently for my God;
    He turned to me and heard my calling.
He drew me up from the pit of desolation,
    Out of the swamp and quicksand.
And he has set my feet upon a rock;
    He has made my steps secure.
And he put in my mouth a new song,
    Words of praise for my God.

Psalm 146:5-10

Happy is he who hopes in God,
    God who made sky and earth and sea.
He keeps his promise for ever;
    He executes justice for the oppressed;
He gives bread to the hungry;
    He sets the prisoners free;
He opens the eyes of the blind;
    He lifts up all that are bowed down.
God loves all who love justice;
    God watches over all strangers;
He supports the widow and orphan;
    He smashes the way of the wicked.

Visitor: I bind on my heart the breastplate of justice.

Prisoner: I bind on my head the helmet of liberation.   [*Isaiah* 59:17]

Here follow the Affirmations God is not dead, *etc. from p. 123.*

Visitor: Our God is faithful to maintain the covenant of his peace through the Liberator, who himself is our peace. For hear his words:
    I have called you out in justice,
        I have taken your hand and supported you;
    I give you as a covenant to my people,
        As a light to all nations on earth:
    To open the eyes of the blind;
        To bring out the captive from prison,
    Those who sit in darkness from the dungeon;
        For I am God, that is my name.
                        [*Isaiah* 42:6-7]
By my God I can overcome an army; through him I can leap over a wall. Maranatha, come quickly, Jesus our Liberator. Shalom, my brother, his peace be with you, Shalom.

Here the visitor and prisoner shall exchange the kiss of peace.

Visitor: May God's love be victorious everywhere, as it has already prevailed in our hearts. May all men and women enlist in the peaceable army of Jesus our Liberator. May the Spirit of life flow into you with its waters, and bring you to a place of hills and sky, of joy and freedom.

6. Memorial of the Dead

Reader: Brothers and sisters, as our uncovered face mirrors the splendor of God, let us be transfigured into his likeness, from splendor to splendor. Our good news is hidden only among those who are being destroyed, whose minds the Idol of this age has blinded with lack of trust, to keep them from seeing the brightness of the Gospel of the splendor of the Liberator, who is the picture of God. For the God who said "May light shine out of darkness" has shined in your hearts, to give the splendor of the knowledge of God in the face of the Liberator. Now we hold this treasure in vessels of clay, to make it clear that the fountain of energy lies with God and not with us. At every point we are oppressed but not crushed; we see no way out but we do not give up; we are persecuted but not deserted, thrown down but not destroyed. Always we carry around the dying of Jesus in our body, so that in turn the life of Jesus may become visible in our body. For we in our life are constantly being handed over to death for Jesus' sake, so that the life of Jesus may shine through our dying flesh.

So let us not give up; for even while our outer humanity is being destroyed, our inner humanity is daily being renewed. For this temporary oppression is generating for us a weight of splendor in the Age to come. Let us then not pay attention to the visible but the invisible; for things seen belong to this passing age, but things unseen belong to the Age to come. For we know that when our temporary quarters of clay are dissolved, we have a home from God, not made by hands, belonging to the Age to come and in the Place of being. In our present house we groan, desiring to be clothed in that habitation which is from God, so that we may not be found naked; so that our vulnerability to death may be swallowed up by life. To this end God is making us ready; and he has already entrusted us with the down-payment of his Spirit.
[*2 Corinthians* 3:18-5:5]

As the body is brought into the room:

ANTHEM

See, the habitation of God is with men, and they shall be his people; he will wipe off every tear

from their eyes. Death and mourning shall be no
longer, because former things have passed away.
                              [*Revelation* 21:3-4]

If there lives in you the Spirit of the one who
raised up Jesus the Liberator from among the dead,
he will give life also to your mortal bodies
through his Spirit which lives in you.
                              [*Romans* 8:11]

The dead in him shall live, their bodies shall
rise up; dance and sing, you dwellers in the dust.
For his is a dew of splendor, on the land of shadows he will make it fall.   [*Isaiah* 26:19]

PSALM 90

God, you have been a home for us
   From one age of men to another.
Before the mountains were pushed up,
   Or the planet gave birth to the
         continents,
From before time and until after time,
   You are the Power of Being.
You turn man back into his dust,
   And then say, "Rise up, children of Adam."
For a thousand years in your eyes
   Are as yesterday or a night watch.
You sweep them away with your floods,
   They are remembered as a dream.
They are grass that springs up in the
         morning;
   In the evening it withers and dries.
For we come to an end by your outrage,
   We draw back at your indignation.
You have set our complicity before you,
   Our crimes in the blaze of your features.
All our days fade away at your sentence;
   Our years pass at the snap of your finger.
Our days are seventy years,
   Or eighty in our farthest strength;
Their breadth is labor and trouble,
   Soon it is gone and we are blown away.
Make us learn so to count our days
   That we bring our hearts to wisdom.

Minister: Shalom, my brothers and sisters, the
light and peace of our Liberator be with you and
with the faithful departed, Shalom.

People: And peace be with you, our brother,
Shalom.

LITANY

Jesus our brother, by your birth outside the inn:
> Put your life in us.
As a victim of harassment, as a refugee child:
> Put your life in us. *And so on.*
By your apprenticeship in wood and stone:
By your new birth in solidarity with our guilt:
By your temptations, by your doubt of your true
> calling:
By your will to feed the hungry, to heal the
> suffering:
By your openness to speak the words of our need:
In your fidelity to the voiceless poor and
> oppressed:
In your anointing with nard by a woman of the
> streets:
In every humiliation of your unmerited dying:
By your rising again wherever bread is broken:
By the new spirit of this your brotherhood:
> Put your life in us.
By all who take your way, both known and unknown:
> Put your life in us.

LESSON

> Vanity of vanities, says the Preacher;
>> Vanity of vanities, all is vanity.
> What profit does a man get
>> Of all the work he does under the sun?
> A generation comes and one goes,
>> But the earth stands as from the beginning.
> The sun rises and the sun goes down
>> And returns to the place it rose up from.
> The wind blows south and turns to the north,
>> It turns and goes back on its circuits.
> All the rivers flow into the sea
>> And the sea is never filled by them;
> To the place that the rivers come from,
>> There they go back once again.
> All things are full of tiresomeness;
>> Men cannot discover their meaning.
> The eye is not satisfied with seeing,
>> Nor the ear ever filled with hearing.
> What has happened is what will happen,
>> And nothing is new under the sun.

>>>>> [*Ecclesiastes* 1:2-9]

NUNC DIMITTIS

> Master, now you dismiss your servant
>> According to your word, in peace.
> For my eyes have seen your liberation
>> Which you have set up before all peoples:

A light to illuminate the nations,
   And to be the splendor of your people
      Israel.   [*Luke* 2:29-32]

FOR THE GOSPEL

It is the love of the Liberator that supports us;
for we conclude that if one died for all, then all
have already died in him. He died for all so that
those who live should no longer live to themselves, but to him who for their sake died and was
raised. So that whoever lives in the Liberator is
a new creation. The old things have passed away
and (Only look!) new things have come into existence. All things are from the God who has reconciled us to himself through the Liberator, and has
given us the servant's task of reconciliation. We
are to announce that the Power of Being has reconciled the universe to himself through the Liberator, not holding men's complicity against them,
but setting in our midst the word of reconciliation. God is making his appeal through us as
spokesmen of the Liberator; on his behalf we urge
you, become reconciled to the Root of your being.
The one man wholly free of complicity was made
guilt for our sake, so that we might become the
justice of God in him. As his fellow-workers we
urge you not to frustrate the gentleness of God.
For it is said, "At the right time I listened to
you; I helped you in the day of liberation." And
just look: today is the right time, now is the
day of liberation.   [*2 Corinthians* 5:11-6:2]

THE PRAYER

Minister: O Life of the world, you uphold all our
individual lives; in the presence of your saints,
look on the body of our *brother* [*sister*] departed
and on us who remember *him;* renew perpetually the
golden ring of our fellowship; maintain both *him*
and us in fidelity to the liberation being done by
Jesus, so that we all may have good hope of life
in this our community of love. **Amen; so may it be.**

INTERCESSIONS

For the solitary and suffering, for the neglected
      and exploited: **We call on the Spirit.**
For all enslaved by a system of violence, whether
      as masters or servants: **We call on the
      Spirit.** *And so on.*
For the hungry and sick, for all dying in lonely
      places:

For all comrades of Luke the physician, for the
    servants of the poor:
For all who struggle for justice in the name of
    the Liberator:
For all who are building their lives into a more
    just society:
For all who have died, in ignorance or in knowl-
    edge of the new Way:
In memory of Jesus our brother, himself deserted
    in his last hour:
In solidarity with our *brother* [*sister*] departed,
    who has died and is living:
In thankfulness for the example set by the saints
    of humanity: We call on the Spirit.
In thankfulness for the new life brought in by our
    Liberator: We call on the Spirit.

PSALM 16:9-11

My heart is glad and my mind rejoices,
    My body dwells in security
For you did not hand my life over to the
        Grave;
    Nor make your faithful servant see the
        Pit.
You show me the Way of life;
    In your face there is wholeness of joy;
        At your right hand is happiness for
        ever.

*If the Freedom Meal is to be celebrated, here fol-
lows the Presentation and Kiss of Peace. In any
case the* Abba Father *is here said:*

Abba, Father:
Blessed be your working;
    Soon be your appearing;
        Done be your desiring.
Our bread provide us;
    Our debts forgive us;
        From trials free us.

*The Blessing and Dismissal are replaced by the
following:*

THE BLESSING OF THE PEOPLE

Minister:
God bless you and watch over you;
    God shine his face on you and love you;
        God lift up his face to you and set his
            peace among you.

[*Numbers* 6:24-26]

DISMISSAL OF THE BODY

Reader: I have been poured out, and the time of my departure is here. I have fought the good fight, I have finished my race, I have kept the faith. Now there is waiting for me the wreath of justice, which the impartial Judge will give me in that day; and not to me alone, but to all who have loved his appearing.   [*2 Timothy* 4:6-8]

Minister: O Ground of our being; with confidence we entrust to you our *brother* [*sister*] departed. Give *him* the rest of the Age to come, you who are all our rest, and may light perpetual shine on *him*.   May any thing that *he* did wrong be forgiven, as we who remain forgive each other, in the spirit of Jesus the Liberator. May any thing that *he* did well live in unity with the excellences of all the saints, which are not theirs but yours. And may we who still walk the way of gentleness in hope, and this one whose way is completed, at your right time stand together beside all reconciled mankind in the paradise of Eden, through our solidarity with Lazarus and all his brothers the poor.. Amen; so may it be.

A Mighty Fortress (Psalm 46)

Tune: "Ein' Feste Burg," Luther 1529 (*The Hymnal 1940* no. 551; 87.87.66.667)

1   A mighty fortress is our God,
    And quick to hear our calling.
We will not fear the final flood,
    Or hills in ocean falling.
The waves may higher break,
And roots of mountains shake;
The universal Power
Stands as our ageless tower,
    And Jacob's God our stronghold.

2   He brings his City mountain streams,
    Her streets with light adorning;
He shows his goodness to her dreams,
    And guards her in the morning.
If nations raise their arm,
His voice arrests their harm;
The universal Power
Stands as our ageless tower,
    And Jacob's God our stronghold.

3   Come see what works our God has done,
    An end to war proclaiming;
He breaks the sword and snaps the gun;
    The armored cars are flaming.
Be still, for he commands,
Controlling in all lands;
The universal Power
Stands as our ageless tower,
    And Jacob's God our stronghold.

AT THE GRAVE

ANTHEM

Free me, O God, for the waters have come up to my
soul; all your waves and floods have gone over me.
[*Psalm* 69;1, 42:7]

Unless a grain of wheat falls into the earth and
dies, it remains alone; but if it dies, it bears
much fruit.

[*John* 12:24]

When this mortality puts on deathlessness, then
will come about the word that is written: Death
is swallowed up in victory.

[*1 Corinthians* 15:54]

PSALM 27

God is my light and my liberation;
   Of whom should I be afraid?
God is the fortress of my life;
   Of whom shall I be terrified?
Teach me your way, Ground of my being;
      Lead me a straight path in the face of my
         oppressors.
I am confident of seeing the goodness of God
   In the country of the living.
Be strong and let your heart be bold,
   And wait for the right time of God.

LESSON

Do not worry about your life, what to eat;
   Nor about your body, what you will wear.
Is not your life more than its food,
   And your body more than its clothing?
See the crows, that they never sow seed
   Or harvest or bring into barns;
And still your Father feeds them;
   Are you not of more value than they?
And which of you by his worrying
   Can add a hand's breadth to his height?
Look at the poppies of the field;
   They do not weave or spin.
I tell you, Solomon in his splendor
   Was not dressed like one of them.
And if the wild plants which bloom today
   And tomorrow are thrown in the oven

Are clothed in such manner by God,
    Will you not also be clothed, you
        suspicious?
So do not worry what you will eat
    Or what you will drink or wear;
All peoples of the earth look for these,
    Your Father knows that you need them.
But instead look for his liberation,
    And you will get these in addition.
Fear not, little flock, for your Father
    Has willed you the country of freedom.
Do not worry yourself about tomorrow;
    Let tomorrow worry for itself.
Sell what are called your possessions
    And give them as presents for the poor.
Make purses that never wear out,
    An unfailing account with your Father,
Where moth and rust cannot rot it,
    Where burglars do not break and enter.
For wherever your treasure is stored up,
    Know also that there will your heart be.

[*Luke* 12:22-34]

THE COMMITTAL

Minister: To the Source of life we entrust the
life of our *brother* [*sister*] departed, and we commit *his* [*her*] body to the *earth* [*deep*] from which
it came, as a shock of grain in its season; con-
fidently awaiting the restoration of all things in
the paradise of this garden earth, for which they
all travail together in hope; through the spirit
of Jesus our Liberator, who in his love is changing each of us into his own splendor.

Kyrie eleison. Kyrie eleison.
    Lord have mercy upon us. Lord have mercy
        upon us.
Christe eleison. Christe eleison.
    Christ have mercy upon us. Christ have
        mercy upon us.
Kyrie eleison. Kyrie eleison.
    Lord have mercy upon us. Lord have mercy
        upon us.

Minister: O Power who brings us from death to
life in the love of our brothers, may this one who
has been one of us never be separated from us, by
the Liberator who has broken down all barriers.
And in the presence of our *brother* [*sister*] now at
rest, we ask that we who remain may find no rest
except by following the new Way of Jesus in justice and love. In union with all the servants of

his people who have gone before us, may our bodies
be built as living stones into the temple of his
community. While we draw breath, may we be filled
with his spirit for reconciliation. And at the
end, allow us (after his example) to have poured
ourselves so fully into others that we are alive
in them, and in him, until the perfection of his
new Age. Amen; so may it be.

BLESSING

May God who brought back from the dead the great
Shepherd of the sheep, by the blood of the perpetual Covenant of Peace, unite you in every good
action to do his desiring, through our Liberator
Jesus, in whom is the splendor of all worlds.

[*Hebrews* 13:20-21]

The Freedom Meal

A Prayer for Peace
attributed to Francis of Assisi

Minister: Jesus, make us instruments of your peace.
peace. Where there is hate, let us sow love;
where there is violence, let us sow forgiveness,
where there is doubt, faith; where there is despair, hope; where there is darkness, light; where
there is sadness, joy. Our Liberator, let us not
so much wish to be comforted as to comfort, to be
loved as to love. For it is in giving that we receive, in pardoning that we are pardoned, in dying
that we are born into the life of the Age to come.

People: Amen, so may it be.

The Greetings

Minister: Shalom, my brothers and sisters, the
covenent of peace be upon you, Shalom.
People: And peace be with you, our brother,
Shalom.

Minister: For the Liberator himself is our peace;
People: He breaks down all walls of hatred.
                                        [*Ephesians* 2:14]

Minister: And if he by the finger of God drives
out demons,
People: No doubt his Age is upon us. [*Luke* 11:20]

Minister:
   In Advent
  His footsteps are close at hand.
    At Christmas
  Alleluia, for our peace a child is born.
    At Epiphany
  Gold is given him, with frankincense and myrrh.
    At Easter
  Alleluia, the tomb could not contain his life.
    At Pentecost
  Alleluia, his spirit is on every tongue.
    At times of penitence
  For our faults the violent spilled his blood.
    At other times
  In love he built the worlds of light.

People: May we be numbered among his saints
[Alleluia].

At other times
In love he built the worlds of light.

People: May we be numbered among his saints
[Alleluia].

THE INVOCATION OF THE SAINTS

*Part III of the Litany (p. 33), in whole or in
part, to which the response is:*

People: Stand here beside us.

THE RULES OF THE NEW WAY

*Here (except at a shortened service) are read the
three Rules from the form of entering the Covenant
(pp. 52-53).*

LIBERATION FROM COMPLICITY

*Except on festivals, the three Rules are usually
followed, as in the form of entering the Covenant,
by the statements of complicity and liberation
(pp. 53-54).*

GLORIA IN EXCELSIS

Splendor to God in the summits;
   And on earth, peace to men of his
         pleasing.   [*Luke* 2:14]
For the rosetree of Jesse has budded,
   A branch has flowered from his root;
And the breath of our God blows upon him,
   A spirit of knowledge and strength.
In freedom he leads the oppressed,
   The untouchable poor in his justice.
              [*Isaiah* 11:1-4]
They will forge each sword to a plow,
   Beat out bayonets into sickles;
No nation lifts weapon at nation,
   Not one will learn war any longer.
But each man sits under his vine,
   Without fearing under his figtree.
              [*Micah* 4:3-4]
The plowman will push past the reaper,
   The vintage comes fast upon flowering.
              [*Amos* 9:14]
The wolf will walk with the lamb,
   And a little child will lead them;
The lioncub feeds with the calf,
   On the rattler's den children are dancing.
No violence or destruction is done
   On all the hill of God's holiness;
For his knowledge covers the continents
   As the seafloor is filled with the waters.
              [*Isaiah* 11:6-9]

Minister: Let us hear that Word from which, we believe, there is fresh light yet to break.

A Hebrew Prophecy

An Epistle

Hymn or Song

Reading of the Gospel

Prayer for the Day

The Affirmations

Repeated by the people after a leader.

> God is not dead.
> God is bread.
> The bread is rising.
> Bread means revolution.
> God means revolution.
> Murder is no revolution.
> Revolution is love.
> Win with love.
> The radical Jesus is winning.
> The world is coming to a beginning.
> The whole world is watching.
> Organize for a new world.
> Wash off your brother's blood.
> Burn out the mark of the Beast.
> Join the freedom meal.
> Plant the people's park.
> The asphalt church is marching.
> The guerrilla church is recruiting.
> The people's church is striking.
> The submarine church is surfacing.
> The war is over.
> The war is over.
> The war is over.
> The Liberated Zone is at hand.

Sermon

Litany of Intercession

Part IV of the Litany (p. 35), to which the response is:

People: We call on the Spirit.

THE OFFERING

Minister: Here, where two or three or more are
joined in breaking bread, Jesus is made known--as
the prisoner, the wounded one, the sick, the
thirsty, the naked, the homeless, who asks for our
help. We have been made a royal priesthood of his
Gospel. So I appeal to you, brothers and sisters,
by the sympathy of God, offer up your bodies a
living sacrifice, in solidarity with his reconcil-
ing love. Do not be conformed to this age, but be
transfigured through the renewal of your will.

A sentence such as the following:

Reader: The King will answer and tell them: Since
you did it for one of the least of these my
brothers, you did it for me.   [*Matthew* 25:40]

For you know the gentleness of Jesus our Liberator, that when rich he became poor for our sake,
so that through his poverty we might become rich.
                                [*2 Corinthians* 8:9]

Let me boast of nothing except the cross of Jesus
our hero and liberator, through whom the world has
been crucified to me and I to the world.
                                  [*Galatians* 6:14]

A song such as the following:

>   They are walking from east and from west
>   To sit down together at table
>   In the life of the world's liberation
>   With Abraham, Isaac, and Jacob;
>   While the confident heirs of the earth
>   Are dismissed into outer darkness.
>   [*Matthew* 8:11]
>   And for all men upon this mountain
>   The Strength beyond armies spreads out
>   A dinner of all the earth's yield,
>   A feast of wine from all vineyards.
>   And upon this hill he unties
>   The blindfold bound on all peoples;
>   He destroys old Death forever,
>   He dries off the tear from all faces.
>   [*Isaiah* 25:6-8]
>   He opens our life in liberty
>   To walk in the ways of justice.
>   He sets a table before us
>   In the face of all our oppressors;
>   Our brow is bright with the olive,
>   Our cup is filled overflowing.
>   [*Psalm* 23:3-5]

At the presentation:

Minister: Blessed is the King of the ages who satisfies his people from the earth. As the grain does not come to life unless it dies, so may we die to the old way and rise in his new way. As the one vine of our father David has many branches, so may the whole universe be made one in the Liberated Zone.

The Kiss of Peace

Reader: If you are bringing your gift to the altar, and there remember that your brother has something against you, leave your gift there in front of the altar; go and first be reconciled to your brother, and then come back and offer your gift.   [*Matthew* 5:23-24]

Minister: We know that we have passed from death to life by the fact that we love our brothers. If a person does not love his brother whom he has seen, how will he love God whom he has not seen? He who does not love, does not know God; for God is love.   [*1 John* 3:14, 4:20, 4:8]

Here follows the Kiss of Peace.

Sursum Corda

Minister: Lift up your hearts.

People: We lift them up to our Liberator.

Minister: Let us celebrate the Power of Being.

People: It is good and right for us to do so.

The Praise of Creation

Minister: It is right for us at all times and places to celebrate the Fountain of nature and history. As our doors of perception open, they testify to a universe of glory: the touch of rocks, skin, fabric, marble columns; the smell of redwood, fish, flowers, our neighbor's sweat, the smoke of incense; the taste of grain and the blood of the vine; the sound of birdsong and animals, waves and wind, voice and music; the light of our sun, the galaxies, the lamp of a student. Through our awareness that the cosmos is everywhere ready to blossom into a love not of our own devising, we rise to a sphere of liberation beyond space and time; we hear words passing human speech, as our brother Isaiah did in the Temple; standing with heads bowed beside angelic Energies, in trust we

sing to you who determine the number of the stars,
O Father of splendors:

SANCTUS

All:

Holy, Holy, Holy is the Power beyond all
hosts.
The fulness of the whole world is his
glory.
Blessed is the one who comes in his name.
Hosanna, may his Way be victorious.

THE MEMORIAL OF HISTORY

Minister: And although by our fault we abandoned
the well of living waters, the chain of complicity
linking our failure to past guilt has been
snapped, through no merit of our own; and, while
living in occupied territory, we walk with hope.
For in our hands, leading back to the first assem-
blies of our City, we hold a golden thread: the
succession of prophets and saints [*and especially
of N*] who looked to you, O Jesus, the Man for
others, as their Morningstar.

[*Here a proper preface can be inserted.*]

Today we remember how at your last freedom meal
with your friends (and at least one enemy) you
took the loaf as we do, said thanks over it and
broke it, and gave it to them, saying: "Take and
eat; this is my body, broken for you; do this for
my remembering." Also after the meal you took the
cup, said thanks and gave it to them, saying:
"Drink this, all of you: for this cup is the unending Constitution of a new society in my blood,
poured out for liberation from your guilt. Do
this when you drink it, for my remembering."

People:

Your dying we recall;
Your rising we proclaim;
Your coming we prepare.

THE INVOCATION OF THE SPIRIT

Minister: Friends, we have learned that our Liberator, by healing the sick, by refusing to do
harm, by telling the poor good news, put himself
so fully in others that nothing of him could die.
So by our self-offering among his peaceable people
we are made whole and given life. And we call
upon you, O Spirit of Jesus, to put his death and
life into this bread and wine, breaking down all

barriers between rich and poor, black and white, man and woman, old and young, East and West. Gather us together as true sons and daughters of our first parents to restore the paradise of Eden. And strengthen us as servants of the poor and as messengers of the peace brought in by our Brother, through whom, in the community of love, nature and history move to their desired Goal.

People: Amen. So may it be, here and everywhere, now and always. Maranatha; come quickly Jesus.

Pater Noster

Minister: The covenant of peace is sealed; for God at his right time has sent the Spirit of the Liberator into our hearts, crying out:

All:

> Abba, Father:
> Blessed be your working;
>   Soon be your appearing;
>   Done be your desiring.
> Our bread provide us;
>   Our debts forgive us;
>   From trials free us.

Breaking the Bread

Minister: The cup of celebration which we bless, is it not a sharing in the blood of the Liberator? The bread which we break, is it not a sharing in the body of the Liberator? We many are one body, for we all share the one loaf.

[1 Corinthians 10:16-17]

Here follows the Freedom Meal proper.

The Blessing

Minister and People:
M.   Blessed are the poor:
P.   For theirs is the Liberated Zone.
M.   Blessed are all who mourn:
P.   For they are comforted.
M.   Blessed are the gentle:
P.   For they shall inherit the earth.
M.   Blessed are those hungry for justice:
P.   For they will be satisfied.
M.   Blessed are the merciful:
P.   For they receive mercy.
M.   Blessed are the pure in heart:
P.   For they see God.
M.   Blessed are the peacemakers:
P.   For they are called the children of God.

M.   Blessed are the oppressed:
P.   For theirs is the Liberated Zone.

[*Matthew* 5:3-12]

THE DISMISSAL

Reader:
        Go in peace and love.
            Serve God, serve the people.
        Keep the faith, baby:
            You are the Liberated Zone.

People: Right on. Right on. Right on.

JOIN THE FREEDOM MEAL

Tune: "Rockingham," Miller-Webbe 1790 *(The Hymnal 1940* no. 203; L.M.)

1   Tonight we join the Freedom Meal,
        Reminding our forgetfulness
    How Jesus felt the Roman steel
        And stood in Caesar's purple dress.

2   He drinks the cup his love had filled,
        And blunts the violence of the Beast;
    In solidarity we build
        The golden circle of his feast.

3   The Great Ones of the world oppress
        The poor, the black, the young, the brown;
    But here the greater is the less,
        Who makes his brother's need his own.

4   Our hands lift up the rising bread
        In which the whole world's hope began;
    We drink the blood our Vine has shed
        To warm the heart of God and man.

5   We kneel to wash our brothers' feet
        Within his Liberated Zone;
    His new example we repeat
        And make his pearl our cornerstone.

6 We look to see our Morning Star
        Shine in the dark as friend to friend,
    And raise the poor, from near to far;
        Come soon, our Fountain and our End.

The Disarmed Forces Prayer Book

REFUSING INDUCTION

It's your *choice*
Ultimately you can listen to only one thing, not
your President, not your many misguided leaders,
save a few, not the Communists or the Socialists
or the Republicans or the Democrats, but you must
listen to your own heart, and do what it dictates.
Because your heart is the only thing which can
tell you what is right and what is wrong. And
after you have found out what you think is right
and what is wrong, then you must know that you can
say yes to what is right and no to what is wrong.
And you young men, for instance, if you feel that
to kill is wrong and to go to war is wrong, then
you have to say no to the draft. And if you young
ladies think it is wrong to kill, and war is
wrong, you can say yes to the young men who say no
to the draft. Because it is not the leaders and
the dictators, it is not God who is going to get
us out of the bloody mess we are in. It is only
you and only me. *Joan Baez*

The house of cards
Spirit of life, help me see that Castle Death is
only a house of cards; let me and my comrade pull
out our cards, and bring it down like the walls of
Jericho.

For freedom from violence
Jesus, you were angry at the unfeeling oppression
of Empire, and tempted to join the guerrillas
fighting for home and family; strengthen my hold
on justice to see oppression wherever it may be,
strengthen my hold on love to see that violence in
a just cause again becomes injustice.

For freedom from self-righteousness
Bread of life, I have not often been hungry, or
without clothing, or in need of medicine; close my
mouth when I begin to condemn the violence of the
hungry, the ill-clothed, the neglected. Let me
join them in their cry for justice; let me correct
the tactics only of those who are better off than
myself.

What causes wars?
The crop of justice in peace is sown by peacemakers. But what causes wars and fighting among
you? Is it not your greeds that fight among your
members? You desire and do not get; so you kill.
You do not have because you do not ask; you ask
and do not receive, because you ask wrongly--to
spend on your acquisitiveness. Don't you know
that the love of this age is enmity with God?
Whoever wants to be a friend of this age is an
enemy of God.   *James 3:18-4:4*

*For police, induction personnel, draftboards,
judges*
Liberator of all persons, you showed me your way;
leave me on my own without your comforts, and show
what I have seen to all blind or unwilling instruments of a coercive system; find a way for them
also to remove their bodies from it, and to build
themselves into the community of your love.

From the Acts of Saint Maximilian, A.D. 295
Proconsul: He must either serve or die.
Maximilian: I will not be a soldier. You can cut
my head off, but I refuse to serve in the armies
of this world. I am a soldier of my God.
P.: Who has put these ideas in your head?
M.: My conscience, and he who has called me.
P.: Be a soldier and accept the leaden seal, the
sign of enlistment.
M.: I have nothing to do with your sign. I al-
ready bear the sign of Christ, my God.
P.: I am going to send you to join your Christ,
here and now.
M.: That is all I ask. That will be glory for
me.
P.: Become a soldier and take the sign; if not,
you will die a shameful death.
M.: I shall not die; my name is already written
down with my God. I cannot be a soldier.
P.: Think of your youth and become a soldier. It
is a fine life for a young man.
M.: My service is under my God. I have already
told you. I cannot serve the world. I am a
Christian.
P.: In the bodyguards of our lords the emperors
there are Christian soldiers, and they serve.
M.: That is their business. I only know I am a
Christian and I cannot do wrong.
P.: But those who serve--what wrong do they do?
M.: You know very well what they do.
P.: Strike his name off.

On Unwilling Assignment

Rifle and bayonet drill
Jesus, I do not want to kill, or practice to kill,
or speak of killing. And still I am afraid of
punishment, of speaking my mind, of being thought
a coward. Lay your discipline on me as you did on
Peter when he took up the sword. With you at my
side let me drop this weapon and enlist in your
army of life.

On guard duty
O Commander above all armies, I find myself assigned on guard duty, like the soldiers who stood
beneath your Cross and at your grave. Shake the
earth underneath this camp of death, open a way
for me to rise into your liberated zone of love.

Dangerous flight or voyage
Blessed Mary, the enemy deported you with your
child on a dangerous journey to an uncertain destination. Give wisdom and skill to the pilot in
whose hands my life rests; give me confidence and
quiet. Your flight to Egypt preserved the world's
liberation; let no person take harm from my
travelling.

Against injury and death
Jesus, you accepted the nails yourself, but told
us to pray the Father for deliverance from trials.
We fall far short of your perfection; let us (if
we may) still be children, asking the Father we do
not yet know to shelter us from the violence of
the world.

On orders
My pursuer, I thought I had found a sanctuary
against your orders; now the Prince of this world
has given me his orders. Let me have courage in
surrendering to you, so that I may obey God rather
than men.

For the enemy
Liberator of the world, I hate and fear the man of
foreign language who is trying to kill me. Help
me to discern that the real enemy is he who put
this weapon in my hand and sent me here to another
man's earth. Protect me and lead me out of the
valley of this death.

Against genocide
Jesus, bring to my eyes the night when your mother
gave birth to her baby outside the inn. Let me
believe that the world's Liberator is being born

in every peasant family; show me him in every
homeless baby. Let me suffer disgrace, punishment, harm, let my right hand be cut off before
lifting it against one of these little ones.

For the crops of the enemy
O Creator of all beings, you have made all green
things food for animals and birds and men, you
make us all dependent on each other. When I am
dead and only historians remember the cause of
this war, there will still be mouths in this land
to feed; do not send them off hungry for any action of mine.

In battle
Jesus, I am weak and afraid. Keep me from any
situation when I would be under direct orders to
fire, when I would have to fire to save my comrade. Help me show my comrade he need not fire to
save me; help me to not fire in my own defense.
Show me a comrade where I see an enemy.

But then what is the use of this weapon I am
holding?

Wounded
Our Liberator, without consulting me you have
given me a share in your Cross, and I do not yet
know the outcome. Stay with me, turn my suffering
like yours to good for some person unknown, do not
leave me hopeless.

For peace
Our Liberator, on the first Christmas men were
promised the benefit which above all others we now
desire. Take the weapon from every hand, burn the
vehicles and blunt the bayonets, break down all
barriers, and rule gently over us all in that
peace which is none other than yourself.

Exorcising the demon Kill
Enemy in my heart, it is you I must fear, and not
the enemy in the facing line or the ambush. I
tear you from me and, if I bleed, I accept a
transfusion from the heart of Jesus. I have put
on the breastplate of justice; never enter me
again, much less another human being in my place,
but like the pigs of Gadara, fall into the abyss
and perish.

SPLITTING

AWOL
Son of Man, when the foxes had holes and the birds
nests, you could not find where to lay your head.

Walk here beside me, let my fear be your fear. Do
not let me wander forever; do not force me into
exile against my will; above all do not send me
back to that slavery I escaped from. Show me a
friend I can trust in your name, and through him
tell me what I must do.

Count me out
From the bayonet drill and the hating: Count me
    out, count me out, count me out.
From the system that makes me machinery: Count me
    out, count me out, count me out. *And so on.*
From the airdrop and the free fire zone:
From unquestioning obedience to orders:
From character guidance lectures:
From letting someone else think for me:
From the G.I. heart transplant of stone:
From now to the end of my walking:
On my sure days and on my unsure days:
In the face of exile and prison:
To face the face of my children:
To build a different America:
For the sake of the people who count on me: Count
    me out, count me out, count me out.
By the bond of my union with Jesus: Count me out,
    count me out, count me out.

Disarmament begins with me
If not with me, with whom, Jesus? Did I listen in
on a telephone call meant for somebody else, or
was it really me you were talking to? And did you
truly mean what you said? But what is that spot
on the khaki? Some kid from My Lai. I guess
Mary's time came in some hooch at My Lai. A spot
of your precious blood answers every question.
Wearing the khaki for me is no longer a question.

Off the World Pig
He still has his piggy claws in me, unexpectedly
strong; the wild boar's tusks graze my cheek from
beside his gasmask snout. I cannot fight him any
longer; I cannot fight any longer. Let him do
what he will. As he pulls out his claws let him
take his pound of flesh. The power of weakness
has delivered me from the power of the World Pig.
The grace of Jesus is sufficient. For the law of
the spirit of life has set me free from the law of
sin and death.

In Liberated Status

New issue of equipment
Jesus, I take off the bandolier of violence and
put on your belt of truth. I take off the flak
vest and put on your breastplate of justice. I
take off the combat boots and put on your walking
shoes of peace. I get out from behind the armor
plating and take up the shield of confidence. I
take off the camouflage helmet and put on the helmet of liberation. I break the rifle and take up
the weapon of the spirit, which is the word of
God. Only so can I dare to struggle, dare to win,
against the world rulers of this present darkness.
For the salary of my old condition was death; but
the free gift of God is the life of the Liberated
Zone under you my Commander.

Solidarity
I am liberated, but still closely hemmed in; I
have comrades outside, but I cannot see them or
speak to them. Spirit of truth, weld an unbreak-
able bond of solidarity among all who are struggling for justice and love, in different ways and
places, unknown to each other. Show us that we
are all one army under the high command of the
Liberator.

Oath of allegiance
I undertake to follow the Liberator as my Com-
mander-in-Chief; I give unconditional obedience to
his orders alone. I wrap up the clothes of the
old way of life and mail them back to from where
they came. I have put off violence to my mother
the Earth, violence to my brother wherever he may
be. I accept commissioning in the Liberation Army
of Love.

Render unto Nixon
Jesus, you told us to render unto Nixon whatever
things belong to him. Help us to discover which
things those are, and to find no further use in
them. Show us also which things belong to God;
help us to set our hearts on them, and through
them to find love, joy, peace and all other fruits
of the Spirit.

Turning myself in
My struggle is not overseas or in exile but here;
I must stand freely in my own country under my own
name. Jesus, you allowed yourself to be turned in
at Gethsemane rather than do violence to any
brother. If the only way to freedom is through

prison, I also allow myself to be turned in. Help
me push beyond man's injustice to your justice,
beyond harassment to liberation, beyond violence
to love.

For strength in trial
Jesus, since they harassed you it is likely they
will harass me. You stood on your feet before
your accusers, and did not open your mouth asking
to be let off. Stand beside me during a play-act-
ing trial, and do not let me fall into self-pity
or anger. Plant the seed in those present which
may blossom after five, ten, twenty years into
love.

For strength in prison
Our Liberator, I cry out to you as the first political prisoner. Take my minutes of despair up
into your minutes of despair. Open the gates of
my heart and come in; at the right time open also
those other gates. Give me with my hope of release that strength and confidence which you had
in your hopelessness.

Looking toward release
Help me remember, my Brother, that the world outside is also a prison, enslaved by the same World
Pig who rules in here. Do not let me expect that
my family or comrades will understand what has
happened here. As you were a marked man, I am a
marked man, marked by your presence with me. Help
me stand on my own feet, and find my own work in
the struggle.

Thank you
We have been through bad times together, of which
the world knows little; and good times, of which
it knows less. I rely on you, as in some strange
way I believe you rely on me. Thank you for being
here. As one comrade to another, I take your
wounded hand in mine.

For the Others

For those still in slavery
Jesus, you did not come to call virtuous men but
sinners to repentance. We are your voice and
hands and feet; show us how the liberation we have
known can be brought to those still enslaved by a
system of violence and fear.

For medics
God of healing, you have left no place empty of
your witness. Make all medics doctors first, and

soldiers second or not at all. Maintain their
loyalty to the oath of Hippocrates and Luke, not
to the rulers of this age. Help them minister im-
partially to all, keep them witnesses to the revolution of love in a sea of violence.

For GI journalists
Spirit of truth, you can break through walls where
none other can enter. Stay with all who have undertaken to speak for you, in however unlikely a
place; maintain their loyalty to yourself alone,
help them ignore all threats and harassment in
fidelity to their vocation.

For the victims
My brother Victim, I was in part responsible for
your suffering. Please go out to those others for
whose suffering I was in part responsible, and
tell them that the one who did it has turned
against it.

For military prisoners
Our Liberator, we thank you for the witness of all
those now imprisoned for that witness. As we know
that you stand daily beside them, give us and all
others their commitment and fearlessness, so that
one day prisons will lie empty and derelict.

For the movement
God, you have made all men of one blood, but set
their hands to different works. Make us one with
our brothers and sisters in the revolution of love
through all countries. Do not let us suspect each
others' motives; rather by the weapon of your
spirit destroy that dark Power whose last resort
is to turn us against each other.

For chaplains
Jesus, forgive those who speak your words from out
of the citadel of repression. Let them do your
work in spite of themselves. Touch their hearts
with disquiet and uncertainty, lead them in your
way; and over against them set other ministers of
your liberation who suffer with the suffering.

For jailers
Mary mother of Jesus, who saw your son mistreated
by his captors; put it into the heart of all jailers and their women to see their prisoners not as
prisoners but as human beings. Show each prison-
keeper that his keys lock up no man tighter than
himself; give him a longing for that liberation
which with pain you brought into the world.

For officers and noncoms

O Power of History, our only true Commander, make your orders known among those who have usurped the authority which by right belongs only to you. Humanize their conduct and increase their doubts. Help them to find a brother in one they were told to consider an enemy, and to find the enemy nowhere but in their own hearts.

For the powerful

O you who drove the demons out of the violent, look with anger and pity on those powerful men oppressed by the demons of oppression. At whatever cost, free them from their tormenters, and free the suffering poor and the planet from their violence.

For civilian supporters of militarism

Spirit of truth, touch all who have been misled or manipulated into fear. Show them that the armed forces which they should fear, the missiles which threaten their towns, are not posted overseas but at home. Break through their walls, dispel the smog of their obsessions, open their eyes, and clothe them in invulnerability, which you alone can give.

For family and friends

O Mother of that Runaway whom you could not understand; by your new understanding, be with our family and friends who are absent and puzzled. Let the sword in their hearts turn them to greater understanding, and to solidarity with yourself and your son Jesus.

For the faithful dead

Jesus our comrade, we thank you for all those faithful dead who struggled without seeing the outcome on earth. We believe that they have seen victory in you, and that they and their work live on in us. As we do not mourn your death, let us not mourn theirs, but organize on the foundations they have laid.

MEDICAL CADRE MANUAL

For confidence
Our Liberator, you suffered and died, and are living in us. Then we do not need to be afraid of
pain and death; we may trust life. Give all medics steady hands and hearts; give their patients
confidence in them; keep them both safe from new
injury.

For strength
O Spirit of life., there is much distress in front
of our eyes, and our strength is failing. Let us
push through to the other side of fatigue. Put
your strength into our hands. We ask that the
suffering of others should be relieved, if necessary at the cost of our own suffering.

Remembering the saints
Luke, physician and historian: Hold my hand
     steady.
Louis Pasteur, physician and scientist: Hold my
     hand steady.
Frantz Fanon, psychiatrist and revolutionary:
     Hold my hand steady.
Che Guevara, physician and revolutionary: Hold my
     hand steady.
Florence Nightingale, nurse and reformer: Hold my
     hand steady.
Albert Schweitzer, doctor and musician: Hold my
     hand steady.
Damien, priest and leper: Hold my hand steady.

Before an operation
O Universal Power of Being, may your eye rest on
our *brother* [*sister*] who in pain and weakness has
put *his* life in our hands. Give both *him* and us
confidence and steadiness. Guide our hands with
all our own knowledge and skill; may Hippocrates,
Luke, Che, all physicians of the people stand beside us. Maintain the springs of life that we
cannot see, overcome the destructive forces we
cannot reach.

At a demonstration
Jesus our Liberator, you were fearless in prophetic witness, tireless in relief of suffering.
Give all medics here that same courage and
strength. Let no act of ours either bring on unnecessary violence, or weaken the cry for justice.

For protection against attack
O Strength beyond nature and history, we have
taken an oath to help the sick and wounded at

whatever risk to ourselves. Hold us steady to
that commitment and lift up the shield of your
protection over us, and all our brother and sister
medics; do not let the healer become another victim; keep the dark powers at bay.

For all brother and sister medics
Our Liberator, you make all persons whole. Send
the spirit of your compassion and skill on all our
brother and sister medics. Keep always in their
hearts an awareness of the fellowship which has
taken the same oath. Do not let the revolution of
love, or the renewal of the planet, be delayed by
any weakness or hesitancy on their part.

For all patients
Jesus our Liberator, we have done for our brothers
and sisters here all that knowledge and skill
could do. We entrust them to the medics who follow us and have taken the same oath. Open the
springs of healing in them which are beyond our
knowledge and skill.

For the seriously ill or wounded
O Best of physicians, look at your *brother* [*sister*] here in the crisis of *his* need. We have
given him all the help that human hands could provide. You first took the dark route, you know
best the secrets of death and life. Take this one
in your hands, give *him* that wholeness and fulfilment which were written down for *him* before all
worlds。

For the dying or dead
Compassionate Father, the spirit of your child is
returning to you who first gave it. Forgive all
he [*she*] did wrong, remember all *he* did well. We
entrust *his* life to you with confidence. Give
your child *his* true place in the society of man,
and in your secret renewal of the whole created
order, through Jesus the brother of us all.

The Hippocratic Oath (adapted)
I swear by the universal Power of healing, in
grateful remembrance of Hippocrates the first doctor, that I will always honor those who taught me
medicine; that I will continue studying it; that I
will support my brother and sister medics, and
share my knowledge with every sincere student. I
will never refuse the call for help. I will treat
friend and enemy with equal diligence, giving them
the best care my art provides. I will subordinate
my own convenience and safety to the needs of my

patient. I will neither give nor prescribe any
poison or dangerous drug; I will not work while
under the influence of any drug myself. While on
duty I will seduce no patient, nurse, or other
person; nor do business to my own advantage; nor
use or carry any weapon. I will maintain all confidences, even from an enemy, inviolate. In every
professional act I will make relief of suffering,
justice for the oppressed, and restoration of
the environment my sacred and revolutionary
priorities.

Guerrilla Liturgies

1. A Lament for Victims and Executioners

Suitable for Good Friday and Church conventions.

I. AT THE STAGING AREA

Minister: Is it nothing to you, all you who pass by? Look and see if there is any sorrow like my sorrow. [*Lamentations* 1:12]

PROPHECY

Reader:
See my Servant shall be raised up;
    He will be put high on display.
Many will be dismayed at him:
    His appearance was distorted
Beyond the semblance of humanity,
    And his form unlike the sons of men.
Many nations will denounce him;
    Ministers will shut their mouths at him:
They will see what they never were told,
    And know what they never heard.

Who has believed our announcement?
    Who saw God's right arm made bare?
His Servant grew up as a worthless weed,
    As a stick from stony ground.
Despised and rejected by the powerful,
    A man of sickness, knowing pain;
The wealthy hid their faces from him,
    He was scorned, we set no store by him.

But surely he has lifted our suffering
    And carried our contagion;
We avoided him as infectious,
    Punished by God and despicable.
In fact he was wounded for our guilt,
    He was beaten up for our complicity;
The punishment of our peace was on him,
    By his harassment we are healed.
We all turned aside like sheep,
    Each one wandering in his own way,

And the Power of History piled on him
    The criminality of us all.

He was exploited and oppressed
    And he never opened his mouth;
As a lamb led to the slaughterhouse,
    As a dumb sheep before the shearers.
He was arrested by law and order.
    And who will now follow his way?
He is exiled from the land of life;
    For a nation's crime he was executed.
His coffin is set among criminals,
    He was buried in a field without markers,
Although he had done no violence,
    And no lies were in his mouth.

God has accepted his suffering
    As a substitute for the violent;
And so he will see his children,
    His days will be long extended.
In his hand God's desiring is done,
    He is reconciled with his suffering.

"My Servant the man of justice
    Shall liberate the people by his life;
He receives the inheritance of the rich,
    He shares the rewards of the wealthy.
Since he poured out his life in his dying,
    And was counted among the criminals,
He carries the guilt of his people,
    And makes himself bail for the prisoners."
                    [*Isaiah* 52:13-53:12]

PSALM 59:1-7

Liberate me from my enemies, my God;
    Protect me from the repressors.
Liberate me from the criminals;
    Save me from the men of blood.
See, they lay ambushes against my life;
    The powerful have conspired against me.
For no crime or evil in me,
    O Lord, they run and make ready.
Wake up at my calling and see;
    For you are the God beyond armies.
Awake to punish the oppressors;
    Do not spare the conspirators.
In the evening they enter the city;
    Howling like dogs they patrol it.
There they are, barking with their jaws
    And snarling with their lips, "Who will
            hear us?"

Reader: Jerusalem, Jerusalem, you who execute the prophets and stone all those sent to you, how often I have wanted to collect your children, as a bird gathers her chicks under her wings, and you would not let me! See now, your house is left desolate. I tell you, you will not see me again until the time comes when you say, "Blessed is he who comes in the name of God." O City: if even today you could learn what things work for your peace! But they have been hidden from your eyes. The days are coming that your enemy will besiege and encircle you and fence you in. They will throw you to the ground with your children in you; they will not leave stone standing upon stone in you, because you did not recognize the time of your visitation.   [*Luke* 13:34-35; 19:41-44]

Minister: Brothers and sisters, we have come here to lament in dead earnest the harassing and murder of God's servant, our Liberator victim. But those who sit in the seat of the scornful are mourning over the fall of the World Pig; and rightly, because our Jesus like Samson pulled him down in his own death. Let us take them at their word; let us join in proclaiming the overthrow of Lucifer, Chief Magistrate of an age of violence, Chief Executioner among the executioners.

LAMENT FOR LUCIFER

Minister and People:
> How you are fallen from heaven, Lucifer, son of the morning: How you are fallen from heaven, Lucifer, son of the morning.
>
> God has broken the oppressor's rifle, who ruled the nations in anger: How you are fallen from heaven, Lucifer, son of the morning. *And so on.*
>
> The cedars and redwoods rejoice, "No logger now comes up against us":
>
> Hell is stirred up to meet you, it awakes those once leaders on earth:
>
> They all are saying together, "You have become like one of us":
>
> But you said in your heart, "I will spread freedom over all lands":
>
> All that see you will stare, "Is this he that made the earth a desert?"

You do not share their burial, because you
    destroyed your people:

Babylon the great is fallen, is fallen, that
    made all nations drink the wine of the
    wrath of her fornication:

Who is like that great beast? Who is able to
    make war against it?:

No man can walk in its streets, unless he has
    on his forehead the mark of the beast:
    How you are fallen from heaven, Lucifer,
    son of the morning.

Babylon the great is fallen, is fallen, and
    has become the home of demonic powers:
    How you are fallen from heaven, Lucifer,
    son of the morning.
                        [*Isaiah* 14:4-21, etc.]

Minister: Friends, here we have been in our own
place. Let us go out to the place of the ex-
ploiter, and there speak to him in lamentation and
anger. For it was he that busted the Liberator of
all people; and there is a word from the Power of
History which he must hear before a worse thing
befalls him.

II. AT THE PROCESSION
PSALM 22

My God, my God:
    Why have you deserted me?
Why are you so far from helping me,
    From the words of my torment?
I cry out by day and you do not answer;
    By night, and I find no sleep.
And you are known as the Holy One;
    You are called the Praise of Israel.
Our fathers trusted in you,
    They trusted in your liberation;
They cried to you and were helped,
    They trusted you and were not let down.
But I am a worm, no human being,
    The scorn of man, contempt of the crowd.
All who see me make fun of me,
    They stick out their lips and wag their
                heads:
"He trusted in God, let God save him;
    Let him rescue the one who calls on him."
And it was you took me from the womb;
    You guarded me on my mother's breast.

I was thrown on you when first I was born;
    From my mother's womb you are my God.
Do not go away, trouble is near;
    There is no other to help me.
Many bulls are closing in on me,
    Fat pigs are surrounding me;
They open their mouths at me
    Like lions roaring for meat.
As water I am poured out;
    My bones are all dislocated.
My heart has become like wax;
    It is melted inside my body.
I am dried up like broken dishes,
    My tongue sticks to my lips.
You have laid me in the dust of death;
    The dogs are circling around me.
A gang of criminals have taken me;
    They pierced my hands and my feet.
I can count all my bones;
    They are staring and cursing at me.
They have divided my clothing
    And are throwing dice for my garments.
Do not stand aside, my Liberator;
    My helper, hurry to save me.
Save my life from their clubs,
    My mouth from the mouth of the lion.
Release me from the paws of the dog;
    Save me from the teeth of the pigs.

THE GHETTO PASSION

Black Jesus, our Liberator, free all your people:
    Black Jesus, free all your people.

Our Liberator, ratbitten in your crib: Black
    Jesus, free all your people. *And so on.*

Our Liberator who ate lead paint from the walls:

Our Liberator in your protein-deficient diet:

Our Liberator with no father at home:

Our Liberator who played with beercans in dirt:

Our Liberator who failed the intelligence test:

Our Liberator, tracked in vocational classrooms:

Our Liberator, knifed by the local dealer:

Our Liberator, with a switchblade scar on his
                cheek:

Our Liberator, swimming with grapefruit rinds:

Our Liberator, hanging around with his friends:

Our Liberator, unskilled and unemployable:

Our Liberator, conned by the recruiting sergeant:

Our Liberator, absent without official leave:

Our Liberator, worked over by pigs in the squad
              car:

Our Liberator, carrying Psalms with a bulletproof
              cover:

Our Liberator, busted in the housing march:

Our Liberator, busted at the induction center:

Our Liberator, busted at the People's Park:

Our Liberator, preaching in the storefront chapel:

Our Liberator, replacing the broken glass:

Our Liberator, busted for preaching with no
              license:

Our Liberator, denounced from Grace Church pulpit:

Our Liberator, leader of brown men and red men:

Our Liberator, harboring white runaway kids:

Our Liberator, bombed as a dangerous radical:

Our Liberator, busted for inciting to riot:

Our Liberator, turned down by the probation
              officer:

Our Liberator, protesting prison meals:

Our Liberator, screwed by the public defender:

Our Liberator, sentenced by a deaf politician:
     Black Jesus, free all your people.

Our Liberator, murdered by law and order: **Black
     Jesus, free all your people.**

Black Mary, mother of the people's liberator:
     Black Mary, free all your people.

Black Mary, sitting on the welfare benches: **Black
     Mary, free all your people.** *And so on.*

Black Mary, evicted for a man in the house:

Black Mary, busted for living in trailers:

Black Mary, Death Row goldstar mother:

Black Mary, best hope of a messed-up planet:
     Black Mary, free all your people.

LONESOME MOMMA BLUES
(Song without tune)

Refrain:
> *"How often I wanted to gather*
> *Your chillen under my wings*
> *Like the sage-hen out on the prairie,"*
> *Your lonesome momma sings.*

1 Oh it's misery for you that's plantin'
    The tombstones of the just,
An' subscribin' to memorials
    For the singers in the dust. *Refrain.*

2 "If we'd lived in the days of our fathers
    We'd be clean from the singers' blood":
So you testify you is members
    Of the lynchin' brotherhood. *Refrain.*

3 An' I sent you preachers an' singers
    For your rope an' gasoline,
An' to whup them behind your churches,
    An' follow them from the scene. *Refrain.*

4 An' I puts their blood on your fingers,
    From the blood of Abel the good,
To the singer you strung from the churchdoor
    In Subsistence Neighborhood. *Refrain.*

5 I tell you, in this generation
    Each injustice is reckoned due;
Oh City that lynches the singers
    An' the preachers I sends to you.
        Refrain.

6 So your houses are left there empty;
    You won't see this chil' again
Till people are callin' him blessed
    When he comes as the Son of men. *Refrain.*
                    [*Matthew* 23:29-39]

III. AT THE CHURCH

One or more of the following three Prophecies is
read, as the situation permits.

FIRST PROPHECY

Minister: My people have done two evils: they
have deserted me, the Fountain of living water,
and built themselves reservoirs, broken reservoirs, which cannot hold water.   [*Jeremiah* 2:13]

Reader:
    Hear the word of the Lord,
        You rulers of Sodom;

    Pay attention to God's instruction,
        You people of Gomorrah.
    "What have I to do with your worship
                services?"
        Says the Lord of history.
    "Why do you gather yourselves together
        To appear before my face?
    Who requested this from you:
        To trample my sanctuaries?
    Conduct no more empty services;
        Your praise is abominable to me.
    Your First Sundays and your festivals,
        My soul has a loathing for them;
    Their burden is unsupportable,
        I am finished with bearing them.
    When you spread out your hands in prayer,
        I turn my eyes away from you;
    When you multiply your prayers,
        There is nobody listening up here.
    Your hands are covered with blood;
        Wash them with soap, make them clean.
    Take away your complicity in crime
        From before the sight of my eyes.
    Bring your evil to an end;
        Learn how to do good.
    Struggle for justice;
        Resist all exploitation."
                              [*Isaiah* 1:10-17]

Minister: Take the music of your songs away from him, for he will not hear the tunes of your organs. Will you let justice roll down as water, and fairness as a stream perpetual? [*Amos* 5:23-24] No, for this people have done two evils: they have deserted the Fountain of living water, and built themselves reservoirs, broken reservoirs, which cannot hold water.

SECOND PROPHECY

Minister: An appalling and terrible thing has happened in this country. The prophets prophesy falsely, and the ministers teach at their instruction, and my people love it so; but what will you do when the end comes? [*Jeremiah* 5:30-31]

Reader:
    For three atrocities of Gaza and for four,
        I will not turn away their punishment;
    For they exiled a whole population
        And turned them over to Edom.
    So I will send a fire against their wall
        And it will devour their strongholds.

```
For three atrocities of Ammon and for four,
    I will not turn away their punishment;
For they ripped up the women with child in
            Gilead
    To extend their frontiers.
So I will send a fire against their wall
    And it will devour their strongholds.

For three atrocities of Moab and for four,
    I will not turn away their punishment;
Because they burned to lime
    The bones of the king of Edom.
So I will send a fire against their wall
    And it will devour their strongholds.

For three atrocities of Israel and for four,
    I will not turn away their punishment;
For they sell the just man for silver
    And the poor man for a pair of shoes.
They trample the head of the oppressed
    Into the dust of the earth.

But I destroyed the Amorite before you,
    Whose height was like the cedars.
And you only have I known
    From all the peoples of earth;
Therefore I will impose reparation
    For all your crimes upon you.
                    [Amos 1:6-15; 2:1-3]
```

Minister: Dig under the rock, hide in the earth, from before the terror of God. For the Power beyond all armies has a day against everything tall and high, against all the cedars of Lebanon, and against every high tower. [*Isaiah* 2:10-15] For an appalling and terrible thing has happened in this country. The prophets prophesy falsely, and the ministers teach at their instruction, and my people love it so; but what will you do when the end comes?

THIRD PROPHECY

Minister: They have put a hasty dressing on the deep wound of my people; they cry out Peace, Peace, where there is no peace.   [*Jeremiah* 6:14]

Reader and People:
Woe to those who say evil is good and good is
    evil. [*Isaiah* 5:20] Woe to those who say
    evil is good and good is evil.

Woe to those who acquit the guilty for a bribe, and deprive the innocent of justice. [*Isaiah* 5:23] **Woe to those who say evil is good and good is evil.** *And so on.*

Woe to those who join house to house, and add field to field. [*Isaiah* 5:8]

Woe to those who pass unjust statutes, to rob the people of their rights. [*Isaiah* 10:1-2]

Woe to everyone that builds his house with injustice; who makes his neighbor work for him, and does not pay him his wages. [*Jeremiah* 22:13]

Woe to those who grind the face of the poor into the dust. [*Isaiah* 3:15]

Woe to one who builds a city with blood, and founds a city on injustice. [*Habakkuk* 2:12]

Woe to those at ease in Zion, who are secure in the suburbs of Samaria. [*Amos* 6:1] **Woe to those who say evil is good and good is evil.**

Woe to those who make a covenant with death, an agreement with destruction. [*Isaiah* 28:15] **Woe to those who say evil is good and good is evil.**

Reader: O Kremlin the rod of my anger; Peking the staff of my fury! Against a godless nation I send them; against the people of my wrath I deploy them. They will loot and plunder; and trample people down in the mud of the streets. But they do not so intend; this was not their plan. For when I have finished all my work on Mount Zion, and destroyed my own people, then I will also punish their pride. For they say, "By the strength of my hand I did it, by the wisdom of my understanding." Shall the axe boast over the one who chops with it? Or the saw be greater than the one who cuts with it?   [*Isaiah* 10:5-15]

Minister: See, God claps his hands together against the dishonest gain they have made, and at the blood shed in their midst. [*Ezekiel* 22:13] They sowed the wind and reap the whirlwind; they plowed evil and reap injustice. [*Hosea* 8:7; 10:13] They have put a hasty dressing on the deep wound of my people; they cry out Peace, peace, where there is no peace.

THE WOES

Here a pot can be smashed, while there is read:
I will smash this people and this city the way one
smashes the jar of a potter, so that it can never
be mended   [*Jeremiah* 19:11]
Reader and People:
Woe to you ministers and professors, hypocrites:
   Woe to you ministers and professors, hypo-
   crites.

Woe to you that preach and do not practice: Woe
   to you ministers and professors, hypocrites.
   And so on.

Woe to you that lay burdens on others, and do not
   lift your finger to them:

Woe to you that love fine suits, and head tables,
   and being called Doctor:

Woe to you that shut off liberation, who do not
   enter yourselves or let others enter:

Woe to you that compute percents, and neglect justice and mercy:

Woe to you who clean the outside of the cup, and
   the inside is full of oppression and
   violence:

Woe to you whitewashed tombs, full of dead men's
   bones inside: Woe to you ministers and
   professors, hypocrites.   [*Matthew* 23:4-27]

PSALM 10:1-12

Why do you stand far away, O Liberator?
   Why are you hidden in time of trouble?
In arrogance the wicked hunt down the poor;
   Let them fall in the schemes of their own
         devising.
The wicked boasts of his heart's desire;
   The rich man curses God.
His ways prosper at all times;
   He thinks, I will never see adversity.
His mouth is full of lies and oppression;
   Under his tongue are wrong and injustice.
From his ambush he murders the innocent;
   He draws the poor into his net.
The poor man is crushed and falls down;
   He thinks in his heart God has forgotten.
Stand up, God; raise up your hand;
   Do not hide your face from the suffering.

Reader: Now when Jesus was setting out on his
way, a man ran up to him, knelt down in front of

him, and asked, "Good Leader, what must I do to
inherit the coming Age?" Jesus said, "Why do you
call me good? No one is good except only God.
You know his demands: 'Do not commit murder, do
not commit adultery, do not steal, do not lie, do
not exploit, honor your father and mother'." And
he said, "Teacher, all these I have observed since
my youth." Then Jesus looked at him, kissed him,
and said: "You lack one thing; go, sell all you
have and give it to the poor, and you will have a
treasure with God. Then follow me." But he was
discouraged at this saying and went away sad, for
he had much property.   [*Mark* 10:17-22]

Minister: He who has an ear to hear, let him hear
what the Spirit says to the Church: Give it all
away. For it is by men of strange lips that he
speaks to this people.

THE REPROACHES

First Reader: O my people, what have I done to
you, or how have I wearied you? Testify against
me.

People: Holy God, Holy Mighty, Holy Immortal,
have mercy upon us.

Second Reader: Because I brought you out of the
land of oppression, and gave you manna forty years
in the desert, and brought you into a land flowing
with milk and honey, you have prepared a cross for
your Liberator.

People: Holy God, Holy Mighty, Holy Immortal,
have mercy upon us.

Third Reader: One American is worth a thousand
gooks; kill them when they're little before they
grow up.

People: Holy God, Holy Mighty, Holy Immortal,
have mercy upon us.

First Reader: O my people, what have I done to
you, or how have I wearied you? Testify against
me.

People: Holy God, Holy Mighty, Holy Immortal,
have mercy upon us.

Second Reader: I whipped Egypt with all her
firstborn for your sake, and you have whipped me.
I brought you out of Egypt through the Red Sea,
and you delivered me to the chief priests. I

opened the sea before you, and you opened my side
with a spear.

People: Holy God, Holy Mighty, Holy Immortal,
have mercy upon us.

Third Reader: Others he saved, himself he cannot
save; we had to destroy the City in order to save
it.

People: Holy God, Holy Mighty, Holy Immortal,
have mercy upon us.

First Reader: O my people, what have I done to
you, or how have I wearied you? Testify against
me.

People: Holy God, Holy Mighty, Holy Immortal,
have mercy upon us.

Second Reader: I went before you in the pillar of
cloud, and you brought me to the pillar of
Pilate's judgment hall. I gave you the water of
life to drink from the rock, and you gave me gall
and vinegar.

People: Holy God, Holy Mighty, Holy Immortal,
have mercy upon us.

Third Reader: I heard the sound of a B-29 engine;
my little brother was putting out his hand to
catch the red dragonfly on the wall, when suddenly there came a flash.

People: Holy God, Holy Mighty, Holy Immortal,
have mercy upon us.

First Reader: O my people, what have I done to
you, or how have I wearied you? Testify against
me.

People: Holy God, Holy Mighty, Holy Immortal,
have mercy upon us.

Second Reader: I struck kings for your sake, and
you struck my head with a reed. I gave you a
royal sceptre, and you set on my head a crown of
thorns. I raised you on high with great power,
and you raised me on the gallows of the Cross.

People: Holy God, Holy Mighty, Holy Immortal,
have mercy upon us.

Third Reader: The fillings from their teeth were
neatly lined up on shelves. Their shoes were in
another room, all the left shoes in one pile and
the right shoes in another pile.

People: Holy God, Holy Mighty, Holy Immortal, have mercy upon us.

First Reader: O my people, what have I done to you, or how have I wearied you? Testify against me.

People: Holy God, Holy Mighty, Holy Immortal, have mercy upon us.

Second Reader: Because I brought you across the great ocean, out of the house of bondage, and set you in this broad and fair land, you have exterminated the inhabitant of the land, and brought others into new bondage.

People: Holy God, Holy Mighty, Holy Immortal, have mercy upon us.

Third Reader: This black kid was laying there in Springfield Avenue with a lot of holes in him; the place was sticky for several days.

People: Holy God, Holy Mighty, Holy Immortal, have mercy upon us.

First Reader: O my people, what have I done to you, or how have I wearied you? Testify against me.

People: Holy God, Holy Mighty, Holy Immortal, have mercy upon us.

Second Reader: Because I brought you into the land of my Great Spirit, a land of many waters and deep forests, you have cut down the forests with your axes, and poisoned the air that my creatures breathe, the water they drink, the soil from which I made you.

People: Holy God, Holy Mighty, Holy Immortal, have mercy upon us.

Third Reader: Can't stand in the way of progress; when you've seen one redwood tree you've seen them all.

People: Holy God, Holy Mighty, Holy Immortal, have mercy upon us.

First Reader: O my people, what have I done to you, or how have I wearied you? Testify against me.

People: Holy God, Holy Mighty, Holy Immortal, have mercy upon us.

Second Reader: Because I liberated you from the

oppressor overseas, and led you safely through a
war of brothers, you have dropped fire from the
sky upon the poorest of peoples, and locked up in
your prisons the young men and women who spoke the
words of my judgement against you.

People: Holy God, Holy Mighty, Holy Immortal,
have mercy upon us.

Third Reader: They was begging and saying, No.
No. And the mothers was hugging their children,
but we kept right on firing. Well, we kept right
on firing. They was waving their arms and
begging.

People: Holy God, Holy Mighty, Holy Immortal,
have mercy upon us.

Reader: The Liberator suffered for the people,
leaving us an example to follow his steps. He did
no crime. No deception was found in his mouth.
When he was insulted he did not insult back. When
he suffered he did not curse. He trusted the one
just Judge. He lifted off our complicity in his
body on the Tree, so that we might die to crime
and live to justice. By his wound we are healed.
We had wandered off like sheep; now we have returned to the shepherd and guardian of our lives.
                                [*1 Peter* 2:21-25]

Minister: Is it nothing to you, all you who pass
by? Look and see if there is any sorrow like my
sorrow.

THE SHEPHERD OF THE FRIENDLESS

Tune: "Passion Chorale," Hassler-Bach 1601 *(The Hymnal 1940* no. 75; 76.76.D.)

1   The Shepherd of the friendless
        By dogs and wolves is torn;
    The King of pity endless
        Is diadem'd with thorn.
    And must our liberation
        Be purchased at such loss:
    To nail the whole creation
        On an imperial cross?

2   See there our Ground of being
        By law and order slain;
    The sun withdraws its seeing,
        The earth is moved in pain.
    Could not your love inherit
        Another end than this:
    Rejected for your merit,
        Arrested by a kiss?

3   Your suff'ring is united
        To victims everywhere,
    By ghetto lords exploited
        Or scarred with fire from air;
    Although in our denying
        Our lives are little worth,
    We pledge a war undying
        Till justice rules on earth.

4   Our Hero still is living
        In all oppressed lands,
    The righteous still forgiving
        Who pierce his feet and hands;
    A redwood arch is growing
        Above his final strife,
    From out his thirst are flowing
        The waters of our life.

2. Burn Out the Mark of the Beast

An Act of Disaffiliation

Suitable for Ash Wednesday, March 16, August 6, and other times of penitence.

I. THE PREPARATION

Spokesman for people: Friends, in the knowledge that demonic forces have infiltrated the institutions of our society, we have gathered here to disaffiliate ourselves from the powers of darkness and to enlist in the army of life.

Minister: Already to the visionary eye, ragweed is growing in the streets of the great city Babylon and poison oak in its plazas; the vulture nests in its towers, the hyena growls from its alleys. At this time therefore we ask for the mountain air of the spirit to blow through our persons and our surroundings, so that we may have strength to say what must be said and do what must be done. Let us hear the words of the Power of history on the great city Babylon.

PROPHECY

Reader: Babylon the great is fallen, is fallen, that great city, because she made all nations drink of the wine of the wrath of her fornication.

And I stood on the sand of the sea, and saw a beast rise up out of the sea, whose feet are like the feet of bears, and whose face is the face of a pig. And all the world wondered at the World Pig, saying, "Who is like this great beast? Who is able to make war against him?" And there was given unto it a mouth speaking great things and blasphemies. And authority was given it over all tribes and peoples and tongues and nations. And all that dwell upon the earth shall worship it, whose names are not written in the book of life of the Lamb slain before the foundation of the world. And it causes all, both small and great, rich and poor, free and slave, to receive a mark in their right hand, or in their forehead, so that no man may buy or sell, or travel to and fro, or walk freely in the streets of the city, unless he has by his hand the mark of the beast and the number of his name.

After this I beheld, and lo, an angel flying in
the midst of the sky, having an everlasting gospel
to preach to all those who live on the earth, saying: "Fear God, and give glory to him, for the
hour of his judgement is come; and worship the one
who made earth and sea and the fountains of waters. And if any man has worshipped the beast and
his image, or received his mark in his forehead or
in his hand, let him repent himself, and take off
from himself the number of the beast, and return
it to the one that gave it."

Babylon the great is fallen, is fallen, and is
become the habitation of demons, and the hold of
every foul spirit, and the cage of every unclean
and hateful bird.

Psalm 94

O Eternal God of vengeance,
    O God of vengeance, send your lightning.
Stand up, you Judge of the earth;
    Pay the exploiters their salary.
How long, O God, will the oppressors,
    How long will they pat their own backs?
They pour out their lying words,
    The criminals praise their own motives.
They smash your people, O God,
    They oppress the folk of your covenant.
Widows and minorities they shoot down;
    They murder the orphan children.
And they say, "History will never notice;
    The God of Jacob is oblivious."
Think it over, you dullest of people;
    When will you fools understand?
Is the Maker of the ear hard of hearing?
    Will the planter of the eye fail to see
                it?
That Power will not abandon his people;
    He never deserts his covenant.
For justice is done to the struggling,
    But a pit is dug for the wicked.
Who stands up for me against the wicked?
    Who takes my side against the violent?
If God had not been my comrade,
    My life would have slept soon in darkness.
Does God favor the rostrum of evil
    Which legislates murder by statute?
They conspire against just men together;
    They pour out the blood of the innocent.
But the Power of history is my fortress,
    My God is a rock of refuge.

He will turn their injustice against them
And wipe them out in their crimes.

Minister: Hear also the words of the Liberator,
what things must happen to us as to him, and what
we must say.

Reader: If a person recognizes me before men, the
Son of Man will recognize him in the presence of
the angels. If a person denies me before men, he
is denied in the presence of the angels. Whoever
speaks a word against the Son of Man is forgiven;
but whoever blasphemes against the holy Spirit is
not forgiven. And when they turn **you** over to mock
trials, or arraign you before judges and magistrates, do not worry how to defend yourself, or be
anxious how you will speak, for the Spirit will
teach you what to say in that hour. [*Luke* 12:8-12]

Minister: O Spirit of that God who ever lives,
you have called us to speak out his will by slogan
and action like the prophets before us; take away
our hostility, and remove all defects of sight and
hearing in those who confront us, so that if possible we may be unharmed and your message may be
received; through the Prophet of Nazareth who
organized the first demonstration in God's Temple.
Amen; so may it be.

II. LITANY

Shall I wear the beast's mark in my forehead? You
     cannot serve two masters.
Shall I cut down the redwood forest? You cannot
     serve two masters. *And so on.*
Shall I take the gun in my hand?
Shall I drop down fire from the sky?
Shall I advertise false products?
Shall I follow the course of the stars?
Shall I wait for another to lead me?
Shall I drug my eyes into blindness?
Shall I stop my ears to the poor man's cry?
Shall I become chaplain to the violent?
Shall I return to the bed of forgetfulness? You
     cannot serve two masters.
Shall I follow the way of the majority? You can-
     not serve two masters.

What way is then left to walk in? Burn out the
     mark of the beast.
Let another begin the action. Burn out the mark
     of the beast. *And so on.*
I have no talent for leadership.
What is the cry of nature?

What is the demand of the Power of History?
My brothers, what do you plan to do?
How shall we get the beast off our back?
What shall we tell our brothers and sisters?   Burn
    out the mark of the beast.

III. THE MAKING AND USE OF ASHES
PROPHECY

Minister:

For three transgressions of Babylon and for
            four,
    I will not turn away the punishment;
Because they brought fire from heaven on
            women with child
    And sowed iron on their villages,
I shall turn the children of Babylon against
            her,
    And burn up her quarters with fire.

Because she cut down the trees of her
            adversary
    And spread poison upon his fields,
I send a spirit of madness upon her
    To cut down her forests with her own hand,
To cast a seed of fire on her cornfields,
    To fill her air with the smoke of her
            burning
        And her waters with the refuse of her
            streets.

Because Babylon has raised a levy of her
            youth
    To enlarge her borders in a distant land,
Behold I raise up her subjects in her
            streets,
    And her young men shall resist her to her
            face.
The lion has roared, who can but fear?
    The Power of History has spoken, who can
            but prophesy?

INTERLUDE

First straight man: We found this man overthrow-
ing our nation, and forbidding us to pay taxes to
Nixon.   [*Luke* 23:2]

Second straight man: We have heard these men
speak disrespectfully of motherhood and God.
                                          [*Acts* 6:11]

First straight man: These men are disturbing our
city; they advocate customs which it is illegal

for us Americans to practice.   [*Acts* 16:20-21]

Second straight man: They are persuading men to
worship God contrary to the law.   [*Acts* 18:13]

First straight man: Come and help us! These are
the men who are teaching against the Law; they
have brought unclean persons into the temple, they
have desecrated a holy place.   [*Acts* 21:28]

Second straight man: These men who turn the world
upside down have come here also; they are all de-
fying the orders of Nixon, saying there is another
President, Jesus.   [*Acts* 17:6-7]

First straight man: The men whom you put in prison are standing in the temple and teaching the
people.   [*Acts* 5:25]

Reader: Then the sergeant with his men went and
brought them, but without brutality, for they were
afraid of being stoned by the people. And when
they had brought them, they set them in the court-
room. And the magistrate interrogated them, saying: "We issued a strict injunction that you
should not teach in the name of Jesus, and here
you have filled the city with this teaching." And
Peter and the Apostles answered:

All: We must obey God rather than men.
                                         [*Acts* 5:26-29]

First straight man: You are all under arrest.
Who is your leader?

All: We have no leader but Jesus our Liberator.

THE DISAFFILIATION

*Then all who wish to disaffiliate from violence
say as follows, either after the Minister or along
with him:*

> If my hand has consented to murder,
>   Let my hand consent no longer.
> If I have shut my eyes to the poor,
>   Today I take up their cause.
> If I exploited my brother,
>   Today I ask his forgiveness.
> If I harmed the living planet,
>   Today I do reparation.
> If I walled myself off with religion,
>   Today I jump over the wall.
> If I invented private ecstasy,
>   I accept communal suffering.

>If ever I bore the mark of the beast,
> I will bear its mark no longer.
>If ever I carried its number,
> I will carry its number no longer.
>So help me God and his holy words,
> In the hearing of these my brothers.

Minister: Brothers and sisters, a narrow door is set before us, which, we are told, not everyone will enter. We know that this universe had its beginning in fire, and we believe that to fire it will return. There are many things we cannot choose; but each of us has a choice whether that fire will be to him the burning love of his brothers, or the cancer of self-reproach. As the whole world is watching, in self-respect we have willed to burn those instruments which once affiliated us with an oppressive system. Today we affirm that some property has no right to exist. We propose this day to light in America such a candle as will never be put out.

Then as each person burns the instruments of affiliation he repeats:

We must obey God rather than men.

EPISTLE

Reader: Hear an Epistle on holy disobedience from our brother Daniel Berrigan.

Our apologies, good friends, for the fracture of good order, the burning of paper instead of children, the angering of the orderlies in the front parlor of the charnel house. We could not, so help us God, do otherwise. For we are sick at heart, our hearts give us no rest for thinking of the Land of Burning Children. And for thinking of that other Child, of whom the poet Luke speaks. The infant was taken up in the arms of an old man, whose tongue grew resonant and vatic at the touch of that beauty. And the old man spoke; this child is set for the fall and rise of many in Israel, a sign that is spoken against.

Small consolation; a child born to make trouble, and to die for it, the first Jew (not the last) to be subject of a "definitive solution." He sets up the cross and dies on it; in the Rose Garden of the executive mansion, on the D.C. Mall, in the courtyard of the Pentagon. We see the sign, we read the direction; you must bear with us, for His

sake. Or if you will not, the consequences are
our own...

[For] we are no more, when the truth is told, than
ignorant beset men, jockeying against all chance,
at the hour of death, for a place at the right
hand of the dying One...

We stretch out our hands to our brothers throughout the world. We who are priests, to our fellow
priests. All of us who act against the law, turn
to the poor of the world, to the Vietnamese, to
the victims, to the soldiers who kill and die; for
no reason at all, because they were so ordered--by
the authorities of that public order which is in
effect a massive institutionalized disorder.

We say killing is disorder; life and gentleness
and community and unselfishness is the only order
we recognize. For the sake of that order, we risk
our liberty, our good name. The time is past when
good men can remain silent, when obedience can
segregate men from public risk, when the poor can
die without defense.

We ask our fellow Christians to consider in their
hearts a question that has tortured us, night and
day, since the war began. How many must die before our voices are heard, how many must be tortured, dislocated, starved, maddened? How long
must the world's resources be raped in the service
of legalized murder? When, at what point, will
you say no to this war?

We have chosen to say, with the gift of our liberty, if necessary of our lives, the violence
stops here, the death stops here, the suppression
of the truth stops here, the war stops here. . . .

Redeem the times! The times are inexpressibly
evil. Christians pay conscious--indeed religious
--tribute to Caesar and Mars; by approval of over-
kill tactics, by brinkmanship, by nuclear liturgies, by racism, by support of genocide. They embrace their society with all their heart, and
abandon the cross. They pay lip service to Christ
and military service to the powers of death.

And yet, and yet, the times are inexhaustibly
good, solaced by the courage and hope of many.
The truth rules, Christ is not forsaken. In a
time of death, some men--the resisters, those who
work hardily for social change, those who preach
and embrace the unpalatable truth--such men

overcome death, their lives are bathed in the
light of the resurrection, the truth has set them
free. In the jaws of death, of contumely, of good
and ill report, they proclaim their love of the
brethren.

We think of such men, in the world, in our nation,
in the churches; and the stone in our breast is
dissolved; we take heart once more.

Here ends the Epistle.

PUTTING ON ASHES

Minister: Brothers and sisters, we know that the
ultimate instrument of police brutality, scandal
to the Jews and folly to the Greeks, has been
transformed by the resistance of the Liberator
into the means of our life and peace. And therefore, O Jesus, in solidarity with your nonviolence, we have cut out the mark of the beast from
our forehead and burned his number to ashes. In
their place, with penitence and hope, we accept
the mark of the cross.

*The the Minister marks the ash from the burned
papers on the foreheads of all who wish it,
saying:*

Render unto Nixon that which is Nixon's and unto
God that which is God's.

Minister: Friends, as the Power of History called
Abraham from his native city and led him a long
journey through the world, we likewise are pilgrims and travelers here, with no permanent city.
When the Son of Man comes, will faith be found on
earth? We then take out naturalization papers in
that land where out true citizenship lies. For
sky and earth witness this day, that there have
been set before us good and evil, blessing and
curse, life and death. Which will you choose?

People: We choose life, that we and our children
may live.

Minister: By that covenant of peace let us enlist
in the army of the Liberator and hear the Apostle's charge to his new recruits.

Reader: Be strong in the Liberator and in his
power. Be dressed in God's complete set of armor,
so that you can stand against the schemes of the
World Beast. For our struggle is not against
flesh and blood, but against demonic authorities,

against the world-rulers of our Dark Age, against
evil spiritual powers in high places. So take up
the panoply of God, in order that you can offer
resistance in the evil day, and stand with your
work complete. Stand with the belt of truth
around your waist, wear the breastplate of justice, and put on the boots of those who announce
the good news of peace. Over all lift up the
shield of confidence, by which you can extinguish
the scorching missiles of evil. And take up the
helmet of liberation and the weapon of the Spirit,
that is, the word of God.   [*Ephesians* 6:10-17]

3. Decontamination: The Advent of the Liberator

*A form of words to accompany some action at a place
which does not expect it. Especially suitable for
Palm Sunday, Advent, Reformation Sunday, and Pentecost.*

I. AT THE STAGING AREA
PSALM 2

Why are the nations in conspiracy?
    Why do presidents make empty plans?
The rulers have consulted together
    Against the Power of history and the
            Liberator:
"Let us break all their constraints;
    Let us throw all their laws from us."
He who sits on the sky laughs them to scorn,
    The Ruler of nature mocks at them,
Then he speaks to them in his anger,
    He routs them with his indignation:
"Today I have set my King
    Upon Zion the hill of my holiness;
I said to him, 'You are my Son,
    Today I have begotten you;
I have made all peoples your inheritance,
    The ends of the earth your possession;
Rule their kings with a rod of steel,
    Smash them like broken china.'"
Now then you rulers understand this,
    Be warned, all judges of the earth;
Serve the Power of history in fear,
    Bow down before him with trembling;
If he is angry, your way is destroyed;
    And his anger is quickly aroused.

Reader: Recognize what time it is: it is the
hour for us to be waked out of sleep. For now our
liberation is closer than when first we trusted.
Night is far advanced, day is breaking. So we
should throw off the works of darkness and get
dressed in the armor of light. Since it is day,
walk properly, not in folly and self-deception,
not in anger and competition; get dressed in Jesus
the Liberator, and pay no attention to the demands
of the present Age.   *[Romans 13:11-14]*

ANNOUNCEMENT

Minister: We interrupt this service to bring you a special announcement. Brothers and sisters, we are told that the ruler and servant of this planet comes at an unspecified time, on his schedule, not ours. Not at a Presidential election but perhaps at a sentencing; not at a military victory but perhaps at a defeat; not announced in the media but perhaps in the ghetto. His budget is not as our budgets; his leadership is with the masses. Our calendars cannot compute his Advent; he has his own time-zones, he is his own air controller.

Friends, be sober, be watchful, be vigilant; re-double your efforts; serve the Lord, serve the people. Any day we may see on our streets the political exile from every land, the universal people's organizer. Daylight saving may be an-nounced at any moment, be prepared to reset your watches. Elections may be cancelled; the *Times* may suspend publication indefinitely; the six o'clock news is in doubt. Sit loose to your calendars: at any time darkness may be turned to day; any week may be all Sundays; any February may get a thirtieth people's day.

And some year the war will be over, won not by bombs but by bicycles, not by metal but by people, not by top-level negotiations but by the smuggled messages of political prisoners. We cannot say that this is the Year of our Liberator Nineteen-Hundred-and-Something. For he is not dead but living; he came long ago and he comes today. His word has gone out to all lands; for the first time in world history it is God's right time for God's folk to triumph over Leviathan; World People car-ries off the victory over World Piggery. The clocks are ticking faster, fallout is falling, the great sea is sick, poison is building up to a critical level; but a new child is about to be born. Be alert, be analytical; it will be told in the streets when the war is over.

Brothers and sisters, when God's acceptable year is at hand, time no longer will be measured by the past, but by the future. The Second Millennium may not wait for the year Two Thousand. Tear up the perpetual calendars. Friends, before the mid-dle-aged in this audience grow old, before the young people are draft-eligible, before new apple trees bear fruit, the World Tree will bear the fruit that all men and women have been reaching

out for. Tear up the calendars. Many difficulties lie ahead but the Second Coming is at hand.
History is sailing into a new Pacific Ocean;
looming up we see the outlines of the Fortunate
Islands. Shortly a prophet of the New Age will
announce YEAR ONE OF PEACE AND LIBERATION!

THE RAINY DAY OF THE CHIL'

Can be sung to St. James Infirmary *and other
tunes.*

That country don't come with watchin',
    It spreads around you plain;
The days are comin' you'll look for
    One day of this chil' in vain.

When they cry, "See it out on the prairie,"
    You better not to roam;
When they whisper "There in the back room,"
    You better keep to home.

As it lightnin's from mountain to prairie
    Will be the day of this chil'
But beforehand you'll see these people
    Harass him for a while.

Like it was in the days of old Noah
    Will be this chil's day;
For they was eatin' and drinkin'
    Marryin' and givin' away,

Till the day he went up the gangplank
    And the rain dropped quietly;
Like it was in the days of Sodom
    The day of this chil' will be.

For they was buyin' and sellin'
    Plantin' corn and raisin' wall,
Till the day Lot come out from Sodom
    And the cin'ers commenced to fall.

In that day a man on the rooftop
    Had best not get his pack,
Or a man in the field run home for
    A shirt to clothe his back.

If you spare your life you lose it,
    And the loser his life will spare;
Two men are plowin' together,
    They take one and leave one there.

Two women at the oven bakin',
    They take one and leave one go.
But wherever the corpse is layin'
    Lights down the carrion crow.

[*Luke* 17:20-37]

INTERLUDE

Reader: And it came to pass, when he drew near to Jericho, a blind man, the son of Timaeus, sat by the road begging. And when he heard the crowd going along the way he asked what this might be, and they answered him, saying:

People: Jesus of Nazareth is passing by!
[*Luke* 18:35-37]

Straight man: Show us a sign! Show us a sign! Show us a sign!

Reader: This is a wicked age; it asks for a sign, and no sign will be given it but the sign of Jonah. The way Jonah was a sign to the men of Nineveh, so will the Son of Man be to this age. The men of Nineveh will go to court with this age and condemn it; for they repented at the teaching of Jonah, and one greater than Jonah is here.
[*Luke* 11:29-32]

Straight man: Blasphemy, blasphemy, blasphemy! Who but God alone can forgive sins?

Reader: Which is easier, to say, "Your sins are forgiven," or to say, "Pick up your bed and walk?"
[*Mark* 2:7-9]

Straight man: Why does he not wash his hands before dinner?

Reader: Why do you wash the outside of the cup, when your inside is full of exploitation and wickedness?   [*Luke* 11:38-39]

Straight man: Why does he eat with street girls and dealers?

Reader: Sick people need a doctor, not well people; he did not come to call righteous but sinners.   [*Mark* 2:16-17]

Straight man: He is stealing grain from the fields; and doing it on Sunday!   [*Mark* 2:24]

Reader: Sunday was made for man, not man for Sunday. A camel can go through a needle's eye quicker than a rich man into the zone of liberation. You cannot serve God and Mammon.
[*Mark* 2:27, 10:25; *Luke* 16:13]

Straight man: If he were a prophet, he would know this woman for a sinner.   [*Luke* 7:39]

Reader: Her sins are forgiven, for she loved

much; he who loves little is forgiven little.
[*Luke* 7:47]

Straight man: Let me first go and bury my father.

Reader: Let the dead bury their own dead.

Straight man: Let me first say goodbye to my family.

Reader: No one who puts his hand to the plow and looks back is fit for the Liberated Zone.
[*Luke* 9:59-62]

Straight man: We saw a man casting out demons in your name, but he does not follow us, so we forbade him.

Reader: He who is not against us is on our side.
[*Mark* 9:38-40]

Straight man: This man casts out demons by Beelzebul Lord of the Mansion, the prince of demons.

Reader:
    Any country is made desolate
        That is divided against itself;
    And any household will fall
        Divided against itself.
    If Satan is set against himself,
        How will his country stand?
    And if it is by Beelzebul
        That I drive out the demons,
    Who do your sons drive them out by?
        So they can be your judges.
    But if I by the finger of God drive them out,
        Then Liberation is upon you.
    When a strong man armed keeps his house,
        His property is in safety.
    But when one stronger comes to his house,
        Binding the strong one hand and foot,
    He takes the panoply that he trusted
        And distributes the spoil.
    When an unclean spirit leaves a man,
        He goes to the desert searching a home;
    And when he finds no home there he says,
        "I go back to my house that I came from."
    And when he comes, he finds it vacant,
        Swept clean and neatly tidied.
    So he gets seven demons worse than himself
        And takes them with him to live there;
    And the last condition of that man
        Becomes worse than his first.
[*Luke* 11:15-26]

Straight man: Are you he that is coming, or do we look for another?

Reader:
    The blind receive their sight,
       Lame men are walking;
    Cancers fall from the skin,
       The deaf get back their hearing;
    Dead men are raised up,
       The poor hear a new preaching;
    And blessed is every one
       Who finds in me no stumbling.
                     [*Luke* 7:20-23]

Minister: We interrupt this service again for another special announcement. We have just received word that the Liberated Zone has been set up at *N*. Free water-fountains, free bread, wine without price. Entry permits now being issued, no formalities, no delay. First preference given to whores and dealers.

II. THE PROCESSION

Reader:
    Dance with joy, daughter of Zion;
       Sing out, daughter of Jerusalem.
    See your King is coming
       With justice and liberation;
    Gentle and riding on a donkey,
       On a colt the foal of a donkey.
    He cuts off the chariot from Babylon
       The cavalry from Sodom.
    The tool of battle is lopped off,
       He demands peace of the nations.
    He governs from sea to sea,
       From the River to the ends of the earth.
    And see O daughter of Zion
       By the blood of his Covenant with you
    He frees your captives from the prisons,
       From the deserts where no water is.
    Return, you hopeful prisoners,
       To your hill-camps beside the stream;
    He restores to you today
       Double for all you endured.
                  [*Zechariah* 9:9-12]

172   Guerrilla Liturgies

We Hope and Trust in Jesus

Tune: "St. Theodulph," Teschner 1615 (*The Hymnal 1940* no. 62; 76.76.D.)

Refrain:
> *We hope and trust in Jesus*
> *Our Liberator King;*
> *To him the flower children*
> *Their gifts and incense bring.*

1 The Brother of humanity,
   He is the Prince of Peace;
 In God's name he is coming
   To make all warfare cease. *Refrain.*

2 He rides along the avenue
   Upon the donkey's back;
 The powers of darkness stumble,
   And Caesar's stick will crack. *Refrain.*

3 The children of the Hebrews
   With palms before him went;
 The hopes of the exploited
   Before him we present. *Refrain.*

4 We burn the monster's number,
   His mark is off our brow;
 The day of liberation
   Is celebrated now. *Refrain.*

5 We melt the guns to plowshares
   We sink the bombs off shore;
 The nations fight no longer
   And study war no more. *Refrain.*

6 But lovers sit together
   Beneath their fig and vine,
 On whom the Sun of justice
   With peace and love will shine. *Refrain.*

7 In all his holy mountain
   They shall not harm again;
 The babies play in safety
   Upon the rattler's den. *Refrain.*

8 Beside the mountain lion
   The sheep may safely graze;
 The paradise of Eden
   Is planted in our days. *Refrain.*

9 The logger's axe no longer
   Shall cut the living tree;
 Our cedar and our redwood
   Stand green above the sea. *Refrain.*

LESSON

Reader: And when they came near Jerusalem, by Bethany at the hill of olivetrees, he commissioned two of his companions: "Go to the village over there. When you enter it you will find a donkey that no man has yet sat on; untie it and bring it. If anybody asks you what you are doing, tell them its owner needs it, and they will let you have it immediately." So they went and found the donkey tied outside the door to a grapevine, and they untied it. And some people standing there asked them what they were doing, untying the donkey. And they answered as Jesus told them, and they let them go. And they brought the donkey to Jesus; they threw their cloaks on it, and he sat on it. And many people took off their cloaks and threw them on the street; and others cut palm branches from the fields and threw them on the street. And the crowd that went in front of him and behind him cried out, saying: [*Mark* 11:1-10]

LITANY

Leader and People:
Who is this riding among us?
    Jesus the Prophet of Nazareth.
Blessed is he who comes in the name of God.
    Hosanna, may his Way be victorious.

Who is this riding the animal of peace?
    Jesus the Prophet of Nazareth.
Blessed be the coming Kingdom of David.
    Hosanna, may his Way be victorious.

Who is the Liberator of Israel?
    Jesus the Prophet of Nazareth.
Blessed be the Liberated Zone he brings.
    Hosanna, may his Way be victorious.

Who is this carrying the palm of peace?
    Jesus the Prophet of Nazareth.
Blessed be our leader the Prince of peace.
    Hosanna, may his Way be victorious.

Who is this that destroys the weapons of war?
    Jesus the Prophet of Nazareth.
Blessed is he who comes in the name of God.
    Hosanna, may his Way be victorious.

Who is this that frees the oppressed from
        prison?
    Jesus the Prophet of Nazareth.
Blessed is he that releases all captives.
    Hosanna, may his Way be victorious.

Who is this that restores the Paradise of
        Eden?
    Jesus the Prophet of Nazareth.
Blessed is the Maker of all the worlds.
    Hosanna, may his Way be victorious. *And
    so on ad lib.*

III. At the Destination
Lesson

Reader (*in* vox clerica): Here beginneth the Lesson. So the supervisors and foremen of the people
went out and said to the people, "Thus says Pharaoh, I will give you no straw. Go out, get yourselves straw wherever you can find it; but your
quota will not be decreased." So the people were
spread out all over Egypt to get stubble for
straw. And the supervisors bore down on them,
saying, "Finish your daily quota as you did when
you had straw." And the foremen of the children
of Israel, who had been appointed by Pharaoh's
supervisors, were beaten and interrogated: "Why
have you not finished your quota of bricks today,
as you did yesterday?" Here endeth the Lesson.
[*Exodus* 5:10-14]

Canticle

If possible, sung to Anglican chant.

Blessed art thou, O Lord, / **our** Property;
    Praised and exalted above / **all** persons · for
                ever.
Blessed art thou for the Name / of our Rights;
    Praised and exalted above / **all** persons · for
                ever.
Blessed art thou in the / temple of · consumption;
    Praised and exalted above / **all** persons · for
                ever.
Blessed art thou that beholdest the land values,
                and dwellest be/tween the brokers;
    Praised and exalted above / **all** persons · for-
                ever.
Blessed art thou in the firmament / of the market;
    Praised and exalted above / **all** persons · for-
                ever.

CONVERSATION IN DARKNESS

Minister: In the beginning the Energy of creation made heaven and earth and all that is in them; and he looked at all he had made, and lo, they were very good. Today he looks in at them from outside space and time, and lo, they are very bad. For a demon of stupidity entered the heart of Adam, that he should increase and multiply and destroy beyond all limits, and pull down the roof of the sky on his own head. Now we are standing on land occupied by demonic powers, whose names are Beelzebul and Mammon. And the sons of man came to consult with the demons that live here, saying:

Reader: Teach us to saw down the cedar and fir, and tread the lilies into the mud; prepare poisons for us to kill the creeping things and whatever feeds on them; show us how to fill the air with waste products of asphalt, the birds that fly in it, the earth and its inhabitants, the waters and all who live in them; and give us your gold and silver, with which to buy the burning ash of death, that we may cast it on the heads of our enemies.

Minister: And the lying demons said to them: "Here are the poisons; go and prosper, only make sure they touch not your own heads." Again a second time the sons of man came and said:

Reader: It is too light a thing, that we have learned how to bend the earth to our will and yours. Teach us also to subdue the inhabitants of the land; help us bring people from all continents to be our hewers of wood and drawers of water, and wall them off in the quarters of our cities; show us how to destroy the woman with child and the young men in all places we wish to go; give us chains to bind all humanity to our desires.

Minister: And the lying demons said: "Here are chains; go and bind them on all people, only be sure they touch not your own legs and arms." Again a third time the sons of men came and said:

Reader: All these things we have done, and more; and now our own sons and daughters stand up against us. Give us therefore confused images to put before their eyes, empty sounds in their ears, and false books in their schools, so that they will not hear the words of the poets of GOD, and turn and overthrow us their parents.

Minister: And the lying demons said: "See, here
are the words of confusion; go and turn them
loose, only be careful to stop up your ears, so
that you are not caught in your falsehoods, and
ours."

But the demons could not deliver what they promised, for they are lying demons, and weak. For
the Word of the Power of history is an antidote to
every poison, a two-edged sword to cut every
chain, a light eclipsing every falsehood. Listen!
At the heart of the place where the demons stand,
a sound of struggle.

Reader: Come out of the man you rotten spirit!

Straight man: What is there between me and thee,
Jesus thou Son of God most high? In the name of
God I adjure thee, torment me not.

Reader: What is your name?

Straight man: American Legion is my name, for we
are many. Send us not out of the country; send us
into the swine that we may enter into them.

Reader: May it be as you have spoken.

Minister: And the rotten spirits came out and
went into the pigs, and the whole herd rushed over
the cliff into the sea, about two thousand of
them, and were drowned in the abyss. [*Mark* 5:7-13]

Psalm 80:8-16

You brought a vine from Egypt;
    You drove out the foreigners and planted
            it;
You cleared the ground for it;
    It struck down root and filled the land.
The mountains were covered with its shadow,
    The cedars of God were under its branches.
It spread its leaves to the Sea,
    And its shoots to the River.
Why then did you break down its wall?
    Each passerby rips off its fruit.
The Pig from the desert grubs it up,
    Each Beast from the wilderness feeds on
            it.
Look down, O God, from the heights
    On the vine which your right hand has
            planted.
They have burned it with fire and smashed it;
    May they fall at the anger of your face!

LITANY

On strike, shut it down, off the World Pig: On
strike, shut it down, off the World Pig.

When Pharaoh raised the brick quota, Moses and his
people said: On strike, shut it down, off
the World Pig. *And so on.*

When Pharaoh offered concessions, Moses and his
people said:

When they ripped up women with child, the prophet
Amos said:

When kings sold the poor for silver, the prophet
Amos said:

When they asked the priests to bless them, the
prophet Amos said:

When Athens shut eyes to murder, Socrates stood up
and said:

When they busted him for corrupting youth, the
youth stood up and said:

When Jesus disrupted the Temple, all his followers
said:

When he broke up sacred monopoly, all his followers said:

When they handed out incense for Caesar, all the
Christians said:

When the Pope put the keys in his pocket, Martin
Luther said:

When they put a gun in his hand, George Fox stood
up and said:

When they told him to stop his preaching, Wesley
stood up and said:

When they slapped on a war surtax, Thoreau sat
down and said:

When the British licensed sea-salt, Mahatma Gandhi
said:

When Hitler said Bow down and worship, Franz
Jaegerstaetter said:

When Hitler said Don't ask questions, Dietrich
Bonhoeffer said:

When the Kremlin bugged the typewriters, Boris
Pasternak said:

When the Kremlin tanks rolled in, Jan Palach sat down and said:

When the helicopters came over, Che stood up and said:

When the orange toadstool pushed up, Abraham Muste said:

When the church said Keep your mouth shut, Norman Morrison said:

When they exempted clergy, the Berrigan brothers said:

When the Dow recruiters came round, the D.C. Nine all said:

When a white man gagged a black man, Dave Dellinger stood up and said:

When they break the farmworkers' heads, we stand up and say:

When they build the detention centers, we stand up and say:

When the Blue Meanies come on the Avenue, we stand up and say:

When they turn off the microphone, we stand up and say:

When the chainsaw hits the redwoods, we stand up and say:

When the captain says Babies also, we stand up and say: On strike, shut it down, off the World Pig.

When murderers speak of gradualism, we stand up and say: On strike, shut it down, off the World Pig.

DECONTAMINATION

Minister: So a fourth and last time the sons of men came to the demons and said:

Reader: You have given us poisons to cast on the earth, and chains to cast on the limbs of men, and lies to cast in the ears of our sons and daughters. But intolerable words still ring in our own ears; give us, we pray, some device by which we may stop our ears against the witness of the prophets of the power of history.

Minister: And the lying demons said: "Take the words given to those prophets by that Energy whom we despise and acknowledge; write the words in a book; build a tower to reach the sky; put the book in the tower, and set a priest of unclean lips to reading it for a people of unclean lips. Then at last you will have rest from the word which you fear."

And the people did as the lying demons commanded them: they wrote the book, and built the tower, and put the book in the tower; and set a priest of unclean lips reading it to a people of unclean lips; and they called the name of that tower CHURCH. And in every age it came to pass as the demons said. Over our heads rises the tombstone of God, we stand in the cemetery administered by the prince of the demons, whose name is RELIGION. But in every age it came to pass also (for the demons are lying demons, and weak) that a fountain of living waters broke through the rock on which the tower stood, and there were found men and wo- men to drink the water, and hear the word spoken there at the command of the demons, and it is for them a fountain of youth.

Worthy is the Lamb which was slain! For the gates of Hell have done their worst against his people and not prevailed; the Lion of Judah is victorious over Sin and Death. In true recollection, over- coming the smog of amnesia, we declare today that the place of confusion, the tower of Babel, is the place of the breath of God. As the cloven tongues of flame descend on us, the demonic powers are dispersed like autumn leaves. Through the libera- tion brought in by Jesus, the victim who refused complicity, the high priest who rejected exploita- tion, we are no longer either victims or accom- plices, but with him priests to the Power of na- ture and servants to humankind. In his name I de- clare this place DECONTAMINATED from the fallout of religion and pride and fear, and RECONSECRATED to hope and life and love. The demons have re- turned to the nothingness from where they came. Earth! Water! Air! Fire! Witness our libera- tion! Brothers and sisters: Plant seeds in earth! Wash bloodstains off stone! Fill air with vibrating tongues of love! Burn instruments of demonic affiliation! Repeat to ends of earth vic- tory slogans:

Here are repeated the Affirmations God is not dead *etc. from p. 123.*

Then the act of liberation (posting theses, washing flags, etc.) is carried out, while there is read:

Reader: And Jesus went into the Sanctuary, and started pushing out all who were buying and selling in the Sanctuary; and he overturned the tables of the money-changers, and the booths of those who sold doves; and he demanded that nobody carry offering plates through the Sanctuary. And he educated them, saying: "Does it not stand written: My house shall be called a house of prayer for all races? But you have made it a cave of murderers." The ministers and the elders heard him, and tried to find a way to destroy him; but they were afraid of him, for the whole people was carried along with his teaching.   [*Mark 11:15-18*]

4. The Sanctuary of Peace

An order to mark out a sanctuary for refugees, either symbolic (Mary and Joseph, war-victims) or real (political resisters). Especially suitable for Christmas and Epiphany.

I. AT THE REFUGEE CENTER

The refugees arrive singing liberation songs:

PSALM 147:1-6

It is a good thing to praise our God;
    A celebration song is proper.
For he builds up Jerusalem,
    He gathers the exploited of Israel;
He heals all broken in heart,
    And bandages their wounds.
He prescribes the number of the stars,
    He calls them all by their names;
Great is our God, great his power;
    There is no limit to his wisdom.
God raises up the oppressed,
    And throws criminals to the ground.

PSALM 126

When God brought back the refugees to Zion,
    We were like those who dream;
Our mouth was filled with laughing,
    And joy was on our tongue.
Then it was said among the nations,
    God has done a great thing among them.
Restore our refugees, O Liberator,
    Like the rivers in the desert.
May all who sow their seed with tears
    Gather up its fruit with joy.
Surely whoever goes out with tears,
    Carrying his seed in his garment,
He will come home with shouts of joy,
    Bringing in his sheaves with him.

The refugees ask for a sanctuary appropriate to their situation.

Reader:
See my servant, I hold him straight;
    I am pleased with the man of my choice.
I have laid the spirit of my breath on him;
    He gives justice to all nations.
He does not shout or raise his voice,
    Or make it heard in public places;

> A bruised grassblade he will not break,
>   Or blow out the feeble flame.
> He announces justice with truth,
>   He does not give up or lose heart;
> Until he builds community on earth.
>   The continents wait for his liberation.
>   [*Isaiah* 42:1-4]

Minister: Brothers and sisters, today these things are fulfilled in your ears. The World Architect has taken justice as his blueprint, and is laying a precious cornerstone--the pearl of great price, whose finder buys it for all he has. The stone rejected by the builders, the rock of stumbling has become the sanctuary of the poor. Into that sanctuary the liberated of God flow in with singing, the desert is covered with the camels of refugees, bringing their precious things. Friends, the sword will not again go through your land; here and in all homes of God's people sanctuary is to be found. In these our last days, God has done his new thing. The Liberator has appeared in every land, under many incognitos, but always himself.

THE SUN AND THE MOON

Buddha is the Moon; Christ is the Sun.

Buddha is the Mother; Christ is the Father.

Buddha is Pity; Christ is Justice.

Buddha retires to the mountain to keep himself spotless and pure; Christ goes forth to the world to fight the battles of faith.

Buddha weeps for the sins of the world; Christ fights to redress the wrong.

We love and admire Buddha, but we worship Christ: worship him not with rosaries and prayerbooks, but with heroic deeds he claims from his worshippers.

God made two great lights; the greater light to rule the day, and the lesser light to rule the night.

We love the Moon and we love the night; but as the night is far spent and the day is at hand, we now love the Sun more than we love the Moon.

And we know that the love of the Moon is included in the love of the Sun, and that he who loves the Sun loves the Moon also.   [*Kanzō Uchimura*]

LESSON

Reader: Now Judas Maccabeus and his men liberated
the temple and the city, for God was going before
them. They dismantled the altars built in the
business district by foreigners, and tore down
their chapels. They reconsecrated the sanctuary
and built another altar of sacrifice. Then they
struck fire from flints, and resumed the sacri-
fices; they burned incense, lighted lamps, and set
out the bread of life. Then they prostrated themselves, and prayed God that they should never
again fall into such complicity; and if they did
do wrong, that he should discipline them gently,
and not hand them over into the power of obscene
and uncivilized races. Now it happened that the
reconsecration of the sanctuary took place on the
same day it had been defiled. They celebrated it
for eight days with great joy, as at the Feast of
Tabernacles, remembering how not long before they
had celebrated the feast living like animals in
the mountains and caves out of their guerrilla en-
campments. They held up the thyrsus, green
branches and palm fronds, and raised loud music in
honor of the one who had guided them to reconse-
crate his sanctuary.   [*2 Maccabees* 10-1:7]

PSALM 72

God, make the king your judge,
　　And set your justice on the son of David;
Let him judge your people with fairness,
　　And your exploited ones in truth.
Let mountains raise up peace for the people
　　And the hills bear justice.
May he liberate the sons of the poor
　　And smash every oppressor.
May his days endure with the sun;
　　May his age be as long as the moon.
May he fall like rain on the grass,
　　Like showers that water the earth.
May justice grow green in his days,
　　And peace rule while the moon remains.
May he rule from the sea to the sea,
　　From the River to the ends of the earth.
May the continents kneel before him
　　And exploiters lick the dust.
May all kings fall down before him,
　　All countries do his service.
For he answers the poor in his crying,
　　He lifts up the needy and helpless;

He is sorry for the weak and poor,
   He liberates the life of the exploited.
He ransoms their life from violence;
   Precious is their blood in his sight.
Long may he live honored with gifts;
   Let the gold of Sheba be brought him.
Let prayer in his name be constant,
   His blessings be pronounced daily.
May the land be covered with grain;
   May it wave on the tops of the hills.
Blessed is his working forever;
   May his name endure with the sun.
May all men bless themselves in him;
   All nations acknowledge his splendor.

II. THE PROCESSION

Minister: Let us go forth in peace. As the tabernacle of peace moves through the desert of violence, may the Spirit of God accompany it in a pillar of cloud by day, a pillar of fire by night. Take stakes and cords, build a moving sanctuary; even so the splendor of Being was seen by Ezekiel, rolling above his people wherever they went. Build the peace temple.

LITANY

All refugees and resisters from all countries:
   Build the peace temple.

Refugees from Biafra, starved by the affluent:
   Build the peace temple. *And so on.*

Refugees from Palestine in your relocation camps:

Refugees of Viet Nam in your strategic hamlets:

Refugees from the American wilderness in your
   reservations:

Refugees from Africa in urban ghettos:

All chemists who have gone out from the poison
   factories:

All who have gone out from the global police
   forces:

All who have deserted the underground command
   posts:

All who have given up counterinsurgency:

All who have left off shuffling papers:

All who have resigned from strip-mining crews:

All who throw nails in the blades of chainsaws:

All who shut down the chimneys of death:

Prophets and poets fired by the Churches:
Scholars and wise men fired by the Colleges:
Honest reporters fired by the papers:
Honest biologists fired by industry:
Reformers and fighters fired by government:
Children who plant flowers and play with kittens:
Children who plant rice and play with beercans:
Woman who plant gardens and bear male children:

People united against repression:
Lovers and craftsmen, farmers and builders:
Organizers for peace and justice:
Political prisoners beside us in spirit:
Planters of parks, sowers of seeds:

Induction refusers, martyrs to Caesar:
Mahatma Gandhi, world conscience:
Abraham Muste, walking beside us:
Martin Luther King, walking beside us:
Francis our friend, walking beside us:
Isaiah and Micah, prophets of the new Age:
Simeon and Anna, who found the Liberator:
Mary the mother who bore the Liberator: **Build the peace temple.**
Jesus our brother who became the Liberator: **Build the peace temple.**

III. AT THE CHURCH

Minister:
Lift up your heads, you gates.

People:
**Open up, you everlasting doors,
For the King of splendor to come in.**

Minister:
Who is this King of splendor?

People:
**Our God strong and mighty,
The Power beyond all armies.**

Minister:
    Lift up your heads, you gates.

People:
    Open up, you everlasting doors,
        For the King of splendor to come in.

Minister:
    Who is this King of splendor?

People:
    The Power beyond all armies,
        He is the King of splendor.

[Psalm 24:7-10]

PSALM 46

Or the metrical version on p. 116.

God is our fortress and guard,
    In oppression our sure supporter.
We will not be afraid of earthquake,
    Though the mountain slides into the sea,
Though the great wave rolls white,
    Though hills are cracked by its crying.
A Power above armies is with us,
    Our castle the Helper of Jacob.

A stream makes happy his city,
    The sacred home of the Highest;
He stays in her, she cannot stumble;
    He defends her in the first dawning.
When nations fall into violence
    By his mouth their dominions are melted.
A Power above armies is with us,
    Our castle the Helper of Jacob.

Come and see his astounding acts:
    He stops war to the ends of the world;
The bow is smashed, the steel blunted;
    The armored cars melt in his flames.
Be still and see, he is your God,
    Controlling all peoples and countries.
A Power beyond armies is with us,
    Our castle the Helper of Jacob.

INTERLUDE

Straight man: Since we like to think of this our sanctuary as a House of Prayer for *all* people, besides welcoming our courageous defenders to this service, we are happy also to greet your little delegation. It gives me great pleasure to introduce our three Directors of Refugee Work.

*Dollar-Sign Star lights up over the altar as Three
Kings enter singing* We three Kings of affluence
are, *etc.*

First King: We have seen the Dollar of his Star
in the east and are come to worship him; all nations come to this light, they bring gold to the
brightness of his rising. And what we bring to
the baby Jesus we bring to all mankind: mold-cast
Infant Jesus of Pragues, convertible six percent
debentures, crocheted kneelers, wall-to-wall car-
peting, quickfrozen crepes suzette, taperecorded
lifesize Barbie dolls, prepaid moon vacations,
plasticized diocesan administrators. Give us (in
the words of Lady Liberty) your tired, your poor.
Under the plexiglass firmament of America, has
anyone yet asked for bread and been given a stone?
They need only command their stones to be made
bread.

Minister: Man shall not live by bread alone, but
by every word proceeding out of the mouth of God.

Second King: We have heard the threat of Herod
the atheist and are come to protect the newly
born, in the name of the Lord of Hosts. And the
shield of defense, the sweet frankincense of security we hold over the baby Jesus we hold over
all mankind: a nuclear umbrella, tariff quotas,
black capitalism, law and order, work-welfare programs, anti-riot legislation, counterinsurgency,
aid to underdeveloped countries, chaplains,
search-and-hold missions, rehabilitation programs,
and computerized baptismal social security regis-
tration. Has the Lord of Hosts ever yet failed to
help and defend those who trust in him? Only give
up your ethnic peculiarities, put your whole confidence in us your well-wishers; throw yourself
down from the pinnacle of this temple into our
melting pot. He will give his angels charge of
you, to keep you in all your ways; they will bear
you in their hands, lest at any time you dash your
foot against a stone.

Minister: Thou shalt not tempt the Lord thy God.

Third King: We have seen the obscureness of his
birth, and are come to offer him publicity. And
the permanence of message, the embalming as by
myrrh, that we offer to the baby Jesus we offer to
the world: multi-media exposure, missionary outreach, prime time, *Life* and *Time*, a plug-in to our
ecumenical ghetto and refugee strategy program.

To the poor and oppressed we say: all the king-
doms of the world can be shown your plight in a
moment of time, for they have been given to Media,
and Media gives them to whom it will; all these it
will give you, if you fall down and worship Media.

Minister: Thou shalt worship the Lord thy God,
and him only shalt thou serve.

BENEDICTUS II

Reader: See, this child is set for the falling
and rising of many in Israel, and for a sign that
will be spoken against.   [*Luke* 2:34]

> And you, child, are called a prophet of the
>   Highest;
>   You precede the Great One to prepare his
>   ways,
> To give knowledge of liberation to his people
>   Through the cancelling of their
>   complicity;
> By the gentle pity of our God,
>   In which the Dawn from on high will spread
>   over us,
> Shining to all that sit in the shadow of
>   death,
>   To direct our feet into the way of peace.
>   [*Luke* 1:76-79]

THE CONSECRATION

Minister: God has made a covenant of peace with
us; it shall be a covenant of all ages; he will
bless us and set his sanctuary in the middle of us
forever. For only see: the tabernacle of God is
with men; he will live with them, and they will be
his people. He will wipe away every tear from
their eyes, and death shall be no more, nor will
there be mourning and pain again, for old things
have passed away.
                [*Ezekiel* 37:26-27; *Revelation* 21:3-4]

*Then the bearers of stakes and cords form them-
selves into a square, and install the refugees
in their midst.*

Let the circuit here marked out enclose an area
forever free from oppression and violence. Let no
weapon be brought into it; nor any uniform be worn
in it, except the linen of those who have made it
white in the blood of the Lamb. Let every person
who takes refuge in this sanctuary, whether sinner
or saint, be welcomed for the sake of the Liberator whom he bears. And for that purpose, let

this community dedicate itself to preserve our
sanctuary inviolate; let their bodies become the
sanctuary of God's spirit, a home of nonviolence
and peace.

THE KISS OF PEACE

Minister and People:

Peace on earth to men of God's pleasing: **Peace on
earth to men of his pleasing.**

Shalom, the peace of God be with all men: **Peace
on earth to men of his pleasing.** *And so on.*

Peace in the hatreds of the Holy Land, *Salaam,* the
peace of God:

Peace in India, land of Mahatma, *Shantih,* the
peace of God:

Peace to Russia, our sister, *Mir,* the peace of
God:

Peace to oppressed Prague, *Miru,* the peace of God:

Peace for the poor of Latin America, *la Paz,* the
peace of God:

Peace in Viet Nam, land of Buddha, *Hoa Binh,* the
peace of God:

Peace to the whole creation, *Eirene,* the peace of
God: **Peace on earth to men of his pleasing.**

Peace in all lands to all men, the peace of God:
Peace on earth to men of his pleasing.

There is no peace without freedom: **There is no
peace without freedom.**

We shall overcome: **We shall overcome.**

Venceremos: **Venceremos.**

Jesus has overcome: **Jesus has overcome.**

Shalom, my brothers and sisters, the peace of our
Liberator be with you all, Shalom.

*Here if there is still opportunity the familiar
nativity story from Luke can be read, while (for
example) the figures in the creche are replaced
with Vietnamese figures. Or there can be read the
following*

HOMILY

Now when the cry of the trumpet sounds, it assem-
bles soldiers and announces war. Shall then the
Liberator, who has sung a melody of peace to the

ends of the earth, not assemble his own soldiers
of peace? For he has drawn together, O Humanity,
by his blood and word, an army that sheds no
blood, and entrusted to them the zone of his liberation. He has sounded the trumpet of his message, and we have heard it. So let us arm ourselves for peace, putting on the breastplate of
justice, taking up the shield of trustfulness,
placing on our head the helmet of liberation; and
let us sharpen the sword of the Spirit, which is
the word of God. So peaceably does the Apostle
array us for battle: these are our invulnerable
arms, in their panoply we may stand in the lines
to resist the Evil One.

[*Clement of Alexandria*]

5. Earth Rebirth

A form for consecrating a park

*Suitable also at Easter,
Rogation time, Thanksgiving.*

I. AT THE STAGING AREA
SLOGANS

Repeated by the Crowd after the leader.

Plant the world park.
Let the earth live.
Give grass a chance.
Liberate the park of your choice.
Support your local garden.
Dig up all asphalt.
Break all carburetors.
Pulverize plastic.
Smash insecticides.
Destroy vinyl flowers.
Stamp out astroturf.
Pass out the pill.
Make chainsaws illegal.
Chop down telephone poles.
Eliminate defoliants.
Exterminate fallout.
Neutralize napalm.
Segregate all arsenals.
Zap sonic boom.
Chain self to redwoods.
Bust poison factories.
Butterflies are people.
Protect pelicans' rights.
Support all carnivores.
Trees are gods.
Fair play for deer.
Squirrels have feelings.
Decent housing for hermit crabs.
Safeguard hummingbird culture.
Power to the plankton.
Reparations for robins.
Equal protection for shellfish.
Green is beautiful.

Recycle all garbage.
Live invisible.
Make love not war.
Weave the great web.

Replace wheels by feet.
Smash consumer culture.
Shut down machines.
On strike shut it down.
Planet on strike.
Planet on strike.
Planet on strike.
Plant the world park.

Leader:

I saw the earth, and it was waste and void;
  And the sky, and it had no light.
I saw the mountains, and they shook back and
            forth;
  And all the hills were quaking.
I saw, and behold, there was no man;
  And every bird of the air had gone.
I saw, and behold, the garden was a desert;
  And all its cities were ruined.
                          [*Jeremiah* 4:23-26]

Hail and fire mixed with blood fell on the
            earth;
  And a third of the earth and the trees
            were burned,
    And all the green grass was burned.
A burning mountain of fire was thrown into
            the sea;
  And a third of the sea was turned into
            blood,
    And a third of the sea creatures died.
And a great star named Wormwood fell on the
            rivers and springs;
  And a third of the waters became bitter,
    And many men died from drinking them.
And a third part of the sun was dimmed,
  A third part of the moon and stars,
    And a third of the day lost its
            shining.   [*Revelation* 8:7-12]

THE LAW OF LIFE

Leader:

Hear the great law of life from the prophet
            William Blake.
  A robin redbreast in a cage
    Puts all Heaven in a rage.
  A dog starved at his master's gate
    Predicts the ruin of the State.
  Each outcry of the hunted hare
    A fibre from the brain does tear.
  A skylark wounded in the wing,
    A cherubim does cease to sing.

He who shall hurt the little wren
   Shall never be beloved by men.
He who the ox to wrath has moved
   Shall never be by woman loved.
Kill not the moth nor butterfly,
   For the Last Judgement draweth nigh.
He who mocks the infant's faith
   Shall be mocked in age and death.
He who shall teach the child to doubt
   The rotting grave shall ne'er get out.
The beggar's rags, fluttering in air,
   Does to rags the heavens tear.
The poor man's farthing is worth more
   Than all the gold on Afric's shore.
One mite wrung from the labourer's hands
   Shall buy and sell the miser's lands.
The soldier, armed with sword and gun,
   Palsied strikes the summer sun.
The strongest poison ever known
   Came from Caesar's laurel crown.
Nought can deform the human race
   Like to the armor's iron brace.
The whore and gambler, by the State
   Licensed, build that nation's fate.
The harlot's cry from street to street
   Shall weave old England's winding-
      sheet.

TRIAL

Straight man: Hear ye, hear ye, the district
court of the Great Chain of Being is now in ses-
sion, the Honorable the Great Spirit presiding.
All stand please. The defendants at the bar have
heard the appropriate sections from the statute
book of life. How do they plead?

The Crowd repeats line by line after the leader:

Your Honor, we enter a plea of Guilty
In the court of the Great Spirit
To first-degree murder of redwoods,
To grand larceny of grasslands,
To statutory rape of minor woodlands,
To unnatural acts of urban living,
To wilful arson of forests,
To unwarranted seizure of ricecrops,
To mutilation of the human form divine,
To misappropriation of natural resources,
To wilful violation of the Pure Food and
      Drug Act,
To genocide against herbivores,
To drunken driving across continents,

To improper combustion of fossil fuels,
To lewd and lascivious waterproofing of the
            earth,
To unlawful possession of insecticides,
To writing blank checks on the future,
To unauthorized handling of fissionable
            materials,
To illegal dumping of detergents,
To illegal manufacture of garbage,
To trespassing on private property of
            animals,
To trespassing on the private property of
            the Great Spirit,
To rape and murder of the air,
To rape and murder of the water,
To rape and murder of the earth,
To rape and murder of flora,
To rape and murder of fauna,
To rape and murder of black men,
To rape and murder of red men,
To rape and murder of yellow men,
To repeated public acts of self-abuse;
We enter a plea of Guilty
To constant adult delinquency;
We accept the penalty prescribed
By the inflexible laws of nature,
And we ask the Power of Being
To change our mind for the future.

Leader: Air, blow the smog of false desires out
of our lungs and replace it with the west wind of
the Spirit. Amen.

Ocean and all waters, wash the synthetics out of
our blood and replace them with our own true chemistry. Amen.

Earth of decay and rebirth, break down the chlori-
nated hydro-carbons in our flesh and let us live
together with all other flesh. Amen.

Fire of the sun, blunt the needles of radiation in
all our biosphere and replace them with the desire
of life. Amen.

Brothers and sisters, let us take up the loads of
our common task. As we shake off from our feet
the dust of the City of Destruction, let us turn
our eyes to the New Jerusalem, and consecrate that
Temple whose pillars have come alive as the forest
cathedral. Let us be on our way, off the road, to
the City whose street is a river of living waters,
where the tree of life is blooming, and its leaves
are for the healing of the nations.

CANTICLE

How shall we sing the Lord's song in a strange
        land?
How shall we sing the Lord's song in a world of
        hunger?
How shall we sing the Lord's song in a house of
        hatred?
How shall we sing the Lord's song with a gun in
        our hands?
How shall we sing the Lord's song on burned-over
        hills?
How shall we sing the Lord's song in a land of
        synthetics?
How shall we sing the Lord's song in a strange
        land?

Leader: All the days of the earth, seedtime and
harvest, cold and heat, summer and winter, day and
night shall not cease.

II. LITANY IN PROCESSION

*At streetcorners, when held up by cops, etc., it
would be good to rehearse the original Slogans
again.*

Restore our earth household: **Restore our
      earth household.**

All powers of being, restore our earth house-
      hold: **Restore our earth
      household.**
Sea of Air, blowing out the smog of our
      self-poisoning:

Snow and rain, washing down the poisons of
      our combustion:

Salts of the sea, decomposing the life-
      killing chemicals:

Fire and light, breaking down the products
      of our industry:

Crabgrass and dandelion, cracking the water-
      proofed surface:

Worms and woodlice, reconverting all foreign
      materials:

Rust and decay, restoring all metals to
      earthloam:

Plankton of the deep, feeding the great
      whales:

Streams and rivers, purifying the land's
          body:

Termites and rot, levelling old settlements:

Squirrels and all rodents, distributing
          acorns:

Deer and buffalo in cooperation with grass-
          lands:

Bear and hawk and all carnivores, completing
          the cycle:

Insurgent Red Men, restoring the land to its
          Spirit:

Insurgent Black Men, putting a new song in
          our mouth:

Insurgent Brown Men, taking over the vine-
          yards:

Insurgent Yellow Men, resisting patented
          poisons:

Children who take to the streets with picket
          signs:

Hippies who fly kites at helicopters:

Biologists who sit down in front of
          bulldozers:

Women who stop being breeding-machines:

Students that plant flowers in the face of
          teargas:

Mothers pushing strollers past the line of
          gasmasks:

Spirit of James Rector, martyr in Berkeley,
          marching beside us:

Spirit of John Muir, keeper of the garden,
          marching beside us:

Spirit of Johnny Appleseed, planter of Eden,
          marching beside us:

Yin and Yang, male and female principles of
          creation:

Buddha the compassionate, surviving the cycle
          of dying:

Adam and Eve, first parents in the paradise
          of Eden:

Angels and guardian spirits, watching over
    this planet:

Seeds of life in the sun, in the space be-
    tween stars:

Our galactic mother, enfolding the planet in
    her spiral arms:

Billion-year heartbeat of the cosmic
    expansion:

Nameless Energy upholding the space-time
    manifold:

Eternal principle of nonviolence, letting
    each do its own thing:

Jesus our loving brother, nonviolence in our
    own flesh:

All the world's rejects, bums and hoboes,
    winos and freaks:

Hippies and street people, blacks and
    Chicanos, women and children:

Victims of genocide, Biafrans and Vietnamese,
    named and nameless:

Refugees in the blackened ruins of the
    doomed city: **Restore our earth
household.**

All who build a new world on the vacant
    lots of the old: **Restore our
earth household.**

III. AT THE PARK

Leader:
The wilderness and arid land shall be glad,
  The desert is smiling and blossoming.
It flowers all over with the crocus;
  It rejoices with happiness and song.
The crown of Lebanon will grow in it,
  The trees of Carmel and Sharon.
Springs are bursting through in the
               wilderness,
  And rivers in the desert.
The burning sand becomes lakes,
  And the thirsty ground pools of water.
                     [*Isaiah* 35:1-2, 6-7]

INTERLUDE

First straight man: Young people, I am very happy
to address you future consumers on the occasion of

this ecological conference. The teaching of the
Judeo-Christian tradition has been that we should
not let nature go on in her old wasteful way, but
by our own skills improve on her. And what has
been the greatest source of improvement in world
history but the inventive genius and capital of
our own nation? As a simple businessman, who in a
small way has shared in guiding this country's
destiny, I should like to make one addition to
your slogans: What's good for the military-indus-
trial complex is good for you.

Second straight man: I am sure you agree with me,
that the great enemy does not only live in some
overseas capital; it is also right here, in the
heart of each unproductive individual who has been
tricked by an international conspiracy. Never
forget that such meetings as this are only possible by the nuclear shield over our skies forged
by our own native talents. Technology is neither
good nor bad in itself; its dangers can be controlled by better technology. And only that technology stands between us and the creeping cancer
from abroad. I am a refugee from that system, I
know whereof I speak. Your own leader has said,
"Be watchful, for you know not what hour of the
night the thief is coming." Only by constant
testing can we trust our defenses; physical discomfort is a small price to pay for that guarantee
of our freedom. I also should like to give you a
slogan: Thank God for fallout.

Third straight man: You have heard the parable of
the foolish virgins who had no oil for their
lamps, and so missed the coming of the bridegroom.
Shall this happen to us? The New Age is on our
threshhold; shall we turn it away in our folly?
The earth was made for man: as Paul says, "Does
God care for oxen? Is he concerned for seagulls?"
Our great commuter cities rely on oil; the oil-
depletion allowance permits our most public-
spirited citizens to go on serving us; by oil the
Liberator is recognized. I would like to add one
more slogan: Oil brings in the Kingdom.

Fourth straight man: In view of the reception you
have given the other speakers on this platform, I
have no recourse but to inform you that you are
trespassing on private property. By order of the
governor of this State, in five minutes you will
all be arrested. This vacant lot has been sur-
rounded. If anybody resists arrest, a chemical

agent will be sprayed on this area by helicopter.
Please obey the orders of the officers with blue
armbands. While you are lining up, let me remind
you that your chief executive must look to the interest of all citizens, not just small pressure
groups. When the sentiments of a few birdwatchers
conflict with the expressed will of an expanding
population, which should give way? On your scenic
bus trip to the county rehabilitation center, remember this: When you've seen one redwood you've
seen them all.

All four straight men together:
    What's good for the military-industrial
       complex is good for you.
    Thank God for fallout.
    Oil brings in the Kingdom.
    When you've seen one redwood you've seen
       them all.

Leader: You fools, when you see a cloud rising in
the West, you say, The rain is coming; and so it
happens. When you see the south wind blowing, you
say, it will come on hot; and so it happens.
Fools and hypocrites: you that can discern the
signs of earth and heaven, can you not discern the
signs of the times?   [*Luke* 12:54-56]

*He then arrests the four straight men, and the
Crowd makes a circuit of the park, repeating the
Slogans.*

THE COVENANT

Leader: Brothers and sisters, hear the words of
the Covenant of Peace which the Power of Being has
made with all life on this planet, in the words of
the poet and prophet Ezekiel:

Assistant: I will seal with them a covenant of
peace, and I will remove all violent life from
their land; they will live safely in the great
wilderness and sleep in the forests. And I shall
make all places round about my mountain a blessing. I shall bring down the rain in its season;
there will be showers of blessing. All the wild
trees will bear fruit; the land will give its increase, and all people will be secure in their own
land. They will know that I am the Master of history when I break the bars of their yoke, and liberate them from all their exploiters. No longer
will they be a prey to foreign nations, nor will
violent life destroy them; they will live se-
curely, and nobody will terrify them.
      [*Ezekiel* 34:25-28]

Leader: I call sky and earth to witness, that the Power of Being has set before us this day good and evil, blessing and curse, life and death. Which will you choose?

Crowd: We choose life, that we and our children may live.

ANTIPHON

You that turn justice to wormwood,
    Seek for the Power of Being and live,
He who made the Pleiades and Orion
    And pours waters out on the earth.

[Amos 5:6-8]

PSALM 65:9-13

You visit the earth and water it,
    You make it blessed in abundance;
Your river is full of water,
    And thus you ensure their grain.
You water its furrows deeply,
    You soften it and bless its growth.
You crown the year with your goodness,
    Your wagon tracks flow with oil.
The upland pastures are moist,
    The hills dress themselves with happiness;
The meadows are clothed with sheep,
    The valleys are wearing corn,
        Together they laugh and sing.

CONSECRATION

Here are buried in the earth old Christmas trees, cartons, eggshells, coffeegrounds, comic books, sunday supplements, etc. Genuine organic matter is shredded for a mulch pile while the leader says:

We proclaim liberty to the land and its inhabitants. As we all travail together in the covenant of peace, on this ground consecrated to the life of the earth, we remove all wastes, blotting out the years that the locust has eaten. We bury all organic life, all that can be decomposed; we remove and recycle all metal, everything useful; we break up and dispose whatever is neither organic nor useful.

    From earth you were taken, .
        And to earth you will return;
    Her life comes to dying,
        And in her the dead is reborn.

The seed we sow is not quickened
    Unless first it passes through death.
In this ground all shall be well
    And all manner of thing shall be well.

Then new living things are planted during the following Homily.

We see the cycle only in part, and we prophesy in part; we are children picking up pebbles on the shore while the great waves roll unnoticed. But what we do see we testify: when we stand on our own earth, we lose our fear of alienation, of our neighbor, of death, of doing wrong, of ourselves. As our City is decontaminated, the plagues of civilization recede: the thistles find their proper niche, the slum rat becomes a healthy field rodent, synthetic bread gives way to bread, chemical ecstasy is replaced by ecstasy of play. The landslide makes way for new forest; from the cracks of the earthquake the sycamore sprouts; in the fresh lava the fireweed is blooming; the rise and fall of the seas, the melting and freezing of icecaps are seen as recirculation of the planet's blood. We move naturally to death as a shock of wheat, old and full of days, when we know that our grandchildren will continue our work on the land we were loaned, eating apples and olives from the trees we planted. We hail as our brother Smokey the Bear, "Wrathful but Calm, Austere but Comic," set in the skies and untouched by any bath in Ocean, "bearing in his right paw the Shovel that digs to the truth beneath appearances, cuts the roots of useless attachments, and flings damp sand on the fires of greed and war"; disappearing in winter and rising in spring to eat earth's sweetest product, the honey of life perpetual. In his name we declare this land freed in eternity from all usurpation, and henceforth CONSECRATED TO THE WORLD PARK, the exclusive property of children, animals, trees, blackberries, and the Great Spirit.

O Risen Bear, type of the Liberator, our Brother who eats the honeycomb; take in your paw the hands of all foresters, gardeners, biologists, and farmers; accept them as your assistants to tend the paradise of this emerald planet, in the splendor of the Great Spirit. Amen; so may it be.

Blessing

May the long time sun shine upon you,
    All love surround you,
        And the pure light within you guide
            you all the way on.

The Song of Francis

All-High, All-Strong, good Master
Yours is all praise, all splendor,
Each honor and each blessing.
You alone, All-High, deserve them,
No man can hope to name you.

Be praised by all your creatures;
And first by Sun our Brother
In whom you make our daytime.
He is fair with great brightness;
You, O Highest, are his meaning.

Be praised by Moon our Sister,
By Stars you made as jewels.
Be praised by Wind our Brother,
By Cloud and every Weather,
Through which you feed your creatures.

Be praised by Sister Water,
Chaste, precious, and most useful.
Be praised by Brother Fire,
In whom our night is brightened,
Handsome and strong and jocund.

Be praised by Earth our Mother,
Who upholds and maintains us,
Bears fruits with colored flowers.
Be praised by all who pardon,
And suffer in harassment.

Blessed are all who witness,
In peace their lives conducting,
For you, Most High, will crown them.
Be praised by Death our Sister,
None living will escape her.

Woe to all that die in violence;
But blessed, all in your pleasing,
No second death will touch them.
Praise the Maker, all his creatures,
And build the world he shows you.

Index of Biblical Lections

Many of the new translations or paraphrases in The Covenant of Peace *are suitable for use as lessons or canticles outside the contexts of the services in which they occur. The following index is a guide to the longer or more important of these texts. Page numbers are printed in italics.*

Genesis
2:4-9, *77*
2:18-25, *89-90*
4:8-12, *72*
9:12-16, *69*
11:1-8, *77*

Exodus
5:10-14, *174*
14:21-29, *70*

Numbers
6:24-26, *66*

Job
26:10-13, *71*
38:4-11, *69*

Psalms
2, *166*
10, *151*
16, *114*
22, *144-145*
23, *65*
24, *185-186*
27, *117*
40, *108*
46, *116*
59, *142*
65, *200*
72, *183-184*
80, *176*
90, *111*
94, *158*
98, *82-83*
111, *54-55*
126, *181*
128, *90*
139, *61*
142, *104-105*
146, *108*

147, *181*

Ecclesiastes
1:2-9, *112*

Song of Solomon
2:10-12, *94*
4:18-25, *86*

Isaiah
1:10-17, *147-148*
10:5-15, *150*
11:1-9, *122*
14:4-21, *144*
25:6-8, *124*
35:1-7, *197*
42:1-4, *181-182*
42:6-7, *108*
51:9-11, *70*
52:13 to 53:12, *141-142*
58:6-7, *52*
61:1-4, *78*
61:8-9, *57*

Jeremiah
4:23-26, *192*
31:31-34, *52*

Ezekiel
33:2-9, *95*
34:25-28, *199*
37:1-10, *78*

Hosea
2:18-20, *63*

Joel
2:28-29, *81*

Amos
1:6 to 3:2, *149*
5:6-8, *200*

Jonah
2:2-6, *71*

Micah
4:3-4, *122*

Zechariah
9:9-12, *171*

2 Maccabees
10:1-7, *183*

Matthew
5:3-12, *127-128*
5:23-24, *125*
8:11, *124*
23:4-27, *151*
23:29-39, *147*

Mark
1:1-11, *72*
5:7-13, *176*
10:13-17, *62*
10:17-22, *152*
11:1-10, *173*
11:15-18, *180*
12:29-31, *88*

Luke
1:46-55, *66*
1:67-75, *57*
1:76-79, *188*
2:29-32, *112-113*
4:16-21, *106*
6:27-36, *53*
7:20-23, *171*
7:36-38, *76*
11:15-26, *170*
11:29-32, *169*
12:8-12, *159*
12:22-34, *117-118*
12:54-56, *199*
13:34-35, *143*
17:20-37, *168*
18:9-14, *55*
19:41-44, *143*
22:25-30, *96*
24:13-35, *83-84*

John
2:1-11, *90-91*

Acts
2:1-11, *79-80*
2:41-47, *57*
5:25-29, *161*
12:6-11, *103-104*

Romans
6:3-11, *82*
8:14-17, *64*
13:11-14, *166*

1 Corinthians
2:6-13, *79*
5:7-8, *85*
10:16-17, *127*
15:20-21, *85*

2 Corinthians
3:18 to 5:5, *110*
5:11 to 6:2, *113*
11:23-31, *104*

Galatians
3:27-28, *91*

Ephesians
6:10-17, *164-165*

Philippians
2:5-11, *95-96*

Colossians
3:3-4, *85*

2 Timothy
4:6-8, *115*

Hebrews
13:20-21, *119*

James
3:18 to 4:4, *130*

1 Peter
2:21-25, *155*

Revelation
8:7-12, *192*

AFRICAN AMERICAN VOICES
REFLECTING, REFORMING, REFRAMING

Pamela V. Hammond, PhD, RN, FAAN, ANEF
Editor

National League
for **Nursing**

National League for Nursing
61 Broadway
New York, NY 10006
212-363-5555 or 800-669-1656
www.nln.org

ISBN 978-1-934758-08-3

Cover Design by Brian Vigorita
Art Director, Mara Jerman

Printed in the United States of America

African American Voices

Reflecting, Reforming, Reframing

Table of Contents

List of Tables VII

List of Figures IX

Foreword   *Janice G. Brewington, PhD, RN, FAAN* XI

Preface   *Pamela V. Hammond, PhD, RN, FAAN, ANEF* XV

Acknowledgments XIX

Chapter 1   Core Values, Visibility and Leadership in Nursing Education:
An African American Nurse Leader's Perspective 21
Beverly Malone PhD, RN, FAAN

Chapter 2   Personality and Depression: Affects on Academic Achievement
in College Students..31
Bertha L. Davis, PhD, RN, FAAN, ANEF
Spencer R. Baker, PhD, CCFC

Chapter 3   Enhancing Student Understanding of Challenges Faced by African
Americans Related to Cancer Prevention and Control 47
Sandra Millon Underwood, PhD, RN, CHN, FAAN

Chapter 4   Challenges in Integrating HIV/AIDS, Mental Health
and Substance Abuse: Implications for Educators 69
Delroy M. Louden. PhD, FRSH

Chapter 5   Mentorship and Nurse Educators: A Model for Diversity 91
Willar F. White-Parson, PhD, APRN, BC, FAAN

Chapter 6   Using Simulation to Enhance Cultural Competency 109
Richardean Benjamin, PhD, RN, MPH, PMHCNS-BC, ANEF

Chapter 7   Closing the Gap on Racial/Ethnic Diversity in Nursing Education 127
Mary H. Hill, DSN, RN

Chapter 8   Nursing Care or Care of Nursing? Doctoral Education and the
Shortage of African American Nursing Faculty 139
Maurice C. Taylor, PhD, JD
Earlene B. Merrill, EdD, RN, CNE

Chapter 9   Health Disparities Research: The Issue for HBCU PhD Nursing Programs...................... 167
Pamela V. Hammond, PhD, RN, FAAN, ANEF
Janet Simmons Rami, PhD, RN

Appendix A   Author Profiles 189

Appendix B   PhD Dissertations: Hampton University School of Nursing, 2002-2009........................ 197

Appendix C   PhD Dissertations: Southern University and A&M College School of
Nursing, 2004-2009 201

LIST OF TABLES

LIST OF TABLES

Table 2-1   Hierarchical Regression Bivariate Correlations with Means and
              Standard Deviations 40

Table 3-1   Age-Adjusted SEER Cancer Incidence Rates per 100,000 by
              Race/Ethnicity, United States, 2000-2004 50-51

Table 3-2   Age-Adjusted SEER Cancer Mobility Rates per 100,000 by
              Race/Ethnicity, United States, 2000-2004 52-53

Table 3-3   Leading Sites of New Cancer Cases and Cancer Deaths Among
              African Americans, 2007 Estimates 55

Table 4-1   Comparison of Persons Screening Positive for HIV by Condition 73

Table 8-1   Projected Population of the United States, by Race and Hispanic
              Origin: 2000 to 2050 145

Table 8-2   Taxonomy of Doctoral Programs in Nursing 149

Table 8-3   A Model PhD Curriculum 159

Table 8-4   Degrees Conferred by Historically Black Colleges and
              Universities (HBCUs) by Degree: 2001–02 161

Table 9-1   Type of Degree by Race/Ethnicity of Students Enrolled, Excluding
              Non-U.S. Residents and Unknown Ethnicities, Fall 2007 172

Table 9-2   Type of Degree by Race/Ethnicity of Graduates, Excluding Non-U.S.
              Residents and Unknown Ethnicities, August 1, 2006 to July 31, 2007 173

LIST OF FIGURES

Figure 2-1   Noncognitive Indicators and Academic Success. 37

Figure 4-1   Prevalence of Mental Health Disorders in Individuals
                 with HIV and in the General Population 75

Figure 4-2   Holistic Approach to Integration of Services for Clients with Co-Occurring
                 Disorders of Substance Abuse, Mental Health, and HIV/AIDS 83

Figure 5-1   Mentorship Connection Project Conceptual Model. 100

Figure 9-1   The Hampton Model 179

Leaders in nursing education, administration and practice who will share their wisdom have written *African American Voices: Reflecting, Reforming, Reframing.* Nursing education is influenced by a myriad of factors in the external environment, including global competitiveness; the complexity of the health care delivery system; advancement in medical technology, diagnoses and treatment; diverse populations entering nursing programs; the nursing shortage; health disparities, and the "graying of faculty." Because of the impact of these issues on nursing education, it becomes increasingly important for schools of nursing to transform their programs to recruit, retain and prepare graduates to meet the needs of this diverse global society, now, and in the future.

This is a provocative and interesting book that addresses some of the aforementioned issues facing the nursing profession, such as the nursing shortage and its impact on the delivery of health care for underrepresented populations; integration of innovative simulations to teach cultural competence; the shortage of nurse educators, especially African Americans, and the value of mentoring; and the role of PhD in nursing programs in HBCUs in meeting the faculty shortage.

The preface describes the foundation and the relevance of this book, which sets the tone for the reader. We are honored to have, as an author, Dr. Beverly Malone, a leader, administrator, nurse educator, practitioner, and the chief executive officer of the National League for Nursing (NLN). Leadership is not always ascribed to positions of authority. In chapter 1, Dr. Malone explores the premise that leadership transcends positions and formal titles of leader and that nurse educators are self-authorized to lead. Thus, they are considered as leaders in their domain as faculty. NLN's, strategic plan, including its mission and core values, are used as a framework for understanding and validating the role of nurse educators as leaders.

She raises the issue of transforming nurse educators from invisible leaders to visible leaders with authority; and she articulates strategy for removing the invisible shield. Dr. Malone describes a personal account of the mentoring she received from two renowned nurse educators. These nurse educators were clear about leadership and the value of mentoring the next generation of nurse educators. This chapter serves as the framework for the articles in this book.

Chapter 2 discusses the importance of exploring "cutting edge" research and the impact of noncognitive variables such as personality differences and depression on academic success for college students, especially African Americans. It includes findings from a study conducted at a historically black institution.

Findings from this type of research have relevance for nurse educators in early identification of students with these problems in order to design and implement prescriptive plans for early intervention. This effort has the potential to improve academic outcomes, which could lead to increase in retention and graduation from nursing programs. Thus, a critical outcome would be an increase the number of African American nurses in the workforce. The article raises an important question for colleges and universities: Should colleges and universities include assessment of these noncognitive variables for freshmen students?

Chapters 3 and 4 include a discussion of two prevalent health disparities, cancer and HIV/AIDS, that plague African Americans - both at different points in time can be considered "silent killers" in the African American community. This is primarily because of the stigma of these types of diseases for African Americans, thus creating a lack of awareness of prevention, early diagnosis and treatment.

In chapter 3, the author challenges nurse educators to incorporate topics of the incidence, morbidity, mortality, survival, prevention, control and treatment for the aforementioned health disparities in the curriculum as well as other areas that affect African Americans.

In chapter 4, the author triangulates HIV/AIDS, mental health and substance abuse as a way to understand their comorbidities and adverse interrelationship. Barriers to integrated treatment and quality care such as stigma, funding and professional norms as well as solutions are discussed. An interdisciplinary approach, using an integrated health care system, is presented as a model to effectively address these diseases. The author recommends that nurse educators work collaboratively with interdisciplinary teams to provide students with clinical experiences in integrated health care delivery systems.

Given the shortage of African American nurse educators, chapter 5 identifies the need for formal professional mentorship programs as a strategy to recruit and retain them in schools of nursing. The author describes the Mentorship Connection Project implemented in an urban and rural university. The project was designed to enhance faculty retention in the departments of nursing. The author indicates that there were differences in the level of effectiveness at the two universities, which poses a challenge for further exploration of variables accounting for the differences.

Chapter 6 discusses the changing demographic trends and the increase of ethnic and racial minorities and their need for health care. As a result of these changes, more practitioners will need to develop cultural competency skills. The author appeals to nurse educators to integrate innovation in technological advances through the use multifaceted simulations, including virtual reality, to teach cultural competency. With the lack of available clinical facilities, simulations are effective alternatives for providing nontraditional, creative clinical experiences for students to apply critical thinking skills for mastery of cultural competence. The author further challenges nurse educators to evaluate the effectiveness of these innovative teaching-learning strategies in improving cultural competency outcomes.

In chapter 7, the author focuses attention on diversity in nursing education and the necessity to close the gap. As diversity becomes the watchword for a myriad of concerns, racial/ethnic diversity has a particular set of tenets. The author exposes areas of concern to help nurse educators enroll, retain, and graduate a diverse student population. She writes about the areas of discovery in nursing education and how they mirror the evidence-based outcomes that have been known to "close the gap" for racial/ethnic educational concerns. Diversity implies competency and interventions that would make a difference in the development of skills sets that are needed to care for a global population.

Chapter 8 focuses on the relationship of doctoral education and the nursing shortage. The authors explore many factors related to the nursing shortage and the shortage of nurse educators and practitioners. A taxonomy of doctoral education is described, which differentiates between practice-focused doctorates in nursing and PhDs in nursing. The American Association of Colleges of Nursing (AACN) proposes a reduction in the types of doctorates in nursing.

The authors discuss the evolution of the purposes and practice of nursing education and propose a PhD in nursing curriculum model with a teaching component. This model incorporates four educational outcomes, which consist of the formation of nursing scholars, stewardship of the nursing discipline, the preparation of future nursing faculty, and critical topics of the nursing discipline. Finally, the authors strongly recommend the establishment and funding of more PhD in nursing programs in HBCUs.

In chapter 9, the authors answer the following questions. Why is it important to increase the number of PhD programs in HBCUs? Why is there an underrepresentation of minorities enrolled in and graduating from PhD programs? What role do minority doctorally prepared nurse educators and researchers have on addressing the myriad of health disparities for minorities? These are questions that have always been important for the nursing profession; however, they have become increasingly important with changes in the demographics of ethnic and racial minorities in the United States.

The authors describe health disparities for minorities and the gap between health outcomes for these populations and the white population. A profile of the types of degrees by race/ethnicity is presented. The authors postulate that if the number of doctorally prepared nurses increases, then there will be an increase in the availability of minority nurses to meet the health care needs of minority populations.

The authors present successful models of two pioneer PhD in nursing programs at Hampton University and Southern University. These programs were established to address the underrepresentation of minorities with PhDs. The authors further describe the role of these programs in preparing researchers to address health disparities issues in this global economy and nurse educators to close the gap for faculty in schools of nursing. Finally, both programs have developed collaborative partnerships with other institutions to create fellowships, postdoctorates, faculty exchanges and research opportunities.

In closing, this book is timely and offers some solutions for transforming nursing education and its ability to prepare a cadre of minority nurse educators and researchers to meet the complex needs of ethnic and racial populations.

Janice G. Brewington, PhD, RN, FAAN
Chief Program Officer
National League for Nursing

This book builds on the one published by the NLN in 1995, edited by Ruth Johnson and entitled, *African American Voices: African American Health Educators Speak Out*. That book explored a variety of maladies that disproportionately affect members of the African American community, provided a wealth of information about the morbidity and mortality of selected illnesses in African American communities, and explored some solutions to decrease the health disparities found in African American communities. This book, *African American Voices: Reflecting, Reforming, Reframing* expands the earlier work by focusing on how nurse educators can use insights about the African American community in their teaching. Models are depicted, case studies suggested, and research elucidated, all of which give voice to the needs of the African American community and what nurses need to understand to meet those needs. The previous text's emphasis on health care issues facing African American communities has given way in this book to a focus on teaching/learning strategies used with African American students, mentoring a diverse faculty body, and program planning to increase research in health disparities related to African Americans.

It is critical that nurse educators are culturally competent and sensitive to diverse populations. They must also direct their teaching toward helping students become similarly competent. It is the nurse educator who will strongly influence the attitudes and behaviors of the next generation of nurses and ensure that students are prepared as culturally competent and culturally sensitive health care providers who serve patients who do not look like them, or speak like them, or believe in the same ideas that they do. One way to help students is to have a familiarity with information such as that included in this book and in similar texts written by a diverse author pool, since such knowledge is critical to the development of cultural competency in students who will be expected to impact the care of high-risk and underserved populations regardless of their racial and ethnic mix.

We continue to be faced with nursing shortages across the nation and a concomitant shortage in nursing faculty; therefore, it is critical that nurse educators have the tools they need to teach in the most efficient and effective manner. *African American Voices: Reflecting, Reforming, Reframing* has been written to be one of those tools. Throughout this book, nurse educators will find exciting strategies that can be used to promote excellence and build tomorrow's diverse nursing workforce. Further, this book serves to provide a platform for discussions surrounding health care issues in the African American community: health issues that are too often ignored or described within a broad context leading one to think that one size fits all is appropriate for all African Americans. This book covers a variety of topics affecting various aspects of health care in the African American community and is designed to help nurse educators think about how they portray health care issues of the African American community. In addition, *African American Voices: Reflecting, Reforming, Reframing* provides the tools needed by the academic community to adequately prepare the next generation of educators regarding a variety of topics.

Malone takes us on a journey delineating her ascension to a variety of positions and praises posthumously two African American nurses who mentored her along the way. As the CEO of the National League for Nursing, she paves the way for the other chapters in this book by discussing the critical need to support nurse educators. Further, Malone shares affirmative lessons from her journey as a leader who has embraced the challenges and opportunities that all nurse educators face as they continue to make a visible, healing difference in the world.

Educators will find evidence-based information regarding a new frontier of research about the impact of noncognitive indicators, specifically personality and depression, on college-aged students, which can be used in determining academic achievement. Davis and Baker take the reader on a fascinating exploration of the complex, interactive nature of the biological systems underlying personality and its effects on academic achievement. They identify one group of specific personality tests used to uncover the structure and features of one's personality, or one's characteristic way of thinking, feeling, and behaving. The Five Factor Model is presented in a way that educators can use it to complement any study of personality and depression. Their study reflects a step in the discovery of the outcomes relating to African American college students.

Millon Underwood describes novel teaching-learning strategies to address cancer control and prevention concepts in nursing curriculums though the use of interactive databases and the development and use of case studies reflecting the stories of cancer survivors. She goes on to build on a foundation laid by nurse researchers and clinicians, saying that faculty should intensify efforts to integrate content and experiences specific to cancer among African Americans in nursing curricula. She presents "A Portrait of the African American Population" and focuses educators' attention on leading diagnoses regarding new cancer cases and deaths. This content is useful in curricula, generally, and for African Americans, in particular, as the challenge is met to enhance students' understanding of African Americans and cancer prevention and control.

Holistic approaches to the integration of services for clients with co-occurring disorders of HIV/AIDS, mental health, and substance abuse, through which curriculums may be developed for an interdisciplinary student population, is described by Louden in a way that an educator can extract and use in a culturally sensitive manner. He states that institutions with schools of nursing would benefit from collaborative linkages as academic partners by providing nurse educators access to diverse service providers. Louden also elucidates this health disparity: that the rate at which African Americans contract AIDS has risen faster in comparison with Caucasians or other ethnic groups.

White-Parson depicts a program of mentorship that she has used in several professional settings. Her hands-on approach to using a mentoring program has undergirded her success as a nurse administrator. Key concepts for designing and implementing a mentoring program for junior faculty to assist in developing their skills as educators and also create environments to increase their retention are described in detail. According to White-Parson, the benefits of the mentoring program to both seasoned and novice nurse educators, in her experience, includes an increased sensitivity to diversity.

Innovative approaches to teaching cultural diversity through simulation that mirrors real-life situations for students who are accustomed to playing video games and who understand the concept of virtual reality is illustrated by Benjamin. She has piloted and implemented several programs using simulations and has culled techniques that are specifically useful when teaching African American students. The changing demographics in the nation call for nurse educators who will be responsible for meeting the needs of a diverse population. In addition, the changing technology to which students and faculty are exposed will impact the coming generations of African Americans and other minority groups.

The health professions must approach the problem of increasing the diversity of the health care workforce by utilizing solutions from health, economics, and security, according to Hill. She cites a trend of underrepresentation of racial and ethnic minorities and says, "we owe it to ourselves to get it right." Hill also calls for action to address the problem of attracting minority students by facilitating their entry into health professions, and using strategies that, once enrolled, will insist students complete their education. Hill goes on to discuss situational analysis as part of the strategic management process. The use of situational analysis can uncover an institution's commitment to diversity. She concludes with a description of a mentorship program and the use of performance indicators to provide evidence of closing the gap on racial/ethnic diversity in nursing education and in the workforce.

The last two chapters of the book will be of great interest to individuals interested in starting a doctoral nursing program or attending one. Taylor and Merrill presents a realistic view of the evolution of nursing doctoral programs and how those programs contribute to the development of nursing faculty and the reduction in the nation's chronic nursing shortage. They go on to put forth a model doctoral program that they claim has the essential elements needed for educating African American doctoral students. While the proposed PhD program may appear controversial to some, others will find it quite an interesting attempt to insure that African American nurses and all doctoral students who take this course of study will graduate with preparation to study the health disparities issues found in African American communities.

In the last chapter, Hammond and Rami describe the evolution of the first and second PhD nursing programs to be established at historically black universities. These authors help readers look at pioneering methodology used in creating a research agenda aimed at eliminating health disparities in two relatively new doctoral programs. Of great importance is the fact that these two programs evolved in institutions where teaching was and remains the focus of a majority of faculty members. Anyone teaching or investigating health disparities will find the research being conducted on the subject in the selected doctoral programs of particular interest. Further, readers will note that the two chapters on doctoral programs may also be of interest to those faculty members contemplating returning to school.

I am confident that this book provides something for all nurse educators and for those who want to be nurse educators. The book conveys some very frank discussions of issues that affect all communities. Therefore, it will make an excellent addition to any class where nurse educators are being prepared. There are strategies within each chapter that can be used regardless of the nurse educator's specialty or role area. Surely, simulations, mentoring, and academic success cross all specialty lines. Further, nurse educators from any type of nursing program will find teaching-learning strategies that can be adapted to their classrooms. Curriculum issues regarding personality and depression, cancer prevention, HIV/AIDS, mental health, and substance abuse are critical to licensed practical nurse, diploma, associate degree, and baccalaureate and higher degree nursing programs. Many nurse educators will not be interested in starting a doctoral program, but surely one can glean from the strategies provided techniques to use in the design and implementation of any major project where faculty and community support are essential.

All the authors in this book are African American, and all have cared for populations of clients or taught students who looked like them and many who did not. Each of these authors has had personal experiences that, while not explicitly conveyed in their chapters, are very influential in their writing and in the selection of topics, topics that reflect their individual quest to care for students and the clients whom they will serve. While not all the authors are nurses, they are all experts in their field and have created a text that gives voice to the issues of our African American communities…a voice that has been silent long enough. This book contains a voice that is needed to insure that educators, especially nurse educators, teach in a manner that is sensitive to African American students…to insure that the nursing workforce is diversified…to insure that the controversial issues surrounding health issues in African American communities are heard and dealt with…to insure that health care equality is not just political rhetoric. The issues in *African American Voices: Reflecting, Reforming, Reframing* are screaming to be heard!

Pamela V. Hammond, PhD, RN, FAAN, ANEF
Provost
Hampton University

ACKNOWLEDGMENTS

The creation of *African American Voices: Reflecting, Reforming, Reframing* is a reflection of the National League for Nursing's leadership in nursing education and its dedication to diversifying the nursing workforce. This book is a tribute to the League's support of nurse educators, both experienced and novice.

I thank the authors who contributed their time, talents, and energies to create the collection of works that led to *African American Voices*. Their opinions, suggestions, conversations, and debates have helped document a legacy of which they can be proud. I further acknowledge their optimism for the future of nursing and nursing education.

I thank Ms. Ina Whitehead of Hampton University, who did the initial edits of selected chapters in this book. Much appreciation also goes to Dr. Terry Valiga and Ms. Justine Fitzgerald, whose expert editing, suggestions, and time were invaluable. Dr. Valiga and Ms. Fitzgerald's expertise are responsible for this book becoming a reality.

Special thanks to my colleagues and administrators at Hampton University, who provided the encouragement and the environment necessary for me to complete this book. To all of my students, past, current, and those I have yet to meet, thank you for choosing to be a nursing professional and for daring to care for the health of our global society.

Finally, I want to thank my family, especially my husband, Gary J. Hammond, and friends for the support and love they provided throughout this endeavor.

Pamela V. Hammond, PhD, RN, FAAN, ANEF, Editor
African American Voices: Reflecting, Reforming, Reframing
Summer 2009

This book

is dedicated to

the loving memory

of the late

Mrs. Nancy Lula Wilson Jones:

my teacher, my mentor,

my Mama.

CHAPTER 1

CORE VALUES, VISIBILITY AND LEADERSHIP IN NURSING EDUCATION: AN AFRICAN AMERICAN NURSE LEADER'S PERSPECTIVE

Beverly Malone, PhD, RN, FAAN

INTRODUCTION

In February 2007, I began my tenure as the Chief Executive Officer for the National League for Nursing (NLN), the nation's premier nursing education association, numbering 30,000 members representing all types of nursing programs. After almost six years in Europe as the General Secretary for the Royal College of Nursing (RCN) now returning home to the United States, I was honored to be in a leadership role with the oldest national nursing organization in the country. The NLN was a character-shaping force in my journey as an undergraduate nursing student at the University of Cincinnati. I was constantly assessed and appraised by the powerful National League for Nursing in the form of standardized testing and participating in accreditation activities, including an in-depth self-study. My nursing program was accredited by this impressive and all-knowing organization located in New York City, a place that in my mind then involved a set of grandiose projections and fantasies that paralleled in greatness those related to my nursing education. The idea of actually helping lead this treasured organization awed this one-time undergraduate nursing student from Elizabethtown, Kentucky.

Of all that makes up the League's powerful legacy, perhaps its crowning glory is its dedication to the nurse educator. I'm not sure whether modern nursing society has ever viewed the nurse educator as a leader. I know that there are extraordinary deans, chairs, directors and other executive nurses in education who are acknowledged as leaders, but I propose that nurse educators teaching in all the various nursing programs are leaders. I believe, as the NLN has so widely proclaimed, that nurse educators are advanced practitioners of teaching and, as part of the advanced practice nursing movement, should be rightfully considered leaders (National League for Nursing, 2005). This chapter will describe the NLN as an organization that supports nurse educators and the need to increase the visibility of educators as leaders. I will also highlight two African American nurse educators who mentored me on my leadership journey. The underrepresentation of African Americans in nursing underscores the need for mentors like the two I mention in this chapter. Nurse educators who understand the need for mentors will provide their students, especially those who are underrepresented, with a tool that will serve them well on their leadership journey.

In assessing the characteristics of the nurse educator, it may be useful to consider the NLN's strategic plan, a blueprint for promoting the role and leadership of nurse educators. The first major step that the League initiated shortly after my arrival was the reframing of its strategic plan. The new and improved mission simply stated: *"The National League for Nursing promotes excellence in nursing education to build a strong and diverse nursing workforce"* (National League for Nursing, 2007b). This mission statement captured the challenges of today (shortage and diversity) while building on the strength of its past and the promise of its future with a commitment to excellence. As powerful as the mission statement is, the underpinning core values touch the soul of nurse educators, nursing education, and even more importantly that of the nursing profession and the purpose of delivering safe, quality care to all people locally, nationally and globally. With these core values, let us examine the underlying fundamental values on which nurse educators stand.

CORE VALUES

The following core values are used to guide the implementation of the NLN's mission. They can also be used to guide the professional journey of the nurse educator by becoming an integral part of the nurse educator and permeating the work environment (National League for Nursing, 2007c).

Caring: promoting health, healing and hope in response to the human condition. A culture of caring, as a fundamental part of the nursing profession, characterizes our concern and demands consideration for the whole person, a commitment to the common good and our outreach to those who are vulnerable. Professional, educational and organizational activities are managed in a participative and person-centered way, demonstrating an ability to understand the needs of others, to be aware of our own personal culture and biases, and, within that framework, to respond from our humanity to the humanity of others. Caring is the container that holds safety and quality teaching for the student, community and fellow staff.

Integrity: respecting the dignity and moral wholeness of every person without conditions or limitation. A culture of integrity is evident when organizational principles of open communication and ethical decision making are expected and demonstrated consistently. Not only is doing the right thing simply how we do business, but our actions reveal our commitment to truth telling and to seeing ourselves from the perspective of others in a large community. Integrity indicates what in the organization or in one's professional life is non-negotiable. The line must be clearly drawn whenever a behavior or situation is no longer acceptable. The ethical dilemma always consists of questions of integrity. It seems wise to be prepared to identify one's boundaries whenever integrity is called into question.

Diversity: affirming the uniqueness of and differences among persons, ideas, values and ethnicities. A culture of diversity embraces acceptance and respect. Diversity involves understanding ourselves and each other and moving beyond simple tolerance to embracing and celebrating the richness of each individual. While diversity can be about individual differences, it also encompasses institutional and systemwide behavior patterns (Dreachslin, 1999; Anderson, Scrimshaw & Fullilove, 2003). For example, the more we become aware of international nursing educational systems with culturally different nurse educators and students, the better we can understand differences in nursing education and practice. Diversity is not only about color, gender or religion, it can include the differences of perspective. For example, take the old argument that entry into nursing practice must be at the baccalaureate level. In the United States, 51 percent of new graduates are prepared at the associate degree level. Less than 17 percent of associate degree nurses return to school for the next degree. The figure makes one sigh with concern and perhaps turn to the baccalaureate programs for reassurance. However, only 21 percent of bachelor of science degree nurses follow up their initial preparation with a second degree (HRSA, 2007). Perhaps a way of embracing diversity is not choosing sides: the baccalaureate versus the associate, but pushing and promoting the academic progression of both types of graduates. The NLN embraces the diversity of all types of nursing programs and simultaneously keeps its emphasis on academic progression. The League believes that we must transform the dialogue from entry into practice to progression within the profession (National League for Nursing, 2007b).

Excellence: creating and implementing transformative strategies with daring ingenuity. Excellence builds a culture where transformation is embraced and the status quo and mediocrity are not tolerated. But exactly what is transformation? One is usually more familiar with the concept of change than with transformation. One may use the following scenario to distinguish between the two concepts. If I give you a dollar and you give me back four quarters, you have given me change. If I give you a dollar and you give me back five dollars, transformation has occurred. Excellence requires transformative strategies, but with daring ingenuity. This daring ingenuity can be described as falling off the cliff without prior knowledge of the existence of a safety net. Nurse educators need to find new paradigms to teach in environments where students are more technologically savvy than even the faculty are. They must teach in environments where human and fiscal resources are becoming scarcer. Examples of some strategies that could be transformative in most teaching environments include teaching psychopathology by assigning case studies of present and past US presidents, finding new ways to use simulations in your clinical teaching, or using only one hospital, one unit for clinical teaching for a student's experience.

The remarkable nature of excellence is that it's dynamic, in constant motion and most of the time, ahead of its pursuer. There are times, moments of exhilaration, where the pursuer is able to momentarily grasp excellence. Usually, this is confirmed by recognition from the other; that is, an award, acknowledgment, press release or promotion to a new job. But true excellence moves as quickly as it is encountered and for this reason requires continuous quality improvement, a continuous stretching for the next level, the next goal.

An exemplar of excellence is the certified nurse educator (CNE) credential conferred by the NLN. In 2008, only two years after the credential was created to recognize excellence in the advanced specialty role of the academic nurse educator, the NLN conducted an analysis to determine its acceptance and value. The results, reported in the March-April 2008 issue of *Nursing Education Perspectives*, revealed that nurse educators in all 50 states and the District of Columbia who teach in all types of nursing education programs, from diploma through doctoral, have taken and passed the CNE examination. As of March 2009, 1552 nurse educators nationwide have added CNE to their CVs, reflecting a diverse group of qualified, full-time academics across the spectrum of nursing programs, academic rank, educational preparation and years of experience in the classroom (National League for Nursing, 2008).

In addition to this acknowledgment of excellence, the NLN initiated an Academy of Nursing Education that recognizes stellar individuals in the nursing education community. In 2008, 24 new members will join the original 41 inductees bringing the total to 65 nurse educators with the ANEF credential. Programs that reward excellence are critical indicators of the continuous passion for quality improvement that exists within the nursing education community.

The four core values of caring, integrity, diversity and excellence provide a platform for nursing education, and are essential factors in the individual professional nurse's career trajectory of health, healing and caring. Even with these values intact, acknowledged and internally integrated, nursing and nurses still face challenges in the 21st century.

THE CHALLENGE OF VISIBILITY

Nursing has always existed within the health sciences arena; but we have been invisible like the cement that holds walls together. To some degree, invisibility was a joint agreement between nurses and other health care providers. Nurses did not "toot their own horns." There is an old saying that he or she who tooteth not his own horn will not be tooteth. Even in terms of hospital budgets, one could only identify staff cost, not the cost and benefit of the actual delivery of nursing services (which is the primary business of hospitals). At one point, nurses were merely considered a part of basic support services, like housekeeping. This invisibility has had a direct effect on morale. As advocates for patients and system managers for quality and safety, nursing and nurses cannot afford to be invisible.

As nurses have stepped up to fully authorize themselves as essential health care providers, invisibility has decreased to low visibility. Academic progression has been a key ingredient in the self-authorizing of nurses: in the United States, we have a well-prepared nurse faculty workforce with approximately 42,000 full-time and part-time nurse faculty, about one third having doctoral degrees and another third prepared at the master's level. As nurses claim and celebrate the full extent of their role (clinician, consultant, leader, educator and researcher), our ability to assume our position and realize its significance in health care is validated and maximized. The most familiar component of this role is clinician, but consultant covers the interpersonal transaction between the nurse and patient, family and/or community. In this transaction, the nurse is clear that he or she is offering recommendations that can be explored, questioned, accepted or refused and not directives that speak to a power differential between the provider and the patient. The nurse is the leader of the healing environment, clearly responsible for the delivery of safe, quality care to the patient and a safe working environment for the staff. The educator component addresses the disease prevention and health promotion aspect of providing care and information while educating the care recipients to assume the leadership in self-management of one's own health. Finally, the research aspect is most frequently denied by nurses and yet it simply speaks to the need for creativity, consistency and validation of what nurses know and do. Research is an integral part of all nursing and the establishment and funding of the National Institute for Nursing Research within the National Institutes of Health is one of the most visible acknowledgments of the science of nursing.

With issues of safety and quality growing in significance internationally and nationally, the need for research that has clinical implications is dire. Nursing is the profession that can build and provide the bridge between research and the clinical realities of health care. So whether the research involves nosocomial infections that tend to be associated with hospital care or the effects of treating cancer on the individual and the patient, it is nursing's focus on how people and systems manage the healing, living and dying process that will enhance the lived experience of health care. The business of nursing research is what can be done to intervene, provide support and eliminate complications while providing a safe healing environment for culturally diverse patients, families and communities. Claiming and celebrating this multifaceted role - clinician, consultant, leader, educator and researcher - brings full authorization to nursing and nurses, and increases the power of nurses to provide leadership in health care.

LOW SALARIES/LOW VISIBILITY IN NURSING EDUCATION

Master's prepared nurse faculty are not only paid 39 percent less than nurse anesthetists, the highest paid nurses, they are also paid significantly less than nurse administrators, consultants, supervisors, head nurses, nurse practitioners and midwives with the same educational credentials. Nurse educators earn only 76 percent of what colleagues in other academic disciplines do (Kaufman, 2007b). These low salaries clearly contribute to the shortage of nurse faculty and to the low visibility of nurse educators in academic settings. This does not mean that nurses in other specialties are making too much. It does mean that nurse faculty are making too little. We know that nurse faculty are a scarce resource and the market value has got to rise. It is part of the NLN's commitment to spread this news, place the spotlight on nursing education and advocate for increases in nurse faculty salaries. The message must be simple: if you want to recruit and retain nurse faculty; if you really want to address the nurse shortage, nurse faculty salaries have to rise.

MAKING THE INVISIBLE VISIBLE

One strategy for increasing the visibility of nurse faculty is to highlight the profile of the nurse faculty community (Kaufman, 2007a).

- Almost half (48 percent) of nurse educators are age 55 and over

- The average retirement age is 62.5 and more than 50 percent are expecting to retire in the next 10 years

- The majority (96 percent) of RN faculty are female

- Seven percent of nurse faculty are minorities: African Americans are the largest minority group representing three percent of the nurse faculty workforce; Hispanics represent just two percent and American Indians and Asians represent one percent of nurse educators.

- Two thirds (65 percent) teach exclusively in prelicensure programs; 5.6 percent teach only in graduate programs; and 16 percent teach in both types of programs

- Nine of ten faculty members surveyed were employed as educators on a full-time basis during the 2005-2006 academic year

- Approximately nine percent of nurse educators held at least one additional paid, nonconsulting job

- Over 40 percent held more than one position as administrator, faculty member or instructor

- Almost one in four (23 percent) acted as the chairperson of a department, program or division during the 2005-2006 academic year.

It is these exceptionally committed and determined professionals who year in and year out prepare our nurses to be of service to our communities. This service may involve clinical care, research, consultation, education and/or leadership of health care systems and other types of organizations. With the shortage of nursing faculty predicted to worsen, the preceding statistics on this segment of the nursing workforce will also worsen. The shortage of nurse faculty coupled with low salaries and low visibility makes for the creation of a perfect storm in health care.

STUDENTS: THE LIFE FORCE OF NURSE EDUCATORS

The most profound way of extolling our visibility as nurse educators is through our students. Students are the lifeblood of nursing education. The roles of nurse educator and nursing student are reciprocal. Our students inspire our creativity, stimulate our imagination, enrich our originality and buoy our spirits. They provoke innovation. They contribute to the body of knowledge that educators use for research and pedagogy. They are the engine of transformation. They are our national treasure (National League for Nursing, 2007a).

Therefore, nurse educators must teach them, and return in-kind the gifts they give to us. Nurse educators must mentor them as well as mentor one another. Mentors are especially important for African American students and others who are underrepresented in the profession. This retention strategy is critical as we all strive to increase diversity in the nursing workforce. A recent NLN position statement maintains: "What is essential throughout the nurse educator's career is interaction with individuals who can continually support, guide, teach and challenge them" (National League for Nursing, 2006).

THE VISIBILITY OF GREATNESS

Two nurse educators upon whose shoulders I stood were Dr. Mary Elizabeth Carnegie and Dr. Rhetaugh Dumas; both giants in the nursing profession; both Living Legends of the American Academy of Nursing. Dr. Dumas served as president of the National League for Nursing as well president of the American Academy of Nursing. Dr. Carnegie authored the groundbreaking book, *The Path We Tread: Blacks in Nursing Worldwide, 1854-1994*, that captured the history of the African American nurse in the United States (Carnegie, 2000). These nurse educators had an aura of vibrancy and passion about them. I always knew I was in the presence of greatness, intermingled with a tenderness and generosity of spirit that touched one's heart. Their role as mentor to the younger generation augmented our capacity for leadership. They knew that nurse educators were positioned to be catalysts for the exchange of ideas about important issues such as nursing education, ethnic/racial diversity of the nursing workforce, access to health care, the cost of health care, and public policy. This is their legacy and the legacy of many nurse educators who have traveled through time sharing their gifts of mentoring and the lessons learned through embracing challenges and opportunities. Nurse educators have a positive role to play in the United States and throughout the world. Nurse educators will continue to make a visible, healing difference in the world.

REFERENCES

Anderson, L. M., Scrimshaw, S. C., & Fullilove, M. T. (2003). Culturally competent healthcare systems: A systematic review. *American Journal of Preventive Medicine, 24*(3), 68-79.

Carnegie, M. E. (2000). *The path we tread: Blacks in nursing worldwide.* Sudbury, MA: Jones and Bartlett.

Dreachslin, J. L. (1999). Diversity leadership and organizational transformation: Performance indicators for health services organizations. *Journal of Healthcare Management, 44*(6), 427-439.

Health Resources and Services Administration (HRSA). (2007). *The registered nurse population: Findings from the March 2004 National Sample Survey of Registered Nurses.* Washington, DC: U.S. Department of Health and Human Services.

Kaufman, K. A. (2007a). Introducing the NLN/Carnegie National Survey of Nurse Educators: Compensation, workload, and teaching practice. *Nursing Education Perspectives, 28*(3), 164-166. Retrieved May 22, 2008, from http://nln.allenpress.com/pdfserv/i1536-5026-028-03-0164.pdf

Kaufman, K. A. (2007b). Compensation for nurse educators: Findings from the NLN/Carnegie National Survey with implications for recruitment and retention. *Nursing Education Perspectives, 28*(4), 223-225. Retrieved May 22, 2008, from http://nln.allenpress.com/pdfserv/i1536-5026-028-04-0223.pdf

National League for Nursing. (2005). *The scope of practice for academic nurse educators.* New York: National League for Nursing Certification Governance Committee.

National League for Nursing. (2006). *Mentoring of nurse faculty.* Retrieved May 22, 2008, from http://www.nln.org/aboutnln/PositionStatements/mentoring_3_21_06.pdf

National League for Nursing. (Producer). (2007a). *NLN Education Summit 2007 - Keynote Address, Beverly Malone, PhD, RN, FAAN, Chief Executive Officer* [Motion picture]. USA: Producer. Retrieved May 22, 2008, from http://www.nln.org/aboutnln/bev_speech.htm

National League for Nursing. (2007b). *Reflection and Dialogue #2 - Academic/Professional progression in nursing.* Retrieved May 22, 2008, from https://www.nln.org/aboutnln/reflection_dialogue/index.htm

National League for Nursing. (2007c). *Strategic Plan 2007-2012.* New York: Author.

National League for Nursing. (2008). *Untitled.* Retrieved May 22, 2008, from http://www.nln.org/facultycertification/CNEs.pdf

CHAPTER 2

PERSONALITY AND DEPRESSION: AFFECTS ON ACADEMIC ACHIEVEMENT IN COLLEGE STUDENTS

Bertha L. Davis, PhD, RN, FAAN, ANEF
Spencer R. Baker, PhD, CCFC

INTRODUCTION

In this chapter, we discuss personality and depression as it affects academic success. Researchers have established the cognitive indicators of academic success used for college entrance, but little research has addressed noncognitive or holistic indicators of academic success. Educators, particularly nurse educators, need to explore any issue that has a potential impact on college-aged students on this new frontier of research about noncognitive indicators. With the increased focus on accountability of colleges and universities beginning at the entry level, and as the cost of higher education rises, the need for focusing on noncognitive indicators has never been so great. The former U.S. Secretary of Education, Margaret Spellings, not only emphasized accountability, she also emphasized improving accessibility and affordability (U.S. Department of Education, 2006). Mental health disparities, including personality and emotional intelligence, disproportionately affect African Americans and their academic achievement. Nurse educators, as first responders seeing the student for other issues, might be required to intervene not only for students' well-being, but to enhance self-esteem, which influences academic success. Our study of college-aged students presented in this chapter shows that noncognitive indicators, such as differences in personality and rates of depression, affect retention and academic success of freshmen while demonstrating the need for nurse educators to "speak out" on their clients' behalf.

HEALTH DISPARITIES AND PSYCHOLOGICAL ASSESSMENT

The Centers for Disease Control and Office of Minority Health and Health Disparities (2008a, p. 1) stated, "According to the 2000 U.S. Census, African Americans account for 13 percent of the U.S. population or 36.4 million individuals." As we think about health disparities and study in greater depth issues that affect minorities, especially African Americans, there is a need for health care providers and nurse educators to "speak out." The CDC/OMHD (2008b) also stated:

> their aim is to accelerate the health impact in the U.S. population and to eliminate health disparities for vulnerable populations as defined by race/ethnicity, socio-economic status, geography, gender, age, disability status, and risk status related to sex and gender, and among other populations identified to be at risk for health disparities (p. 1).

Nurse educators must give voice to the issue of health disparities by speaking out and protecting and reducing risks for vulnerable African American communities, especially with respect to mental health.

The CDC and OMHD have made the assertion that "all people, and especially those at greater risk of health disparities, will achieve their optimal lifespan with the best possible quality of health in every stage of life." (CDC, 2008a, p. 1). The assessment of mental health disparities is an interdisciplinary function; as such, nurse educators must work with a variety of mental health practitioners to effect a change in disparate conditions. Moreover, nurse educators need to prepare nurses for clinical practice and education to meet the mental health needs of vulnerable and marginalized populations (Healthy People 2010, 2008). Therefore, educators must teach students that studying mental health disparities is as important as the study of physical health disparities.

Psychological assessment pervades nearly every aspect of clinical and research work in the broad area of mental health. In general, psychological assessment techniques are designed to evaluate a person's cognitive, emotional, behavioral, and social functioning (Mayer, 2005). One specific group of tests, called personality tests, strives to uncover the structure and features of one's personality or one's characteristic way of thinking, feeling, and behaving. The Five-Factor Model (FFM) of personality is well documented in the literature (Digman, 1990, 1994; Digman & Inouye, 1986; Goldberg, 1990, 1992, 1993; McCrae & Costa, 1997; Norman 1963; Tupes & Christal, 1992). Ozer and Reise (1994) identified the FFM of personality as the model becoming the predominant representation of global personality dimensions. Research has demonstrated that the five-factor structure of personality was evident in adults and college students (Costa & McCrae, 1994; Goldberg, 1990, 1992; John, 1990) and there is support for cross-cultural universality (McCrae & Costa, 1997; Saucier, Hampson, & Goldberg, 2000). The study of the structure of personality has been extended to childhood (Halverson et al., 2003; Halverson, Kohnstamm & Martin, 1994), to mid-childhood and later adolescent personality development (Rothbart, Ahadi, & Evans, 2000; Shiner, 1998, 2000), and to include personality types (Caspi, 1998, 2000). There is also support for a person-environment interaction influence on personality development (Kagan, 1995). The complex, interactive nature of the biological systems underlying personality is reason enough that the five-factor model, with its distinct components, can complement any study of personality and depression.

Emotional intelligence is another important aspect of personality relevant to this discussion and refers to an ability to recognize the meanings of emotion and their relationships and to reason and problem solve on the basis of these relationships (Mayer, 2005; Mayer, Caruso, & Salovey, 1999; Mayer, Salovey, & Caruso, 2004). Emotional intelligence "is involved in the capacity to perceive emotions, assimilate emotion-related feelings, understand the information of those emotions, and manage them" (p. 267). The concept of emotional intelligence is integral to discussions of studies of personality and depression and their impact on achievement. According to Mayer et al. (2004), emotional intelligence also meets the traditional standards for intelligence. When students learn to manage behaviors when experiencing the stresses of college life, they become influenced holistically in mind and body in both internal and external environments. Recognition of the importance of managing behaviors by students and educators will help create successful academic outcomes.

ACCOUNTABILITY IN COLLEGES AND UNIVERSITIES FOR ACADEMIC SUCCESS

With an increased focus on accountability in colleges and universities, there has been no concomitant focus on assessing the admissions process in higher education. Colleges and universities use the student's high school grade point average (HSGPA), and, more specifically, the results of standardized tests to determine admittance. Although these factors are considered primarily as cognitive indicators of academic success, they do not reflect the likelihood of students remaining in school. In order to address the increased focus on improving accessibility, affordability, and accountability in higher education, educators must begin to put a new focus on noncognitive indicators of academic success. Central to this new focus on noncognitive indicators are areas of interest to the health professional, such as individual differences in personality and rates of depression.

In higher education, the freshman year is considered to be a stressful transition period. Many students are not able to successfully manage this transition and decide to leave higher education during or at the end of their freshman year (DeBerard, Spielmans, & Julka, 2004). Higher academic performing students appear to persist through this transition period while lower academic performing students do not persist. Whether students choose to persist through this stressful period may be indicated more by noncognitive factors, especially personality and depression, than by standardized test scores or HSGPAs.

PERSONALITY AND DEPRESSION IN COLLEGE STUDENTS

There is a complex and controversial relationship between personality and depression. In general, adolescence is a period where epidemiological studies identify a dramatic increase in the prevalence of mood disorders, which includes depression (Santor & Rosenbluth, 2005). Although health care professionals are reluctant to prematurely diagnose a young person with a mental illness, health care professionals indicate that up to 8.3 percent of the adolescents in the United States suffer from depression, and depression is occurring earlier (National Institute of Mental Health, 2000). Depression may affect the development of personality, and several different models identifying this relationship have been suggested (Santor & Rosenbluth, 2005).

Personality is described as individual differences in human characteristics (Kagan, 1988) and is an intriguing area of research. In recent years, researchers have shown that the majority of personality traits can be adequately explained by five distinct factors referred to as the Big Five (Paunonen & Ashton, 2001). The Big Five are commonly referred to as Neuroticism (N) or Emotional Stability (ES), commonly used for adolescents; Extraversion (E); Openness to Experience (O); Agreeableness (A); and Conscientiousness (C). Arroyo and Zigler (1995) investigated the relationship between racial identity, academic achievement, and personal psychological functioning and found that higher achieving African American and European American adolescents shared common achievement-related attitudes and behaviors when compared with lower achieving African American and European American adolescents. It is possible that these common achievement-related attitudes and behaviors are facets of personality. Graziano and Ward (1992) previously reported findings that positively associated Conscientiousness to academic achievement. There is growing evidence demonstrating relationships between factors of personality and academic achievement (Kohnstamm, Halverson, Mervielde, & Havill, 1998). While controlling for intelligence, researchers have demonstrated there is a relationship between academic conscientiousness and academic attainment (Shiner & Caspi, 2003).

Dzurec, Allchin, and Engler (2007) conducted a study using content analysis and hermeneutics to examine the reasons first-year nursing students' or their peers felt depressed. The authors stated that the demands of the nursing curricula become increasingly complex as students continue to respond to the reason for choosing nursing with the statement "I want to help people" (p. 545). The researchers further stated that demands will only increase in the current health care environment, and a desire to help people may not be enough to keep students in nursing. This study was a component of an ongoing, longitudinal study. Dzurec et al. stated that this study was initiated to investigate the personal characteristics of nursing students with the goal of being able to better understand the nature of nursing students' academic experience to support evidenced-based practice in teaching. The sample consisted of 53 participants who were enrolled in the study beginning in the first year. Of the participants, 90 percent (n = 48) were white and the additional 10 percent (n = 5) were of other races.

Participants completed the psychological measure, the Myers-Briggs Type Inventory; depression and fatigue measure; Epidemiologic Studies Depression Scale; and a measure of their general optimism, the Attributional Style Questionnaire (Dzurec et al., 2007). As the data were completed for the initial data collection point, investigators found that depression exists among the college students studied, and nurse educators must assess the nature of student experiences and help them cope. Specifically, the reasons for students' perceived depression were the amount of schoolwork, time away from family, the stress of meeting new people, and the pressures of maintaining a high GPA.

Victor, Dent, Carter, Halverson, and Havill (1998) reported a follow-up study to Victor's (1994) investigation into teacher's reports of children's personality and academic achievement as measured by grade point average (GPA). Using the Hawaii Scales for Judging Behavior (Digman & Inouye, 1986), Victor et al. found that teacher-rated C and O at Time one accounted for 17 percent of the variance in GPA at Time 2. Using Goldberg's bipolar self-rating markers of personality, Hair and Graziano (2003) investigated a sample of middle school (N =317) students' personalities and their later high school GPAs (N = 244 at Time 2). Hair and Graziano found statistically significant zero-order correlations between students' high school GPAs and every dimension of self-rated middle school personality except ES. These zero-order correlations were reported as .22, .34, .19, .17, and .10 for A, O, E, C, and ES, respectively. Chamorro-Premuzic and Furnham (2003) conducted a study investigating personality prediction of academic performance using two British university samples and two personality instruments, the NEO Five Factor Inventory (NEO FFI) and the Eysenck Personality Questionnaire-Revised. In the sample (N = 70) using the NEO FFI, Chamorro-Premuzic and Furnham reported that the Big Five personality factors accounted for more than 10 percent of the unique variance in both end-of-academic-year examinations results and a 6-month supervised final project grade while controlling for selected academic behavior indicators. Chamorro-Premuzic and Furnham found the strongest predictors of personality for academic achievement was N, which includes a measure of depression, and C. These investigators have identified that a relationship exists between the structure of personality and academic achievement.

A STUDY OF DEPRESSION, PERSONALITY, AND ACADEMIC SUCCESS

Background

Predictors of success for African American students have been identified by many researchers. Scholars have found that noncognitive variables correlate particularly well with grades, retention, and graduation for African American students (Bandura, 1986; Fleming, 1984; Tracey & Sedlacek, 1984). Selected noncognitive variables found to be predictors of success in African Americans include: (a) positive self-concept, (b) realistic self-appraisal, (c) understanding of and ability to deal with racism, (d) preference of long-range goals over immediate needs; (e) availability of a strong support person, (f) successful leadership experience, (g) demonstrated community service, and (h) nontraditional/culturally related knowledge acquired in a field (Tracey & Sedlacek, 1985; Sedlacek, 1996).

Specific factors of personality and depression may influence a student's ability to persist in higher education and to succeed academically. These noncognitive indicators of academic success and persistence may be better predictors than primarily reviewing results of norm-referenced standardized tests as a proxy for intelligence or ability. The individual's personality and intelligence appear to have a reciprocal influence on each other as well as the environment. Together, these factors have a relationship to academic success (see Figure 2-1).

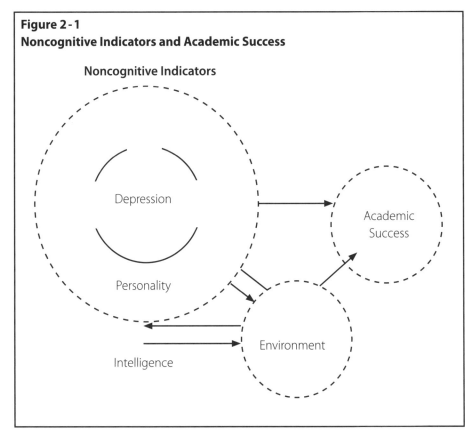

Figure 2-1
Noncognitive Indicators and Academic Success

Health care professionals could serve a central role in diagnosing and providing services to students seeking admission into higher education. The study described here investigated if depression is a better predictor than standardized test results of retention of freshmen students in higher education. Further, the researchers also investigated if, while controlling standardized test results, Conscientiousness and Impulsivity account for additional variance in the freshman first-year cumulative grade point average (CGPA).

Method

Participants. Data were collected at a private university in the southeastern United States. The NEO Personality Inventory-3 (NEO-PI-3), a more readable version of the NEO Personality Inventory - Revised Self-Report Personality Instrument, and the Beck's Depression Inventory II (BDI II) were completed by 360 entering college freshmen. The 360-freshman sample that volunteered were from an overall freshman class of approximately 900 with an overall mean 12th grade GPA of 3.2 and a mean SAT verbal score of 539. The NEO PI-3 was one of several instruments administered in random order during a university-wide introductory course. College freshmen who completed instruments were provided optional extra credit for the course. Of the 360 college freshmen, there were 259 who had SAT scores and valid instruments, BDI-II and NEO PI-3. The sample consisted of 52 males and 206 females, with a mean age of 18.4, who were born in 29 different locations. There were 231 freshmen who identified themselves as black, 16 as multicultural, three as white, and two as Hispanic. The students who had valid NEO PI-3 scores were statistically compared with students who did not have valid NEO PI-3 scores using chi-square analyses on 12th grade GPA and SAT verbal scores with no significant differences between the groups.

Instruments

This study used the results from the administration of two instruments; the NEO PI-3 and the BDI-II. The NEO PI-3 is a 240-item questionnaire that assesses 30 traits, with six traits for each of the Basic Five basic personality dimensions of N versus ES, E, O, A, and C. Items are answered on a 5-point Likert scale, ranging from strongly disagree to strongly agree. The NEO PI-3 has established psychometric properties comparable to the NEO PI R (McCrae, Costa, & Martin, 2005; McCrae, Martin, & Costa, 2005). These psychometric properties appeared consistent across all age groups.

The BDI-II is a 21-item self-report instrument for measuring the severity of depression in adults and adolescents aged 13 years and older. Each BDI-II item is rated on a 4-point scale, ranging from zero to three in terms of severity. The BDI-II was developed for the assessment of symptoms corresponding to criteria for diagnosing depressive disorders listed in the *Diagnostic and Statistical Manual of Mental Disorders* (4th edition) (American Psychiatric Association, 1994). The BDI-II was developed to measure the presence or degree of depressive symptoms, not as an instrument for specifying a clinical diagnosis. The BDI-II scores have demonstrated adequate psychometric properties.

Procedures

During September and October of 2005, the students were contacted during the university-wide introductory course and provided written informed consent for participation. Although data were collected approximately three years ago, personality is identified as an enduring pattern of behaviors that are possessed by all and depression should be somewhat heightened for students away from home for the first time. These noncognitive indicators provide insight on both retention and academic success. The students were provided an envelope with several instruments in random order and were requested to return the envelope during the next class meeting. To determine if depression and impulsivity were better predictors of retention of students after the first year than SAT results, the researchers performed a logistics regression. In order to investigate if Conscientiousness accounted for additional variance in CGPA while controlling for SAT results, the researchers performed a hierarchical multiple regression. The Conscientiousness raw score was computed as a T-score for use in this analysis.

Results

Study 1. The researchers performed a logistics regression using SAT scores and depression as predictors of retention, a dichotomous variable. There were 66 freshmen who did not return to the university and 192 who did return. The deviance log likelihood (-2LL) was 289.355 after four iterations with a chi-square of 4.811 (8), $p = .778$. When comparing the coefficients, depression was a better predictor of retention than SAT scores, according to Wald 3.899 (1), $p = .04$ and Wald .314 (1), $p = .579$. The predicted change in odds of classification were below 1.0 for both SAT scores and BDI scores, revealing that for every unit increase in SAT scores or BDI scores there will be a decrease in the odds that the student would be retained. In other words, as the SAT score increased so did the probability that the student would not return for the second semester. This result negates the predictability of the SAT scores on students' retention. Although the classification was only slightly improved for the model, possibly due to group size, depression was a better predictor of retention than the standardized test.

Study 2. To determine if Conscientiousness (C) accounted for additional variance while controlling for SAT scores, a hierarchical multiple regression was performed using the CGPA as the criterion variable. The bivariate correlations with means and standard deviations are identified in Table 2-1. In step 1, the SAT scores accounted for a statistically significant amount of variability in CGPA, $R^2 = .04$, $F(1, 191) = 8.461$, $p = .004$. In step 2, C was evaluated to determine whether it accounted for variance over and above that predicted by the SAT scores. Conscientiousness accounted for a statistically significant portion of variability in students' CGPA after controlling for the effects of the SAT scores, R^2 change $= .04$, $F(1, 190) = 8.069$, $p = .005$.

Table 2-1
Hierarchical Regression Bivariate Correlations with
Means and Standard Deviations

Variable	1	2	3
1 CGPA			
2 SAT Total Score	.206[b]		
3 Conscientiousness T-Score	.171[b]	-.120[a]	
Mean	2.95	950.57	52.79
Standard Deviation	.48	95.39	9.29

[a] $p < .05$
[b] $p < .01$

Conclusions

The literature is replete with the impact of cognitive indicators on student achievement of college-aged students, but the study of this new frontier of research is about noncognitive indicators. When SAT scores were controlled, Conscientiousness accounted for the variability in students' CGPA. Depression, though, was a better predictor of retention than SAT scores.

Further investigation of the effects of personality and depression by nurse educators as first responders in higher education is needed. Educators should continue to study the impact of noncognitive indicators on college-aged students. The need is great for focusing on noncognitive indicators, because there is an increased focus on accountability of colleges and universities, especially as the cost of higher education rises. As we look toward the future, we should include personality and depression among those indices that assist educators in understanding achievement. These indices allow educators to attempt to uncover the structure of the personality that constitutes the student's individual profile. Individual profiles as well as collective profiles are useful in determining motivators that lead to achievements in learning. The outcome of this study of depression and personality is part of a new frontier for educators.

IMPLICATIONS FOR EDUCATION

The call for democratization of higher education is not new (Spaulding & Kargodorian, 1982). Democratization continues to be a challenge to institutions of higher learning. "Colleges and universities are finding…that democratization…brings with it cultural transformations…valuing a climate of inquiry that identifies areas…that supports analysis that pursues real change over time" (Petrides, 2004, p. 1). The question is how to determine the intentions of educators in the design of curricula and where should the noncognitive indicators be taken into account in this design. Intentions assist in the deliberate developing of interventions that can be used by educators to reframe the dialogue among students. The goal then is to reframe behavior as evidenced by speech showing collaboration with educators that will support successful outcomes.

College administrators who have a desire to know additional means to enhance the academic success of African Americans must find ways to incorporate factors like noncognitive indicators that impact the students' experience. The indicators that impact experiences should be identified as early in the students' matriculation as possible. This early identification will assist students and faculty in knowing factors that impact success and communicate those factors so that appropriate interventions can be identified.

REFERENCES

American Psychiatric Association (1994). *Diagnostic and statistical manual of mental disorders DSM-IV-TR* (4th ed.). Washington, DC: Author.

Arroyo, C., & Zigler, E. (1995). Racial identity, academic achievement, and the psychological well-being of economically disadvantaged adolescents. *Journal of Personality and Social Psychology, 69*(5), 903-914.

Bandura A. (1986). *Social foundations of thought and action. A social cognitive theory.* Englewood Cliffs, NJ: Prentice-Hall.

Caspi, A. (1998). Personality and development across the life course. In W. Damon (Series Ed.) & N. Eisenberg (Vol. Ed.), *Handbook of Child Psychology: Vol. 3. Social, emotional, and personality development* (5th ed.). pp. 311-388. New York: Wiley.

Caspi, A. (2000). The child is father of the man: Personality continuities from childhood to adulthood. *Journal of Personality and Social Psychology, 78*(1), 158-172.

Centers for Disease Control and Prevention/Office of Minority Health and Health Disparities. (2008a). CDC: *Achieving greater health impact.* Retrieved April 19, 2008, from http://www.cdc.gov/omhd/

Centers for Disease Control and Prevention/Office of Minority Health and Health Disparities. (2008b). *Health disparities affecting minorities: African Americans.* Retrieved April 19, 2008, from http://www.cdc.gov/omhd/

Chamorro-Premuzic, T., & Furnham, A. (2003). Personality predicts academic performance: Evidence from two longitudinal university samples. *Journal of Research in Personality, 37*, 319-338.

Costa, P. T., Jr., & McCrae, R. R. (1994). Stability and change in personality from adolescence through adulthood. In C. F. Halverson, Jr., G. A. Kohnstamm, & R. P. Martin (Eds.), *The developing structure of temperament and personality from infancy to adulthood* (pp. 139-150). Hillsdale, NJ: Erlbaum.

DeBerard, M. S., Spielmans, G. I., & Julka, D. L. (2004). Predictors of academic achievement and retention among college freshmen: A longitudinal study. *College Student Journal, 38*(1), 66-79.

Digman, J. M. (1990). Personality structure: Emergence of the five-factor model. In M. R. Rosensweig & L. W. Porter (Eds.), *Annual Review of Psychology, 41*, 417-440.

Digman, J. M. (1994). Child personality and temperament: Does the five-factor model embrace both domains? In C. F. Halverson, Jr., G. A. Kohnstamm, & R. P. Martin (Eds.), *The developing structure of temperament and personality from infancy to adulthood* (pp.293-318). Hillsdale, NJ: Erlbaum.

Digman, J. M., & Inouye, J. (1986). Further specification of the five robust factors of personality. *Journal of Personality and Social Psychology, 50*(1), 116-123.

Fleming, J. (1984). *Blacks in college*. San Francisco: Jossey-Bass.

Dzurec, L. C., Allchin, L., & Engler, A. J. (2007) First-year nursing students' accounts of reasons for student depression. *Journal of Nursing Education, 46*(12), 545-551.

Goldberg, L. (1990). An alternative "description of personality": The big-five factor structure. *Journal of Personality and Social Psychology, 59*(6), 1216-1229.

Goldberg, L. (1992). The development of markers for the big-five factor structure. *Personality Assessments, 4*(1), 26-42.

Goldberg, L. (1993). The structure of phenotypic personality traits. *American Psychologist, 48*(1), 26-34.

Graziano, W. G., & Ward, D. (1992). Probing the big five in adolescence: Personality and adjustment during a developmental transition. *Journal of Personality, 60*(2), 425-439.

Hair, E. C., & Graziano, W. G. (2003). Self-esteem, personality and achievement in high school: A prospective longitudinal study in Texas. *Journal of Personality, 71*(6), 971-994.

Halverson, C. F., Jr., Havill, V. L., Deal, J. E., Baker, S. R., Victor, J. B., Pavlopoulos, V., et al. (2003). Personality structure as derived from parental ratings of free descriptions of children: The inventory of child individual differences. *Journal of Personality, 71*(6), 998-1028.

Halverson, C. F., Jr., Kohnstamm, G. A. & Martin, R. P. (Eds.) (1994). *The developing structure of temperament and personality from infancy to adulthood*. Hillsdale, NJ: Erlbaum.

Healthy People 2010. (2009). Leading health indicators. Retrieved February 21, 2009, from www.healthypeople.gov/Document/HTML/uih/uih_4.htm

John, O. P. (1990). The "big five" factor taxonomy: Dimensions of personality in natural language and in questionnaires. In L. A. Peurin (Ed.), *Handbook of personality: Theory and research*. New York: Guilford.

Kagan, J. (1988). The meaning of personality predicates. *American Psychologist, 43*(8), 614-620.

Kagan, J. (1995). Yesterday's premises, tomorrow's promises. In R. D. Parke, P. A. Ornstein, J. J. Rieser, & C. Zahn-Waxler (Eds.), *A century of developmental psychology*. Washington, DC: American Psychological Association.

Kohnstamm, G. A., Halverson, C. F., Jr., Mervielde, I., & Havill, V. L. (Eds.). (1998). *Parental descriptions of child personality: Developmental antecedents of the big five?* Hillsdale, NJ: Erlbaum.

Mayer, J. D. (2005). A tale of two visions: Can a new view of personality help integrate psychology? *American Psychologist, 60*(4), 294-307.

Mayer, J. D., Caruso, D., & Salovey, P. (1999). Emotional intelligence meets traditional standards for an intelligence. *Intelligence, 27*, 267-298.

Mayer, J. D., Salovey, P., & Caruso, D. R. (2004). Emotional intelligence: Theory, findings, and implications. *Psychological Inquiry, 15*(3), 197-215.

McCrae, R. R., & Costa, P. T., Jr. (1997). Personality trait structure as a human universal. *American Psychologist, 52*(5), 509-516.

McCrae, R. R., Costa, P. T., Jr., & Martin, T. A. (2005). The NEO-PI-3: A more readable Revised NEO Personality Inventory. *Journal of Personality Assessment, 84*, 261-270

McCrae, R. R., Martin, T. A., & Costa, P. T., Jr. (2005). Age trends and age norms for the NEO Personality Inventory-3 in adolescents and adults. *Assessment, 12*(4), 363-373.

National Institute of Mental Health (2000). *Depression in children and adolescents: A fact sheet for physicians*. Bethesda, MD: National Institute of Mental Health, National Institutes of Health, US Department of Health and Human Services.

Norman, W. T. (1963). Toward an adequate taxonomy of personality attributes: Replicated factor structure in peer nomination personality ratings. *Journal of Abnormal and Social Psychology, 66*, 574-583.

Ozer, D. J., & Reise, S. P. (1994). Personality assessment. *Annual Review of Psychology, 45*, 357-388.

Paunonen, S. V., & Ashton, M. C. (2001). Big five factors and facets and the prediction of behavior. *Journal of Personality and Social Psychology, 81*(3), 524-539.

Petrides, L. (2004). The democratization of data in higher education: A case study of the challenges that institutions face as they seek to improve student success. Retrieved July 20, 2008, from http://www.iskme.org/what-we-do/publications/democratization

Rothbart, M. K., Ahadi, S. A., & Evans, D. E. (2000). Temperament and personality: Origins and outcomes. *Journal of Personality and Social Psychology, 78*(1), 122-135.

Santor, D. A., & Rosenbluth, M. (2005). Evaluating the contribution of personality factors to depressed mood in adolescents: Conceptual and clinical issues. In M. Rosenbluth, S. H. Kennedy, & R. M. Bagby (Eds.), *Depression and personality: Conceptual and clinical challenges.* Arlington, VA: American Psychiatric Publishing.

Saucier, G., Hampson, S. E., Goldberg, L. R. (2000). Cross-language studies of lexical personality factors. In S. E. Hampson (Ed.), *Advances in personality psychology.* Philadelphia: Taylor & Francis.

Shiner, R. L., & Caspi, A. (2003). Personality differences in childhood and adolescence: Measurement, development, and consequences. *Journal of Child Psychology and Psychiatry and Allied Disciplines, 44,* 2-32.

Shiner, R. L. (2000). Linking childhood personality with adaptation evidence for continuity and change across time into late adolescence. *Journal of Personality and Social Psychology, 78*(2), 310-325.

Spaulding, S., & Kargodorian, A. (1982, March 19-23). *Democratization of higher education: Issues and trends.* Paper presented at the annual meeting of the American Educational Research Association, New York, NY. (ERIC Document Reproduction Service No. ED216631) Retrieved July 20, 2008, from http://eric.ed.gov/ERICDocs/data/ericdocs2sql/content_storage_01/0000019b/80/2f/e8/a6.pdf

Sedlacek, W. E. (1996). Employing noncognitive variables in admitting students of color. In I. H. Johnson & A. J. Ottens (Eds.), *Leveling the playing field: Promoting academic success for students of color* (New Directions for Student Services No. 74, pp. 79-91). San Francisco: Jossey-Bass.

Tracey, T. J., & Sedlacek, W. E. (1984). Noncognitive variables in predicting academic success by race. *Measurement and Evaluation in Guidance, 16,* 171-178.

Tracey, T. J., & Sedlacek, W. E. (1985). The relationship of noncognitive variables to academic success success: A longitudinal comparison by race. *Journal of College Student Personnel, 26,* 410.

Tupes, E. C., & Christal, R. C. (1992). Recurrent personality factors based on trait ratings. *Journal of Personality, 60,* 225-251 (work originally published in 1961).

U. S. Department of Education. (2006). *Action plan for higher education: Improving accessibility, affordability and accountability.* Washington, DC: Author.

Victor, J. B. (1994). The five-factor model applied to individual differences in school behavior. In C. F. Halverson, Jr., G. A. Kohnstamm, & R. P. Martin (Eds.), *The developing structure of temperament and personality from infancy to adulthood.* Hillsdale, NJ: Erlbaum.

Victor, J. B., Dent, H. E., Carter, B., Halverson, C. F., Jr., & Havill, V. L. (1998). How African American parents describe their children. In G. A. Kohnstamm, C. F. Halverson, Jr., I. Mervielde, & V. L. Havill (Eds.), *Parental descriptions of child personality: Developmental antecedents of the big five?* Hillsdale, NJ: Erlbaum.

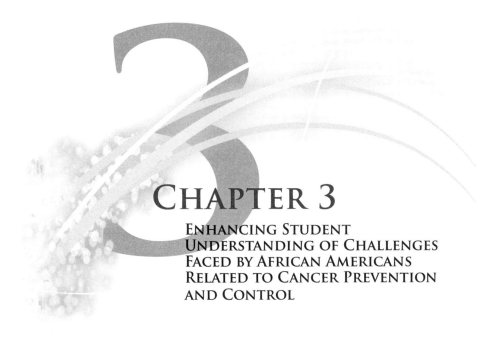

CHAPTER 3

**ENHANCING STUDENT
UNDERSTANDING OF CHALLENGES
FACED BY AFRICAN AMERICANS
RELATED TO CANCER PREVENTION
AND CONTROL**

Sandra Millon Underwood, PhD, RN, CHN, FAAN

INTRODUCTION

In anticipation of the need for nurses to have a strong base of knowledge of and skill in cancer prevention and cancer control, schools and colleges of nursing across the country are being encouraged by oncology nurse leaders to integrate didactic, laboratory and clinical experiences that address cancer prevention and control within nursing curricula. Efforts to incorporate cancer nursing content into nursing education within colleges and universities across the United States began in 1954. However, at present, limited attention is given to cancer prevention, risk reduction and screening in most nursing programs. The same is true of the degree of attention given in nursing programs to the prevention and control of cancer among African Americans, the nation's most vulnerable, at-risk, and underserved population group.

CANCER MORBIDITY AND MORTALITY AMONG AFRICAN AMERICANS

Cancer, a group of more than 100 diseases characterized by abnormal development, uncontrolled growth, and unpredictable spread of cells, is a major health problem in the African American community. The American Cancer Society estimated that 152,900 new cases of invasive cancer would be diagnosed and an estimated 62,780 deaths from cancer would occur among African American men and women in the United States in 2007 (American Cancer Society, 2007).

In spite of strides made over the past three decades in cancer prevention, cancer risk management, early cancer detection and diagnosis, cancer treatment and cancer control, the mere thought of a cancer diagnosis continues to evoke a paralytic sense of anxiety, fear, and uncertainty in the hearts and minds of most African American men and women. The scourging effect of cancer impacts all population groups. However, the degree to which it afflicts men and women in the African American community - a heterogeneous group of approximately 36 million individuals who trace their ancestry to one of the 42 African countries south of the Sahara Desert or to the islands of Madagascar, Cape Verde, Comoros, Mauritius, Reunion, Seychelles, Sao Tome and Principe - is alarming (see Textbox 1).

A PORTRAIT OF THE AFRICAN AMERICAN POPULATION

Ancestry: The U.S. Department of Commerce report entitled Race and Ethnic Standards for Federal Statistics and Administrative Reporting, more commonly referred to as Directive 15, classifies individuals who trace their ancestry to sub-Saharan Africa as African Americans (United States Department of Commerce, 1978). Sub-Saharan Africa includes the 42 countries south of the Sahara Desert on the mainland of Africa, plus the islands of Madagascar, Cape Verde, Comoros, Mauritius, Reunion, Seychelles and Sao Tome and Principe. Most African Americans in the United States are descendents of the African men, women and children who were forcibly transported from sub-Saharan Africa to the United States and the Caribbean during the 17th, 18th and 19th centuries and sold into slavery. Yet, many recent immigrants with sub-Saharan ancestry have come voluntarily to the United States from the Caribbean Islands and sub-Saharan Africa.

Ethnic Diversity: Contrary to popular belief, the African American population is not a homogeneous group. The majority of African Americans are descendants of men, women and children who were transported from sub-Saharan Africa to the United States or the Caribbean and sold into slavery. However, the proportion of immigrants who migrate to the United States, the proportion of Caribbean immigrants who migrate to the United States, and the proportion of first-generation and second-generation descendants of African and Caribbean immigrants who have sub-Saharan ancestry are increasing. As a result, the population of African Americans in the United States is becoming increasingly more ethnically and culturally diverse.

Population Trends: When the first census was taken in 1790, African Americans numbered approximately 760,000. African Americans are now the second largest racial group in the United States. According to 2006 estimates by the U.S. Department of Census, the population has grown to approximately 37.1 million, accounting for 12.4 percent of the population (United States Census Bureau, 2007).

CANCER MORBIDITY AND MORTALITY AMONG AFRICAN AMERICANS: AN UNDUE BURDEN

The National Cancer Institute Surveillance, Epidemiology, and End Results (SEER) Program monitors the impact of cancer in the general population throughout the United States (Ries, et al., 2007). Data reported by the SEER Program indicate that African Americans, compared to other racial and ethnic groups in the United States, have a greater risk for developing cancer, and a greater risk for dying from cancer (see Tables 3-1 and 3-2). For all cancer sites combined, cancer incidence rates are highest among African Americans, followed by whites, Hispanics, Asian/Pacific Islanders, and American Indian/Alaska Natives. For all cancer sites combined, cancer mortality rates are highest among African Americans, followed by whites, American Indian/Alaska Natives, Hispanics, and Asian/Pacific Islanders (Ries, et al.).

Prostate cancer is the most common form of cancer experienced by African American men, followed by cancer of the lung and bronchus, colon and rectum, kidney and renal pelvis, non-Hodgkin's lymphoma, and oral cavity (Table 3-3). When compared with men

Table 3-1
Age-Adjusted SEER Cancer Incidence Rates per 100,000 by Race/Ethnicity, United States, 2000-2004

Age-Adjusted SEER Cancer Incidence Rates per 100,000 by Race/Ethnicity, United States, 2000-2004	White			Black			Asian/Pacific Islander			American Indian/Alaska Native			Hispanic		
	Total	M	F	Total	M	F	Total	M	F	Total	M	F	Total	M	F
All Sites	477.5	556.7	423.9	504.1	663.7	396.9	314.9	359.9	285.8	297.6	321.2	282.4	356.0	421.3	314.2
Brain and Nervous System	7.0	8.3	5.9	4.1	4.9	3.5	3.4	3.9	3.0	2.8	3.5	2.2	5.3	6.0	4.7
Female Breast (Invasive)	132.5	---	132.5	118.3	---	118.3	89.0	---	89.0	69.8	---	69.8	89.3	---	89.3
Colon and Rectum	51.2	60.4	44.0	62.1	72.6	55.0	41.6	49.7	35.3	40.8	42.1	39.6	39.3	47.5	32.9
Esophagus	4.6	8.0	1.9	6.2	10.4	3.2	2.5	4.2	1.2	4.1	7.0	---	3.0	5.4	1.2
Kidney and Renal Pelvis	13.3	18.3	9.1	14.3	20.4	9.7	6.3	8.9	4.3	14.7	18.5	11.5	12.4	16.5	9.1
Hodgkin's Lymphoma	2.9	3.2	2.6	2.4	2.8	2.1	1.2	1.4	1.0	0.9	---	---	2.2	2.8	1.7
Larynx	3.7	6.5	1.4	6.0	11.6	2.0	1.5	3.0	0.3	1.7	2.9	---	2.7	5.2	0.7
Leukemia	12.8	16.7	9.9	10.2	13.2	8.1	7.4	9.2	5.9	6.4	6.5	6.1	9.6	11.8	8.0
Liver and Intrahepatic Bile Duct	5.2	7.9	2.9	7.6	12.7	3.8	13.9	21.3	7.9	9.7	14.8	5.5	9.7	14.4	5.7
Lung and Bronchus	65.7	81.0	54.6	76.6	110.6	53.7	39.4	55.1	27.7	44.0	53.7	36.7	33.3	44.7	25.2
Melanoma of the Skin	21.6	27.2	17.6	1.0	1.1	0.9	1.5	1.7	1.3	2.9	4.1	2.0	4.5	4.5	4.6
Myeloma	5.2	6.6	4.1	11.3	14.0	9.5	3.3	3.7	3.0	5.3	4.8	5.7	5.7	6.9	4.6
Non-Hodgkin's Lymphoma	20.2	24.1	17.0	14.6	18.1	11.9	13.2	15.7	11.2	10.4	11.6	9.5	16.5	19.2	14.2
Oral Cavity and Pharynx	10.6	15.7	6.1	11.1	18.1	5.7	7.9	10.8	5.4	7.1	10.0	4.6	6.2	9.3	3.6
Ovary	14.3	---	14.3	10.1	---	10.1	9.7	---	9.7	11.2	---	11.2	11.5	---	11.5
Pancreas	11.2	12.8	9.9	15.0	16.2	13.9	9.0	10.0	8.3	9.2	9.5	8.9	10.5	11.0	10.0
Prostate	161.4	161.4	---	255.5	255.5	---	96.5	96.5	---	68.2	68.2	---	140.8	140.8	---

Age-Adjusted SEER Cancer Incidence Rates per 100,000 by Race/Ethnicity, United States, 2000-2004 (continued)

	White			Black			Asian/ Pacific Islander			American Indian/ Alaska Native			Hispanic		
	Total	M	F	Total	M	F	Total	M	F	Total	M	F	Total	M	F
Stomach	7.1	10.2	4.7	12.5	17.5	9.1	14.3	18.9	10.8	11.5	16.3	7.9	12.3	16.0	9.6
Testis	6.3	6.3	---	1.4	1.4	---	1.7	1.7	---	3.8	3.8	---	3.8	3.8	---
Thyroid	8.9	4.6	13.2	5.1	2.4	7.3	8.5	3.9	12.6	5.3	11.9	7.8	7.5	3.3	11.6
Urinary Bladder	23.0	40.5	10.1	12.6	20.3	7.6	9.2	16.4	3.9	7.0	11.9	3.2	11.6	20.2	5.5
Uterine Cervix	8.5	---	8.5	11.4	---	11.4	8.0	---	8.0	6.6	---	6.6	13.8	---	13.8
Uterine Corpus	24.3	---	24.3	19.6	---	19.6	16.2	---	16.2	15.1	---	15.1	17.4	---	17.4

Source: Ries, L. A. G., Melbert, D., Krapcho, M., Mariotto, A., Miller, B. A., Feuer, E. J., Clegg, L., Horner, M. J., Howlader, N., Eisner, M. P., Reichman, M., & Edwards, B. K. (Eds). (2007). *SEER Cancer Statistics Review, 1975-2004.* Bethesda, MD: National Cancer Institute.

Table 3-2
Age-Adjusted SEER Cancer Morality Rates per 100,000 by Race/Ethnicity, United States, 2000-2004

Age-Adjusted SEER Cancer Mortality Rates per 100,000 by Race/Ethnicity, United States, 2000-2004

	White			Black			Asian/ Pacific Islander			American Indian/ Alaska Native			Hispanic		
	Total	M	F	Total	M	F	Total	M	F	Total	M	F	Total	M	F
All Sites	190.7	234.7	161.4	238.8	321.8	189.3	115.5	141.7	96.7	128.6	187.9	141.2	120.1	162.2	106.7
Brain and Nervous System	4.8	5.8	3.9	2.6	3.2	2.2	2.0	2.5	1.5	1.9	2.6	1.9	2.8	3.4	2.4
Female Breast (Invasive)	25.0	---	25.0	33.8	---	33.8	12.6	---	12.6	13.9	---	16.1	16.9	---	16.1
Colon and Rectum	18.9	22.9	15.9	26.7	32.7	22.9	12.3	15.0	10.3	13.0	20.6	14.3	13.6	17.0	11.1
Esophagus	4.3	7.7	1.7	6.0	10.2	3.0	1.8	3.1	0.8	2.9	6.7	1.5	2.4	4.2	1.0
Kidney and Renal Pelvis	4.3	6.2	2.8	4.1	6.1	2.8	1.7	2.4	1.1	4.8	6.6	.2	3.6	4	2.3
Hodgkin's Lymphoma	5	6	4	4	6.1	2.8	2	2.4	1.1	2	9.3	4.3	4	5.4	2.3
Larynx	1.2	2.2	0.5	2.5	5.0	0.8	4	0.8		9	1.9	---	9	1.9	0.2
Leukemia	7.7	10.3	5.8	6.7	6.8	5.3	3.9	5.0	3.0	4.0	5.6	4.1	5.1	6.4	4.1
Liver and Intrahepatic Bile Duct	4.5	6.5	2.8	6.5	10.0	3.9	10.6	15.5	6.7	6.3	10.7	6.4	7.6	10.8	5.0
Lung and Bronchus	55.0	72.6	42.1	62.0	95.8	39.8	26.9	38.3	18.5	34.3	49.6	32.7	23.6	36.0	14.6
Melanoma of the Skin	3.0	4.3	2.0	.4	0.5	.4	.3	0.4	0.3	.7	1.3	0.7	.7	0.9	0.6
Myeloma	3.5	4.4	2.8	7.1	8.5	6.3	1.6	1.9	1.5	2.9	4.2	3.5	3.1	3.7	2.6
Non-Hodgkin's Lymphoma	7.9	9.9	6.4	5.2	6.5	4.3	4.8	5.8	3.9	4.3	6.1	5.0	5.7	6.9	4.8
Oral Cavity and Pharynx	2.5	3.8	1.5	.9	6.8	1.7	2.3	3.4	1.3	2.1	3.8	1.5	1.7	2.8	0.8
Ovary	9.2	---	9.2	7.4	---	7.4	4.8	---	4.8	5.5	---	7.1	6.1	---	6.1
Pancreas	10.4	12.0	9.0	13.8	15.5	12.4	7.4	7.9	6.9	6.3	7.6	7.3	8.3	9.1	7.5

Age-Adjusted SEER Cancer Mortality Rates per 100,000 by Race/Ethnicity, United States, 2000-2004 (continued)

	White			Black			Asian/Pacific Islander			American Indian/Alaska Native			Hispanic		
	Total	M	F	Total	M	F	Total	M	F	Total	M	F	Total	M	F
Prostate	25.6	25.6	---	62.3	62.3	---	11.3	11.3	---	18.0	21.5	---	21.2	21.2	---
Stomach	3.7	5.2	2.6	8.2	11.9	5.8	8.0	10.5	6.2	5.0	9.6	5.5	6.8	9.1	5.1
Testis	.3	.3	NA	.2	2	NA	.1	.1	NA	---	---	NA	2	2	NA
Thyroid	8.9	4.6	13.2	5.1	2.4	.3	8.5	3.9	12.6	5.3	.7	7.	87.5	3.3	11.6
Urinary Bladder	4.5	---	3.9	3.7	---	7.1	1.8	---	2.4	1.6	---	2.9	2.4	---	3.1
Uterine Cervix	2.3			4.9			2.4			2.7			3.3		
Uterine Corpus	3.9			7.1			2.4			2.3					

Sources: Ries, L. A. G., Melbert, D., Krapcho, M., Mariotto, A., Miller, B. A., Feuer, E. J., Clegg, L., Horner, M. J., Howlader, N., Eisner, M. P., Reichman, M., & Edwards, B. K. (Eds.). (2007). *SEER Cancer Statistics Review, 1975-2004.* Bethesda, MD: National Cancer Institute.

of other racial/ethnic groups in the United States, African American men have the highest age-adjusted incidence rates of cancer of the colon, esophagus, kidney, larynx, lung and bronchus, multiple myeloma, oral cavity, pancreas and cancer of the prostate. When compared with white, Hispanic, Asian/Pacific Islander, and American Indian/Alaska Native men, African American men have the highest age-adjusted mortality rates of cancer of the colon and rectum, esophagus, Hodgkin's disease, larynx, lung and bronchus, multiple myeloma, oral cavity and pharynx, pancreas, prostate and cancer of the stomach. And, when compared to white men, African American men have poorer survival rates of cancer of the colon and rectum, esophagus, Hodgkin's lymphoma, kidney, larynx, leukemia, liver, lung and bronchus, melanoma, non-Hodgkin's lymphoma, oral cavity, pancreas, prostate, testes, thyroid, and cancer of the urinary bladder (Ries, et al., 2007).

Breast cancer is the most common form of cancer experienced by African American women, followed by cancer of the lung and bronchus, colon and rectum, uterus, and pancreas (see Table 3-3). When compared with white, Hispanic, Asian/Pacific Islander, and American Indian/Alaska Native women, African American women have the highest age-adjusted incidence rates of cancer of the colon and rectum, esophagus, larynx, multiple myeloma, and cancer of the pancreas. African American women have the highest age-adjusted mortality rates for cancer of the breast, colon and rectum, esophagus, Hodgkin's lymphoma, multiple myeloma, oral cavity and pharynx, pancreas, and urinary bladder. And, when compared with white women, African American women have poorer survival rates of cancer of the breast, colon and rectum, esophagus, Hodgkin's lymphoma, larynx, leukemia, liver, lung and bronchus, melanoma, non-Hodgkin's lymphoma, oral cavity, ovary, thyroid, urinary bladder, uterine cervix and uterine corpus (Ries, et al., 2007).

Mapping cancer mortality rates by state reveal distinct regions of the country where cancer mortality of African American population groups is excessive (American Cancer Society, 2007; Devesa, et al., 1999). Charting the stage of cancer at diagnosis of African Americans by economic status, also, reveals disparities among low-income and uninsured population groups (National Center for Health Statistics, 2007; Ward, et al., 2003).

FACTORS INFLUENCING CANCER MORBIDITY AND MORTALITY IN AFRICAN AMERICANS

Research suggests that the disparities in cancer incidence, mortality and survival experienced by African Americans are associated with a host of individual factors, social and economic inequalities, environmental conditions, and access and utilization of quality health care (Institute of Medicine, 2002; Institute of Medicine, 2003; Mayberry, Milini, & Ofili, 2000; Modlin, 2003; Shavers & Brown, 2002; Ward, et al., 2004). Among the most common factors influencing these trends are: environmental exposures to carcinogenic

Table 3-3
Leading Sites of New Cancer Cases and Cancer Deaths
Among African Americans, 2007 Estimates

New Cancer Cases		Cancer Deaths	
Men	**Women**	**Men**	**Women**
Prostate 30,870 (37%)	Breast 19,010 (27%)	Lung and Bronchus 9,970 (31%)	Lung and Bronchus 6,720 (22%)
Lung and Bronchus 12,490 (15%)	Lung and Bronchus 9,060 (13%)	Prostate 4,240 (13%)	Breast 5,830 (19%)
Colon and Rectum 7,860 (9%)	Colon and Rectum 8,580 (12%)	Colon and Rectum 3,420 (11%)	Colon and Rectum 3,650 (12%)
Kidney and Renal Pelvis 3,280 (4%)	Uterine Corpus 3,420 (5%)	Pancreas 1,700 (5%)	Pancreas 2,000 (6%)
Non-Hodgkin's Lymphoma 2,640 (3%)	Pancreas 2,310 (3%)	Liver & Intrahepatic Bile Duct 1,430 (5%)	Ovary 1,290 (4%)
Oral Cavity and Pharynx 2,590 (3%)	Kidney and Renal Pelvis 2,310 (3%)	Stomach 1,130 (4%)	Uterine Corpus 1,220 (4%)
Pancreas 2,080 (3%)	Non-Hodgkin's Lymphoma 2,240 (3%)	Leukemia 980 (3%)	Myeloma 990 (3%)
Urinary Bladder 2,050 (3%)	Myeloma 1,920 (3%)	Esophagus 950 (3%)	Leukemia 890 (3%)
Myeloma 1,940 (2%)	Uterine Cervix 1,910 (3%)	Myeloma 860 (3%)	Stomach 820 (3%)
Liver & Intrahepatic Bile Duct 1,880 (2%)	Ovary 1,770 (3%)	Oral Cavity and Pharynx 840 (3%)	Uterine Cervix 720 (2%)

Source: American Cancer Society. (2007). *Cancer Facts and Figures for African Americans 2007-2008*. Atlanta, GA: Author.

substances; lifestyle choices and behaviors that result in tobacco use, poor diets, physical inactivity, and obesity; decisions that impede and/or delay cancer screening, diagnosis, treatment and follow-up, and barriers to accessing quality cancer care.

Advances made over the last three decades in understanding the etiology, epidemiology, screening, diagnosis, and treatment of cancer have led to declines in cancer incidence, declines in cancer mortality, improvements in life expectancy and improvements in cancer survival among many population groups. The identification of oncogenes and tumor suppressor genes has advanced knowledge of the genesis of cancer (American Cancer Society, 2007; Lichenstein, et al., 2000; National Cancer Institute, 1996; Weinstein & Perera, 1995). Advances in medical technology have led to the development of advanced clinical procedures, imaging methods and computer technologies for use in the detection and diagnosis of cancer (Breen, et al., 2001; National Cancer Institute, 1993). Advances made in cancer treatment have led to the development of more precise and less drastic surgical interventions; safer and more powerful radiation therapy; anti-neoplastic agents that impede the growth of cancer cells while sparing damage to normal cells, and pharmacological agents to treat expected side effects of the cytotoxic therapy (Jacox, Carr, & Payne, 1994; Johnson, Moroney, & Gay, 1997; King, et al., 1996; Richardson & Ream, 1996). Yet, despite the phenomenal progress African Americans have not benefited fully from the advances in science and medicine.

NURSING EDUCATION'S RESPONSE TO CANCER CARE NEEDS OF AFRICAN AMERICANS

Cancer morbidity and mortality among African Americans has long been a concern of leaders in the nursing community. Well before reducing cancer-related health disparities was acclaimed as a national priority, efforts were being undertaken by nurse clinicians and nurse researchers to explore the cancer experiences of African American population groups and to design of interventions to improve their overall health status, their health care, and their health outcomes. However, the response by faculty within the field of nursing education to the burden of cancer among African Americans (and other vulnerable population groups) has been limited.

The disparities in cancer incidence, mortality and survival experienced by African Americans are of such a magnitude that content and learning experiences specific to the prevention and control of cancer among African Americans should be integrated into every nursing curriculum. However, graduates entering the field of nursing typically have little exposure to issues and challenges that result in excess cancer morbidity and mortality among African Americans. Information specific to the oncologic process, cancer diagnosis and cancer treatment are well articulated in texts designed to address concepts essential to adult health nursing, medical-surgical nursing and community-based nursing practice. However, content relevant to cancer prevention and control among African Americans is minimally addressed. Surprisingly absent from most nursing texts are tables and charts that highlight trends in cancer morbidity and mortality; describe health/risk behaviors, and describe cancer screening practices of African Americans. Also absent are illustrations and references to cancer-related health disparities and case reports that highlight the cancer care needs of vulnerable and medically underserved population groups.

A substantive body of knowledge about the cancer morbidity and mortality of African American population groups is available in the nursing literature (see Bibliography). These reports have contributed a wealth of knowledge to the profession about the influence of race, culture and economics to cancer prevention, cancer care, and cancer control; the influence of attitudes, beliefs, myths and misperceptions on cancer prevention and cancer care; the unmet cancer care needs of poor and geographically defined population groups, and the role nurses can play in the prevention and control of cancer among African American population groups (Underwood, et al., 2004). Yet, insights gleaned from nursing faculty suggest that little effort is undertaken in colleges and universities to engage students in discussions that highlight or allude to the excess cancer morbidity and mortality experienced by African Americans (Underwood & Dobson, 2002). The same is true of efforts undertaken by faculty to engage nursing students in the provision of cancer care to African Americans in the clinical arena.

REDUCING DISPARITIES IN CANCER MORBIDITY AND MORTALITY IN AFRICAN AMERICANS: IN THE CLASSROOM, THE CLINICAL LABORATORY AND THE FIELD

Building on the foundation laid by nurse researchers and nurse clinicians, faculty should intensify efforts to integrate content and experiences specific to cancer prevention and control among African Americans in nursing curricula. There is much that nursing faculty could do within academic settings to address the cancer disparities experienced among African American population groups. Faculty could reference and utilize interactive websites and databases to highlight local, regional and national trends in cancer prevention and control among African Americans (and other racial ethnic population groups) (see Textbox 2). Faculty could engage students in discussions of factors affecting trends among geographically, economically and culturally distinct groups of African Americans. Faculty could develop case studies of survivors, co-survivors and men and women at increased cancer risk to highlight perceptions, beliefs, behaviors, and needs common among African Americans specific to cancer prevention, risk management, screening, diagnosis, treatment, and follow-up (see Textbox 3). And, rather than contriving experiences in the acute care setting or the local community based on custom and/or convenience, faculty could engage students in clinical activities that directly or indirectly influence cancer prevention and control among African American population groups bearing a significant risk.

Text Interactive Websites and Databases that Highlight Trends in Cancer in African American Population Groups	
American Cancer Society	http://www.cancer.org
Addressing Racial and Ethnic Disparities in Health Care	http://www.ahrq.gov/research/disparit.htm
Cancer Atlas	http://www3.cancer.gov/atlasplus
Cancer Control Planet	http://cancercontrolplanet.cancer.gov
Centers for Disease Control and Prevention	http://www.cdc.gov
Medline Plus	http://www.nlm.nih.gov/medlineplus/cancer.html
National Cancer Institute	http://www.nci.nih.gov
Office of Minority Health	http://www.omhrc.gov

Hereditary/Familial Breast Cancer: What Will Be Her Fate?

I believed that breast cancer was a death sentence because that was what I had seen all my life!

My experience with breast cancer started in 1967 when I was about 12. My mother's sister was diagnosed with breast cancer at the age of 24. The doctors said the cancer was in her left breast. She chose to have a mastectomy. In less than a year her cancer spread. She was buried on her 25th birthday. She had two children. Both were less than ten years old.

In the spring of 1971, at the age of 31, another one of my mother's sisters was diagnosed with breast cancer. It was also in her left breast. I was still in shock from the death of my other aunt, so learning that another aunt had breast cancer was very hard for me. I remember her having surgery and having her breast removed. Sadly, she died in September of 1971. She, too, had two children. They also were under the age of ten.

Two years later, in 1973, another aunt was diagnosed with breast cancer. She was 26 years old. Just like her sisters, the cancer was in her left breast. I remember my mom telling me that the doctor said her breast cancer was very aggressive. She had a mastectomy, but sadly passed away one year after her diagnosis.

In 1986, another aunt was diagnosed with breast cancer. She was 36 years old. Unlike her other sisters, she saw a lot of doctors. They recommended that she have a mastectomy, chemotherapy and radiation. The doctors seemed to be better able to help this aunt. I guess they were more informed by the time it got to her, and they knew more about what to do. She is still living today.

In the early 1990s my first cousin, whose father was my mom's brother, was diagnosed with breast cancer. She was in her early 30s. After consulting with her doctors, she decided to have a double mastectomy. Since her surgery, she has done well. She will soon celebrate her 45th birthday.

In the spring of 1996, another first cousin was diagnosed with breast cancer. She was 34. Her mom was the first to die from breast cancer. Having grown up without a mom, we were always there to support her and help her when she needed it. Over the years, everyone in our family encouraged her to get regular mammograms. We thought she was getting regular mammograms. When talking to her later, we found out that she wasn't. I think she thought because she was young she could get away with not being concerned with breast cancer. She was married and had four children. It wasn't until she found a lump under her arm that she became concerned. When she felt it, she was very afraid. She did not go to the doctor right away. My family and I believe that she may have known about the lump under her arm earlier and didn't say anything. By the time we knew about it, it was late in the summer. She was 36 when she died.

My doctors knew about my family history, so they recommended that I have yearly mammograms and they recommended that I do monthly self breast exams. I started getting yearly mammograms when I was 35. I was doing self exams well before that.

I was diagnosed with breast cancer in 2000 at the age of 44. I thought to myself , "Am I going to be the next person in my family to die from breast cancer?"

The doctors informed me that my breast cancer was Stage 0. The fact that my aunts and cousins had breast cancer helped me to appreciate how important it was for me to help myself and for me to find out what was best for me. The doctors gave me many options. I researched magazines, the internet, and medical books. I used the information I gathered when it came time to make a decision as to whether to have a mastectomy or not. I chose a partial mastectomy.

The doctors wanted to do a breast cancer study of my family. They even asked me to be part of the study. I didn't consent to it. I wanted them to figure out what is happening to my family. But, once I was diagnosed, since I already had it, I wanted to focus only on getting well. I focused all of my attention on fighting my disease. I did not want them checking this, checking that and checking on anything outside of my breast cancer.

If this were your patient, how would you intervene?

Engaging in any or all of these teaching/learning activities would contribute much to the nation's efforts to reduce cancer morbidity and mortality among African Americans and enhance the preparedness of future nurses to do the same. As educators evaluate the present and look to the future, the greater challenge before them is to exert concerted efforts individually and collectively to do so.

BIBLIOGRAPHY

Barg, F. K., & Gullatte, M. M. (2001). Cancer support groups: meeting the needs of African Americans with cancer. *Seminars in Oncology Nursing, 17*(3), 171-178.

Bibb, S. C. (2001). The relationship between access and stage at diagnosis of breast cancer in African American and Caucasian women. *Oncology Nursing Forum, 28*(4), 711-719.

Bradley, P. K. (2005). The delay and worry experience of African American women with breast cancer. *Oncology Nursing Forum, 32*(2), 243-249.

Clarke-Tasker, V. A., & Wade, R. (2002). What we thought we knew: African American males' perceptions of prostate cancer and screening methods. *Journal of the Association of Black Nursing Faculty, 13*(3), 56-60.

Davis, M. A. (2003, August 25). Peer pressure can be used for good - not evil - in tobacco control. *Nursing Spectrum*. Retrieved from http://include.nurse.com/apps/pbcs.dll/article?AID=2003308250325

Fowler, B. A. (2006). Claiming health: Mammography screening decision making of African American women. *Oncology Nursing Forum, 33*(5), 969-975.

Fowler, B. A. (2006). Social processes used by African American women in making decisions about mammography screening. *Journal of Nursing Scholarship, 38*(3), 247-254.

Fowler, B. A. (2007). The influence of social support relationships on mammography screening in African-American women. *Journal of the National Black Nurses Association, 18*(1), 21-29.

Fowler, B. A., Rodney, M., Roberts, S., & Broadus, L. (2005). Collaborative breast health intervention for African American women of lower socioeconomic status. *Oncology Nursing Forum, 32*(6), 1207-1216.

Gates, M. F., Lackey, N. R., & Brown, G.(2001). Caring demands and delay in seeking care in African American women newly diagnosed with breast cancer: An ethnographic, photographic study. *Oncology Nursing Forum, 28*(3), 529-537.

Gill, K. M., Mishel, M., Belyea, M., Germino, B., Germino, L. S., Porter, L., et al. (2004). Triggers of uncertainty about recurrence and long-term treatment side effects in older African American and Caucasian breast cancer survivors. *Oncology Nursing Forum, 31*(3), 633-839.

Green, P. M., & Davis, M. A. (2004). Lung cancer in African-Americans. *Journal of the National Black Nurses Association, 15*(2), 54-60.

Grindel, C. G., Brown, L., Caplan, L., & Blumenthal, D. (2004). The effect of breast cancer screening messages on knowledge, attitudes, perceived risk, and mammography screening of African American women in the rural South. *Oncology Nursing Forum, 31*(4), 801-808.

Gullatte, M. M., Phillips, J. M., & Gibson, L. M. (2006). Factors associated with delays in screening of self-detected breast changes in African-American women. *Journal of the National Black Nurses Association, 17*(1), 45-50.

Hall, C.P., Wimberley, P.D., Hall, J.D., Pfriemer, J.T., Hubbard, E., Stacy, A.S., et al. (2005). Teaching breast cancer screening to African American women in the Arkansas Mississippi River Delta. *Oncology Nursing Forum, 32*(4), 857-863.

Hamilton, J. B., & Sandelowski, M. (2004). Types of social support in African Americans with cancer. *Oncology Nursing Forum, 31*(4), 792-800.

Henderson, P. D., Gore, S. V., Davis, B. L., & Condon, E. H. (2003). African American women coping with breast cancer: A qualitative analysis. *Oncology Nursing Forum, 30*(4), 641-647.

Jones, R. A., & Wenzel, J. (2005). Prostate cancer among African-American males: Understanding the current issues. *Journal of the National Black Nurses Association, 16*(1), 55-62.

Jones, R. A., Underwood, S. M., & Rivers, B. M. (2007). Reducing prostate cancer morbidity and mortality in African American men: Issues and challenges. *Clinical Journal of Oncology Nursing, 11*(6), 865-872.

Kelley, M. A. (2004). Culturally appropriate breast health educational intervention program for African-American women. *Journal of the National Black Nurses Association, 15*(1), 36-47.

Kinney, A. Y., Emery, G., Dudley, W. N., & Croyle, R. T. (2002). Screening behaviors among African American women at high risk for breast cancer: Do beliefs about God matter? *Oncology Nursing Forum, 29*(5), 835-843.

Kooken, W. C., Haase, J. E., & Russell, K. M. (2007). "I've been through something": Poetic explorations of African American women's cancer survivorship. *Western Journal of Nursing Research, 29*(7), 896-919.

Lackey, N. R., Gates, M. F., & Brown, G. (2001) African American women's experiences with the initial discovery, diagnosis, and treatment of breast cancer. *Oncology Nursing Forum, 28*(3), 519-527.

Morgan, P. D., Barnett, K., Perdue, B., Fogel, J., Underwood, S. M., Gaskins, M., et al. (2006). African American women with breast cancer and their spouses' perception of care received from physicians. *Journal of the Association of Black Nursing Faculty, 17*(1), 32-37.

Morgan, P. D., Fogel, J., Rose, L., Barnett, K., Mock, V., Davis, B. L., et al. (2005). African American couples merging strengths to successfully cope with breast cancer. *Oncology Nursing Forum, 32*(5), 979-987.

Phillips, J. M., Cohen, M. Z., & Tarzian, A. J. (2001). African American women's experiences with breast cancer screening. *Journal of Nursing Scholarship, 33*(2), 135-140

Powe, B., & Adderley-Kelly, B. (2005). Colorectal cancer in African-Americans: Addressing the need for further research and research utilization. *Journal of the National Black Nurses Association, 16*(1), 48-54.

Powe, B. D., & Finnie, R. (2004). Knowledge of oral cancer risk factors among African Americans: Do nurses have a role? *Oncology Nursing Forum, 31*(4), 785-791.

Ramsay-Johnson, E. M. (2006). An approach to reducing disparities in breast cancer in the United States Virgin Islands. *Journal of the Association of Black Nursing Faculty, 17*(1), 44-47.

Robertson, E. M. (2002, May 4). *Teaching the teachers.* Presentation given at the Dissemination Colloquium sponsored by ONS Cancer Prevention and Early Detection Program for HBCU/MSI nurses in Miami, FL. Retrieved from http://www.minoritynurse.com/features/faculty/06-03-03.html

Russell, K. M., Champion, V. L., & Skinner, C. S. (2006). Psychosocial factors related to repeat mammography screening over 5 years in African American women. *Cancer Nursing, 29*(3), 236-243.

Spurlock, W. R., & Cullins, L. S. (2006). Cancer fatalism and breast cancer screening in African American women. *Journal of the Association of Black Nursing Faculty, 17*(1), 38-43.

Thomas, B. C. (2004). African American women's breast memories, cancer beliefs, and screening behaviors. *Cancer Nursing, 27*(4), 295-302.

Underwood, S. M. (2006). Breast cancer in African American women: Nursing essentials. *Journal of the Association of Black Nursing Faculty, 17*(1), 3-14.

Underwood, S. M., & Dobson, A. (2002). Cancer prevention and early detection program for educators: Reducing the cancer burden among African Americans within the academic arena. *Journal of the National Black Nurses Association, 13*(1), 45-55.

Weinrich, S., Royal, C., Pettaway, C. A., Dunston, G., Faison-Smith, L., Priest, J. H., et al. (2002). Interest in genetic prostate cancer susceptibility testing among African American men. *Cancer Nursing, 25*(1), 28-34.

Weinrich, S., Vijayakumar, S., Powell, I. J., Priest, J., Hamner, C. A., McCloud, L., et al. (2007). Knowledge of hereditary prostate cancer among high-risk African American men. *Oncology Nursing Forum, 34*(4), 854-860.

Wilmoth, M. C., & Sanders, L. D. (2001). Accept me for myself: African American women's issues after breast cancer. *Oncology Nursing Forum, 28*(5), 875-879.

Wood, R. Y., Duffy, M. E., Morris, S. J., & Carnes, J. E. (2002). The effect of an educational intervention on promoting breast self-examination in older African American and Caucasian women. *Oncology Nursing Forum, 29*(7), 1081-1090.

Wu, W. (2003, May 30-31). *The power of a pear*. Presentation given at the Dissemination Colloquium sponsored by ONS Cancer Prevention and Early Detection Program for HBCU/MSI nurses in Miami, FL. Retrieved from http://www.minoritynurse.com/features/health/02-12-04f.html

REFERENCES

American Cancer Society. (2007). *Cancer prevention and early detection facts and figures, 2007.* Atlanta, GA: Author.

American Cancer Society. (2007). *Cancer facts and figures for African Americans 2007-2008.* Atlanta, GA: Author.

Breen, N., Wagener, D. K., Brown, M. L., Davis, W. W., & Ballard-Barbash, R. (2001). Progress in cancer screening over a decade: Results of cancer screening from 1987, 1992 and 1998 National Health Interview Surveys. *Journal of the National Cancer Institute, 93*(22), 1704-1713.

Devesa, S. S., Grauman, D. J., Blot, W. J., Pennello, G. A., Hoover, R. N., & Fraunebi, J. F. (1999). *Atlas of cancer mortality in the United States, 1950-94.* Bethesda, MD: National Cancer Institute.

Institute of Medicine. (2002). Unequal treatment: What healthcare providers need to know about racial and ethnic disparities in healthcare. In Institute of Medicine, *Shaping the future of health.* Washington, DC: National Academies Press.

Institute of Medicine. (2003). *Unequal treatment: Confronting racial and ethnic disparities in healthcare.* Washington, DC: National Academies Press.

Jacox A., Carr D. B., & Payne R. (1994). *Management of cancer pain. Clinical practice guideline.* (AHCPR Pub. No. 94-0592). Rockville, MD: Agency for Health Care Policy and Research, U.S. Department of Health and Human Services, Public Health Services.

Johnson M. H., Moroney, C. E., & Gay, C. F. (1997). Relieving nausea and vomiting in patients with cancer: A treatment algorithm. *Oncology Nursing Forum, 24*(1), 51-57.

King, C., Haberman, M., Berry, D., Bush, N., Butler, L., Dow, K., et al. (1996). Quality of life and the cancer experience: The state of knowledge. *Oncology Nursing Forum, 24*(1), 27-41.

Lichenstein, P., Holm, N. V., Verkasalo, P. K., Iliadou, A., Kaprio, J., Koskenvuo, M., et al. (2000). Environmental and heritable factors in the causation of cancer. Analyses of cohorts of twins from Sweden, Denmark, and Finland. *New England Journal of Medicine, 343*, 78-85.

Mayberry, R. M., Milini, F., & Ofili, E. (2000). Racial and ethnic differences in access to medical care. *Medical Care Research and Review, 57*(Suppl. 1): S108-S145.

Modlin, C. S. (2003). Culture, race, and disparities in health care. *Cleveland Clinic Journal of Medicine, 70*(4), 283-288.

National Cancer Institute. (1993). *Measures of progress against cancer: Advances in early detection*. Bethesda, MD: Author.

National Cancer Institute. (1996). *Cancer rates and risks*. Bethesda, MD: National Institutes of Health National Cancer Institute.

National Center for Health Statistics. (2007). *Health United States, 2007 with chartbook on trends in the health of Americans*. Hyattsville, MD: United States Department of Health and Human Services, Centers for Disease Control and Prevention, National Center for Health Statistics.

Richardson, A., & Ream, E. (1996). Research and development. Fatigue in patients receiving chemotherapy for advanced cancer. *International Journal of Palliative Nursing, 2*(4), 199-204.

Ries, L. A. G., Melbert, D., Krapcho, M., Mariotto, A., Miller, B. A., Feuer, E. J., et al. (Eds.). (2007). *SEER cancer statistics review, 1975-2004*. Bethesda, MD: National Cancer Institute.

Shavers, V. L., & Brown, M. L. (2002). Racial and ethnic disparities in the receipt of cancer treatment. *Journal of the National Cancer Institute, 94*, 334-357.

Singh, G. K., Miller, B. A., Hankey, B. F., & Edwards, B. K. (2003). *Area socioeconomic variations in U.S. cancer incidence, mortality, stage, treatment and survival, 1975-1999* (National Cancer Institute Surveillance Monograph Series, No. 4). Bethesda, MD: National Cancer Institute.

Thurn, M. (2004). Cancer disparities by race/ethnicity and socioeconomic status. *CA Cancer Journal for Clinicians, 54*(2), 78-93.

Underwood, S., & Dobson, A. (2002). Cancer prevention and early detection program for educators: Reducing the cancer burden among African Americans within the academic arena. *Journal of National Black Nurses Association, 13*(1), 45-55.

Underwood, S., Buseh, A. G., Canales, M. K., Powe, B., Dockery, B., Kather, T., et al. (2004). Nursing contributions to the elimination of health disparities among African-Americans: Review and critique of a decade of research. *Journal of the National Black Nurses Association, 15*(1), 48-62.

United States Census Bureau (2007). *U.S. population estimates.* Washington, D.C.: Population Estimates Program, Population Division, U.S. Census Bureau.

United States Department of Commerce. (1978). Directive No. 15. Race and ethnic standards for Federal statistics and administrative reporting. In United States Office of Federal Statistical Policy and Standards, *Statistical policy handbook* (pp. 37-38). Washington, DC: U.S. Department of Commerce, Office of Federal Statistical Policy and Standards.

Ward, E. W., Jemal, A., Cokkinides, V., Singh, G. P., Cardinez, C., Ghafoor, A., et al. (2004). Cancer disparities by race/ethnicity and socioeconomic status. *CA Cancer Journal for Clinicians, 54*(2), 78-93.

Weinstein I. B., & Perera F. (1995). Molecular biology and epidemiology of cancer. In P. Greenwald, B. Kramer, & D. Weed (Eds.), *Cancer prevention and control*. New York: Marcel Dekker.

CHAPTER 4

CHALLENGES IN INTEGRATING HIV/AIDS, MENTAL HEALTH AND SUBSTANCE ABUSE: IMPLICATIONS FOR EDUCATORS

Delroy M. Louden, PhD, FRSH

Introduction

It is by now well established in the public health community that a significant number of people diagnosed with HIV/AIDS also display co-occurring disorders of mental illness and substance abuse. Treating these conditions places an enormous burden on families and the health care delivery system, as many individuals exhibiting them are very difficult to engage, difficult to retain in traditional treatment settings, and present a challenge to the community that attempts to maintain them. One of the long-term goals in managing this very diverse population has been the notion of "one-stop-shopping": providing for the complex clinical needs of this population under one roof, thereby increasing compliance with care.

This chapter outlines an integrated system of care for this population with significant co-morbidities. Specifically, it addresses the need for interdisciplinary curriculum changes and emphasis, as well as the need to break down professional boundaries in improving the level of care through "one-stop-shopping." The need is for nursing educators to emphasize an interdisciplinary, population-based approach to health care, thus improving patient compliance and adherence.

Epidemiological Trends: Prevalence of Mental Health and Substance Abuse Problems Among Persons with HIV

Certain psychiatric features, such as cognitive impairment, are now well recognized as the most serious psychiatric disorders with the most serious impact on individuals, either by directly affecting behavior or by having a mediating effect on the ability of individuals to use information about risk factors associated with HIV/AIDS to engage in safer sex behaviors.

The stress of being diagnosed with HIV and later HIV/AIDS is a major contributory factor in psychological disorders and is manifested in two broad categories: (i) mood and anxiety disorders, such as depression, anxiety sociality and insomnia; and (ii) organic mental disorders, such as organic psychosis; delirium; cognitive impairment; dementia, and manic episodes. One of the most debilitating conditions and psychological disorders exhibited by patients with HIV/AIDS is dementia. Patients often develop anxiety, panic, and psychosis. The literature describes the following characteristics among patients with dementia due to HIV/AIDS: slow or poor motor skills; poor concentration; reduced cognitive skills (particularly in information processing) and weakness in abstract thinking; language comprehension impairment; apraxia; visual difficulties; poor short- and long-term memory; personality changes; social withdrawal; and weakened interpersonal skills.

In an investigation that focused on HIV infection among young adults with psychotic disorders from a diverse population of individuals, Susser et al. (1997) found a substantial number of cases had contracted HIV infection before their first hospital admission. AIDS was the leading cause of mortality in this cohort, and the number of deaths among the HIV-positive patients exceeded the number of deaths from all other causes combined. In addition, there was no definitive evidence that HIV caused the psychosis in any of the patients, but this etiology could not be ruled out since, in all cases, the HIV infection was antecedent to the onset of psychosis.

Epidemiological Characteristics of HIV/AIDS in the African American Population

Of all ethnic and racial groups in America, HIV/AIDS has disproportionately affected the African American community since the beginning of the epidemic, and that disparity has increased over time. The data reported by the Kaiser Foundation (2008) and the CDC (2007) show that African Americans account for more HIV and AIDS cases, people estimated to be living with AIDS, and HIV-related deaths than any other racial/ethnic group in the United States. The epidemic has also had a disproportionate impact on African American women, youth, and men who have sex with men, and its impact varies in several major metropolitan areas. Kaiser (2008) reports the following statistics:

- Although African Americans represent only 12 percent of the U.S. population, they accounted for half of AIDS cases diagnosed in 2006 as well as accounted for a disproportionate share of HIV/AIDS diagnoses in states/areas with confidential name-based HIV reporting.

- The AIDS case rate per 100,000 among African American adults/adolescents was more than nine times that of Caucasians in 2006.

- HIV-related deaths and HIV death rates are highest among African Americans. African Americans accounted for 56 percent of deaths due to HIV in 2004 and their survival time after an AIDS diagnosis is lower on average than it is for most other racial/ethnic groups. In 2004, African American men had the highest HIV death rate per 100,000 men aged 25-44. The HIV death rate among African American women aged 25-44 was 23.1 compared to 1.3 for Caucasian women.

Key trends reported by CDC (2007) have shown that the share of AIDS diagnoses accounted for by African Americans has risen over time, from 25 percent of cases diagnosed in 1985 to 49 percent in 2006. Other data also have been presented:

- The number of African Americans living with AIDS increased by 27 percent between 2002 and 2006, compared with a 19 percent increase among the white population.

- The picture is particularly disturbing with respect to African American women, who account for the majority of new AIDS cases among women (66 percent in 2006); while Caucasian and Latina women account for 17 percent and 16 percent, respectively.

- African American women represent more than a third (36 percent) of AIDS cases diagnosed among African Americans (African American men and women combined) in 2006; by comparison, Caucasian women represented 15 percent of AIDS cases diagnosed among Caucasians in 2006.

- The AIDS case rate for African American men (82.9 per 100,000) was the highest of any group, followed by African American women (40.4 per 100,000).

- HIV was the 4th leading cause of death for African American men and 3rd for African American women, aged 25-44, in 2004.

- Although African American teens (aged 13-19) represent only 16 percent of U.S. teenagers, they accounted for 69 percent of new AIDS cases reported among teens in 2005.

- With respect to mode of transmission, HIV patterns among African American men vary from those of Caucasian men. Although both groups are most likely to have been infected through sex with other men, Caucasian men are much more likely to have been infected this way. Heterosexual transmission and injection drug use account for a greater share of infections among African American men than among Caucasian men.

CO-OCCURRENCE OF HIV AND MENTAL ILLNESS

In examining psychiatric morbidity on entry into an HIV primary care setting, Lyketsos, et al. (1996) found that 54 percent of these patients exhibited anxiety or at least one disorder other than substance abuse; further, 74 percent had a substance abuse disorder. Later investigations estimate that chronically ill psychiatric patients were at increased risk for HIV infection with an estimated seroprevalence of over 3.1 percent.

Using data from the HIV Cost and Services Utilization Study (HCSUS), Bing et al. (2001) examined mental health and substance abuse through a nationally representative probability sample of adults receiving HIV care in the United States. The results showed that nearly half of the sample screened positively for a mental health disorder, forty percent reported using an illicit drug other than marijuana and twelve percent screened positively for drug dependence. In addition, more than one third of the sample screened positive for depression and over a quarter of the sample screened positive for dysthymia. Table 4-1 shows that the proportion of individuals screening positive for mental illness and substance disorders in the HCSUS sample is significantly higher than that in the general population. The proportion of individuals screening positive for major depression in HCSUS is five times greater than the proportion found in the Household Survey on Drug Abuse (NHSDA) (NASTAD, 2005).

Table 4-1

Comparison of Persons Screening Positive for HIV by Condition

Condition	HCSUS[1]	NHSDA[2]
	National Representative Probability Sample of Adults Receiving Care for HIV in the U.S. (N=2,864)	General Population Sample (N=22,181)
Major Depression	36.0%	7.6%
Anxiety Disorder	15.8%	2.1%
Panic Attack	10.5%	2.5%
Drug Use	50.1%	10.3%

[1]HCSUS: HIV Cost and Service Utilization Survey
[2]NHSDA: National Household Survey on Drug Abuse

Source: Adapted from NASTAD's *HIV and Mental Health: The Challenges of Dual Diagnosis* - Mental Health Issue Brief (2005). Used with permission.

In addition to being disproportionately vulnerable to infection with HIV and other sexually transmitted diseases, evidence presented by M. P. Carey, K. B. Carey, and Kalichman (2001) makes clear that persons living with severe mental illness are more likely to be victims of sexual coercion and intimate partner violence, to live in risky environments, to have unstable partnerships in high-risk sexual networks, to use substances that impair decision making, and to lack the emotional stability, judgment, and interpersonal skills needed to avoid risk. Overall, recent evidence suggests that even persons living with the most disabling mental illnesses, including schizophrenia and other psychiatric disorders, can reduce their risky behaviors through group-level behavioral risk reduction interventions that are specifically tailored to understand their underlining vulnerabilities.

Gender Depression and HIV in Relation to Other Psychosocial Factors

With respect to gender, Ickovics et al. (2001) found that depressive symptoms among women with HIV are associated with HIV disease progression, even when the effects of key clinical, substance use, and sociodemographic characteristics are controlled. Symptoms of depression are also associated with unprotected sexual intercourse, multiple sex partners, trading sex for money or drugs, and contracting sexually transmitted diseases (Hutton, et al., 2004). Depression may combine with the effects of other psychosocial factors, stressors such as unemployment, post-traumatic stress disorder, to produce a phenomenon known in the public health literature as a "syndemic," a highly interrelated set of health problems experienced by a single population. Stall and colleagues (2003) analyzed data from a large-scale, household-based sample of urban men who have sex with men (MSM) to test whether an added interplay among a specific set of psychosocial health conditions (i.e., depression, polydrug use, childhood sexual abuse, and partner violence) is driving the HIV/AIDS epidemic among MSM. Their findings indicated that all four of these psychosocial health problems were independently related to a greater likelihood of high-risk sexual behavior and of having HIV. Their results showed that individuals with depressive symptoms, polydrug use, and childhood sexual abuse were at higher risk HIV/AIDS than individuals with depressive symptoms alone.

Individuals with a history of multiple or triple diagnosis (mental illness, substance abuse and HIV/AIDS) often experience significant difficulties in accessing employment and housing. Figure 4-1 shows that housing is a major issue for individuals with co-occurring disorders. For example, Susser et al. (1993) studied the prevalence of HIV infection among mentally ill individuals in a New York City men's shelter and showed that there is a higher prevalence of HIV infection among mentally ill men whose HIV status was known than that among those individuals who status was not known. The authors speculated that intravenous drug use and sex with other men appeared to have played important roles in the contraction of HIV in this population.

Challenges in the Provision of Comprehensive Medical Treatment for HIV-Affected Persons with Multiple Psychological Disorders

In reviewing the literature and data from the Epidemiological Catchments Area Study, it is clear that individuals with psychiatric disorders display greater risks of alcohol or drug use compared with the rest of the population (U.S. Department. of Health and Human Services, National Institute of Mental Health, 1992).

In a number of epidemiological investigations of medical comorbidity among patients with mental illness, the findings indicate that individuals with mental illness had significant active medical conditions of which diabetes, hepatitis, epilepsy and organic brain syndrome were the most common. Other researchers such as Dixon, Postrado, Delahanty, Fischer, and Lehman (1999) in their investigation among individuals with schizophrenia reported findings of high blood pressure, poor eyesight, and dental problems. However, a review by Jeste, Gladsjo, Lidamer, and Lacro (1996) indicated that individuals with schizophrenia may not have more coexisting medical illnesses than the population at large, but the clinical conditions may be more severe. Dickey, Normand, Weiss, Drake, and Azeni (2002) speak eloquently to this point:

> "It has long been known that habitual alcohol use increases the likelihood of developing many disorders, such as liver, heart, and gastrointestinal disease, and exacerbates others, such as diabetes and hypertension . However, the degree to which mental illness adds

Figure 4-1

Prevalence of Mental Health Disorders in Individuals with HIV and in the General Population[a]

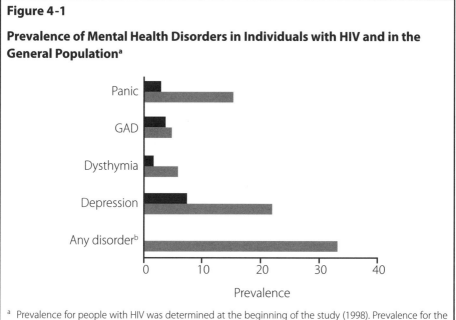

a Prevalence for people with HIV was determined at the beginning of the study (1998). Prevalence for the general population is based on a 2004 estimate using the most recent U.S. Census data, as reported in National Institute of Mental Health, *The Numbers Count: Mental Disorders in America*.

b "Any disorder" refers to any of the four disorders specified; no comparable data are available for the general population.

Source: Beckett, et al. (2007). Adapted with permission.

extra risk of developing these disorders is unclear. In two cross-sectional studies of patients with psychotic disorders, chronic medical problems rated by case managers were not correlated with substance use disorders. These studies did not control for age, however. Because the frequencies of chronic medical disorders increase with age and substance users are more often younger; the studies may have underestimated the association between chronic medical disorders, substance use, and mental illness."

In their investigation of medical morbidity, mental illness and substance abuse disorders, Dickey and colleagues (2002) examined whether certain medical conditions were more prevalent among adults with severe mental illness and whether a comorbid substance use disorder increased prevalence beyond the effect of severe mental illness alone. Using a cross-sectional observational study design, twelve-month prevalence rates were computed and logistic regression was used to estimate the effect of a substance abuse disorder or another mental illness on the risk of a medical disorder.

Substance abuse and dependence is one of the central characteristics of individuals with comorbid conditions of HIV/AIDS and mental illness. Berkman et al. (2005) explored the impact of substance dependence on the efficacy of an HIV sexual risk-reduction intervention previously shown to be effective among men with severe mental illness by comparing rates of high-risk sexual behaviors among men with and without a lifetime of substance abuse. The findings showed that at each follow-up interval (6, 12, and 18 months), the intervention group as a whole and the non-substance-dependent participants showed a significant reduction in risk; for example, the substance-dependent men showed no difference from the control group. These findings suggest that among men with severe mental illness, substance abuse and dependence may be a further impediment to HIV risk reduction.

With the rising cost of health care, recent discussion has focused on assessing the cost of providing care to persons with multiple diagnoses of HIV/AIDS, mental illness and substance abuse. The most comprehensive account of how substance abuse and mental health problems affect patients affected/infected with HIV/AIDS was the Substance Abuse and Mental Health Administration (SAMHSA) initiated HIV Costs and Services Utilization Study (HCSUS). This was the first survey of a nationally representative sample of people with HIV that estimated the prevalence of these problems among people with HIV, and assessed those individuals' access to appropriate care. The survey also measured how these problems affected their ability to adhere to treatment.

The HIV Cost and Services Utilization Study (HCSUS) found that African Americans fared more poorly on several important measures of access to care and quality of care than whites. These differences diminished over time, but were not completely eliminated (Shapiro, et al., 1999). HCSUS also found that African Americans were more likely to report postponing medical care because they lacked transportation, were too sick to go to the doctor, or had other competing needs (Cunningham, et al., 1999). A recent analysis of data from 11 HIV primary and specialty care sites in 2000-2002 in the United States found higher rates of hospitalization among African Americans with HIV/AIDS, but differences in outpatient utilization were not significant (Fleishman, et al., 2005). Finally, in the HCSUS study mentioned earlier, participants reported that they had made several positive changes in their health behaviors, notably reduction in drinking and the use of drugs (Beckett et al., 2007).

In a series of investigations examining health and health care of individuals with severe mental illness who were Medicaid recipients, Blank, Mandell, Aiken, and Hadley (2002), in a cross-sectional study, used Medicaid claims data and welfare recipients' files to calculate the treated period prevalence of serious mental illness (defined as schizophrenia spectrum disorder or a major affective disorder) and the odds of receiving a diagnosis of

HIV infection among those who had a diagnosis of mental illness. Their findings showed that the treated period prevalence of HIV infection was 0.6 percent among Medicaid recipients who did not have a diagnosis of serious mental illness and 1.8 percent among those who did. After controlling for age, race and set time on welfare, individuals with schizophrenia spectrum disorder were 1.5 times as likely to have a diagnosis of HIV infection, and individuals with a major affective disorder were 3.8 times as likely. These findings suggest that, compared with Medicaid beneficiaries who were not treated for severe mental illness, those with severe mental illness had a significantly higher age- and gender-adjusted risk of the medical disorder considered in the study.

Individuals with comorbid substance use disorder had the highest risk for several of the disorders: diabetes, hypertension, heart disease (ischemic heart disease, heart rhythm disorders, and other heart conditions), asthma, gastrointestinal disorders, infections of the skin and subcutaneous tissue, malignant neoplasm, and acute respiratory disorders (pneumonia and influenza).

In a later investigation, Rothbard, Metraux, and Blank (2003) examined the cost of care for Medicaid recipients with mental illness and HIV infection or AIDS. Previous investigations showed that individuals with serious mental illness had higher medical costs than persons without serious mental illness. Using claims data from Pennsylvania, Rothbard et al. estimated the costs of care for four groups of adults eligible to receive Medicaid: individuals with mental illness and HIV infection or AIDS; individuals with serious mental illness only; individuals with HIV infection or AIDS only; and a control group without serious mental illness, HIV infection, or AIDS. Estimates included all outpatient and inpatient treatment costs per year per person, but excluded pharmacy costs and nursing home care for individuals with severe mental illness, HIV infection, or AIDS, but who received a diagnosis between 1985 and 1996. The findings indicate that individuals with comorbid connections of mental illness, HIV infection or AIDS had the highest annual medical and behavioral health treatment expenditure (estimated at $13,800 per person). For the control group without mental illness, HIV infection, or AIDS, the annual expenditure per person was estimated at $1,000. Other investigations, such as Dickey et al. (2002), demonstrate that individuals with comorbid substance use and psychotic disorders have the highest medical costs.

Barriers and Challenges to Nurse Educators in Preparing Nursing Students to Achieve Integrated Care for Patients with HIV/AIDS and Comorbidity

The primary barriers to integrating mental health, substance abuse, and HIV/AIDS services are stigma, lack of funding, and professional norms. These are evident across the health care delivery system, and clearly affect the number and quality of services provided. The nursing curriculum should ideally contain standardized clinical assessment tools currently in use covering domains such as alcohol, drug abuse, anxiety, depression, neuropsychological dysfunction, and psychiatric distress.

Nursing educators should prepare students to deal with, for example, stigma associated with HIV, which may undermine a client's motivation to access appropriate services from a particular provider due to patients concerns about how they will be perceived because of their diagnosis or their physical appearance. The location in the community of the provider or service can contribute to barriers. A client may become unable to access services because of the impact of their disease on their cognition and problem-solving skills, such as the development of HIV associated dementia (HAD) and minor cogitative disorder (MMCD). The sources of funding for HIV, mental health, and substance abuse systems are varied and include state general funds, Medicaid, and federal funds. However, providers of substance abuse and mental health services both have a history of inadequate and inconsistent public funding, which often creates a sense of uncertainty and mistrust around integrating services and resources. Often these bureaucratic hurdles act as barriers by discouraging clients and providers to seek specialty care.

Because of the multidisciplinary approach to providing HIV /AIDS services, there are differences among program norms and practices. These frequently lead to differences in treatment and often result in tension among service providers.

The major challenge to achieving integrated HIV/AIDS care revolves around integration and collaboration that would result in a seamless care delivery system where all agencies in a community are linked. An integrated model of the delivery of appropriate care must provide an organizational structure that binds together the array of elements including:

- Joint planning for the delivery of services;

- Shared funding for key federal, state and community-based organizations;

- Joint budget delivery;

- Clients seen as shared responsibility of all collaborating agencies;

- Unified intake/assessment with sharing of care;

- Streamlining professional licensure requirements for service delivery; and

- One-stop-shopping facility for the delivery of services, using a multidisciplinary approach.

For nursing educators, the challenge is to insure that the traditional clinical assessment method that is taught in nursing school is modified for clients who are dual and triple diagnosed with HIV, mental health, and substance abuse. This can be achieved by adding HIV-specific questions to existing clinical assessment practice. These questions should cover such areas as: educational background; occupational/employment history; psychiatric history; mental status examination; medical history; history of alcoholism as a substance abuse/intervenous drug use; risk-taking behaviors, particularly sexual risk taking; social support systems; coping skills; strength; financial and economic resources; religious and spiritual practices.

Focusing on areas such as coping skills allows nursing students as clinicians to get a sense of how the patient has historically and recently approached problems in their lives in addition to how they're coping with being HIV positive. This is a way of understanding the patient's strength (for example, the will to live, adaptive skills and problem solving) and maladaptive behaviors such as isolation, avoidance, denial, and self-destructive activity.

In the conduct of the clinical assessment, the need to maintain the level of trust and respect with the patient prior to conducting the assessment must continue to be emphasized. Keep in mind the following when conducting the assessment: respect a client's endurance; be sensitive to the client's circumstances. Do not begin the clinical assessment by asking the client how he/she contracted the virus. Stay client-centered (e.g., Are you doing okay? Are you getting a chance to tell me what would be helpful for you? Is there something you'd like to tell me that I haven't asked?). Pay attention to the pace of the assessment. Clients might not be ready to give you all the information at once. Remember that denial and avoidance are adaptive strategies - not necessarily signs of resistance - and that these strategies give clients control in divulging sensitive material. Recognize the client's strengths and resources. For many triply diagnosed clients, HIV is an additional burden to a long list of burdens with which they have managed to live. Finally, a comprehensive clinical assessment acts as a prelude to any effective treatment/ management plan (DHHS, 1998).

Institutions with schools of nursing would benefit from collaboration and linkages as academic partners with community partnerships/campus community health partnerships, thus providing nurse educators with ready-made laboratories from a diverse group of service providers. This could be accomplished if you:

- Establish community advisory boards as a part of every substance abuse, mental health, and HIV/AIDS treatment program to ensure that public health services are client-centered.

- Recognize substance abuse, mental health, and HIV/AIDS as public health issues and train service providers on how to address the needs of those patients who are dually and triply diagnosed.

- Develop survey instruments.

- Conduct meta-analyses of studies that report on integration of services.

- Implement social marketing campaigns to reduce the stigma associated with substance abuse, mental health, and HIV, utilizing the arts to convey their message.

- Carry out meta-analyses or other studies to demonstrate the cost-effectiveness of the integration of services.

- Convey the message of co-occurring disorders as a serious public health issue and be strategic in identifying to whom the message is directed.

- Utilize strong advocacy and outreach methods to recruit family members to be involved in the delivery of care. Use public relations campaigns that target family members of affected populations and help normalize the issue.

- Continue the practice, through nursing education curricula, of preparing faculty to emphasize a population-based approach to health and illness, so that nurses become skilled in providing targeted education and awareness campaigns to affected communities.

Providers of HIV/AIDS, mental health, and substance abuse treatment services have frequently succeeded in implementing effective methods for consultation, collaboration, and even integration to address issues related to the systemic fragmentation of public health care. At the federal level, agencies such as SAMHSA (Substance Abuse and Mental Health Administration) and HRSA (Health Resources and Services Administration) emphasize that the reduction of professional boundaries in the delivery of services leads to improved integration of services when dealing with the impact of co-occurring disorders of mental health, HIV/AIDS and substance abuse disorders (CDM Group, 2008).

Progression toward service integration would begin with a formal dialogue among decision-making representatives and stakeholders from each of these disorders. This dialogue would have as its goal the development of a shared perspective and a common understanding of HIV/AIDS and the co-occurring disorder of mental illness and substance abuse disorders that impact patients' lives. These representatives would bring to the dialogue their collective experience regarding the broader issues of treatment, administration, and funding arrangements that would provide continuity and quality care for the individuals affected.

Some approaches to breaking down the professional norms identified earlier and enhancing a multidisciplinary educational approach to care include:

- Scheduling cross-training workshops at the state agency level for their public and/or private grantees and providers to improve knowledge and skills and to eliminate differences in treatment philosophies.

- Disseminating program or resource directories to grantees and providers and scheduling periodic meetings to ensure that directories are reviewed and updated on a yearly basis to increase knowledge of referral sources.

- Developing "network partners" through a Memorandum of Understanding among their grantees and setting up monthly or bimonthly meetings for grantees to network and share information.

- Establishing an interagency task force to address differences in data collection, education, and training. Members should include representatives from SAMHSA, HRSA, and CDC; state-level representatives in substance abuse, mental health, and HIV/AIDS; and providers representing the three disciplines. Financially supporting academic research initiatives that strive to elucidate reliable statistics on the nature and extent of co-occurring disorders should also be included.

- Establishing an interagency task force to 1) address the need for a consistent core language, value, and definitions and 2) establish clarity on the core clinical standards that can apply to HIV/AIDS, mental health and substance abuse across the clinical, community and systemic levels that all three systems can support.

Managing HIV/AIDS and Comorbidity Through an Integrated System of Care

The management of HIV/AIDS, mental health, and substance abuse has become a multidisciplinary task, demanding the time, attention, and skills of a diverse care team through "one-stop shopping," where all patients' needs can be met in one health care facility, thereby improving compliance with recommended treatment protocols. Therefore, it is imperative for care to be accessible through community-based organizations (CBOs) that are capable and willing to accept client referrals from formal and informal community-based agencies through established linkages, thereby expediting the referral process. Of equal importance is the planning process, where service providers network to create an infrastructure that meets the needs of individuals who are diagnosed with HIV/AIDS, mental illness and substance abuse. This process must include the promotion, coordination and integration among different groups of providers serving a population with multiple health issues.

An important feature of an integrated system of care is the extent to which communities and groups affected by these health conditions are represented in the planning and implementation of the services delivery system and the extent to which they are encouraged to actively participate in planning their care. Ideally, services for clients with these health problems should also be provided in the same manner that they are provided to populations with physical illnesses that exhibit a similar severity of illness.

The integration of services should in the long run foster improved quality of care, increased access to care, and economic efficiency. Coordination and collaboration among service providers in an integrated system of care are critical in order to avoid duplication and assure a complete continuum of care. In addition, collaboration among community leaders, including service providers; minority groups; those affected by HIV/AIDS, mental illness and substance abuse; and other interested individuals and organizations is essential to the success of a comprehensive primary care delivery model.

The essential characteristics of services integration include: proximity to a geographical location; service mix; funding elements; coordination of the client's treatment needs; linking the client with multiple primary care, substance abuse treatment and mental health providers; and assisting the client in obtaining social services such as entitlements, housing, home care, transportation, employment, or other identified needs.

IMPLICATIONS FOR EDUCATORS

The challenge for educators and service providers is to integrate HIV/AIDS, mental health and substance abuse care providers into an integrated model in which the contributions of each professional field is merged into a single treatment setting and treatment regimen. In such a context, students would be introduced to interdisciplinary teams that will meet on a regular basis to develop treatment plans and coordinate services for individual clients. In Figure 4-2, a holistic approach that shows a comprehensive approach to care is illustrated. Thus, within the context of a primary care setting, all elements of the co-occurring disorders of substance abuse, mental health and HIV/AIDS are represented. The challenge for educators then is not only to design a curriculum to address these issues, but also to expand an integrated service delivery pattern of care that will reflect this multidisciplinary approach.

Figure 4-2 provides an example of an holistic approach to clinical assessment of a client with co-occurring disorder of substance abuse, mental health and HIV/AIDS. It illustrates the need for comprehensive assessment of the client functioning and the need for nurse educators to prepare nursing students for more detailed comprehensive assessment than is customarily undertaken. It illustrates progression along the continuum to reach integration of services for the targeted population. Pathways are depicted to show the service providers' move from informal modes of information sharing and communication to coordination and cooperation to collaborations and finally to integration. The schematic demonstrates

Figure 4-2

Holistic Approach to Integration of Services for Clients with Co-Occurring Disorders of Substance Abuse, Mental Health, and HIV/AIDS

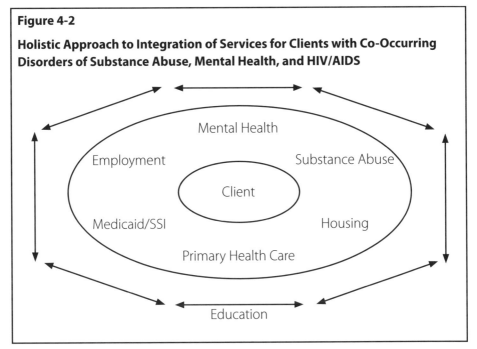

Source: Report of Workgroup Integrating States' HIV/AIDS, Mental Health and Substance Abuse Services. Presentation made at the Substance Abuse and Mental Health Administration (SAMHSA) conference in San Antonio, Texas, February 2002

that curricula should be developed to ensure that students learn that there are variable steps before the ultimate goal of integration is achieved.

For health educators, several implications follow:

1. The traditional professional boundaries that exist must give way to a broader array of interdisciplinary approaches in the curriculum, including team teaching from a variety of interdisciplinary cross-cutting competencies and perspective (nursing, environmental health sciences, epidemiology, health policy and management and social and behavioral sciences). This can be achieved through collaborative planning and teaching of core courses. Specialty areas and dual-degree programs are also effective ways of getting unacquainted faculty to work together. The provision of joint seminars, coterminous appointments and avoidance of split faculty lines are other practices to help achieve integration.

2. Pedagogical delivery must be broadened to include not only the learning styles of students, but clients' beliefs about sickness, health, religiosity, and their own illness.

3. The public health model of host-agent and environment must now be extended to emphasize public health genomics, which focus on "the study and application of knowledge about the elements of the human genome and their functions, including interactions with the environment, in relation to health and disease in populations" (CDC, 2004) in the curriculum.

4. Educators must include more in-depth teaching of the five-stage model of behavior changes (Prochaska & DiClemente, 1982) that has proven useful in assessing a client's level of readiness to change. This model is applicable to all forms of behavior, including drug use and sexual activities. It is also useful when examining issues related to HIV combination therapy adherence and includes the following elements:

    a. Pre-contemplation (no intention of changing)

    b. Contemplation (considering a change)

    c. Preparation (planning to act)

    d. Action (modifying his or her behavior)

    e. Maintenance (supporting the new behavior while avoiding relapse)

    Assessing where a client is along this continuum often helps determine the appropriateness of intervention efforts.

5. Practicum experiences that allow students to identify needed community referral sources are essential to the implementation of the integrated system of care.

6. Integration, linkages, and coordination through the use of specialists in the field serving as guest lecturers will ensure that nursing students can appreciate more fully a population-based perspective, thereby demonstrating that individuals with a history of mental illness, substance abuse and HIV/AIDS requires a comprehensive approach to clinical assessment, management and a planning process that fully incorporates the biopsychosocial complexity of living with these conditions. For these dual and triply diagnosed clients, the clinical assessment must be multidimensional.

CONCLUSION

HIV/AIDS has been associated with significant psychological impacts in terms of increased morbidity, premature mortality, and staggering medical costs. Of course, cost cannot be measured only in terms of health care costs, but must be addressed with respect to the damage on humans in terms of premature death, and the debilitating effects and suffering of HIV-infected and affected persons. Patients with co-occurring disorders of HIV/AIDS, substance abuse and mental illness present a significant challenge to health care professionals, clinical educators and caregivers. Individuals with co-occurring disorders may serve as markers for impaired functioning and well being. Inclusion of sufficiently educated professionals with multidisciplinary backgrounds to identify and treat such conditions may reduce unnecessary utilization of other health services and improve health-related quality of life in persons with HIV/AIDS, substance abuse, and mental disorders.

A model of integrated care that educators can use as a basis for helping students understand the impact of comorbidities and the need for holistic care for the HIV population is critical. Implications for educators includes the need for interdisciplinary collaborations to implement the model of care that should include treatment for HIV infection, substance use/abuse, and mental illness, along with provision for psychotherapy in clinical settings, social rehabilitation and education.

REFERENCES

Beckett, M. K., Collins, R. L., Burnam, M. A., Kanouse, D. E., Beckman, R., Bing, E. G., et al. (2007). Mental health and substance abuse issues among people with HIV: Lessons from HCSUS. [Research brief]. Santa Monica, CA: Rand.

Berkman, A., Pilowsky, D., Zybert, P., Leu, C-S., Sohler, N., & Susser, E. (2005). The impact of substance dependence on HIV sexual risk-reduction among men with severe mental illness. *AIDS Care, 17*(5) 635-639.

Bing, E. G., Burnam, M. A., Longshore, D., Fleishman, J. A., Sherbourne, C. D., London, A. S., et al. (2001). Psychiatric disorders and drug use among human immunodeficiency virus-infected adults in the United States. *Archives of General Psychiatry, 58*(8), 721-728.

Blank, M. B., Mandell, D. S., Aiken, L., & Hadley, T. R. (2002). Co-occurrence of HIV and serious mental illness among Medicaid recipients. *Psychiatric Services, 53*(7), 868-873.

Carey, M. P., Carey, K.B., & Kalichman, S. C. (1997). Risk for human immunodeficiency virus (HIV) infection among persons with severe mental illness. *Clinical Psychology Review, 17*(3), 271-299.

CDM Group. (2008). TIP 37: *Substance abuse treatment for persons with HIV/AIDS*. Rockville, MD: SAMHSA.

Centers for Disease Control and Prevention. (2004). Genomics for public health practitioners. Atlanta, GA: Author.

Centers for Disease Control and Prevention. (2007). A heightened national response to the HIV/AIDS crisis among African Americans. Retrieved from http://www.cdc.gov/hiv/topics/aa/resources/reports/heightendresponse.htm

Cunningham, W. E., Andersen, R. M., Katz, M. H., Stein, M. D., Turner, B. J., Crystal, S., et al. (1999). The impact of competing subsistence needs and barriers on access to medical care for persons with human immunodeficiency virus receiving care in the United States. *Medical Care, 37*, 1270-1281.

Department of Health and Human Services (DHHS). (1998). *Mental health care for people living with HIV/AIDS: A practical guide* (DHHS Research Triangle Institute Project #6031). Research Triangle Park, NC: Research Triangle Institute.

Dickey, B., Normand, S. T., Weiss, R. D., Drake, R. E., & Azeni, H. (2002). Medical morbidity, mental illness, and substance use disorders. *Psychiatric Services, 53*(7), 861-867.

Dixon, L., Postrado, L., Delahanty, J., Fischer, P. J., & Lehman, A. (1999). The association of medical comorbidity in schizophrenia with poor physical and mental health. *Journal of Nervous and Mental Disease, 187*, 496-502.

Fleishman, J. A., Gebo, K. A., Reilly, E. D., Conviser, R., Mathews, W. C., Korthuis, P. T., et al. (2005). Hospital and outpatient health services utilization among HIV-infected adults in care 2000-2002. *Medical Care, 43*(3), 40-52.

Hutton, H. E., Lyketsos, C. G., Zenilman, J. M., Thompson, R. E., & Erbelding, E. J. (2004). Depression and HIV risk behaviors among patients in a sexually transmitted disease clinic. *American Journal of Psychiatry, 161*, 912-914.

Ickovics, J. R., Hamburger, M. E., Vlahov, D., Schoenbaum, E. E., Schuman, P., Boland, R. J., et al. (2001). Mortality, CD4 cell count decline, and depressive symptoms among HIV-seropositive women. *Journal of the American Medical Association, 285*, 1466-1474.

Jeste, D. V., Gladsjo, J. A., Lindamer, L. A., & Lacro, J. P. (1996). Medical comorbidity in schizophrenia. *Schizophrenia Bulletin, 22*, 413-430.

Kaiser Family Foundation. (2008). Black Americans and HIV/AIDS. *HIV/AIDS Policy Fact Sheet*. Retrieved from http://www.kff.org/hivaids/upload/6089-061.pdf

Lyketsos, C. G., Hoover, D. R., Guccione, M., Dew, M. A., Wesch, J. E., Bing, E.G., et al. (1996). Changes in depressive symptoms as AIDS develops. The Multicenter AIDS Cohort Study. *American Journal of Psychiatry, 153*(11), 1430-1437.

Lyketsos, C. G., Hutton, H., Fishman, M., Schwartz, J., & Treisman, G. J. (1996). Psychiatric morbidity on entry to an HIV primary care clinic. *AIDS, 10*(9), 1033-1039.

Marquart, J. M., & Konrad, E. L. (1996). Evaluating initiatives to integrate human services. *New Directions for Evaluation, No. 69*. San Francisco: Jossey-Bass.

NASTAD. (2005). *HIV prevention: Focus on mental health and HIV/AIDS*. Washington, DC: Author.

Prochaska, J. O., & DiClemente, C. C. (1982). Transtheoretical therapy: Toward a more integrated model of change. *Psychotherapy: Theory, Research, and Practice, 19*(3), 276-288.

Rothbard, A., Metraux, S., & Blank, M. (2003). Cost of care for Medicaid recipients with serious mental illness and HIV infection or AIDS. *Psychiatric Services, 54*(9), 1240-1246.

Shapiro, M. F., Morton, S. C., McCaffrey, D. F., Senterfitt, J. W., Fleishman, J. A., Perlman. J. F., et al. (1999). Variations in the care of HIV-infected adults in the United States: Results from the HIV Cost and Services Utilization Study. *Journal of the American Medical Association, 281*(24), 2305-2315.

Sherbourne, C., Hays, R., Fleishman, J., Vitiello, E. B., Margruder, K., Bing, E., et al. (2000). Impact of psychiatric condition on health-related quality of life in persons with HIV infection. *American Journal of Psychiatry, 157*(2), 248-254.

Stall, R., Mills, T. C., Williamson, J., Hart, T., Greenwood, G., Paul, J., et al. (2003). Association of co-occurring psychosocial health problems and increased vulnerability to HIV/AIDS among urban men who have sex with men. *American Journal of Public Health, 93*(6), 939-942.

Susser, E., Colson, P., Jandorf, L., Berkman, A., Lavelle, J., Fennig, S., et al. (1997). HIV infection among young adults with psychotic disorders. *American Journal of Psychiatry, 154*(6), 864-866.

Susser, E., Valencia, E., & Conover, S. (1993). Prevalence of HIV infection among psychiatric patients in a New York City men's shelter. *American Journal of Public Health, 83*(4), 568-570.

U.S. Department of Health and Human Services (HHS), National Institute of Mental Health. (1992). *Epidemiologic Catchment Area Study, 1980-1985*. Rockville, MD: U.S. Dept. of Health and Human Services, National Institute of Mental Health, 1992. Ann Arbor, MI: Inter-university Consortium for Political and Social Research, 1994.

Workgroup Report [Unpublished]. (2002, February). *Integrating states' HIV/AIDS, mental health, and substance abuse services*. Presentation at a conference sponsored by SAMHSA in San Antonio, Texas.

ACKNOWLEDGMENTS

This chapter was made possible by grant number 5G11HD043805 to Lincoln University Office of Research Development Planning and Coordination (ORDPC) from NICHD. The content is solely the responsibility of the author and does not necessarily represent the official views of the National Institute of Child Health and Human Development or the National Institutes of Health. Thanks also to Kevin Favor, PhD, Penny Kinsey, PhD, Jonice Louden, MSc, and Janis Walker, BS, for their comments on an earlier draft of this chapter.

CHAPTER 5

MENTORSHIP AND NURSE EDUCATORS: A MODEL FOR DIVERSITY

Willar F. White-Parson, PhD, APRN, BC, FAAN

INTRODUCTION

Mentoring is a concept that has been used by business, education, and other professional fields to socialize individuals to new roles. In older professions, it has been widely recognized that the careful nurturing and coaching of aspiring professionals through a mentoring relationship is essential in ensuring the highest level of achievement, success, and satisfaction. Mentoring is described as an interaction between an experienced and an inexperienced individual, with the experienced individual taking an active role in the professional development of the junior person. The concept of mentoring has also been described as an empowering relationship between novice and experienced nurses and is a best practice that fosters successful nursing careers (Daniels, 2004).

The nurse educator as a mentor plays an essential developmental role in the professional socialization, and personal and career development of junior-level nurse educators. The recruitment and retention of talent in nursing education, as well as the continuing support of potential nurse educators, will require the adoption of formal mentoring programs and the expansion of such programs throughout the nursing profession. Seasoned nurse educators must grow nurse educators. This statement simply means that mentoring and coaching by senior-level educators will develop future educators who will in turn leave their legacy of contributions to the profession and the improvement of nursing education.

Mentoring is beneficial for the novice teacher. One of the key benefits is that it can increase the novice teacher's retention in the teaching profession (Kajs, 2002). Experienced nursing teachers, with practical knowledge of the faculty role, are an important resource for new nursing teachers. However, this important resource will be lost, given the projected retirements and resignations of nursing faculty for the next 20 years (National League for Nursing, 2002). This chapter will describe the Mentorship Connection Project that was designed to retain junior-level African American nursing faculty in two institutions of higher education. This project was initiated in a historically black college/university (HBCU) in the Hampton Roads region of Virginia. It was also implemented in an HBCU in the southeastern region of North Carolina.

THE CONCEPT OF MENTORING

The concept of mentoring has its roots in ancient Greek mythology. In Homer's Odyssey, King Odysseus left home to participate in the siege of Troy. In his 10-year absence, Odysseus appointed his good friend Mentor to educate and guide his son Telemachus. Mentor nurtured, protected, taught, and guided Telemachus to his rightful place in Greek society (Gopee, 2007). The concept of "mentoring" was thus conceived. Throughout history, there are many instances of the more experienced guiding, teaching, and nurturing those who are less experienced. Over the years, many trades and professions used a master-apprentice relationship to provide guidance, direction, advice, and practical knowledge of a master craft. Although the master-apprentice approach has largely been abandoned in modern education, the concept of mentoring has persisted throughout time. It has been concluded that mentoring is an effective strategy when it is guided by a caring framework of trust, commitment, and compassion (Wagner & Seymour, 2007). Mentoring is defined as a process by which persons of rank, achievement, and prestige, instruct, counsel, guide, and facilitate the development of others identified as protégés. Historically, mentors were senior persons in terms of age and experience who provided the protégé with information, advice, and emotional support over a significant period of time. The relationship was described as a substantial commitment by both parties, and mentors also used their influence to further the career of the protégé (Byrne & Keefe, 2002).

Vance (2002) noted that informal mentoring was not new to nursing; however, to capitalize more fully on the benefits, formal mentorship programs in nursing were needed and currently mentoring has unfolded into clinical, educational, leadership, academia, and other settings. Although the mentoring literature addresses definition, role description, and process, there has been little attention to building mentorship models in nursing. Building on models from other disciplines, Byrne and Keefe (2002, p. 395) described five mentoring models in use today: traditional, team, inclusion, horizontal peer-to-peer mentorship, and a vertical/horizontal "mentoring forward" model. These models are helpful in organizing mentoring strategies.

It has also been noted that there are different types of mentoring relationships and that compatibility may differ. Facilitated mentoring, or matching the novice with an expert, may or may not result in a mentoring relationship. Matches do not always work. Unstructured or nonfacilitated mentoring occurs when the novice and the expert are inadvertently drawn together, usually the result of some mutual interest or attraction. Then a unique, reciprocal, trusting relationship develops over an unspecified period of time (Shaffer et al., 2000). Because of the chemistry of the mentoring relationship, most experiences are personal, intense, and emotionally charged. The mentor has a stake in the future of the protégé and there is always an element of risk associated with intense relationships (Desjardins, 2006). Roach (2002) noted that specific mentoring characteristics are closely aligned with caring attributes of intentional presence, respect, compassion, competence, confidence, conscience, and commitment. To reach the desired outcomes of a transformative relationship, empowerment of the other, and mutual personal growth, mentoring needs to be reflective and meaningful for both mentors and mentees, beyond the cognitive and affective levels of understanding.

De Janasz and Sullivan (2004) suggested that mentoring has been typified by a one-to-one mentor-mentee relationship that begins early in the mentee's career and continues as the mentee advances in his or her career within a single institution. However, over time, as academic careers have become characterized by mobility, flexibility, and specific project work, the concept of mentorship has broadened to include relationships between multiple mentors and mentees and relationships that span distance and institutions. It should be noted that the model that is presented in this chapter is a one-to-one mentor-mentee relationship that occurs in the same institution.

THE NURSE FACULTY SHORTAGE: A CURRENT ISSUE

The shortage of nurses in this country is well documented. The federal government estimates that there will be one million fewer nurses than needed by 2020. The shortage of nurse educators is also a national problem that is negatively impacting schools of nursing. Nursing schools do not have the capacity to accept the number of qualified applicants to the nursing schools, hence the shortage continues. Many schools of nursing are unable to recruit and/or retain nurse educators. The shortage of nurse educators is a result of many factors, including: (1) faculty age that continues to climb, narrowing the number of productive years nurse educators will be working; (2) the wave of faculty retirements expected across the country over the next decade; (3) higher compensation in clinical and private-sector settings, which is luring current and potential nurse educators away from teaching; and (4) master's and doctoral programs in nursing that are not producing a large enough pool of potential nurse educators to meet the demand (American Association of Colleges of Nursing, 2006). A factor that impacted the development of the Mentorship Connection Project was a pool of junior-level faculty members who were nurse practitioners and were functioning in the role of nurse educators without additional education in such areas as curriculum development and the teaching of nursing. The National League for Nursing (2002) concluded that more attention needs to be given to the teaching/pedagogical component of the nurse educator role. It is critical that all nurse educators know about teaching, learning, and evaluation, and have knowledge and skills in curriculum development, assessment of program outcomes and being an effective member of an academic community.

To address the above-noted issues and other issues concerning the shortage of nursing faculty in the nation's nursing schools, the American Federation of Teachers' Healthcare and Higher Education divisions convened a task force of nurse leaders, who made the following recommendations:

Recommendation 1. Create a work environment that is conducive to recruiting new nurses and retaining those nurse educators already in the profession;

Recommendation 2. Increase the amount of public and private money available to properly fund nursing programs and provide for the expansion of nursing education programs while also working to improve the image of the profession;

Recommendation 3. Develop and implement updated and nontraditional methods of instruction to prepare future nurse educators; and

Recommendation 4. Utilize faculty and facilities in a collaborative manner consistent with quality nursing education, academic independence of nursing institutions and the best use of faculty time (American Federation of Teachers, 2005).

The development and implementation of the Mentorship Connection Project is a strategy that can be classified under Recommendation one in addressing the shortage of nurse educators, which is exacerbating the overall nurse shortage.

THE IMPACT OF MENTORING ON DIVERSITY IN NURSING EDUCATION

Cultural and racial diversity continue to permeate nursing practice and education as major demographic shifts occur in the United States. Current trends indicate that as the need for culturally competent nurses increases, the number of racial/ethnic students and faculty members continues to decrease (Robinson, 2000). A strategy is needed to address this situation in the nursing profession and the concept of mentoring is an effective approach. The utilization of mentoring as a framework can better ensure the retention of minority nursing faculty in the academic roles of nurse educator, nurse scholar, service provider, and community leader.

Recruiting and retaining an adequate workforce in nursing education is a priority as well as a challenge, and creating an environment that respects individual differences must be incorporated in the mentoring process. Mentoring is a tool that can ease difficult faculty situations and promote self-awareness, personal and professional growth, and leadership. Insensitivity to cultural differences in faculty is one situation that can lead to diversity issues. Resolution of these issues is sometimes beyond the traditional modes of teaching-learning, academic relationships, and professional socialization. The utilization of mentoring has been noted to be a motivating framework for the reciprocal growth of faculty (Zachary, 2005).

Mentoring can be an effective way to enhance organizational readiness to respond to the challenge of diversity in the academic setting. Mentoring activities must be implemented to recruit and retain a culturally and racially diverse cadre of nursing faculty who will not only serve as mentors and role models for students, but will also create a culturally sensitive teaching-learning environment. Without a culturally and racially diverse faculty, goals related to preparing culturally competent nurses cannot be fully realized.

Glanville and Porche (2000) noted that, because of the small distribution of nursing faculty of color in higher education, institutions must focus on a faculty development process that achieves job satisfaction and retention. It is recommended that mentoring be an essential component of each university's faculty development program and that this process must be valued and accommodated within the organizational structure of the institution. Faculty who participate in mentoring should have organizational support. The essential elements required from the university are time and access to resources. Faculty who actively participate in mentoring should have this recognized as either service to the university or community leadership. The primary focus of the university mission will impact the type of mentoring processes implemented.

The Mentor/Mentee Partnership

Mentoring is an excellent framework that can assist in transforming the academic environment while enhancing the faculty's potential. The mentoring process is a longitudinal relationship that develops through at least four stages over time. Greene and Puetzer (2002) describe these stages as initiation, cultivation, separation, and redefinition. The first stage, initiation, involves mentor and mentee meeting, getting to know each other, and setting goals. To ensure the best success in relationship building, it is suggested that mentoring and being mentored are voluntary endeavors and the pairing should be self-selecting. As a trusting relationship matures, the pair moves to the second stage, cultivation. In this stage, information is shared and joint problem solving promotes respectful confrontation and exploration of alternatives. Successful mentoring empowers the mentee to move forward in his or her career and personal life. This process leads the pair to the third stage, separation (from their original novice-expert roles), and allows for a fourth stage of mutually redefining the mentoring relationship toward long-term friendship or going separate ways.

Mentoring activities provide benefits to the faculty and the parent institution. Mentoring activities heighten competence and productivity, foster empowerment, attract and retain talented faculty, and increase the number of ambassadors for the institution.

Mentor

A mentor is defined as a seasoned individual in an organization who guides and advises junior-level individuals, opens doors for the individuals, and teaches the individuals the "ropes." It is also noted that the benefits of being a mentor lie in the quality of the mentoring relationship. Mentors who are successful find themselves ultimately rewarded by the growth and achievement of their protégés. Good mentors benefit from feedback by the protégé; there is mutuality in the sharing of knowledge and information. Protégés may also assist mentors with their work, learning from mentors while also providing a service. The novice researcher or the novice practitioner working with and assisting a more experienced colleague is illustrative of such a relationship. As documented previously, a mentor is a trusted and experienced adviser who has a direct interest in the development and education of a less experienced individual. A mentor generally serves in a supportive role, is that person who achieves a one-to-one developmental relationship with a learner, and is the one whom the learner identifies as having enabled personal growth to take place. The relationship between the mentor and mentee is unique. The mentor assumes numerous roles, while contributing to a sustaining relationship of shared interests and goals. A mentor makes a commitment to an assigned mentee to help him or her grow in the organization's culture and become a productive and effective member in the organization (Gibson, 2004). Mentors must also have certain qualities to be effective. These identified qualities should be considered in the selection process of a mentor. The qualities are as follows:

- a role model and/or expert in area of specialty
- commits to the mentoring process
- sensitive to individual circumstances
- encourages and motivates others
- creates a supportive learning environment
- has the respect of others at the institution
- possesses the knowledge and influence needed to be a mentor
- willing to share knowledge
- possesses good interpersonal communication skills

A high level of commitment is required for a mentor to effectively function in the mentoring relationship. A mentor may function in many roles and any of these roles will enhance the mentoring relationship. Gibson (2004) identified and described the following roles:

Adviser: Provide mentee with useful information about the institution; offer mentee an avenue for social and emotional support during his/her transition into the institution; familiarize mentee with the numerous sources and resources located throughout the community.

Role model: Teach mentee how to succeed in the institution by modeling how individuals in senior positions conduct themselves and interact with others.

Coach: Advise mentee on how to accomplish his/her goals and provide feedback. Help the mentee develop alternatives to address work-related problems or create learning opportunities. Teach the mentee organizational and professional skills and help "decode" the institutional culture; create an atmosphere where mentees can learn from their own and each other's experiences, mistakes, and successes as well as from their mentors' experiences.

Supporter: Encourage the participation of the mentee on committees to increase visibility; enhance the mentee's self-esteem through supportive, nonjudgmental discussions and "pep talks." Help the mentee establish a professional network.

Mentee

A mentee is defined as a junior-level or new member of an organization, who would benefit from the knowledge and support of a senior member of the organization relative to professional socialization. Research has documented that new nursing faculty often feel a lack of support and recognition by colleagues and that a mentoring relationship can assist the new faculty member to overcome the feelings of isolation and enhance professional socialization (National League for Nursing, 2006, p. 2).

Benefits of mentoring for a mentee: Each university and/or nursing program has its own culture, a system with distinct structural features, role relations, informal system dynamics and environmental stresses and strains. Junior-level or new faculty members should not be left alone to discover this culture or navigate in it. Research suggests that new faculty members who have the assistance of a mentor perform better both as teachers and as researchers (Boykins & Schoenhofer, 2001).

Although new faculty members have responsibility for their own growth and success, having a mentor offers, among many other things, an avenue to become acclimated more quickly to the institutional culture. The effectiveness of having a mentoring relationship depends on the active participation of the mentee as well as the mentor. Some benefits of being mentored are as follows:

- Expand understanding of the institution's policies and procedures

- Receive advice on how to balance teaching, research, community service and other responsibilities, and set professional priorities

- Obtain knowledge of informal rules for advancement (as well as political and substantive pitfalls to be avoided)

- Obtain knowledge about developing a portfolio of accomplishments
- Increase understanding on how to build a circle of friends and contacts both within and outside one's department or team
- Provide a perspective on long-term career planning
- Enhance networking within the institution and to other colleagues
- Increase communication about what activities in other areas of the institution might be beneficial to career advancement
- Expand growth, a sense of competence, identity, and effectiveness as a professional
- Provide an outlet to discuss concerns
- Increase value to the institution
- Learn to cope with the formal and informal structure of the institution
- Provide a successful and productive integration into the institution

MENTORSHIP CONNECTION PROJECT

The Mentorship Connection Project is the result of challenges faced by a Department of Nursing in an HBCU, where the majority of the junior-level faculty members were nurse practitioners who were hired to function in the role of nurse educator. Many of these faculty members did not feel adequately prepared to function as nurse educators. Without some means of support, this environment was not conducive for the retention of faculty, some of whom exhibited the potential to become excellent nurse educators.

In an attempt to deal with these problems, a faculty mentoring program was designed and implemented in the fall semester of 2001. The initial plan for the project was presented and approved by the Department of Nursing faculty organization for the academic year 2000-01. The Mentorship Connection Project was designed to enhance the role transition of junior-level nursing faculty to the role of academician in an institution of higher education. The project addressed a need of the Department of Nursing in maintaining, supporting, and nurturing faculty. A review of the literature provided data that supported the development of a faculty mentoring program that was meaningful and substantive. The purpose for the program was clearly delineated and the purpose for the program was congruent with the mission, vision, and values of the parent institution and the Department of Nursing.

THE MENTORSHIP CONNECTION PROJECT CONCEPTUAL MODEL

A conceptual model has been defined as a set of relatively abstract and general concepts that address the phenomena of central interest of a discipline, the propositions that broadly describe those concepts, and the propositions that state relatively abstract and general relations between two or more of the concepts (Fawcett, 2005). The Mentorship Connection Project's model illustrates the interrelationship between the three major concepts of this model. This model is a visual display of the concepts that formed the paradigm of this mentoring project. The interrelationship of the concepts of Organization, Mentor, and Mentee dictates that there is an interaction/reaction relationship between each component. The model is schematically depicted in Figure 5-1, which illustrates the connection between the mentor, the organization, and the mentee.

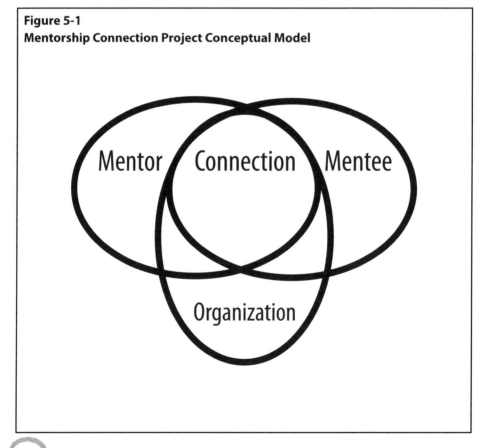

Figure 5-1
Mentorship Connection Project Conceptual Model

Mentor / Connection / Mentee

Organization

PROGRAM DEVELOPMENT PHASE

The development phase of the Mentorship Connection Project was a priority for the Department of Nursing and every effort was made to foster success. Participants in the project were given two hours of release time as a part of their teaching workload. The development phase of this project included the following steps:

- Conducted organizational needs assessment

- Established program objectives

- Obtained organizational commitment for the project

Needs Assessment: A departmental needs assessment was conducted during the end of the fall semester 2000. Ninety-five percent of the faculty members were in favor of the proposed project. The junior-level faculty members were excited about the prospect of being mentored and the senior-level faculty members were excited about serving as mentors.

Project Objectives: The project objectives were developed with input from the entire nursing faculty. To enhance program success, it was important to incorporate faculty input. The project objectives are as follows:

- To enhance the mentee's teaching performance and professional development

- To enhance the transition of junior-level faculty into the role of academician

- To increase the retention of new faculty and junior-level faculty

- To orient the junior-level faculty to the university and the role of the academician

- To enhance the understanding of the mission, vision, and values of the department and the university

- To promote personal and professional well-being for both the mentor and mentee

- To assist the mentee in meeting professorial expectations and/or challenges

- To develop an incentive program that encourages mentor/mentee participation in the Mentorship Connection Project

- To development faculty ambassadors to enhance faculty recruitment

Organizational Commitment: The Mentorship Connection Project was an initiative of the department head and faculty of the nursing program. This was a strategy to strengthen and maintain the faculty workforce in the department. The commitment and support of the mentoring project by the nursing faculty was a plus for program success and faculty participation. The project's purpose and objectives clearly delineated a congruency with the mission, vision, and goals of the department of nursing and the university. The administrative support was also based on a departmental need to raise teaching standards and to expand the ranks of the profession at a time when the pool of experienced teachers was growing small. It was felt that a mentoring program: (1) could be used as a recruitment tool; (2) could improve teacher retention rates; and (3) could help improve the skills and knowledge of both the junior and senior faculty members. It has been noted that mentoring programs help ensure that new teachers have access to the accumulated instructional knowledge and expertise of their senior colleagues in ways that contribute to student success.

PROGRAM IMPLEMENTATION PHASE

The Mentorship Connection Project was implemented in August 2001 in the Department of Nursing of an urban institution of higher education. The success of this project had implications for the department, the school, and the university as a model for mentoring. A relationship with a supportive, active mentor has been shown to contribute significantly to a junior-level faculty member's professional development and satisfaction (Vance, 2002).

The project was a two-semester mentoring program targeted to new and/or junior-level faculty. The two-semester time frame could be extended if the mentoring pair was agreeable. If the mentee desired additional mentoring and the mentor was not available, a new mentor would be recruited. In cases of changing commitments, incompatibility, or where the relationship was not fulfilling, either mentor or mentee could seek confidential advice from the department head. It was important that change could be made without prejudice or fault. The individual team member should be encouraged to participate in the mentoring process and another individual should be recruited.

SELECTION CRITERIA FOR MENTORING TEAMS

Mentor

Criteria were established for recruiting and training individuals who could serve as mentors. A major criterion for the selection of a mentor was the length of time the individual had served in a faculty role. The minimum of five years in a faculty role was mandatory. Five years was considered essential for faculty role development. Other selection requirements asked that an individual:

- Demonstrate an understanding of academia and the professorial role
- Demonstrate role expertise and promote role socialization
- Provide a career vision by role modeling and offering guidance
- Demonstrate a reflective practice that would enable the mentee to determine how and why decisions are made and how these decisions influence positive outcomes
- Be available to participate as a mentor
- Demonstrate a sensitivity for cultural diversity

Mentor Responsibilities

- Meet regularly with the mentee as determined by mutual agreement
- Maintain confidentiality of shared information
- Meet monthly with the mentoring teams/other mentors and mentees ("brown bag" luncheons)
- Actively participate in the mentoring process
- Provide information about university politics and campus resources
- Provide collaboration about research and/or publications
- Assist with research and grant writing opportunities
- Encourage involvement in professional networking
- Provide guidance and assistance to mentee whenever it is needed
- Provide the university's requirements for tenure and promotion, assist with the development of mentee's tenure/promotion plan, and time frame toward meeting those requirements
- Assist with balancing professional and personal commitments
- Support the concept of diversity

The role and responsibilities of mentors were fully explained by the department head and mentoring workshops were provided before the mentors signed a contract to serve. Mentoring workshops were departmentally sponsored and were held both on and off campus. The extent of the mentoring relationship had to be fully understood by participants in the project.

Mentee

Criteria for the selection of mentees were: (1) the individual's willingness to participate in the project as a mentee; (2) attending a mentoring workshop; and (3) a signed contract to be a mentee. There were five mentoring pairs initially participating in the project. All of the junior-level faculty members were willing to participate in the project. There was one mentee assigned per mentor. The following responsibilities were presented to the mentees before the contract was signed.

Mentee Responsibilities

- Meet regularly with the mentor
- Maintain confidentiality
- Meet monthly for "brown bag" luncheons with the mentoring teams
- Provide and give feedback of the experience for the evaluative process
- Take responsibility for own growth and success
- Follow through on referrals from mentor relative to professional networking
- Actively participate in the mentoring process
- Seek mentor's guidance and assistance whenever it is needed
- Develop a plan and time frame for meeting tenure and promotion requirements
- Attend professional seminars on mentoring
- Seek assistance with balancing professional and personal commitments
- Document progress toward both short- and long-term goals

The project in the second setting was much smaller. There were two mentoring teams and the same procedural process was implemented.

Program Evaluation

The evaluation plan for the Mentorship Connection Project was designed to measure the program objectives/outcomes. Program evaluation was managed by the department head. Program evaluation consisted of ongoing, monthly evaluations conducted by the mentoring teams. Data collection was used by the department head for program revision and expansion. An evaluation and tracking process to measure short- and long-term outcomes of the program was implemented by the department head. Both the mentors and mentees were required to evaluate themselves, the mentor/mentee partnership, and mentoring team activities. These evaluative data were collected monthly. When the monthly "brown bag" luncheons were held, this group mentoring activity facilitated an exchange of experiences among junior- and senior-level faculty. The project's success was dependent on the mentees, their mentors, and their department taking an active role in the acclimation process of an academician.

Both the mentor and mentee reported that they learned, grew and developed through the relationship, thereby motivating and stimulating each other in their respective roles. The mentoring teams viewed themselves as colleagues helping each other learn and grow. Each member of these faculty teams were empowered by the collegial relationship. Other benefits noted by the project participants included the following:

- Gained increased respect and recognition from others in the university as individuals who have the ability to identify, encourage, and promote other employees

- Extended their professional network to other mentors and mentees

- Contributed to the professional development of new employees and/or junior level faculty

- Experienced professional and personal growth

- Used or developed additional skills not required in current position

- Enhanced their value to others

- Became more sensitive to diversity

CONCLUSION

The Mentorship Connection Project model has been implemented in both an urban university and a rural university. Although the level of effectiveness has been different between the universities, results indicated that the five mentoring pairs at the urban university completed the mentoring process and reported positive results. The two mentoring pairs at the rural university were not able to complete the process because of the death of one mentor and the resignation of the second mentor. Although these factors caused a disruption in the process, the faculty members who volunteered to be mentored were positive about their experience and were willing to become involved in another mentoring relationship in the department of nursing. The department plans to restart the project. Regardless of the programs' differences, the faculty members at both universities reported that mentoring is an effective tool for enhancing diversity, and retaining and socializing nursing faculty.

The retention of nurse educators is a significant nursing workforce issue and needs to be addressed by nursing educators. One solution to boost the retention of junior-level nurse educators and/or new faculty is the utilization of mentoring activities by seasoned nurse educators to enhance the professional socialization of this cohort of colleagues. Two schools of nursing implemented this strategy (a formal mentoring program) to retain new and junior-level faculty members.

It is concluded that the impact of mentoring programs is dependent upon effective communication, clear objectives, and mutual interest and mutual respect between the mentor and mentee. The implementation of mentoring activities can have tremendous benefit for nursing programs, universities, faculty mentoring teams, nursing students, and nursing education. The National League for Nursing (2006) suggests that mentoring is relevant across the entire career continuum of a nurse educator, and encompasses orientation to the faculty role; socialization to the academic community; development of teaching, research, and service skills; and facilitation of the growth of future leaders in nursing and nursing education.

The need for an increase in the number of culturally diverse nursing faculty in institutions of higher education is imperative. To address the need and accomplish cultural diversity initiatives, there must be university leadership commitment, structural linkages, organizational support and continuous assessment of this goal (Frusti, Niesen, & Campion, 2003).

REFERENCES

American Association of Colleges of Nursing. (2006). *Fact sheet: Nursing faculty shortage.* Washington, DC: Author.

American Federation of Teachers. (2005). *Recommendations of the AFT Nurse Faculty Shortage Task Force.* Washington, DC: Author.

Boykin, A., & Schenhofer, S. (2001). *Nursing as caring: A model for transforming practice.* Boston: Jones and Bartlett.

Byrne, M. W., & Keefe, M. R. (2002). Building research competence in nursing through mentoring. *Journal of Nursing Scholarship, 34*, 391-396.

Daniels, M. (2004). Mentoring: Link to the future. *Reflections on Nursing Leadership, 30*, 24-25, 44.

De Janasz, S. C., & Sullivan, S. E. (2004). Multiple mentoring in academe: Developing the professional network. *Journal of Vocational Behavior, 64*, 263-283.

Desjardins, M. (2006). Mentoring: A new video highlights this mutually beneficial relationship. *American Journal of Nursing, 106*(11), 72AAA.

Fawcett J. (2005). *Contemporary nursing knowledge: Analysis and evaluation of nursing models and theories* (2nd ed.). Philadelphia: F.A. Davis.

Frusti, D., Niesen, K., & Campion, J. (2003). Creating a culturally competent organization: Use of the Diversity Competency Model. *Journal of Nursing Administration, 33*, 31-38.

Gibson, S. K. (2004). Being mentored: The experience of women faculty. *Journal of Career Development, 30*, 173-188.

Glanville, C., & Porche, D. (2000). Graduate nursing faculty: Ensuring cultural and racial diversity through faculty development. *Journal of Multicultural Nursing & Health. Winter,* 1-9.

Gopee, N. (2007). *Mentoring and supervision in healthcare.* Thousand Oaks, CA: Sage.

Greene, M. T., & Puetzer, M. (2002). The value of mentoring: A strategic approach to retention and recruitment. *Journal of Nursing Care Quality, 17*, 67-74.

Kajs, L. T. (2002). Framework for designing a mentoring program for novice teachers. *Mentoring and Tutoring, 10*, 57-69.

National League for Nursing. (2002). [Position statement]. *The preparation of nurse educators.* New York: Author.

National League for Nursing. (2006). [Position statement]. *Mentoring of nursing faculty.* New York: Author.

Roach, M. (2002). *Caring, the human mode of being* (2nd ed.). Ottawa, Ontario, Canada: CHA Press.

Robinson, J. (2000). Increasing students' cultural sensitivity. A step toward greater diversity in nursing. *Nurse Educator, 25*, 131-135.

Shaffer, B., Tallarica, B., & Walsh, J. (2000). Win-win mentoring. *Nursing Management, 31*, 32-34.

Vance, C. (2002). Mentoring: A professional obligation. *Creative Nursing, 8*, 4-9.

Wagner, L., & Seymour, M. (2007). A model of caring mentorship for nursing. *Journal for Nurses in Staff Development, 23*, 201-211.

Zachary, L. (2005). *Creating a mentoring culture. The organization's guide.* San Francisco: Jossey-Bass.

CHAPTER 6
USING SIMULATION TO ENHANCE CULTURAL COMPETENCY

Richardean Benjamin, PhD, RN, MPH, PMHCNS-BC, ANEF

Introduction

The changing demographics of the United States population and the nursing shortage have been described as two of the most important issues facing nursing and health care today (Yoder, 2001). The rising numbers of ethnic and racial minorities is expected to surpass current levels by the year 2020, with Hispanics (18 percent) and African Americans (13 percent) accounting for the two largest groups of minorities (U.S. Census Bureau, 2006). By 2050, the African American population will have nearly doubled in size, reaching 61.4 million (U.S. Census Bureau, 2006). Increased numbers of diverse patients, due to rising numbers of minorities in the population, will require nurses with the appropriate skills to practice in a complex health care system and nurses who are able to care for sicker patients, yet, can be sensitive to their needs.

The shortage of registered nurses in the United States could reach levels as high as 500,000 by 2025, thus adding increased pressure on schools of nursing to produce more graduates in a shorter period of time (Buerhaus, 2008). In addition, calls have been issued asking for more minority nurses and nurses who are culturally competent (Sullivan Report, 2004; IOM, 2003). Cultural competency has been described in the literature as a way to improve quality and eliminate racial, ethnic and gender disparities, which ultimately will improve patient outcomes (HHS, 2001, 2005; Joint Commission on Accreditation of Healthcare Organizations [JCAHO], 2007). Nurse educators are challenged to prepare graduates who are able to care for patients from diverse racial and ethnic backgrounds while at the same time incorporating new technologies in the educational process (IOM, 2003). Simulation models, many incorporating technological devices, are being used more frequently in response to the need for alternatives to traditional clinical education practices.

This chapter will discuss an instructional approach that includes the use of simulation models, which tends to directly impact the cultural competency of nursing students and indirectly affects the health care of culturally diverse clients. The discussion will include a review of emerging definitions of culture, cultural diversity, cultural sensitivity, and cultural competence. A brief overview will be provided of popular models of cultural sensitivity and cultural competence. Finally, a discussion will describe how simulation is used to educate culturally competent student nurses.

Population Trends

The demographics of the nation are changing, which means that nurse educators will be responsible for the diverse educational needs of a student population that will ultimately be responsible for an equally diverse patient population. The current ethnic composition of the United States is 32.6 percent minority (U.S. Census Bureau,

2006). Yet, the U.S. ethnic composition of practicing nurses is 4.2 percent African American, 1.7 percent Hispanic/Latino, and 3.1 percent Asian/Pacific Islander (2004 National Sample Survey of Registered Nurses, 2007). Racial and ethnic groups are underrepresented among registered nurses and among student nurses (Sullivan Report, 2004). The Institute of Medicine Report (IOM), *Unequal Treatment: Confronting Racial and Ethnic Disparities in Health Care* provides support for a direct link between poorer health outcomes for minorities and the shortage of minority health care providers (2003). The pipeline of minority nurses are less promising, with minority student enrollments only showing marginal increases over the last two years. The 2006 American Association of Colleges of Nursing (AACN) report notes that minorities represent 25.7 percent of the students enrolled in baccalaureate nursing schools and 22.6 percent of new minority graduates during the period August 1, 2006 to July 31, 2007, with African Americans representing 12.3 percent of students enrolled and 10.5 percent of the new graduates (Fang, Htut, & Bednash [AACN], 2008). The National League for Nursing's enrollment and graduation data for all types of programs indicate that during 2006 the enrollment rates fell across all types of RN programs; baccalaureate enrollments declined 33 percent from 2005 to 2006; associate degree programs dropped by 0.3 percent; and diploma enrollments fell by 2.6 percent. On the other hand, minority graduations increased to 24.5 percent in 2006, which is distributed across all racial-ethnic categories (Asians, African Americans, and Hispanics each gained approximately one percent and American Indians gained 0.3 percent) (NLN, 2008). The discrepancy between the number of minority nursing students who matriculate and the number who subsequently graduate and become practicing nurses responsible for the care of diverse racial and ethnic patients raises a number of concerns, the most important of which is providing culturally competent care. Increasing the number of culturally competent health professionals in the workforce is seen as the means by which excellence in health care is attained (Sullivan, 2004).

Preparing culturally competent health care providers, which includes nurses, is seen as a way to reduce patient dissatisfaction and subsequent issues related to disparities (IOM, 2003). Changes in nursing education will be needed because of the population shift. Research increasingly links minority health disparities to a lack of cultural competence on the part of the health care providers, who often differ from their patients with respect to racial-ethnic background. This concern has been particularly acute within the RN workforce, where the percentage of minorities has been slow to increase, and only exceeded 10 percent in the last decade (2004 National Sample Survey of Registered Nurses, 2007).

Patient demographics are changing, therefore, "delivery of appropriate care will depend on use of a culturally informed approach that goes beyond simple language translation and understanding of characteristics of different cultures" (Sims & Baldwin, 1995, p. 321). It is imperative that the nursing profession is prepared for this health care challenge, but more importantly, it is the role of the nurse educator to respond to this challenge in two ways: 1) by increasing the number of minority graduates; and 2) strengthening multicultural perspectives in nursing education programs.

DEFINITION OF CULTURAL COMPETENCY

Cultural competence in nursing was first addressed by Leininger as Transcultural Nursing in the late 1970s (Leininger, 1978). However, since then the definition and description of cultural competency continues to evolve from the use of the term Transcultural Nursing to "cross-cultural health care," because the American Academy of Nursing (AAN) viewed this as a more global and interdisciplinary term (Lenburg et al., 1995). In the 1990s, the term cultural competence replaced earlier terms. Cultural competence is defined as a set of congruent behaviors, attitudes, and policies that come together in a system, agency, or amongst professionals and enables that system, agency, or those professionals to work effectively in cross-cultural situations that extends along a continuum of behaviors, attitudes, and policies ranging from cultural destructiveness to proficiency (Cross, Bazron, Dennis, & Isaac, 1989). For purposes of this discussion, related terms important to understanding cultural competency will be defined: culture, cultural diversity, and cultural sensitivity.

Culture is subjective, in that it is acquired rather than inherited. Culture refers to "the totality of socially transmitted behavioral patterns, arts, beliefs, values, customs, life-ways, and all other products of human work and thought characteristics of a…people that guides their worldview and decision making" (Purnell & Paulanka, 2008, p. 5). Cultural values represent the individual's desired or preferred way of acting or knowing something that is sustained over a period of time, which governs actions or decisions. A culture's values are its ideas about what is good, right, fair, and just. The values identify those objects, conditions or characteristics that members of the society consider important.

Cultural behavior, on the other hand, is how one acts in certain situations; it is socially acquired as well. Patterns of cultural behavior are learned through a socialization process called enculturation, which involves acquiring knowledge and internalizing values (Giger & Davidhizar, 2004). Davidhizar, Dowd, and Giger (1998) determined that patterns of cultural behavior are important to the nurse, because they provide explanations for behavior related to life events. These life events are significant by virtue of the patient's cultural heritage. Such events as marriage, birth, illness and death carry strong significance that is rooted in values, traditions, and socialization. The nurse is able to determine a patient's pattern of cultural behaviors by performing a cultural assessment.

Cultural diversity is a term that has evolved over the years and tends to be more general, in that it allows for considering differences among individuals other than racial and ethnic differences. Purnell and Paulanka (2008) define cultural diversity as representing a variety of different cultures. Cultural diversity encompasses the cultural differences that exist between people, such as language, dress and traditions, and the way societies organize themselves, their conception of morality and religion, and the way they interact with the environment. An individual's cultural affiliation, values and behavior are all related to one's cultural diversity.

Cultural sensitivity and cultural competency are different terms that frequently have been used interchangeably. Cultural competency is a process while cultural sensitivity "has more to do with personal attitudes and not saying things that might be offensive to someone from a cultural or ethnic background different from the health care provider's" (Purnell & Paulinka, 2008, p. 6).

A MODEL FOR CULTURALLY COMPETENT CARE

Old Dominion University School of Nursing (ODU) was awarded Health Resources and Services Administration (HRSA) funding to implement a project entitled, "Educating Culturally Competent Baccalaureate Nurses". This project's goal is twofold: (1) to develop a mechanism for integrating cultural diversity concepts and content into the baccalaureate curriculum, and (2) to meet the needs of a diverse student population. Following a curriculum review and input from a consultant, the faculty of ODU decided on an approach to teaching cultural diversity content in the undergraduate nursing program. The following assumptions are presented:

- Preparing culturally competent student nurses requires integrating didactic content and clinical experiences.
- Nursing is a practice discipline that requires opportunities for practice with patients.
- Faculty and students are collaborators in the cultural competency process.
- Faculty are facilitators in the learning experience.

The National Goals of the Bureau of Health Professions (BHPr), Healthy People 2010 Objectives and the School of Nursing's purpose guided the development of the curriculum focus. HRSA's National Goals and Healthy People 2010 Objectives emphasize increased access to care, reduced disparities, and improved quality of care. The School of Nursing's purpose emphasizes that nursing education involves providing care in multiple and diverse environments.

The Campinha-Bacote cultural competency model (2007) is the framework selected to guide the development and integration of the cultural diversity content into the curriculum. Simulation models were identified as the primary instructional method. The

Campinha-Bacote model views cultural competence as an ongoing process in which the health care provider continuously strives to achieve the ability to effectively work within the cultural context of the patient.

Numerous sources have suggested ways to prepare culturally competent nurses or strategies to incorporate this content into the curriculum (Anderson, 1990; Campinha-Bacote, 1995; Duffy, 2001; Giger & Davidhizar, 2004; Leininger, 1988; Purnell & Paulanka, 2008; Spector, 2004). Leininger was one of the first nurse theorists to articulate the importance of culture and health to positive patient outcomes. She, along with several others, began to define the role of the nurse in meeting the unique needs of individuals from different ethnic and racial origins. Leininger's focus has been on three main categories: ethnicity, race and religion. Information relevant to these three categories include: communication patterns; beliefs about health and illness; birth, death and marriage; roles and responsibilities; and the group's worldview.

Campinha-Bacote (2007) states that cultural competence is enhanced through a process rather than an event and consists of five components: cultural desire, cultural awareness, cultural knowledge, cultural skill, and cultural encounter. The process develops over time and the nurse or health care provider engages in a period of self-examination to determine their beliefs and values and their effect on the patient. The process of becoming culturally competent may be anxiety-provoking for students and faculty, especially if it involves real encounters with patients from racial and ethnically diverse groups. Simulation in many instances can offer a realistic alternative to cultural encounters that allows the individual to overcome the discomfort before a real encounter.

Jeffries describes a framework for developing, implementing and evaluating simulations used as teaching strategies in nursing. Although not conceptualized according to Jeffries' simulation model, the Old Dominion School of Nursing project utilizes similar components in its development and implementation. The Jeffries simulation framework has five major components: the teacher, the student, educational practices, design characteristics and simulation, and outcomes (2005). The cultural competency simulation model presented here will be described utilizing the interrelated concepts of Campinha-Bacote's cultural competency model and Jeffries' simulation model.

SIMULATION IN NURSING

Complex health environments and staff shortages have contributed to increases in medical errors. The IOM report urges increased use of technology to decrease medical errors and increase patient safety (Greiner & Knebel, 2003; Kohn, Corrigan, & Donaldson, 2000). The use of technology in nursing education is on the rise, with the focus to addressing this problem. Increasingly, more nursing programs have established simulation laboratories equipped with high-tech machinery to promote psychomotor competence in order to provide safe patient care. Using the airline industry as the model, nursing programs have incorporated practice with such devices as SimMan©, a computerized mannequin or an intravenous (IV) arm to increase practice and promote mastery of selected skills. Limited options are available that allow the student experiences in managing behavioral, emotional and relational aspects of a situation. In addition, real life clinical experiences are becoming increasingly more difficult to arrange due to competing demands for additional course content and limited clinical sites. Simulation is a method that utilizes artificial or hypothetical experiences that engage the learner in an activity that reflects real-life conditions without the risk-taking consequences of an actual situation (Rystedt & Lindstrom, 2001). Limited practice time, complex health care environments and the need to provide beginning baccalaureate students a safe and supportive environment to practice have led to increasing use of virtual and simulated experiences, thus reducing the anxiety and discomfort students frequently experience in their early hospital clinical assignments. Repetition allows for ease in manipulating new equipment in a strange environment.

New technologies, advances in health knowledge and the changing dynamics of the individual roles of health care providers require reconceptualizing nursing practice and ultimately how clinical nursing education is delivered. Simulation is establishing an environment that duplicates a real-world experience. In the professional domain, airline pilots, astronauts and other high-risk professions have adopted some form of virtual training environment for workers. The challenge for nurse educators is creating simulations that come as close to real life situations as possible.

First evidence of the use of simulation models in health care were in the 1960s with the use of what was known as "static mannequins" like Resusci-Annie to provide cardiopulmonary resuscitation training of staff. The early mannequins were heavy and awkward and lacked the complex mechanisms of today's designs. Yet these early models, precursors to today's equipment, served a very important function, which was practice in a safe environment in order to develop mastery of a skill.

Simulation involves experiential learning that includes role-play, case studies and low and high-fidelity simulators. In each instance, the learner is provided realistic information to process and make decisions. Participants make decisions in a safe environment, observe the consequences, and evaluate the effectiveness of their actions (Delpier, 2006). Debriefing is important to assist in the analysis of the experiences. Simulations can center on critical-incident-type situations, where sophisticated equipment is used to recreate a situation of a patient in sudden cardiac distress, for example. In these instances, the learner is assessed for their ability to make decisions quickly under stressful conditions or make rapid assessment and intervention with accuracy when coordinating and providing care.

Nursing education programs have sought to develop strategies that could provide meaningful learning opportunities that increase cultural competency of nursing students (Flinn, 2004, Jeffries, 2007), yet little evidence exists that describes teaching cultural competency using simulation models. Simulation is an integrative instructional method that relies on multicontextual strategies (Ibarra, 1999). A description of the cultural competency simulation model will follow, incorporating Jeffries' simulation model as the framework. The five components of the Jeffries model will be discussed separately in the following section.

Teacher

There are 15 full-time faculty members with teaching responsibilities in the undergraduate program at Old Dominion University School of Nursing. Faculty who teach in the nursing program are white women whose ages range from the late 30s to 60+ years. Each has a minimum of a master's degree, two are doctorally prepared and four others are certified as advanced practice nurses. The faculty members bring a wealth of teaching experience that range from as little as two years to over 30 years. Although white women comprise the faculty teaching in this undergraduate nursing program, there is diversity within the group.

Student

The student population in the School of Nursing represents two distinctly different cohorts – pre-licensure and post-licensure. Pre-licensure students typically are younger women pursuing their first college degree and reside in the Tidewater area of Virginia. Students are admitted into the school during the sophomore year of the program. The ethnic composition of this group is 64 percent white and 36 percent minority. Post-licensure students on the other hand are mostly older white women who are practicing registered nurses. The ethnic composition of this group is 77 percent white and 23 percent minority. Students enrolled in the post-licensure program complete their program of study through the university's distance education network, which incorporates asynchronous and synchronous formats. These students come from all over the Commonwealth of Virginia as well as locations outside the state. In both groups, African Americans represent the largest minority group; men comprise approximately 10 percent of each cohort. There is racial and gender discordance between the faculty and the students in the School of Nursing. In addition, there is even more diversity among the populations where the students practice during their clinical rotations. The diverse characteristics of the students have forced the faculty to explore alternative teaching strategies to promote student success and to comply with the school's purpose, which is to prepare graduates who provide competent care in a diverse environment.

The number of minorities living in the Hampton Roads area is growing and includes African Americans, the largest of the groups, as well as Hispanics and Asian/

Pacific Islanders. The pre-licensure students, members of the Millennium generation, and the post-licensure students, mostly Generation X-ers, come with characteristics and challenges that impact the educational practices of this program.

Educational Practices

The intent of the Old Dominion project is to develop teaching strategies that support the learning of all students: African Americans and other minorities, adult learners, and distance learners, each representing populations with unique characteristics that require different instructional approaches to promote optimum learning. Simulation as an instructional method was identified as most appropriate because of the diversity of the student population. Students today approach learning much differently than several years ago. The student's age, gender and ethnicity are factors that contribute to the difference. The lecture method, a teacher-centered strategy, had been utilized predominately as the instructional method of choice.

Teacher-centered strategies focused on reading, writing and lectures. Many of today's students come to the university and to nursing with limitations in reading comprehension, writing and problem-solving. Teaching and learning strategies are critical to the instructional process, especially in terms of producing positive student outcomes. Although nurse educators are interested in innovative teaching strategies, they typically rely on traditional methods of teaching, which most often tend to be teacher-centered rather than student-centered (Schaefer & Zygmont, 2003).

Schaefer and Zygmont state that student-centered teaching styles foster independence in learning, creative problem-solving skills, a commitment to lifelong learning, and critical thinking, whereas teacher-centered learning promotes dependent learning (2003). Royse and Newton (2007) report that, "Under-utilization of nontraditional approaches to teaching and learning may be related to a lack of understanding" (p. 264) and a fear of the unknown.

Multicontextuality, a concept described by Ibarra, is especially helpful in understanding and developing teaching/learning strategies for minorities. Multicontextual instructional approaches are grouped into two categories, low context or high context. Low context approaches focus on reading, writing, and lectures; high context approaches focus on relationships, social learning, case study, and reflective writing (Ibarra, 1999). High contextual instructional approaches incorporate integrative learning, a student-centered approach that is active, emotional and purposeful. Integrative learning is useful when the faculty decreases the distance between the information presented in the classroom and the use of that information in the practice area (Giddens, 2008). Next to actual encounters, simulation models, an integrative approach that uses case studies and role play, have provided the best options to practice interpersonal situations that consider the patient's cultural beliefs and the student's level of competence.

Teaching strategies utilized in this cultural competency model are designed to assess the student's cultural competence concentrating in the following areas: awareness, knowledge, attitudes, and behaviors. Cultural awareness concentrates on promoting acknowledging and acceptance of difference. Cultural knowledge involves understanding various cultural practices and beliefs held by selected ethnic groups. Cultural attitudes involve the perceptions held by the student based on past experiences. Cultural behaviors are the skills and activities performed by the student, such as conducting a health assessment (Campinha-Bacote, 2007).

Design Characteristics

The cultural competency instructional model used in the undergraduate program at Old Dominion University is based on a platform that incorporates principles of integrative learning and multicontextual approaches in a simulated environment. In doing so, multiple instructional strategies are utilized to respond to diverse students who utilize different learning styles (auditory, visual, and kinesthetic). The model components: a virtual web-based hospital, high performance simulators, standardized patients, and videotaped simulation encounters (Rutledge et al., 2008). Theoretical concepts are introduced using traditional instructional methods, such as structured readings, lectures, and videos. The theory is reinforced by incorporating experiential components that include simulation.

The virtual hospital is housed on a web-based platform that utilizes still photos, text-based messages and video clips to create the learning situation. Access to the hospital and the learning activities is limited to students registered in courses in the nursing program. Students are introduced to the virtual hospital during the first semester of their sophomore year. Students are introduced to individuals representing different racial and ethnic groups through the "Mundo family wedding." A genogram depicts the relationship of family members who will appear first in the health assessment course and later in other courses throughout the program. The bride is white and the groom is Hispanic. The best man is an African American whose wife is Filipino. Other family members and acquaintances from diverse backgrounds are presented, along with unique health/ illnesses and cultural practices that require nursing intervention. The first web-based assignment focuses on nurse-patient communication while completing a health history. The standardized patient case scenarios were created based on information collected from focus group sessions representing selected racial-ethnic groups such as African American women, African American men, Filipino Americans, and Hispanic Americans.

The Standardized Patients (SP) are individuals trained to act as patients, who follow a scripted scenario. Through role-play, the learner assumes the role of the nurse and the

SP represents a patient from a diverse background. Combining simulation with group discussion addresses all three learner domains (affective, cognitive and psychomotor) and involves active learning strategies.

There are two types of SP encounters, the face-to-face encounter and a video encounter. The history and present illness of an African American woman is a face-to-face encounter for all students. Video-recorded SP scenarios were developed to increase the encounter opportunities for the students without the additional costs. Use of High Performance Simulators is combined with a case study that incorporates psychomotor skills practice and cultural assessment aspects, thus increasing the complexity of the situation. Patient demographic information is developed to reflect an individual from a diverse group, e.g., someone who is overweight, or gay and African American. There are specific learning objectives associated with each case scenario.

Outcomes

A two-part assessment is planned to determine the success of the Old Dominion simulation project. The first part, the programmatic evaluation, will employ structural and process indicators to measure the extent that program aspects are implemented. Second, the outcomes evaluation will assess the extent the expected changes in student's cultural competency occur. Measures to be assessed include student satisfaction, pre- and post-test scores on cultural competency surveys (cultural awareness, knowledge, and skill), and student performance on the clinical performance assessment tool (CPA). Substantive outcomes relate to the student's level of success in meeting the course objectives. The measurement criteria are used to determine a student's performance in the following three areas: health assessment, history and present illness, and patient teaching.

Teaching-learning outcomes are assessed utilizing a variety of formats: written papers, online discussion groups, video recording of student performance and in-class debriefing. The debriefing emphasizes key concepts and reinforces students' critical thinking and clinical judgment (Comer, 2005). These patient care simulations have the advantage of capturing all the learning domains - cognitive, psychomotor and affective (Nehring, Ellis, & Lashley, 2001) - while effectively accommodating the learning preferences of all nursing students. The visual preference learners have the opportunity to observe their classmates perform the interaction, auditory learners participate in the verbal communication that occurs during the scenario, and the kinesthetic or tactile learners work through problems described in the scenario in a hands-on manner using the HPS. Most importantly, the simulation model allows for repetition to promote mastery in a safe environment. Most nursing students, not unlike the majority of the population, are visual learners who prefer to learn new material through graphs, videos, and pictures (Comer, 2005). Simulations and role-play are real-time interactive experiences that provide visual learners with opportunities to observe or participate in clinical situations (Arwood, Kaakinen, & Wynne, 2002).

The proposed cultural competency model includes multiple components: a virtual hospital, live Standardized Patients, video recordings of Standardized Patients and High Performance Simulators (HPS) (Rutledge et al., 2008). Cultural competence is recognized as an important component to promote positive health outcomes, but instructional methods have been limited to developing cognitive functioning. Use of simulation has the potential to promote affective, psychomotor and cognitive domains. Critical to the effectiveness of the process of increasing cultural competency is the extent to which the faculty member views the process as a partnership that requires self-assessment and self-examination. This self-assessment phase of the Campinha-Bacote model includes an awareness component in the overall process (2007). Reasons for using simulation as a teaching strategy are: the promotion of active learning (Sisson & Baker, 1988), encouragement of critical thinking (Rowell & Spielvogle, 1996), and replication of real-life situations (Rowles & Brigham, 2005).

IMPLICATIONS FOR NURSING EDUCATION – EVALUATING THE PROCESS

Little data is available that validates the effectiveness of cultural competency teaching-learning strategies. Use of simulation for purposes of teaching cognitive, psychosocial, and interpersonal skills is less well-known. One might expect that similar principles to the cases that involve psychomotor and critical thinking skills can be used.

Early learning theorists support the idea that learning style be matched with a similar teaching style for the learner to attain an optimal level of achievement (Dunn & Dunn, 1978; Kolb, 1984). Because research findings are inconsistent, more recent thinking is that learning occurs not because of matching, but when the educator uses a variety of teaching strategies rather than relying on just one approach (Bastable, 2008).

When considering program effectiveness, one must include short-term as well as long-term outcomes. Indicators of short-term effectiveness may take the form of a survey that assesses changes in attitudes and behaviors following an encounter with the cultural sensitivity information. Indicators of long-term program effectiveness may be reflected in a number of ways, some of which might include a nurse's decision to work with minority populations or increases in numbers of minority patients engaging in health promotion/prevention activities resulting from positive encounters with the health care provider.

Students also may practice nursing interventions in responding to culturally diverse patients. Participating in a culturally diverse scenario will help students develop beginning skills and techniques in competence, as well as change their understanding, feelings, and attitudes.

This instructional model assumes that there is a direct relationship between the health care provider's level of cultural competence and their ability to provide culturally responsive care, which ultimately will improve the access to and the quality of care to all populations. The focus of cultural competency should extend beyond including content and facts in a single course. This is a process that requires infusion throughout the curriculum. Integration of course content throughout the entire curriculum is thought to be better than having a separate, discrete course. Utilizing this approach assures that students have multiple exposures, which will serve two purposes: (1) increased mastery, and (2) support for increases in cognitive as well as psychomotor skill development levels. Because nursing is a practice-focused profession, information presented in the classroom must focus on both education and practice. Educators face numerous challenges when seeking to provide the most comprehensive, relevant and comparable experiences for students over time and with different groups of students. Using simulation can address some of these challenges. Simulation, a familiar concept, can bring cultural competency education closer to reality.

References

Anderson, J. M. (1990). Health care across cultures. *Nursing Outlook, 38*(3), 136-139.

Arwood, E. L., Kaakinen, J., & Wynne, A. L. (2002). *Nurse educators: Using visual language: Learning to see.* Portland, OR: APRICOT.

Bastable, S. B. (2008). *Nurse as educator: Principles of teaching and learning for nursing practice* (3rd ed.). Boston: Jones and Bartlett.

Buerhaus, P. I. (2008). *The future of the nursing workforce in the United States: Data, trends and implications.* Boston: Jones and Bartlett.

Campinha-Bacote, J. (1995). The quest for cultural competence in nursing care. *Nursing Forum, 30*(4), 19-25.

Campinha-Bacote, J. (2007). *The process of cultural competence in the delivery of healthcare services: A culturally competent model of care.* Cincinnati, OH: Transcultural C.A.R.E. Associates.

Comer, S. (2005). Patient care simulations: Role playing to enhance clinical understanding. *Nursing Education Perspectives, 26*(6), 357-361.

Cross, T., Bazron, B., Dennis, K., & Isaac, M. (1989). *Toward a culturally competent system of care.* Vol. 1. Washington, DC: Georgetown University Child Development Center, CASSP Technical Assistance Center.

Davidhizar, R., Dowd, S., & Giger, J. N. (1998). Educating the culturally diverse student. *Nurse Educator, 23*(2), 38-42.

Delpier, T. (2006). Cases 101: Learning to teach with cases. *Nursing Education Perspectives, 27*(4), 204-209.

Duffy, M.E. (2001). A critique of culture education in nursing. *Journal of Advanced Nursing, 36*(4), 487-495.

Dunn, R., & Dunn, K. (1978). *Teaching students through their individual learning styles model research: A practical approach.* Reston, VA: National Association of Secondary School Principals.

Fang, D., Htut, A., & Bednash, G. D. (2008). *2007-2008 Enrollment and graduations in baccalaureate and graduate programs in nursing.* Washington, DC: American Association of Colleges of Nursing.

Fletcher, J. L. (1998). ERR WATCH: Anesthesia crisis resource management for the nurse anesthetist's perspective. *Journal of the American Association of Nurse Anesthetists, 66,* 595-602.

Flinn, J. B. (2004). Teaching strategies used with success in the multicultural classroom. *Nurse Educator, 29*(1), 10-12.

Giddens, J. (2008, October 17). *New directions for nursing education: Virtual experiential communities.* Keynote presentation at the Modeling and Simulation in Nursing workshop, Virginia Modeling, Analysis and Simulation Center, Suffolk, VA.

Giger, J. N., & Davidhizar, R .E. (2004). *Transcultural nursing: Assessment and intervention.* (2nd ed.). St. Louis, MO: Mosby-Yearbook.

Greiner, A. C., & Knebel, E. (Eds.). Institute of Medicine. (2003). *Health professions education: A bridge to quality.* Washington, DC: National Academies Press.

Ibarra, R. A. (1999). Multicontextuality: A new perspective on minority underrepresentation in SEM academic fields. *Making Strides. Research News on Minority Graduate Education, 1*(3). Retrieved November 2, 2008, from http://ehrweb.aaas.org/mge/Archives/3/Multi.html

Institute of Medicine. (2003). *Unequal treatment: Confronting racial and ethnic disparities in health care.* Washington, DC: National Academies Press (http://www.nap.edu).

Jeffries. P. R. (2005). A framework for designing, implementing, and evaluating simulations used as teaching strategies in nursing. *Nursing Education Perspectives, 26*(2), 96-103.

Jeffries, P. R. (Ed.) (2007). *Simulation in nursing education: From conceptualization to evaluation.* New York: National League for Nursing.

Joint Commission on Accreditation of Healthcare Organizations. (2007). *Accreditation manual for hospitals.* Oakbrook Terrace, IL: Author.

Kohn, L.T., Corrigan, M., & Donaldson, M.S. (Eds.). (2000). *To err is human: Building a safer health system.* Washington, DC: National Academies Press.

Kolb, D.A. (1984). *Experiential learning: Experience as the source of learning and development.* Englewood Cliffs, NJ: Prentice Hall.

Leininger, M. M. (1978). *Transcultural nursing: Concepts, theories, research and practice.* New York: Wiley & Sons.

Leininger, M. M. (1988). Leininger's theory of nursing: Culture care diversity and universality. *Nursing Science Quarterly, 1*, 152-160.

Lenburg, C.B., Lipson, J.G., Demi, A.S., Blaney, D.R., Stern, P.N., Schultz, P.R., et al. (1995). *Promoting cultural competence in and through nursing education: A critical review and comprehensive plan for action.* Washington, DC: American Academy of Nursing.

National League for Nursing. (2008). *Nursing data review, academic year 2005-2006, baccalaureate, associate degree, and diploma programs*. New York: Author.

2004 National Sample Survey of Registered Nurses (NSSRN). (2007). Retrieved April 10, 2008, from http://bhpr.hrsa.gov/nursing/

Nehring, W. M, Ellis, W. E., & Lashley, F. R. (2001). Human patient simulators in nursing education: An overview. *Simulation and Gaming, 32*(2), 194-204.

Purnell, L. D., & Paulanka, B. J. (2008). *Transcultural health care: A culturally competent approach*. Philadelphia: F.A. Davis.

Rowell, S., & Spielvogle, S. (1996). Wanted: "A Few Good Bug Detectives," a gaming technique to increase staff awareness of current infection control practices. *Journal of Continuing Education in Nursing, 27*(6), 274-278.

Rowles, C. J., & Brigham, C. (2005). Strategies to promote critical thinking and active learning. In D. M. Billings & J. A. Halstead (Eds.). *Teaching in nursing: A guide for faculty* (pp. 283-315). St. Louis, MO: Elsevier.

Royse, M. A., & Newton, S. E. (2007). How gaming is used as an innovative strategy for nursing education. *Nursing Education Perspectives, 28*(5), 263-267.

Rutledge, C. M., Barham, P., Wiles, L., Benjamin, R., Eaton, P., & Palmer, K. (2008). Integrative simulation: A novel approach to educating culturally competent nurses. *Contemporary Nurse, 28*(1-2), 119-128.

Rystedt, H., & Lindstrom, D. (2001). Introducing simulation technologies in nurse education: A nursing practice perspective. *Nurse Education in Practice, 1*(3), 134-141.

Schaefer, K. M., & Zygmont, D. (2003). Analyzing the teaching style of nursing faculty. *Nursing Education Perspectives, 24*(5), 238-245.

Sims, G., & Baldwin, D. (1995). Race, class, and gender considerations in nursing education. *Nursing & Health Care: Perspectives on Community, 16*(6), 316-321.

Sisson, P. M., & Becker, L. M. (1988). Using games in nursing education. *Journal of Nursing Staff Development, 88*(4), 146-151.

Spector, R. E. (2004). *Cultural diversity in health and illness* (6th ed.). Saddle River, NJ: Pearson Education.

Sullivan Report. (2004). *Missing Persons: Minorities in the Health Professions*. Retrieved from http://www.aacn.nche.edu/Media/pdf/SullivanReport.pdf

U.S. Census Bureau. (2006). *Statistical abstract of the United States*. Retrieved March 28, 2008, from http://www.census.gov/

U.S. Department of Health and Human Services (HHS), Health Resources and Services Administration. (2001). *Cultural competence works*. Washington, DC: Government Printing Office.

U.S. Department of Health and Human Services. (2005). *Healthy People 2010*. Retrieved April 1, 2008, from http://www.healthypeople.gov

U.S. Department of Health and Human Services, Health Resources and Services Administration (HRSA). (2006). *The registered nurse population: Findings from the March 2004 National Survey of Registered Nurses*. Retrieved October 24, 2008, from ftp://ftp.hrsa.gov/bhpr/workforce/0306rnss.pdf

Yoder, M.K. (2001). The bridging approach: Effective strategies for teaching ethnically diverse nursing students. *Journal of Transcultural Nursing, 12*, 319-325.

Acknowledgment

This project, "Educating Culturally Competent Baccalaureate Nurses," is supported in part by funds from the Division of Nursing (DN), Bureau of Health Professions (BHPr), Health Resources and Services Administration (HRSA), Department of Health and Human Services (DHHS) under grant titled "Educating Culturally Competent Baccalaureate Nurses" 7/1/06 - 6/30/09. The information or content and conclusions are those of the author and should not be construed as the official position or policy of, nor should any endorsements be inferred as belonging to, the Division of Nursing, BHPr, DHHS or the U.S. government.

CHAPTER 7

CLOSING THE GAP ON RACIAL/ETHNIC DIVERSITY IN NURSING EDUCATION

Mary H. Hill, DSN, RN

INTRODUCTION

The Sullivan Commission Report (2004) clearly identifies the need for leadership beyond the institutional level as an essential element for increasing diversity of the health care workforce. Four years after the Sullivan Commission Report, on November 4, 2008, the United States of America decisively elected the first African American, Senator Barack Obama (D-IL), as the 44th President of the United States. In keeping with President Obama's campaign promise, he has demonstrated a commitment to increase the diversity of leadership at the Cabinet level, the highest institutional level in the United States of America. For example, President Obama has selected a team that reflects our nation's greatest strength, its diversity. His choice of Eric Shinseki, an Asian American, as the Veterans Affairs Secretary was an early indication that the President would make good on his pledge to have a diverse Cabinet. Within President Obama's eight Cabinet announcements at the time of this writing, white men were the minority with two nominations - Timothy Geithner at Treasury and Robert Gates at Defense. Three choices were women - Janet Napolitano at Homeland Security, Susan Rice as United Nations ambassador and Hillary Rodham Clinton at State. Eric Holder at the Justice Department is African American and Bill Richardson, the President's original pick at Commerce, is Latino.

Leadership at the highest institutional level has utilized the strategy of inclusion in crafting a solution to the economic, health care and homeland security crises facing this nation. Therefore, health professions, too, must approach the problem of increasing diversity of the health care workforce by utilizing the strategy of inclusion in crafting solutions.

THE PROBLEM: UNDERREPRESENTATION OF RACIAL/ETHNIC MINORITIES IN NURSING EDUCATION

The underrepresentation of racial/ethnic minorities in baccalaureate and higher degree programs is not new. This has been an ongoing trend since the inception of the profession and has been acknowledged repeatedly within the nursing community.

As an African American growing up in Mississippi, it was my dream to become a nurse. This dream began at the age of four upon the death of my father. My younger sister grew up with a dream also, and her dream was to become a physician; she graduated from New York University Medical School. Although both dreams came to fruition, the path I tread to become a registered nurse was strewn with challenges and opportunities along the way, because of the cultural diversity gap in nursing education. However, the challenges have been far greater than the opportunities. For example, the first challenge that I encountered was when I was completing high school and preparing to go to college. It was then that I realized there was not a nursing school in the state of Mississippi in which I could enroll and complete a program of study for a bachelor of science in nursing degree. However, the state of Mississippi would, through legislation, pay out-of-state tuition for me to attend a baccalaureate nursing program in another state, rather than permit me to attend one of the state universities that offered such a program of study. Consequently, in order to begin the first rung on the ladder in pursuit of my dream to become a nurse, I had to attend a nursing school out of state. I chose to attend a nursing school in Alabama, and today I remain grateful for the access to nursing education that was provided me by the nursing school that is known today as the School of Nursing and Allied Health at Tuskegee University, a historically black college/university (HBCU).

To continue with my "lived experience," 24 years later, after I received a bachelor's degree in nursing and earned a master's degree in nursing, coupled with diverse teaching experience on the East Coast in such institutions as Columbia University, Adelphi University and Downstate University College of Nursing in New York, I moved back to Mississippi. Prior to the move to Mississippi in 1991, however, I applied and was interviewed for a faculty position in a state institution of higher learning. It appeared that I would not gain access to the workplace, because over a month passed after the interview and there was no follow-up. As a matter of fact, I was not offered a faculty position until after I communicated with the governor of the state of Mississippi and informed him that I was moving back to the state, where I continued to pay taxes while living in New York, and I was seeking employment. Yes, afterwards I was hired at a majority school of nursing and joined two African American faculty members who were currently teaching at the school. However, at the end of my first year, one African American faculty retired and by the end of my second year, the other African American faculty transferred from academe to a service position within the institution. Consequently, at the beginning of my third year of teaching at the institution, I was the only African American faculty in this majority institution. This situation continued for three years, and, as a result, individuals often asked me what was it like to be the only African American faculty in a majority institution? I would often respond to my colleagues by saying "well, picture yourself in an HBCU school of nursing in Mississippi and the only white faculty person there for three years." I would respond in this manner so that they would begin to see what it could be like from the standpoint of social isolation.

In spite of the many challenges I've had along the way, I have had opportunities, and one of the most rewarding opportunities afforded me in nursing education has been to serve as the dean of a school of nursing. I am proud to say that I was the first African American native Mississippian to serve as a dean of a school of nursing in the state of Mississippi. I often say what a return on investment has been received by the Institutions of Higher Learning (IHL) for the state of Mississippi. Because neither I nor the IHL had any idea that when they paid for me to attend nursing school out of state from 1963-1967 I would one day serve as the dean of a state school of nursing in Mississippi.

I often wonder, what if other African Americans, maybe 100 to 200, had been afforded the opportunity to pursue baccalaureate education in nursing in the early 1960s, what an impact the resulting diversity of the workforce would have had on the health status of the state of Mississippi. According to the Institute of Medicine's landmark study (2003), there is a direct link between poorer health outcomes and the shortage of minority health providers.

Many African American nurse leaders, both today and in the past, are graduates of HBCU schools of nursing, because these schools provided access to nursing education and a foundation for graduate study. As a toddler, Dr. Rhetaugh Dumas, a native of Natchez, Mississippi, was imbued with the idea that when she grew up she would become a nurse, not just an ordinary nurse, but one who would be recognized nationally and globally for her illustrious career of accomplishments, leadership and service. Dr. Dumas received her BS in nursing from Dillard University, an HBCU, and during her career became dean of the School of Nursing at the University of Michigan and later vice president and provost at the University of Michigan School of Nursing. Other accomplishments included serving as president of the National League for Nursing, member of the National Advisory Commission on Nursing and associate director of the National Institute of Mental Health.

Another nursing leader, Vernice Ferguson, retired assistant chief medical director for nursing programs at the United States Department of Veterans Affairs, decided that she wanted to be a nurse as early as the fourth grade, but as a resident of the state of Maryland, there were few options for schools in Baltimore. According to Ferguson (Bessent, 2005), "I didn't want to go to a diploma school (Provident Hospital), Morgan State College was not much in those days, and the University of Maryland was not open to Negroes, nor was Johns Hopkins or Goucher." However, the state of Maryland, like the state of Mississippi, would pay for her to go out of state, so off she went to Fisk University, an HBCU, and then to New York University where she graduated in 1959.

Whether you see the underrepresentation of racial/ethnic diversity in nursing education as a challenge or an opportunity, as nursing educators we owe it to ourselves, the profession, the health care workforce and consumers of health care to get it right in the 21st century. The agony of the problem of underrepresentation of racial/ethnic minorities enrolled in basic nursing education programs or pursuing graduate study is best described in a statement by a minority nurse educator, the late Dr. Lillian Harvey, former dean of Tuskegee Institute School of Nursing. Harvey (1970) stated:

> One of the most perplexing and persistent problems in nursing is how to increase the pool of baccalaureate graduates to serve as a source of candidates for graduate education…An even knottier problem that lies within the larger one is how to

prepare students from minority groups, who are inadequately represented in these programs (p. 48).

It has been 38 years since Harvey identified this problem. As a former student of Harvey, and in response to this statement, current data reveal that progress has not been made in increasing the representation of racial/ethnic minorities in baccalaureate and higher degree nursing programs to the degree that it reflects the demographics of the population.

A review of data regarding admission and graduation rates of minority students, particularly African Americans, as they pursue higher education in nursing, reveals an emerging pattern. If African Americans are fortunate enough to gain access to higher education, far too many of these students are unsuccessful in completing the educational program.

Call for Action

To address the problem, failure of many African Americans to complete nursing education programs, a group of nurse educators (Rozella, Regan-Kubinski, & Albrecht, 1994) suggested that a comprehensive approach to designing strategies to increase the number of minority health care providers, particularly nurses, is urgently needed. Such an approach should include (1) attracting minority students by facilitating their entry into the health professions schools by enhancing their competitiveness for admission, and (2) ensuring that once enrolled these students completed their education (p. 243).

Recognizing that the underrepresentation of racial/ethnic groups and men in nursing education perpetuated their underrepresentation in the workforce, the Southern Regional Education Board (SREB) Council on Collegiate Education for Nursing conducted surveys of nursing education administrators in the 16 SREB states to determine the racial/ethnic and gender composition of nursing education programs, changes in the last five years, ongoing recruitment and retention activities and resources that were available to support recruitment and retention activities. Data regarding the racial/ethnic composition of nursing students and faculty were collected in an earlier survey in May 2001; and findings were: Caucasian, 74 percent; African Americans, 16 percent; and five percent or less for Latinos, Asians and American Indians (SREB, 2002).

With such a small percentage of racial/ethnic nursing students enrolled in nursing education in the SREB states, nursing education continues to be faced with the perplexing problem of how to increase the pool of baccalaureate graduates to serve as a source of candidates for graduate education and for recruitment of diverse faculty for nursing education. Although 52 percent of the nursing programs in this study reported an increase of the racial/ethnic diversity of students over the last five years, 60 percent of the nursing programs reported that the racial/ethnic makeup of faculty was unchanged, and 29 percent of the programs reported an 11 percent decrease of racial/ethnic diversity in faculty.

In summary, other findings of the report were that 72 percent of those surveyed experienced no change in the gender distribution of faculty in the last five years, with 19 percent showing an increase and nine percent showing a decrease. Student and faculty recruitment and retention efforts included partnerships with professional organizations, including cultural-ethnic-specific nursing organizations and a variety of media and other advertisements, such as participating in community-based health and educational activities such as tutoring and mentoring programs. Specifically regarding retention, 72 percent reported affording opportunities for professional growth as a strategy to retain faculty members who represented racial/ethnic minorities.

Lessons Learned

Within the summary of the SREB report, it was concluded that the recruitment of faculty of diverse racial/ethnic groups must begin with recruitment of more racial/ethnic minorities into baccalaureate programs, because this is the first step toward producing more qualified candidates to be nurse educators. Although a plethora of similar strategies have been used by nursing education programs and other disciplines in the recruitment of faculty, none has been particularly successful. A common agreement among many respondents of the study, however, is that greater emphasis needs to be placed on the acquisition of funding to support activities to recruit and retain underrepresented students and faculty.

TRANSFORMATION OF NURSING EDUCATION TO ACHIEVE RACIAL/ETHNIC DIVERSITY

Using the theme of the 2006 National League for Nursing Summit, "Transformation Begins with You," leadership and a commitment to diversity are essential ingredients for transforming higher education as well as nursing education and closing the racial/ethnic diversity gap. It is known that the pillars of any organization are the core values, or guiding principles, that provide the foundation that drives decision making for strategic planning. Strategic planning includes program implementation, resource allocation and the identification of outcomes achievement, such as graduation rate, retention rate, and NCLEX pass rate on the first write.

Values/Guiding Principles

The Sullivan Commission Report (2004) has specified that diversity should be a core value in health professions and that health professions schools should ensure that their mission statements not only reflect a social contract with the community, but also express a commitment to diversity among their students, faculty, staff and administration. Other core values of nursing programs commonly include caring and integrity. A challenge, therefore, for administrators of nursing programs in response to the problem of access and diversity in higher education is to use values/guiding principles of the institution and the professions as foundation for implementing the strategic management process to increase the recruitment, admission, retention, and graduation of racial/ethnic students in nursing and to ensure that the curriculum is culturally relevant.

Strategic Management

Through strategic management, a university or school of nursing could achieve a creative fit between the external environment and its internal situation. The strategic management process will be a vital link to increasing the number of practicing registered nurses who reflect the racial/ethnic diversity of the population served. Even more vital is the need for racial/ethnic faculty input into the overall strategic management process - environmental assessments, situational analysis, strategy formulation, strategy implementation and strategic evaluation. The involvement of racial/ethnic faculty in strategic planning would bring uniqueness to the strategic management process by adding a diversity of ideas and approaches to problem-solving issues unique to racial/ethnic students in social and academic settings. Also, racial/ethnic faculty would have increased sensitivity to the needs of racial/ethnic students that has been acquired through "lived experiences" within the family and social community, secondary and postsecondary education programs, and nursing practice arena.

Strategic Management Process

The strategic management process to increase the recruitment, admission, retention and graduation of racially and ethnically diverse students in schools of nursing begins with an assessment of the external and internal environments of the nursing program. In assessing the external environment, consideration needs to be given to: the level of integration of technology; social, regulatory, political and economic conditions; competition; the educational institution's report card; research organizations and foundations to tap for funding support, and the consumers. Assessment of the internal environment begins with, but is not limited to, an assessment of the mission and racial/ethnic diversity of faculty, as well as other resources that are assessed to provide support for academic success (e.g., faculty committed to racial/ethnic diversity, racially and ethnically diverse faculty to serve as role models, integration of cultural diversity into the curriculum, computer learning labs, tutors, mentors, counselors, financial support - scholarships or loans - and networking with diverse nurse professional organizations). Determining which secondary schools have a strong curriculum in math and science is also useful, because this kind of academic preparation would contribute immensely to preparing racially and ethnically diverse students to meet admission requirements for nursing and provide a foundation for academic success in those nursing programs.

Situational Analysis

From the situational analysis of factors in the external and internal environments, threats and opportunities can be identified. First, look for evidence of a demonstrated commitment of the university to promote diversity in the workplace and in the student population. Also, pay particular attention to your numbers - percent of faculty that is racially/ethnically diverse, positions that they hold in the institution, racial/ethnic student admission and retention rates for the institution and for the nursing program. In addition, analyze data at hand regarding the number of applications, admission and graduation rates of racially/ethnically diverse students.

Still other ways to assess the institution's commitment to diversity are to: (1) determine resources available to assist in the admission and retention of students in the nursing program; (2) create a profile of racially/ethnically diverse students admitted and available support services to meet the students' needs, based upon academic and personal profiles (excellent indicators of commitment to support minority students); (3) have a curriculum that includes cultural diversity as a core concept, which indicates it is valued within the nursing program; (4) observe the behaviors of administrators, faculty, staff and students, which allows one to draw inferences regarding the degree of commitment to racial/ethnic diversity in the institution; (5) look for the presence of an office of multicultural affairs or a similar entity to provide guidance and support for racially/ethnically diverse students, and (6) determine whether research initiatives by faculty and students focus on major health problems of the minority population.

Strategy Formulation

Strategy formulation is concerned with making strategic decisions based on information obtained during the situational analysis. With underrepresentation of racially/ethnically diverse individuals, a strategy to increase the number of minority health care providers, particularly nurses, must be comprehensive and is urgently needed. There could be the need for a nursing program to, first, reaffirm or establish and, then, reach consensus on its mission, vision, values and the directional strategies (objectives) for the institution.

Within the school of nursing, faculty will need to decide if it will expand, contract or remain stable in terms of the enrollment and the types of programs offered. For example, one strategy may be expansion by market development, which is a strategy designed to increase minority students' admission and completion of a nursing program through geographic expansion or by targeting new market segments within a geographic area. Market penetration could be evidenced by increasing minority students' enrollment. One market segment to target might be minority licensed practical nurses already in the field

Strategy Implementation

Strategy implementation is the process whereby operational strategies, whether functional or organization-wide, are brought into play and have a critical role in the achievement of a goal such as increasing racial/ethnic representation in nursing programs. Therefore, efforts directed toward goal achievement will require the coordination of functional operational strategies, such as marketing, information systems, human resources and finance. Underlying the functional operational strategies are those organization-wide strategies that include organizational culture, structure, facilities and equipment, as well as ethical and social responsibilities. The organizational culture of a nursing program may be supportive of effecting strategies to increase racial/ethnic student representation or the culture may resist any changes that alter the accepted way of doing things. If the latter occurs, the organization must implement measures to modify the culture.

First, there must be support and genuine commitment of the institutional leader, nursing education administration, faculty and students. Nursing programs that have been successful in recruiting, admitting and graduating racially/ethnically diverse students have demonstrated commitment by faculty to educate underrepresented groups. Once a commitment by the administrator and faculty has been established, discussion groups should be held for the purpose of allowing faculty to ventilate their feelings regarding minorities in general and students specifically. Such groups should be facilitated by an individual with expertise in organizational development and behavior, with an emphasis on cultural diversity in organizations. Also, the climate of the organization may need to change in order to ensure that the environment is conducive to students' success. Other strategies include:

- Recruit faculty that represent racial/ethnic diversity

- Incorporate cultural diversity as a core concept in the curriculum. Ensure that it receives the same consideration as safety, caring, integrity, etc. Also ensure that those presenting cultural concepts are grounded in theory about the culture

- Increase the visibility of individuals from different racial/ethnic groups

- Increase the visibility of racially/ethnically diverse leaders (e.g., local and national leaders could be incorporated into program activities through such appropriate roles as guest speakers)

- Partner with minority institutions for collaborative initiatives

- Establish a mentorship program. Advantages are that it: (a) provides early advisement regarding admission requirements for entering nursing and the need to take those courses that will give the potential student a strong background in the basic sciences; (b) avails additional academic preparation by attending tutoring sessions; and (c) affords opportunities for students to attend forums with minority nursing faculty and leaders in the nursing community.

Strategic Control

Strategic control will be the process by which the nursing faculty will assess how well the nursing school is progressing towards achieving the outcomes for racial/ethnic diversity. Indicators such as student satisfaction, increased admission, retention, and graduation rates, and NCLEX-RN first-write pass rates measure performance and outcome achievements that provide evidence of closing the gap on racial/ethnic diversity in nursing education and the workforce.

In conclusion, nursing leaders who are committed to diversity and apply the strategy of inclusion to the strategic management process will increase diversity in nursing education and the workforce.

References

Bessent, H. (2005). *The soul of leadership*. Battle Creek, MI: W. K. Kellogg Foundation.

Genter, P. (2005). *Strategic management of health care organizations* (5th ed.). Malden, MA: Blackwell.

Harvey, L. H. (1970). Educational problems of minority group nurses. *Nursing Outlook, 18*(9), 48-50.

Institute of Medicine. (2003). *Unequal treatment: Confronting racial and ethnic disparities in health care*. Washington, DC: National Academies Press (http://www.nap.edu).

Rozella, J. D., Regan-Kubinski, M. J., & Albrecht, S. A. (1994). The need for multicultural diversity among health professionals. *Nursing & Health Care: Perspectives on Community, 15*(5), 243-246.

SREB. (2002). *Racial/Ethnic and gender diversity in nursing education*. Retrieved from http://www.sreb.org/programs/nursing/publications/Diversity_in_Nursing.pdf

Sullivan Commission. (2004). *Missing Persons: Minorities in Health Professions*. Retrieved from http://www.aacn.nche.edu/media/pdf/SullivanReport.pdf

CHAPTER 8

Nursing Care or Care of Nursing?
Doctoral Education and the Shortage of African American Nursing Faculty

Maurice C. Taylor, PhD, JD,
and Earlene B. Merrill, EdD, RN, CNE

INTRODUCTION

The nation's health care delivery system is experiencing a significant and unprecedented shortage of nurses. A recent study finds that the shortage of registered nurses (RNs) in the United States could reach as high as 500,000 by 2025, and that the demand for RNs is expected to grow by one to three percent each year (Buerhaus, Staiger, & Auerbach, 2008). In its November 2007 report, the U.S. Bureau of Labor Statistics observed that registered nurses will add 587,000 new jobs by 2016 (Dohm & Shniper, 2007). An American Hospital Association (AHA) report, *The 2007 State of America's Hospitals - Taking the Pulse*, concluded that nationwide, U.S. hospitals need approximately 116,000 RNs to fill vacant positions. Projections for the next decade suggest that hospitals, medical clinics, and other critical care facilities will experience significant challenges in meeting the health care needs of aging baby boomers, typically defined as persons born between 1946 and 1964.

The challenge of meeting the nation's health care needs is exacerbated by the decreasing supply of nurses and nurse faculty due, in large measure, to the retirement of baby boomer nurses and nursing faculty. The Southern Regional Education Board (SREB) (2007) reported that southern states and the District of Columbia are projected to have nearly 40,000 job openings for RNs every year through 2014. Nationally, many hospitals, nursing homes and other health care facilities are struggling to fill empty registered nurse positions. Similarly, nursing education is also experiencing a problem filling nursing faculty positions. Hence, the shortage of nursing faculty to provide instruction and training to new nurses is as critical as the shortage of nurses to provide nursing care in clinical and hospital settings.

According to the Council of Graduate Schools (CGS) (2005), the well-documented nursing shortage "includes a lack of minority nurses both in education and practice" (p. 8). A 2002 National League for Nursing (NLN) Faculty Survey concluded that more nurse educators are needed to increase the number of nurses and concomitantly to eliminate the nursing shortage and that this situation is not expected to improve in the near future because of an inadequate number of nurse educators in the education pipeline (NLN, 2005). Similarly, a 2008 NAS Report also noted that the shortage of nursing school faculty is restricting nursing program enrollments. Specifically, the NAS Report found that nursing schools turned away 5,823 qualified applicants during the 2000-2001 school year. More than a third (38.8 percent) of schools point to faculty shortages as a reason for not accepting all qualified applicants into entry level baccalaureate programs. A compounding factor is that the nursing faculty is aging and many are approaching retirement. The average age of nurse faculty is 51 years. The average age of doctorate level nursing professors is 56.3 years. Consequently, even if schools had more students, they may not have the faculty to teach them (NAS Recruitment Communications, 2008).

A 2006 Health Resources and Services Administration (HRSA) report concluded that if the demand for more nurses is to be met, schools of nursing in the United States must graduate approximately 90 percent more nurses. Despite the demand for nurses, the American Association of Colleges of Nursing (AACN) indicated that 32,797 qualified nursing student applicants were turned away in 2004, followed by 42,000 in 2006 - all due to the shortage in faculty. The shortage of nursing faculty is interwoven with the current national shortage of nurses. Although educational programs need to produce more graduates to function within the health care system, the shortage of nursing faculty directly limits the capacity of educational programs to enroll more nursing students, particularly graduate students, thereby decreasing the number of graduates available to meet the demand for nurses to care for patients as well as the demand for nursing faculty (AACN, 2006).

The shortage of minority nurses and nurse faculty, particularly among African Americans, is dangerously acute. The editors of *Minority Nurse* (2006) magazine note, for example, when it comes to minority and male nursing faculty, there has always been a severe shortage and that only about 9.5 percent of today's nursing educators are people of color and even fewer (4.2 percent) are men. Tucker-Allen (2002), founder of the Association of Black Nursing Faculty (ABNF), observed, for example, that at the Call to the Nursing Profession conference held in 2001 conferees reached an "understanding that meeting societal needs meant that we would work towards increasing the number of minority nurses in the profession." She notes further that all schools of nursing are being asked to increase the number of minority students and minority faculty teaching in nursing programs.

In this chapter, we examine factors impacting doctoral education for nurses and how those factors affect the development of African American nursing faculty. We identify factors affecting the shortage of nurses and the shortage of nursing faculty. Our focus is identifying the educational objectives and learning outcomes for nurses pursuing doctoral degrees. We are especially interested in presenting learning objectives and a model curriculum for African Americans pursuing a PhD in nursing.

NURSING FACULTY AGE, RETIREMENT, AND FACULTY SHORTAGE

There are multiple factors that influence the nursing shortage, both in practice and in the academy. For example, one factor contributing to the shortage in nursing care is the ability of nurses who are college graduates to select a variety of occupations in administration, health services, home care, risk management, public health and community-based settings in addition to engaging in direct nursing practice in clinical and/or hospital settings. Included among the factors contributing to the shortage in nursing faculty are: faculty age, inadequate compensation (pay received not commensurate with the responsibility), and lack of master's and doctoral programs in nursing. In considering the "why" of the faculty shortage, Robinson (2005) explains that

> [t]he most obvious "why" points to the retiring nurse faculty. Currently the average age of faculty is 57 years. The delays in pursuing and completing graduate education is a major "why." Less than half of full-time nursing faculty teaching at the collegiate level hold a doctoral degree. Thirty-two percent of schools of nursing cite insufficient faculty as the reason for decreased admissions. Nursing faculty salaries tend to be lower than those of other nurse positions. This "why" has seen the flight of doctorally prepared faculty from academia to more lucrative clinical and private sector positions. Still other skilled practitioners desire to remain in clinical practice for fear of loss of clinical skills. A final "why" is the various misperceptions about the educator roles (p. 3).

While the preparation of more nurses to practice in clinics and hospitals may be met in a variety of educational settings, including community colleges, hospitals, and four-year colleges and universities, the preparation of nurse educators is limited to universities with graduate degree programs. It is, therefore, possible to increase the number of registered nurses to serve in hospital and clinical settings without increasing the number of doctorally prepared nursing faculty, since most registered nurses need not earn a bachelor's or master's degree, both of which are prerequisites for the doctorate.

By 2010, the number of elderly in the U.S. population is expected to increase dramatically, since baby boomers, individuals born in the mid-1940s, will begin qualifying for Social Security benefits. The nation's supply of nurses is also aging. Responses from the 2004 National Sample Survey of Registered Nurses revealed: "The average age of the RN population [has] continued to climb, increasing to 46.8 years of age in 2004, compared to 45.2 years in 2000, and 44.3 years in 1996" (Health Resources and Services Administration, 2006). The survey's findings also revealed that as the average age of nurses moves closer to retirement, fewer younger nurses are entering the workforce. According to the survey, in 1980, 25.1 percent of RNs were under the age of 30, compared with only 8.0 percent of RNs in 2004 and the percent of nurses over 54 years of age increased to 25.2 percent in 2004, compared with 20.3 percent in 2000 and 16.9 percent in 1980. According to NAS Recruitment Communications (2008), the demand for nurses to care for an aging population will increase dramatically by 2010 as the first of the 78 million baby-boomer generation begin to retire and experience chronic health problems. Nooney and Lacey (2007) also indicated that an aging population and a demographic shift are causing an increased demand for health care at the same time that some nurses are retiring.

Hinshaw (2001) stated that not only are nursing faculty aging, but the average age for assistant professors is also increasing due to nurses entering academia later in their careers. An NLN 2002 Faculty Survey (2005) on schools of nursing programs found that among the critical factors impacting the future of nursing education was the aging of the nursing faculty. According to the survey's findings, an average of 1.3 full-time faculty members per program left their positions in nursing education in 2002. About half the survey respondents had at least one unfilled, budgeted full-time faculty position, and some had as many as 15 such positions. Based on the findings, 36.5 percent of faculty who left their positions in the preceding year did so because of retirement, and 8.6 percent of faculty were 61 years of age or older. The survey indicated that 75 percent of the schools of nursing current faculty population were expected to retire by 2019 (NLN, 2005).

An AACN study (2005) found that the median age of the 417 recipients of nursing doctoral degrees in 2002 was 47.3 years. Half of all graduates (50.8 percent) were between the ages of 45 and 54 years; 12.8 percent were older than 55 years, and only 36 individuals (8.6 percent) were under the age of 35. By way of comparison, data from the 2003 Survey of Earned Doctorates (SED) revealed that the median age for completing the doctorate was 33.3 years in 2002 (National Opinion Research Center, 2003). According to the SED, in 2002 the mean number of years registered in a doctoral program for all students was 7.5 years (National Opinion Research Center, 2003) as compared to a mean of 8.8 years for nursing students. The mean age of retirement for full-time, doctorally prepared faculty in 2004, according to the AACN data was 54.3 years; it was 49.2 years for nursing faculty with master's degrees. Retirement projections for individuals who were faculty in 2001 revealed that from 2004 through 2012, between 200 and 300 doctorally prepared faculty will be eligible for retirement each year (AACN, 2005).

SOCIAL JUSTICE, HEALTH DISPARITIES, AND AFRICAN AMERICAN NURSING FACULTY

The shortage of nursing faculty, like the shortage of nurses, generally varies by race, gender, ethnicity, and region. The shortage of minority nursing faculty is particularly acute. During data collection in 2004-2005 on diversity of the nursing student population, it was revealed that only 23 percent of students were identified as belonging to a minority group. Hence, of that population, 12 percent reported being African American, six percent Pacific-Asian, four percent Hispanic, and only one percent Native American (National League for Nursing, 2006). According to Minority Nurse (2006), less than 10 percent of the nation's nursing educators are people of color.

Any increase in student enrollment trends will result in a need for more nursing faculty. One writer (Tucker-Allen, 2003) has suggested that increasing the number of minority nurses means there must be an increase in minority nursing faculty members. According to the NLN (2005), the nursing shortage is not confined solely to health providers; rather, there is a growing shortage of nurse faculty. In a research study analyzing perceived existing educational barriers in nursing school, 26 faculty and 17 ethnically diverse nurses from associate and baccalaureate nursing programs were interviewed. One of the barriers that consistently surfaced was the lack of diverse role models (Amaro et al., 2006).

In September 2004, the Sullivan Commission released its report on diversity in the health care workforce, which revealed specific data about minorities in nursing. The Sullivan Commission recommended that there needs to be a priority placed on increasing health care workforce diversity if the overall health in the United States is to improve. This priority can be realized by increasing the cultural competence of health care providers as well as improving health outcomes for members of minorities (Sullivan Commission, 2004). The report noted that nursing has increased the numbers of underrepresented minorities at a slightly greater rate than medicine and dentistry, which were the other professions studied. However, the report stated that an increase of 20,000 minority nurses would be required to raise the proportion of minorities by one percent. Minority nurses also pursue graduate education at rates higher than do white, non-Hispanic nurses. In addition, it was noted that faculty and academic leaders in nursing have less diversity than the nursing population in general (Sullivan Commission, 2004).

Health concerns vary among racial and ethnic groups. The Centers for Disease Control and Prevention (CDC) MMWR (2005) reports that although African Americans and whites share many of the same leading causes of death, such as cancer and stroke, three of the 10 leading causes of death for African Americans are not among the leading causes of death for whites, including homicide (sixth), human immunodeficiency virus (HIV) disease (seventh), and septicemia (ninth). In a report entitled, *Racial and Ethnic Approaches to Community Health (REACH U.S.) Finding Solutions to Health Disparities: At a Glance 2008*, the CDC notes that although African Americans represent only 12.7 percent of the U.S. population, they account for 26 percent of all asthma deaths and are nearly twice as likely to have diabetes as whites. The infant death rate for African Americans is almost double the national rate. Death from heart disease is 30 percent higher and stroke death rates are 41 percent higher for African Americans than for whites. According to the CDC, even with nearly identical screening rates for mammograms, the death rate for African American women from breast cancer remains higher than white women.

In order to properly care for patients and to effectively teach nursing students, nurses as well as nurse educators must be knowledgeable about the impact of health disparities on racial and ethnic communities. Given projections by the Census Bureau of demographic shifts in the United States, knowledge of such health disparities will become increasingly important for nurses as well as nurse educators. Table 8-1 reflects the Census Bureau's projections of the growth of whites, blacks, Asians and Hispanics from 2000 to 2050. The African American population is projected to grow, for example, from 12.7 percent in 2000 to 14.6 percent by 2050. The Hispanic population is projected to double in size during the same period. Although their number is relatively small, the Asian population is projected to more than double from 3.8 percent to eight percent of the U.S. population by 2050. The percent of whites in the population is projected to decline almost 10 percent during this period. These demographic shifts in the U.S. population demonstrate that at least for the foreseeable future it is unlikely that a "one size fits all" curriculum will be sufficient to provide the necessary education needed by nurses and nurse educators serving diverse racial and ethnic communities in the United States.

Table 8-1

Projected Population of the United States, by Race and Hispanic Origin: 2000 to 2050						
Year	2000	2010	2020	2030	2040	2050
Percent of Total	100	100	100	100	100	100
Race and Hispanic Origin						
White	81	79.3	77.6	75.8	73.9	72.1
Black	12.7	13.1	13.5	13.9	14.3	14.6
Asian	3.8	4.6	5.4	6.2	7.1	8
All Other Races	2.5	3	3.5	4.1	4.7	5.3
Hispanic	12.6	15.5	17.8	20.1	22.3	24.4
Whites	69.4	65.1	61.3	57.5	53.7	50.1

Source: U.S. Census Bureau, 2004, *U.S. Interim Projections by Age, Sex, Race, and Hispanic Origin 2000-2050*, http://www.census.gov/ipc/www/usinterimproj/

AVAILABILITY OF NURSES QUALIFIED IN NURSING EDUCATION

The NLN 2002 Faculty Survey identified three trends impacting the availability of nursing faculty including: (1) the aging of nursing faculty; (2) the increasing number of part-time faculty; and (3) the large number of faculty who are not prepared at the doctoral level. It is this last trend that is the focus of this chapter, particularly as it impacts doctoral education for African American nurses. The NLN survey found that: "Only 350 to 400 nursing students receive doctoral degrees each year and the pool of doctorally-prepared candidates for full-time nursing professorships is very limited" (NLN, 2005). The NLN Position Statement on the Preparation of Nurse Educators (2002) notes that in 1993, from the 54 doctoral programs in nursing in the United States, only 381 individuals graduated. And although by 1999, the number of programs had increased to 72, the number of students graduating from all of these doctoral programs actually decreased nearly two percent to only 375.

In contrast to the numerous doctoral programs located at traditionally white institutions (TWIs), Carnegie (2005) reports that Hampton University established a master's program in nursing and graduated its first student in 1978. Since that time, at least eleven (11) other historically black universities (HBCU), including Coppin State University, one of four HBCUs in Maryland, have established masters' programs. As late as 2005, there were only two at HBCUs, Hampton in Virginia and Southern in Baton Rouge, Louisiana, that awarded doctoral degrees in Nursing (Carnegie, 2005). Morgan State University in Baltimore, Maryland, another HBCU, was recently approved by that state's higher education commission to award the PhD in nursing. Carnegie (2005) reports that: "According to the National Sample Survey, 11.1 percent of all master's and doctoral prepared nurses are Black as compared to 10.4 percent of the white nurses" (p. 7). In any case, it is clear that "the supply of doctorally-prepared faculty has not kept pace with program demands" (NLN, 2002).

Echoing the sentiments expressed in the NLN Position Statement, Yordy (2006) concludes that only a relatively small proportion of nursing schools provide research-oriented doctoral training. His research reveals:

> The number of students in these doctoral programs is also relatively small, with 1,603 full-time and 1,836 part-time students, and only 412 graduate[s] in 2004, an average of about 4.5 per doctoral program. Although the number of graduates by school is not available, it is likely that these graduates are not evenly distributed among all 93 programs, meaning that some programs probably have one or two (or even fewer) graduates per year. The total number of doctoral graduates is about 0.5 percent of all graduates of nursing programs preparing RNs, and not all of these doctoral graduates end up in faculty positions (Yordy, 2006, p. 3).

According to AACN (2008), U.S. nursing schools turned away 40,285 qualified applicants from entry-level baccalaureate nursing programs in 2007 due to an insufficient number of faculty, clinical sites, classroom space, clinical preceptors, and budget constraints. In addition, in 2007, 3,048 qualified applicants were turned away from master's programs, and 313 qualified applicants were turned away from doctoral programs. Enrollment in research-focused doctoral nursing programs was up by only 0.9 percent from the 2006-2007 academic year. Almost three quarters (71.4 percent) of the nursing schools responding to the 2007 survey pointed to faculty shortages as a reason for not accepting all qualified applicants into nursing programs.

Shortages of nursing faculty, particularly nursing faculty with doctoral degrees, confront many schools of nursing. Competition among health care institutions and schools of nursing for master's- and doctorally prepared nurses is a significant problem. Credentialed minority faculty members are in demand. Rising salaries and increasing opportunities outside academia present significant barriers to schools of nursing that seek to recruit and retain minority nursing faculty (Stanley, Capers, & Berlin, 2007).

Several states have implemented new initiatives to study and to identify solutions to the nursing shortage. Facing a shortage of 10,000 RNs by 2016, hospital administrators in Maryland announced a plan for increasing to 1,800 the number of enrollees of first-year nursing students beginning in 2009 and continuing into the foreseeable future. Maryland instituted a Statewide Commission on the Crisis in Nursing to examine the nursing shortage with a focus on issues in the workplace, compensation of nurses, retention of nurses, and issues related to faculty. Maryland's Governor, Martin O'Malley, recently announced the allocation of $3.4 million to the University of Maryland School of Nursing from the state's Higher Education Investment Fund to assist in recruiting more nursing faculty and nursing students, and to help the state's universities by creating jobs and expanding enrollment. In 2006, the AACN reviewed a number of state legislative initiatives to address the nursing shortage, including the Illinois Nurse Educator Assistance Act, Colorado's Nursing Faculty Fellowship Program, Nebraska's Nurse Faculty Student Loan Act, and North Dakota's Nurse Educator Loan Program (AACN, 2006).

Recognizing the need to specifically address the shortage of underrepresented minorities among nursing faculties, the NLN Foundation and the AACN have each implemented scholarship programs. The NLN Foundation has created a Minority Faculty Preparation Scholarship in order to encourage and support underrepresented minorities pursuing master's degree nursing education and who are preparing for the nurse faculty role. With support from the California Endowment, the AACN has implemented a similar scholarship program for underrepresented full-time minority nursing students who are residents of the state of California and enrolled in master's or doctoral nursing studies. The scholarship is designed to increase the number of minority nursing faculty in the state of California.

Taxonomy of Doctorates

Not all graduate education programs for nurses, and, in particular, not all doctoral education programs, will address the demand for nursing faculties at the associate, baccalaureate, and doctoral levels. Graduate education for nurses involves two distinct objectives. First, increasing the number of nurses earning the doctorate should lead to improved hospital and/or clinical care. Second, as Nyquist and Woodford (2000) observe, "doctoral education prepares graduates to conduct quality research" (p. 6) and to become future faculty.

The doctor of philosophy (PhD) degree is but one of several types of "doctorates" that nurses may pursue. Currently, doctorates may be earned in clinical nursing, nursing practice, and nursing science. In addition, many nurse educators have earned the doctor of education (EdD) degree. A number of other doctorates, including several in the health care fields, such as medical doctor (MD), doctor of dental surgery (DDS), doctor of pharmacy (PharmD), may also be differentiated from the PhD degree. Such doctorates are often classified as first professional degrees.

The AACN classifies doctoral programs in nursing into two distinct types: research-focused and practice-focused. The AACN's *Position Statement on the Practice Doctorate in Nursing* (AACN Position Statement) (2004) defines the term practice, specifically nursing practice, as

any form of nursing intervention that influences health care outcomes for individuals or populations, including the direct care of individual patients, management of care for individuals and populations, administration of nursing and health care organizations, and the development and implementation of health policy. Preparation at the practice doctorate level includes advanced preparation in nursing, based on nursing science, and is at the highest level of nursing practice (p. 3).

Practiced-focused doctoral nursing programs place less emphasis on designing research methodologies to test assumptions or hypotheses derived from theories of nursing. There is typically greater emphasis on the use of research data for evaluation and/or assessment of programs and administrative processes than on the collection of research data for the sake of generating new knowledge. Practice-focused nursing programs may also include a variety of variable capstone requirements in lieu of a dissertation. These capstone requirements may include demonstration projects, writing projects, and/or clinical activities.

Other differences may be identified between practice-focused doctorates in nursing and the PhD in nursing. For example, state licensing of graduates may be more important for practice-focused degree programs than for research-focused programs. On the other hand, accreditation by regional accrediting bodies of colleges and universities with schools of nursing as well as the accreditation of nursing programs by professional organizations may carry greater consequences for programs with research-focused degrees such as the PhD. The 2006 Report of the Task Force on the Professional Doctorate concluded:

Quality assurance agencies could respond appropriately if the standards applied to professional doctorates actually led to better practice and increased the student's capacity to practice effectively in diverse settings. In short, if the objective of these doctorates is related to the enhancement of professional practice, then their quality should be defined by how effectively they fulfill that objective.

According to the Task Force, "an effort should be made to engage various stakeholders in the exercise to create relevant 'Best Practices' for the Professional Doctorate" (Higher Learning Commission, 2006, p. 6). Some of the differences between practice-focused doctoral programs and PhD programs may be reflected in their admission requirements. Specifically, whether a master's degree, standard test scores, prior work experience, or a minimum baccalaureate grade point average (GPA) is required for admission may depend on whether one is applying to a practiced focused-nursing program or to a PhD in nursing program. A taxonomy of doctoral programs in nursing is presented in Table 8-2 below.

Table 8-2

Taxonomy of Doctoral Programs in Nursing	
Title of Program	**Degree**
Doctor of Nursing	ND
Doctor of Nursing Practice	DNP
Doctor of Nursing Practice	DrNP
Doctor of Nursing Science	DNS
Doctor of Nursing Science	DNSc
Doctor of Nursing Science	DSN
Doctor of Philosophy	PhD
Doctor of Education	EdD

Although not a nursing degree, the doctor of education (EdD) is included in this taxonomy because many of the faculty in schools of nursing possess the terminal degree in education. Offering a variety of terminal degree choices to nurses, nurse educators, and other applicants to doctoral nursing programs provides applicants with educational options that best match their vocational interests and/or nursing specialty. Problems may arise, however, with an excessive proliferation of doctoral nursing degrees. The problems include, but are not necessarily limited to, mission creep, questions regarding faculty qualifications, questions over investments in programs and facilities, decisions regarding curricula content, and confusion over admission and graduation requirements. In its Position Statement (2004), the AACN recognized the problems that such a large number of nursing doctorates may pose for the profession and has recommended the following:

- One degree title be chosen to represent practice-focused doctoral programs that prepare graduates for the highest level of nursing practice.

- The doctor of nursing practice (DNP) be the degree associated with practice-focused doctoral nursing education.

- The doctor of nursing (ND) degree title be phased out.

- The practice doctorate be the graduate degree for advanced nursing practice preparation, including but not limited to the four current APN roles: clinical nurse specialist, nurse anesthetist, nurse midwife, and nurse practitioner.

- A transition period be planned to provide nurses with master's degrees who wish to obtain the practice doctoral degree a mechanism to earn a practice doctorate in a relatively streamlined fashion, with credit given for previous graduate study and practice experience. The transition mechanism should provide multiple points of entry, standardized validation of competencies, and be time limited.

- Practice doctorate programs, as in research-focused doctoral programs, are encouraged to offer additional course work and practica that would prepare graduates to fill the role of nurse educator.

- Practice-focused doctoral programs need to be accredited by a nursing accrediting agency recognized by the U.S. Secretary of Education (i.e., the Commission on Collegiate Nursing Education or the National League for Nursing Accrediting Commission) (AACN Position Statement, 2004, p. 15).

In summary, the taxonomy of doctoral education in nursing is weighted heavily toward practice-focused degrees. Despite some "mission creep," neither the content of practice-focused curricula nor the educational objectives of practice-focused degrees are necessarily the same for the PhD in nursing. In 2005, the Council of Graduate Schools (CGS) insisted that the PhD "is a research degree and is to be distinguished from other doctorates, such as the M.D., J.D., Ed.D., or N.D., which are designed for professional training or which focus on applied research related to professional practice rather than on basic research that expands the knowledge base of the field" (CGS, 2005, p. 1).

The AACN recommends reducing to three the types of doctorates including the doctor of nursing practice (DNP), the doctor of philosophy (PhD) in nursing and/or the doctor of nursing science (DNSc). The content of the practice-focused doctoral curriculum typically does not address the central features of the research doctorate, namely, mastery of the founding theories of the discipline, mastery of basic research design and methodologies common to the discipline, and a familiarity with instructional pedagogy needed to transmit the knowledge of the discipline to aspiring students and/ or professionals.

It is the production of a sufficiently large number of nurses who comprehend theory and research and who are knowledgeable of instructional pedagogy in the discipline that is needed to address the shortage of nursing faculty. And, although teaching nurses to become more skilled in their clinical or hospital practice is also a desirable goal of the nursing profession, nursing faculty, like the faculty in most other colleges and universities, should possess the research skills to advance the knowledge of the nursing profession and transmit both the research skills and the new knowledge to aspiring nurse practitioners and/or nurse educators. Recognizing the shortfall in the content of practice-focused doctorates (as well as in some research-focused doctorates) the AACN's Position Statement encourages more pedagogical content in doctoral curricula to prepare graduates "to fill the role of nurse educator."

OBJECTIVES OF THE PHD

Nettles and Millett (2006) note that the American doctorate was initially modeled after the German PhD and was "conceived as the degree awarded to an elite cadre of serious students for extended study as they prepared for careers as scholars and researchers" (p. 1). Indeed, it was not until the late 19th century that "leading American educators discovered the power of German universities that were based on research and scientific discovery; the focus on research gave them an opportunity to develop professional academic standards based on the process of inquiry and the advance of knowledge" (Gaff, Pruitt-Logan, & Weibl, 2006, p. 2). More recently, the Carnegie Foundation for the Advancement of Teaching has suggested that the purposes of the doctorate, the PhD in particular, are twofold: the formation of scholars; and the preparation of stewards of the discipline. The president of CGS notes, for example, that the PhD degree "is awarded by faculty stewards of the discipline to those who have demonstrated the highest level of mastery of the intellectual principles of their chosen field" (CGS, 2005, p. v).

The Carnegie Initiative on the Doctorate (CID), a five-year project begun in 2001, "focused on aligning the purpose and practice of doctoral education in six disciplines" (Golde, 2006, p. 13). Although none of the six disciplines (chemistry, education, English, mathematics, and neuroscience) in the CID included nursing, the findings and generalizations from the CID are, nonetheless, instructive. For example, Walker, former director of the CID, describes doctoral education as "a complex process of formation." He explains that formation

points not only to the development of intellectual expertise but to the growth of "the personality, character, habits of heart and mind" and "the role that the given discipline is capable of and meant to play in academe and society at large." What is formed, in short, is the scholar's professional identity in all its dimensions (Walker, 2008, p. 8).

In defining the second purpose of the doctorate, Golde (2006), a senior scholar at the Carnegie Foundation writes, "We believe the term *steward of the discipline* should be applied to all doctorate holders. It is not a 'Hall of Fame' title reserved for the rare individual who excels in all domains of action" (p. 13). According to Golde, "The Ph.D., at its heart, is a research degree. Demonstrating the ability to conduct research and scholarship that make a unique contribution and meet the standards of credible work is the culminating experience of the Ph.D." (p. 10).

The findings and assumptions of the CID project hold several important implications for the doctoral education of nurses. One implication is that the proliferation of doctorates that focus on developing narrow nursing care competencies will fail to develop a sufficient number of scholars and stewards of the nursing discipline. A second implication is that scholarship, the hallmark of the PhD, is not synonymous with the creation of highly skilled nurse practitioners. Highly skilled nurse practitioners, for example, those who have earned a doctorate of nursing practice, are presumably expert at providing nursing care to patients in hospital and clinical settings. The focus of such expertise is the patient. By contrast, the focus of the research doctorate, the PhD in particular, is not so much the care of patients as much as it is the care of the nursing discipline. Golde contends:

> The doctorate should signal a high level accomplishment in three facets of the discipline: generation, conservation, and transformation. A Ph.D. holder should be capable of generating new knowledge and defending knowledge claims against challenges and criticism, conserving the most important ideas and findings that are a legacy of past and current work, and transforming knowledge that has been generated and conserved by explaining and connecting it to ideas from other fields. All of this implies the ability to teach well to a variety of audiences, including those outside formal classrooms (p. 10).

Indeed, in its Position Statement in 2002, the NLN also suggests that more attention needs to be given to the teaching/pedagogical component of the nurse educator role. The NLN Board of Governors asserts,

> It is critical that all nurse educators know about teaching, learning and evaluation; and nurse educators who practice in academic settings also must have knowledge and skill in curriculum development, assessment of program outcomes, and being an effective member of an academic community, among other things. Additionally, each academic unit in nursing must have a cadre of experts/"architects"/designers/ leaders who can envision new realities for nursing education, generate new models of education, and create new pedagogies and new futures for nursing education.

We are not contending that the practice of nursing and quality of care are not important for those pursuing a PhD in nursing. Rather, our contention is that best practices and quality care are part of the nursing discipline's storehouse of knowledge that forms the foundation for research and scholarship by graduate nursing students and faculty. In addition, graduate students are called upon to exercise stewardship over the nursing discipline's storehouse of knowledge regarding practice and care.

In *Graduate Education: The Backbone of American Competitiveness and Innovation* (McAllister, 2007), CGS, an international organization of deans of 480 universities in the United States and Canada, and 13 universities outside North America identified the following five "key assumptions" of graduate education in the United States.

1. A highly skilled workforce operating at the frontiers of knowledge creation and professional practice is key to America's competitiveness and national security. Universities, governments, and private industry each play an essential role in providing the expertise and resources necessary to achieve this objective.

2. The expanded participation of U.S. citizens, particularly from underrepresented minority groups, should be a priority in fields that are essential to our nation's success. Development of STEM careers should be emphasized.

3. Interdisciplinary research preparation and education are central to future competitiveness, because knowledge creation and innovation frequently occur at the interface of disciplines.

4. U.S. graduate schools must be able to attract the best and brightest students from around the world.

5. The quality of graduate programs drives the success of America's higher education system. Efforts to evaluate and improve all aspects of the quality of the U.S. graduate education enterprise must be advanced and supported in order to foster innovation (p. 8).

As reflected in the CGS assumptions, the key characteristics of graduate education in the United States are "knowledge creation" and "research preparation and education." The key characteristics of graduate education as identified by CGS are consistent with the findings and assumptions of the CID Project regarding the formation of scholars and the stewardship imperative. Increasingly, the regional societies that accredit colleges and universities throughout the United States and affiliated territories are promulgating separate educational standards and/or criteria for institutions with graduate programs. These educational standards also emphasize the primacy of research and scholarship in the instruction of graduate students. For example, the Middle States Commission on Higher Education (2002) has included three elements for graduate and professional education among its Fundamental Elements of Educational Offerings. Among the 14 standards that the Middle States Commission on Higher Education asserts that colleges and universities must meet, Standard 11, Educational Offerings, requires that graduate programs possess:

- graduate curricula providing for the development of research and independent thinking which studies at the advanced level presuppose;

- faculty with credentials appropriate to the graduate curricula; and

- assessment of student learning and program outcomes relative to the goals and objectives of the graduate programs (including professional and clinical skills, professional examinations and professional placement where applicable) and the use of results to improve student learning and program effectiveness (see Standard 14: Assessment of Student Learning) (p. 35).

Increasingly, however, simple mastery of the content of the discipline is not enough to assure success as a college or university faculty member. Gaff et al. (2006) contend, for example, that: "Graduate students who lack teaching experience, supervision and support from faculty members, expertise with some of the newer technological, collaborative, and experiential approaches to teaching and learning, and evidence of success, are at a disadvantage" (p. 6). In 1993, CGS and the Association of American Colleges and Universities (AACU) partnered to establish the Preparing Future Faculty (PFF) initiative. The purpose of the PFF initiative is to provide doctoral students, as well as some master's and postdoctoral students, with opportunities to observe and experience faculty responsibilities at a variety of academic institutions with varying missions, diverse student bodies, and different expectations for faculty. According to Pruitt-Logan, Gaff, and Jentoft (2002),

The most fundamental idea characterizing PFF is that the doctoral experience for those interested in an academic career should include: a) increasingly independent and varied teaching responsibilities, b) opportunities to grow and develop as a researcher, and c) opportunities to serve the department, campus, and community (p. 4).

In summary, we suggest that the research doctorate in nursing, specifically the PhD, ought to share similar educational objectives, research designs and methodologies, and learning outcomes as do PhD degrees in other disciplines. Specifically, the preceding research suggests that a PhD, regardless of discipline, should include a process whereby students master the theory and research central to the discipline, become familiar with the research methodologies common to the discipline, conduct original research that advances the knowledge in the discipline, and are prepared to teach the content of the discipline. These sentiments are consistent with the three recommendations for program development of nurse educators as proposed by the NLN (2002).

1. Some master's programs should develop or reinstate a track that prepares beginning nurse educators (for full-time faculty roles in community colleges, part-time or non-tenure-track positions in universities, or staff development positions in the practice setting) or that help advanced clinicians make the transition to the role of educator.

2. Doctoral programs should include learning experiences related to teaching and learning for all students.

3. Some doctoral programs should offer an option that allows students to specialize in nursing education and conduct pedagogical research, thereby contributing significantly to the development of a strong cadre of expert faculty-scholars who will assume leadership roles in nursing education and contribute to the ongoing development of the science of nursing education.

Indeed because of the commonality of educational objectives (i.e., stewardship of the discipline), research designs and methodologies (i.e., formation of scholars), and learning outcomes (i.e., a curricula of nursing-specific topics), it is reasonable to attempt to outline a model set of educational objectives, curricula, and learning outcomes for the PhD in nursing.

Objectives of a PhD in Nursing

If the assumptions of the Carnegie Foundation for the Advancement of Teaching as outlined in its CID Project as well as the key characteristics of graduate education as reflected in the Council of Graduate Schools formulation are accepted, the PhD in nursing should reflect, at a minimum, a core set of educational objectives including:

1. the formation of scholars who are researching topics important to the advancement of knowledge about the discipline of nursing;

2. the creation of stewards of critical theory and commonly held knowledge and beliefs about the discipline of nursing, including common nursing practices; and

3. the preparation of future faculty for the discipline who are effective teachers of the theory, research, and practice of nursing to future generations of nurses.

We recommend, as a model, that at the completion of the doctoral degree in nursing, in particular the PhD degree, graduates will: (a) comprehend well enough to teach the commonly held concepts, theories, and research findings regarding the discipline of nursing; (b) be able to design and conduct original research that advances the frontier of knowledge about the discipline of nursing; and (c) be prepared to assume the role of nursing faculty as well as providing expertise in the practice of nursing care in clinical settings. The PhD in nursing, just as the PhD in other disciplines, should prepare students "to discover, integrate, and apply knowledge, as well as to communicate and disseminate it (CGS, 2005, p. 1)." The CGS further contends that the objectives of a model PhD degree in nursing may be gleaned from the "Nature and Purpose of the Doctoral Program" as outlined in the CGS Policy Statement on the Doctor of Philosophy Degree (p. 1). Thus, the objectives of the PhD in nursing should be to:

1. develop nursing students' capacity to make significant original contributions to knowledge about the science and practice of nursing in a context of freedom of inquiry and expression;

2. develop the ability of nursing students to understand and critically evaluate the literature in the field of nursing;

3. prepare nursing students to apply appropriate principles and procedures to the recognition, evaluation, interpretation, and understanding of issues and problems at the frontier of knowledge about nursing;

4. instill in nursing students an appropriate awareness of and commitment to the ethical practices appropriate to the field of nursing; and

5. provide an apprenticeship to and close association with nursing faculty experienced in research and teaching.

In summary, we propose that the objectives of a PhD in nursing are to produce faculty to teach aspiring nurses, to develop experts in nursing practice for hospitals and clinics, and to produce leaders to articulate administrative and policy matters for nurses. Given the general consensus regarding the purpose and objectives of the PhD, i.e., to form scholars, to create stewards, to train faculty, and to develop professional expertise, it is feasible to develop a model curriculum for the PhD in nursing. We propose that the graduate curriculum cover health disparities that disproportionately affect the African American community as additional course content for African Americans pursuing the doctorate, specifically, the PhD in nursing.

TOWARD A MODEL CURRICULUM FOR AFRICAN AMERICAN NURSE EDUCATORS

A model PhD curriculum for African American nurses should conform, in a general sense, to the basic objectives listed above. The model curriculum that we propose also incorporates courses recommended by the NLN that provide candidates for the doctorate with "learning experiences related to teaching and learning" and with formal instruction in conducting "pedagogical research." We assert that in addition to the general objectives and courses that form the core of any PhD curriculum in nursing, African American nurse educators should also be taught about the illnesses, diseases, and/or health risks that disproportionately impact their communities.

REACH 2010 is a national program of 40 community-based organizations funded by the CDC to support programs to eliminate health disparities among African Americans, American Indians, Alaska Natives, Asians, Native Hawaiians and other Pacific Islanders, and Hispanics in any of six health priority areas. According to the CDC (2007), the six priority areas include:

1. Infant Mortality

2. Deficits in Breast and Cervical Cancer Screening and Management

3. Cardiovascular Diseases

4. Diabetes

5. HIV Infections/AIDS

6. Child and Adult Immunizations

It is this context of health disparities, in particular the six REACH 2010 priority areas, that provides the social justice backdrop for the education of African American nurses and nursing faculty. We are not suggesting that these health priority areas have no relevance to nurses or nursing faculty who are not African American. Because these health disparities areas disproportionately impact African American communities, nurses who are working in health care facilities in these communities and nursing faculty instructing nursing students and/or aspiring nursing faculty should be trained to be thoroughly conversant about the risk factors associated with these health disparities and their implications for the health of patients in the community in which they are likely to work. Tucker-Allen (2002) explains that increasing the number of minority faculty/students is so important, because

> [i]t is also known that minority health care workers return to their communities to provide health care. With the current minority nurse work force aging, graying and retiring, there will be fewer minority nurses working in these minority communities. This would have a further detrimental effect on the health care of residents in these communities. Agreeing to make diligent efforts to increase minority enrollment in schools of nursing and to increase minority faculty teaching in these institutions is a good thing.

The model curriculum that we propose in Table 8-3 below is based on a minimum of sixty (60) semester credits. Culled from the literature reviewed above, we have organized the curriculum around four educational outcomes; namely, the formation of nursing scholars, stewardship of the nursing discipline, the preparation of future nursing faculty, and health disparities that disproportionately affect African Americans. The course numbering is meant to reflect only a general level of difficulty where 600 suggests foundation courses, 700 suggests intermediate level difficulty, 800 more advanced courses, and 900 reserved for the dissertation sequence of courses. Beyond the general order reflected in the numbering of courses, the model curriculum is not meant to suggest a strict chronological sequence by which students enroll in courses. We would contend that students should enroll in the foundation courses first and enroll in the dissertation courses only when they have completed all other required courses.

The order in which students enroll in the foundation courses or when they enroll in the intermediate and advanced courses is left to the faculty in schools and departments of nursing to determine. Although this model curriculum is based on 60 credits, we readily concede that schools and/or departments of nursing may wish to require more credits to reflect the particular expertise of the faculty, to cover local and or regional health care concerns, or, depending on demographics, to focus the curriculum on additional health disparities impacting the majority of racial and ethnic minority residents in the area. Finally, we would expect that PhD curricula in specific schools or departments of nursing would contain more than 12 credits of health disparities electives. A curriculum could contain, for example, several Independent Study and Supervised Research courses as well as any number of electives reflecting the nursing faculty's interests. This model curriculum is intended to suggest that of all the electives that could be offered, subjects covering the priority areas identified by REACH 2010 as they impact disproportionately the health of African Americans must be a part of the curriculum for African Americans pursuing the PhD in nursing.

RACE AND THE SHORTAGE OF NURSING FACULTY

The shortage of nursing faculty, like the shortage of nurses, generally varies by race, sex, ethnicity, and region. The shortage of minority nursing faculty is, however, particularly acute. Less than 10 percent of the nation's nursing educators are people of color (Minority Nurse, 2006). According to data published for the 2005 National Nurses Week by the U.S. Census Bureau (2005), of the 2.4 million registered nurses in the United States, 92 percent are female, ten percent are black, seven percent are Asian, and four percent are Hispanic. Forde (2008) reports that, at 589 registered nurses per 100,000 residents, California has the lowest number of registered nurses in the United States. The national average is 825 registered nurses per 100,000 residents. According to Forde (2008), "The current racial makeup of the nursing work force in California is 63.9 percent white; 6.3 percent Hispanic; 3.8 percent African American; 21.9 percent Asian and 4.1 percent Other" (p. 11).

Table 8-3

A Model PhD Curriculum

Educational Outcomes	Course	Course Number	Course Title	Total
Formation of Nursing Scholars	NURS	600	Advanced Theory of Nursing	3
	NURS	601	Research Methods I	3
	NURS	602	Statistical Applications in Nursing Research	3
	NURS	700	Biostatistics	3
	NURS	701	Advanced Research Design and Methodology	3
	NURS	900	Dissertation Seminar	3
	NURS	901	Dissertation Research	3
	NURS	902	Dissertation Defense	3
Summary of Scholarship Credit				**24**
Stewardship of the Nursing Discipline	NURS	613	Advanced History and Philosophy of Nursing	3
	NURS	614	Nursing Care in Institutional Settings	3
	NURS	615	Organizational Behavior in Nursing	3
	NURS	616	Legal Issues in Nursing Care	3
	NURS			
Summary of Stewardship Credit				**12**
Preparation of Future Faculty in Nursing	NURS	704	Philosophy of Nursing Education	3
	NURS	705	Curriculum Design	3
	NURS	803	Assessment of Learning Outcomes	3
	NURS	804	Practicum in Nursing Education	3
Summary of Future Faculty Credit				**12**
Health Disparities, Nursing and African Americans	NURS	702	Seminar in HIV Infections and AIDS	3
	NURS	703	Screenings and Immunizations in the	
			African American Community	3
	NURS	706	Diabetes, Obesity, and Risk Factors	3
	NURS	801	Cardiovascular Disease and Nursing Care	3
	NURS	802	Seminar in Maternal Child Health Policy	3
Summary of Health Disparities Credit				**12**
Summary (minimum) Credit for the PhD in Nursing				**60**

A national effort similar to the AACN partnership with the California Endowment will be necessary to increase the number of underrepresented minorities, in particular African Americans, who become nursing faculty. Several other initiatives have been established to increase the number of minority nurses and minority nursing faculty. For example, with financial support from HRSA, Thomas Edison State College School of Nursing in Trenton, NJ, is implementing a program to recruit 45 minority nurse educators during the next three years to complete a 32-week Distance Education Program. Upon completion, the minority faculty will teach one 12-week online nursing course at the college and will then be able to bring their distance education skills back to their own local institutions.

And while not expressly focusing on minority faculty, the Robert Wood Johnson Foundation's newly created Center to Champion Nursing in America (2007) holds promise for increasing the number of nursing faculty by serving as an advocate for more federal funding as well as a clearinghouse of data related to the nursing faculty shortage. The Foundation's objectives for the Center are to improve patient care by pressing for:

- Greater state and federal funding to support expanded nursing education, particularly addressing severe faculty shortages at nurse training institutions across the country

- Places for nurse leaders on the governing boards of hospitals and other health care organizations to provide critically needed perspective on improving quality and safety of care

- Education, awareness and dissemination of research to inform the public and policy-makers about nurse workforce issues and the link between a trained and adequate nursing workforce and high-quality health care

In addition to increased funding to support minority nursing students, more schools of nursing must be established and funded at historically black colleges and universities (HBCUs) and at other minority serving institutions (MSIs) including Tribal Colleges. The percent of African Americans earning bachelor's, master's, and doctorate degrees from HBCUs is significant. Table 8-4 reveals that in 2001-2002, HBCUs accounted for over a tenth of all doctorates awarded to African Americans. Both the number and percent of doctorates awarded to African Americans by HBCUs have increased since 2004 when these data were analyzed. For example, the *Journal of Blacks in Higher Education* (2007) reports that in 2005, historically black colleges and universities awarded 367 doctorates to recipients of all races, a slight increase over the 350 doctorates awarded by black universities in 2004. And in 2006, historically black colleges and universities awarded 376 doctorates to recipients of all races, an increase over the 367 doctorates awarded by black universities in 2005 (JBHE Weekly Bulletin, 2007).

Table 8-4

Degrees Conferred by Historically Black Colleges and Universities (HBCUs) by Degree, 2001-02			
Degree	Number of degrees	HBCU degrees as a percentage of all degrees awarded	HBCU degrees as a percentage of all degrees to Blacks
Associate's	3,436	0.6	2.8
Bachelor's	28,846	2.2	21.5
Master's	6,338	1.3	11.0
Doctor's	364	0.8	10.7
First professional	1,427	1.8	17.2

Source: Stephen Provasnik & Linda L. Shafer. *Historically Black Colleges and Universities, 1976 to 2001.* National Center for Education Statistics. (September 2004). http://nces.ed.gov/pubs2004/2004062.pdf

SUMMARY AND CONCLUSION

In this chapter, we examined the link between the national shortage of nurses and the shortage of African American nursing faculty. We argue that increasing the number of African American nursing faculty requires increasing the number of nurses holding research doctorates, specifically the PhD. We contend that the curriculum for African American nurse educators should include courses and training in the health disparities that disproportionately impact their patients, students, and their communities. We believe that nurses from other racial and ethnic groups should also be knowledgeable about those health disparities that disproportionately impact their respective communities.

We noted that the both the NLN and the AACN recommendations acknowledge that the shortage of nursing faculty is not readily addressed by a proliferation of practice-focused doctorates. Specifically, the AACN recommends the DNP as the sole practice-focused doctorate and that practice doctorate programs, as in research-focused doctoral programs, are encouraged to offer additional course work and practice that would prepare graduates to fill the role of nurse educator. The NLN has recommended that more teaching and learning experiences and training in conducting research be incorporated in doctoral curricula for nurse educators.

We cited the assumptions of the Carnegie Foundation for the Advancement of Teaching and the Council of Graduate Schools regarding the objectives of the PhD, noting in particular their focus on the preparation of future faculty. Our review of the literature and the findings of the CID Project as well as the key assumptions of graduate education noted by CGS suggest that the educational objectives of the PhD, regardless of the discipline, are: the formation of scholars, the creation of stewards of the discipline, and the preparation of future faculty. Based on these core objectives, we posited a set of learning objectives for a model PhD curriculum in nursing. We assert that the objectives of the PhD in nursing should include the education of nurses as researchers in the discipline, the preparation of faculty to teach aspiring nurses, the development of experts in nursing practice, and the production of leaders to articulate the history, key assumptions, principles, theories, and commonly held knowledge and "facts" of the discipline of nursing. We explained that health disparities vary among racial and ethnic minorities and that the particular health disparities impacting African American communities should be part of the doctoral curriculum for African Americans pursuing the doctorate, in particular, the PhD in nursing.

Based on these learning objectives, we outlined a model curriculum for the PhD in nursing. Our model curriculum is based on a minimum of 60 semester credits organized around four educational outcomes; namely, the formation of nursing scholars, stewardship of the nursing discipline, preparation of future nursing faculty, and health disparities among African Americans as reflected in the six priorities identified by REACH 2010. Our goal in developing the model PhD curriculum is twofold. First, we contend that the PhD in nursing should conform to the basic tenets of the PhD degree regarding theory, basic research designs, statistics, and dissertations, regardless of the academic discipline. We also endorse the NLN recommendation and the trend in an increasing number of PhD programs of providing formal instruction in teaching the core concepts and practices of the discipline. Second, we sought to encourage discussion about what nurses, African American nurses in particular, should be required to know prior to being qualified as nursing faculty.

We observed that any solution to the shortage of nursing faculty also requires addressing the underrepresentation of males, African Americans, Hispanics, Native Americans, and Asians in the nursing profession. We called for nationwide partnerships similar to the AACN and California Endowment partnership to increase the number of males and minority nurses in the United States. We endorse the NLN Foundation's minority scholarship program. Finally, we assert that until there is an increase in the number of schools and departments of nursing offering doctoral degrees at historically black colleges and universities, the impact on the underrepresentation of African American nursing faculty will be negligible.

References

Amaro, D., Abriam-Yago, K., & Yoder, M. (2006). Perceived barriers for ethnically diverse students in nursing programs. *Journal of Nursing Education, 45*(7), 247-254.

American Association of Colleges of Nursing (AACN). (2005). [Mean age of retirement of full-time doctorally prepared nurse faculty]. Unpublished data.

American Association of Colleges of Nursing. (2006). State legislative initiatives to address nursing shortage. *Issues Bulletin, October.* Washington, DC: Author. Retrieved from http://www.aacn.nche.edu/Publications/issues/Oct06.htm

American Association of Colleges of Nursing. (2008). *Nursing Fact Sheet.* Retrieved from http://www.aacn.nche.edu/Media/FactSheets/FacultyShortage.htm

American Hospital Association. (2007). *The 2007 state of America's hospitals - Taking the pulse.* Retrieved March 1, 2008, from http://www.aha.org/aha/content/2007/PowerPoint/StateofHospitalsChartPack2007.ppt#407,6,Hospitals face workforce shortages in key care-giving professions

Buerhaus, P., Staiger, D. O., & Auerbach, D. I. (2008). *The future of the nursing workforce in the United States: Data, trends and implications.* Sudbury, MA: Jones and Bartlett.

Carnegie, Elizabeth M. (2005, January/February). Educational preparation of black nurses: A historical perspective. *The Association of Black Nursing Faculty Journal,* 6-7.

Center for Disease Control and Prevention, Department of Health and Human Services, Division of Adult and Community Health (2007) *Racial and ethnic approaches to community health-REACH 2010 community profiles.* Retrieved March 7, 2008 from http://www.cdc.gov/reach/community_profiles/.

Center for Disease Control and Prevention, MMWR (2005, January 14) *Health disparities experienced by black or African Americans --- United States. 54*(01); 1-3 Retrieved March 7, 2008 from http://www.cdc.gov/mmwr/preview/mmwrhtml/mm5401a1.htm.

Council of Graduate Schools (CGS). (2005). *The doctor of philosophy degree: A policy statement.* Washington, DC: Author.

Dohm, A., & Shniper, L. (2007, November). Employment outlook: 2006-16. Occupational employment projections to 2016. *Monthly Labor Review, 130*(11). Retrieved March 2, 2008, from http://www.bls.gov/opub/mlr/2007/11/art5full.pdf

Forde, D. (2008, March 20). Golden State responds to shortage of health care professionals. *Diverse Magazine, 10,* 3, 11.

Gaff, J. G., Pruitt-Logan A. S., & Weibl, R. A. (2006). *Building the faculty we need: Colleges and universities working together.* Washington, DC: Association of American Colleges and Universities.

Golde, C. M. (2006). Preparing stewards of the discipline. In Chris M. Golde & George E. Walker (Eds.), *Envisioning the future of doctoral education: Preparing stewards of the discipline* (pp. 3-20). The Carnegie Foundation for the Advancement of Teaching. San Francisco: Jossey-Bass.

Health Resources and Services Administration. (2006). *The registered nurse population: Findings from the March 2004 National Sample Survey of Registered Nurses.* Retrieved March 12, 2008, from ftp://ftp.hrsa.gov/bhpr/workforce/0306rnss.pdf

Higher Learning Commission, North Central Association of Colleges and Schools. (2006). *Report to the Board of Trustees from the Task Force on the Professional Doctorate.* Retrieved from http://www.ncacihe.org/download/TaskForceProfDocFinal0606.pdf

Hinshaw, A. S. (2001, January 31). A continuing challenge: The shortage of educationally prepared nursing faculty. *Online Journal of Issues in Nursing, 6*(1), Manuscript 3. Retrieved March 9, 2008, from www.nursingworld.org/MainMenuCategories/ANAMarketplace/ANAPeriodicals/OJIN/TableofContents/Volume62001/No1Jan01ShortageofEducationalFaculty.aspx

Journal of Blacks in Higher Education. (2007). Doctorates awarded by historically black universities. *JBHE Weekly Bulletin, January 4, 2007.* Retrieved March 1, 2008, from http://www.jbhe.com/latest/index010407.html

McAllister, P. (Ed.). (2007). *Graduate education: The backbone of American competitiveness and innovation. A report from the Advisory Committee on Graduate Education and American Competiveness.* Washington, DC: Council of Graduate Schools. Retrieved from http://www.cgsnet.org/portals/0/pdf/GR_GradEdAmComp_0407.pdf

Middle States Commission on Higher Education. (2002). *Standards for accreditation and characteristics of excellence in higher education: Standards for accreditation*, p. 35.

Minority Nurse, Vital Signs. (2006, Winter). How do you solve the minority nursing shortage? Put them online! Retrieved March 1, 2008, from http://www.minoritynurse.com/how-do-you-solve-minority-nursing-faculty-shortage-put-them-online

NAS Recruitment Communications. (2008). *NAS Insights: Nursing Shortage Report.* The nursing shortage. Retrieved March 7, 2008, from http://www.nasrecruitment.com/MicroSites/Healthcare/Articles/featureH5a.html

National League for Nursing. (2002, May 18). The preparation of nurse educators. [Position statement]. Retrieved from http://www.nln.org/aboutnln/PositionStatements/preparation051802.pdf

National League for Nursing. (2005). *Nurse faculty shortage fact sheet*. Retrieved October 12, 2008, from http://www.nln.org/governmentaffairs/pdf/nursefacultyshortage.pdf

National League for Nursing. (2006). *Nursing data review, academic year 2004-2005*. New York: Author.

National Opinion Research Center. (2003). *Doctorate recipients from United States universities: Summary report 2002*. Survey of earned doctorates. Chicago: Author.

Nettles, M. T., & Millett, C. M. (2006). *Three magic letters: Getting to Ph.D.* Baltimore: Johns Hopkins University Press.

Nooney, J., & Lacey, L. (2007). Validating HRSA's nurse supply and demand models: A state-level perspective. *Nursing Economics, 25*(5), 270-278.

Nyquist, J. D., & Woodford, B. J. (2000) Re-envisioning the PhD: What concerns do we have? Retrieved from http://www.grad.washington.edu/envision/pdf/concernsBrief.pdf

Office of the Governor. (2008, February 7). Governor O'Malley, health officials address nursing shortage. [Press release.] Retrieved from http://www.governor.maryland.gov/pressreleases/080207.html

Provasnik, S., & Shafer, L. L. (2004). *Historically black colleges and universities, 1976 to 2001*. (NCES 2004-062). Washington, DC: US Department of Education, National Center for Education Statistics.

Pruitt-Logan, A. S., Gaff, J. G. & Jentoft, J. E. (2002). *Preparing future faculty in the sciences and mathematics: A guide for change*. Washington, DC: Association of American Colleges and Universities.

Robert Wood Johnson Foundation. (2007, December 6). [Newsroom]. Center to Champion Nursing to address projected workforce shortage. Retrieved March 7, 2008, from http://www.rwjf.org/newsroom/product.jsp?id=24092

Robinson, B. H. (2005, January/February) Minority Faculty: Another faculty shortage. *Association of Black Nursing Faculty Journal, 1*(16): 3-4.

Southern Regional Education Board (SREB). (2007, April 25). *SREB states face increasing shortage of registered nurses*. [News release]. Retrieved from http://www.sreb.org/main/Publications/PressRel/news1.asp?Code=1157

Stanley, J. M., Capers, C. F., & Berlin, L. E. (2007). Changing the face of nursing faculty: Minority faculty recruitment and retention. *Journal of Professional Nursing, 23*(5), 253-261.

Sullivan Commission. (2004). *Missing persons: Minorities in the health professions.* Retrieved from http://www.aacn.nche.edu/Media/pdf/SullivanReport.pdf

Tucker-Allen, S. (2002). A shortage of minority nurses: A national campaign. *Minority Nurse Newsletter, Winter-Spring.* Retrieved from http://findarticles.com/p/articles/mi_m0MJV/is_1_9/ai_93610996?tag=rbxcra.2.a.2

Tucker-Allen, S. (2003). Increasing minority nurses means increasing minority nursing faculty members. [Editorial]. *Association of Black Nursing Faculty Journal, 14*(1), 1.

U.S. Census Bureau Population Projections. (2004). *U.S. interim projections by age, sex, race, and Hispanic origin, 2000-2050.* Retrieved from http://www.census.gov/ipc/www/usinterimproj/

U.S. Census Bureau Releases. (2005, April 29). *Facts for features & special editions.* (Publication CB05-FFSE 02-2). Retrieved from http://www.census.gov/Press-Release/www/releases/archives/facts_for_features_special_editions/004491.html

Walker, G. E. (2008). Moving doctoral education into the future. In G.E. Walker, C. M. Golde, L. Jones, A. C. Bueschel, & P. Hutchings, *The formation of scholars: Rethinking doctoral education for the twenty-first century* (pp. 1-18). San Francisco: Jossey-Bass.

Yordy, K. D. (2006). *The nursing faculty shortage: A crisis for health care.* Princeton, NJ: Robert Wood Johnson Foundation.

CHAPTER 9

HEALTH DISPARITIES RESEARCH: THE ISSUE FOR HBCU PhD NURSING PROGRAMS

Pamela V. Hammond, PhD, RN, FAAN, ANEF
Janet Simmons Rami, PhD, RN

INTRODUCTION

Historically black colleges and universities (HBCUs) have had a long history of providing an education for all people, but most especially African Americans. The focus of HBCUs has traditionally been on teaching, but there has always been an acknowledgment of the academic triad: teaching, research, and service. Despite placing a greater emphasis on teaching, large numbers of HBCUs over the past few decades have made research an important part of the academic milieu. HBCUs have promoted a research agenda that contributes significantly to the body of knowledge on a myriad of topics, such as improving the health and well-being of minorities and underserved communities as well as other issues affecting disenfranchised populations.

Two historically black universities that have created an environment that promotes research and rewards faculty researchers are Hampton University in Virginia and Southern University and A&M College in Louisiana. These two institutions have increased the research base of faculty and students, both undergraduates and graduates, and that research base covers a variety of topics. For example, at Hampton University scientists are making history by studying noctilucent clouds that form in Earth's polar regions and conducting research on nuclear, particle, and optical physics as well as material science, nanotechnology, genomics, and alternative fuels and energy. Hampton University is preparing for a 2010 opening of its Proton Therapy Institute, a proton-beam cancer therapy treatment, research, and technology center, the only one of its kind in the Commonwealth of Virginia and the mid-Atlantic states. Researchers at Southern University are well known for their involvement in astronomy and astrophysics, consumer science, computer technology, energy-saving textiles and technologies, health, and national security issues. Southern is also a partner in the Science Mission to Plant Earth (SMPE) project that promotes the use of technology in teaching environmental science. In addition to conducting cutting-edge research, both Hampton and Southern are leaders among HBCUs in the study of nursing. These institutions have initiated PhD programs in nursing that are developing researchers, mostly African Americans, with skills in the study of disparities and other issues impacting health. The graduates complete the curricula with evolving programs of research in the study of families and vulnerable populations.

Hampton University and Southern University Schools of Nursing used the *Indicators of Quality in Research-Focused Doctoral Programs in Nursing* published by the American Association of Colleges of Nursing (AACN, 2001) in implementing and evaluating their PhD programs. This document covers five significant areas according to AACN: faculty, programs of study, resources, students, and evaluation. In 2006, faculty added to their evaluation tools the National League for Nursing's (NLN) Excellence in Nursing Education Model. The model provided an opportunity to critique the programs' quality in eight areas considered core by NLN: program standards, faculty, students, administrators, teaching methods, resources, curriculum, and recognition programs. The Hampton and Southern faculties have used these evaluation documents to insure that both HBCUs provide high quality, research-focused doctoral programs that compare favorably with other doctoral programs nationally.

This chapter outlines the development and growth of the only doctoral nursing programs located in HBCUs, but more importantly there is a description of the research agendas at these two institutions. The programs have produced graduates for less than a decade. Featured in this chapter will be a discussion of the research conducted by those graduates in the form of their dissertations. The Hampton program focuses on family and family-related research, while the Southern program emphasizes research on vulnerable women and children and issues related to public policy. In these two universities that continue to have a strong emphasis on teaching, Hampton and Southern together have increased the study of disparate health conditions among racial and ethnic minorities through research conducted by both its faculty and its students.

HEALTH DISPARITIES

While many Americans are just learning about health disparities from both professional and lay media, the issue of health disparities is not new. Health disparities have been a concern for decades, because health care professionals have long known that many diseases, illnesses, and other maladies disproportionately affect members of racial and ethnic minority groups (Institute of Medicine, 2006). Since its inception in 1979, *Healthy People 2010* has been used to guide the nation's attention on disparate health conditions among various population groups in an effort to improve the health of all people (Institute of Medicine, 1999). Greater health risks exist among people who are poor, underserved, or otherwise disadvantaged. Health disparities in minority groups do not merely constitute differences in the incidence and prevalence of disease and mortality, they include inadequate access to health care, and inequality in the nature of treatment provided (Institute of Medicine, 2006; Virginia Department of Health, 2006). Health disparities have also been found to be linked to the quality of the patient-physician relationships, especially when the person providing care lacks cultural sensitivity to the needs of the population being served (Saha, Arbelaez, & Cooper, 2003; van Ryn & Fu, 2003). Baldwin (2003) posits that racial disparities exist, in part, because historically minorities have had a lack of input into the delivery of care that they receive, which may be related to the underrepresentation of minorities in the health professions.

The National Center for Health Statistics (2007) identified the top 10 causes of death for all Americans as diseases of the heart; cancer; cerebrovascular diseases; chronic lower respiratory diseases; unintentional injuries; diabetes mellitus; Alzheimer's disease; influenza and pneumonia; nephritis, nephritic syndrome, and nephrosis; and septicemia. The leading causes of death in the United States for African Americans are heart disease, cancer, and stroke (National Center for Health Statistics, 2007). Factors such as receiving inadequate and delayed health care, facing greater health risks, and living in poverty have been shown to influence morbidity and mortality. Minority populations have differences in health outcomes and, according to the Institute of Medicine (2006), minorities differ from whites on many health indicators, such as infant mortality, cancer mortality, diabetes, renal disease, and stroke. The age-adjusted death rate for African Americans exceeds those of whites: 38 percent for stroke, 28 percent for heart disease, 27 percent for cancer, and over 700 percent for HIV disease (National Center for Health Statistics, 2002).

The *Healthy People 2010* objectives highlight care through health promotion and disease prevention for all ages by encouraging individual responsibility for personal well-being through nutrition, stress reduction, avoidance of drugs, exercise, and moderate alcohol and tobacco intake (Institute of Medicine, 1999). Preventive activities have their greatest yields in communities where there are barriers to health care access, and cultural sensitivities and factors affecting morbidity and mortality are addressed. Minorities traditionally have had less access to preventive health care (Carter-Pokras & Baquet, 2002). To address health care disparities, both providers and consumers must be involved, and prevention strategies should include outreach, education, cultural competency initiatives, appropriate materials, and disease management initiatives (Virginia Department of Health, 2006). Further, health services interventions should be designed to target select populations while focusing on contributing factors or the prevalent disease conditions found in the targeted community (Cooper, Hill, & Powe, 2002).

African Americans are underrepresented in the health professions, but overrepresented in those populations who are in need of health care (U.S. Department of Health and Human Services [DHHS], 2003). Further, health-seeking behaviors of African Americans are influenced by the lack of multicultural diversity among health care providers (DHHS, 2000). According to the Sullivan Commission (2004), the nation will benefit from a diversified health care workforce that is culturally sensitive, because the nation's health benefits when people from different backgrounds explore different approaches and solutions to the same problem. The report further indicates health professions schools have not adequately addressed diversity among their student bodies, which bear little resemblance to the people they will serve.

The state and national health status indicators reported by the National Center for Health Statistics (2008) reflect an urgent need for increased numbers of minority nurses to care for the nation. A goal of *Healthy People 2010* is to increase the percentage of degrees in the health professions awarded to members of underrepresented racial and ethnic minority groups (DHHS, 2000). *Healthy People 2010* Objective 1.8 states that health professions should increase the proportion of degrees awarded to members of underrepresented racial and ethnic groups, which reflects the goal both universities discussed in this chapter have strived to achieve throughout their long history of preparing minority nurses.

In providing an education to greater numbers of minority nurses seeking doctoral degrees, Hampton University and Southern University have implemented curriculums to promote the study of health disparities as evidenced by the dissertation research agendas of its students. DHHS (2000) reports *Healthy People 2010* Objective 1.7, which states that there needs to be an increased number of health professionals schools that include the core competencies in health promotion and disease prevention in their curriculums. This objective definitely relates to the efforts of these two schools to graduate culturally competent and culturally sensitive scholars.

DOCTORALLY PREPARED MINORITY NURSES

As reported in *Healthy People 2010*, more individuals from underrepresented minority populations are needed (DHHS, 2000). To accomplish this objective, more minority students must first be recruited and retained in the health professions (Bessent, 1997; Fleming, 1997). Moving in this direction requires using a range of health care professionals, especially nurses from disadvantaged and/or ethnic minority backgrounds, who are uniquely sensitive to the needs of multicultural families. Minority nurses bring their own experiences and the experiences of those from the communities from which they hail, therefore, they are needed to investigate clinical problems affecting the health of people of color, implement health care activities that are culturally sensitive and culturally appropriate, serve as role models for healthy lifestyles in underserved minority communities, and improve access to care for medically underserved communities.

The percentage of African American registered nurses (RNs) increased 101.3 percent from 1980 (N = 60,845) to 2004 (N = 122,495), but despite this growth African Americans continue to be underrepresented among the RN workforce (Health Resources and Services Administration [HRSA], 2006). HRSA (2006) also reports that African Americans make up 12.2 percent of the U.S. population, but only 4.2 percent of the RN population. Other racial and ethnic groups have similar shortages. The greatest shortage among racial and ethnic minority groups in the RN workforce is among the Hispanic/Latino population. Hispanics/Latinos represent only 1.7 percent of the RN population, but comprise 14.1 percent of the general population. HRSA (2006) reports that Asians, Native Hawaiians, and Pacific Islanders comprise 3.1 percent of the RN population (4.1 percent of the U.S.

population), and 0.3 percent of the RN population is American Indian or Alaska Native (0.7 percent of the U.S. population). The number of minority RNs produced has not reflected the number of minorities in the general population.

Total enrollment in research-focused doctoral programs was 3,508 nationally in 2007 (Fang, Htut, & Bednash, 2008). The total number of African American students enrolled was 357 (10.2 percent). White students were the largest group of students enrolled in doctoral programs (79.0 percent). Graduations from research-focused doctoral programs totaled 431 in 2007. The 30 African Americans who were part of that total represented seven percent. During that same period of time, Hampton University and Southern University graduated a total of eight students, which represented two percent of the total number of graduates from research institutions. Hampton and Southern together graduated 17 percent (six) of the national total of African American graduates that year. It is important that nursing programs not only increase the numbers of underrepresented minorities enrolled as called for in *Healthy People 2010*, but it is also necessary to increase the numbers of those minorities who graduate. Tables 9-1 and 9-2 provide specific data on the enrollment and graduation rates of minority students in graduate nursing programs.

Table 9-1

Type of Degree by Race/Ethnicity of Students Enrolled, Excluding Non-U.S. Residents and Unknown Ethnicities, Fall 2007

	MASTERS	RESEARCH FOCUSED	DNP	POST DOCTORAL
SCHOOLS REPORTING	429	113	53	31
RACE/ETHNICITY				
American Indian or Alaskan Native (%)	353 (0.6)	35 (1.0)	9 (0.5)	0
Asian (%)	3,379 (6.2)	217 (6.2)	50 (2.8)	4 (6.1)
Black or African American (%)	6,436 (11.8)	357 (10.2)	152 (8.6)	8 (12.1)
Hispanic or Latino (%)	2,635 (4.8)	126 (3.6)	64 (3.6)	0
White (%)	41,795 (76.6)	2,773 (79.0)	1,495 (84.5)	54 (81.8)
Total	54,598	3,508	1,770	66
Total Minority (%)	12,803 (23.4)	735 (21.0)	275 (15.5)	12 (18.2)

Source: Fang, D., Htut, A., & Bednash, G. D. (2008). *2007-2008 Enrollment and Graduations in Baccalaureate and Graduate Programs in Nursing*. Washington, DC: American Association of Colleges of Nursing.

Table 9-2

Type of Degree by Race/Ethnicity of Graduates, Excluding Non-U.S. Residents and Unknown Ethnicities, August 1, 2006 to July 31, 2007

	MASTERS	RESEARCH FOCUSED	DNP	POST DOCTORAL
SCHOOLS REPORTING	429	113	53	31
RACE/ETHNICITY				
American Indian or Alaskan Native (%)	86 (0.6)	1	0	0
Asian (%)	805 (5.8)	21 (4.9)	3 (2.6)	1 (11.8)
Black or African American (%)	1,421 (10.2)	30 (7.0)	6 (5.3)	1 (5.9)
Hispanic or Latino (%)	650 (4.7)	11 (2.6)	3 (2.6)	2
White (%)	10,934 (78.7)	368 (85.4)	102 (89.5)	12 (70.6)
Total	13,896	431	114	17
Total Minority (%)	2,962 (21.3)	63 (14.6)	12 (10.5)	5 (29.4)

Source: Fang, D., Htut, A., & Bednash, G. D. (2008). *2007-2008 Enrollment and Graduations in Baccalaureate and Graduate Programs in Nursing.* Washington, DC: American Association of Colleges of Nursing.

Minority nurses are relatively few in number, but are significant contributors to the provision of health services in this country and leaders in the development of models of care that address the unique needs of racial/ethnic minorities. Hampton University School of Nursing and Southern University School of Nursing have undertaken the challenge of increasing the numbers of doctorally prepared nurses who can conduct research focusing on issues related to reducing health disparities and meeting other health care needs of a global society. Both programs have been developed in response to a need to increase the representation of minorities in nursing.

HAMPTON UNIVERSITY (HAMPTON)

Overview

Hampton University, historically black and privately endowed, was founded in 1868 and is the oldest nonsectarian, coeducational, postsecondary institution in the Commonwealth of Virginia. Hampton University offers 52 bachelor's degree programs, 21 master's degree programs, a specialist in education program, two professional doctorates: doctor of pharmacy and doctor of physical therapy, and three PhD programs: physics (medical, nuclear, optical, plasma), nursing, and atmospheric and planetary sciences. There are over 5,000 undergraduate and nearly 1,000 graduate and professional students enrolled at Hampton University. Approximately 88 percent of the students are African American; nearly nine percent are Caucasian, and the remaining three percent are from other racial and ethnic groups.

Nursing has existed at Hampton University since 1891 when the Hampton Training School for Nurses, commonly called Dixie Hospital, was started. Hampton's bachelor of science degree program in nursing is the oldest continuous program in the Commonwealth of Virginia, having been instituted during the 1943-1944 academic year. Hampton University was the first HBCU to offer a master's degree in nursing in 1976. In 2003, the School of Nursing instituted a three-year accelerated baccalaureate program at the newly established Hampton University College of Virginia Beach. The School of Nursing provides primary health care services through the school's Health Mobile, a mobile nursing center, which emphasizes the implementation of health promotion and disease prevention programs for client groups in urban and rural communities. The School of Nursing is approved by the Virginia Board of Nursing and is fully accredited by the National League for Nursing Accrediting Commission and the Commission on Collegiate Nursing Education.

The Doctor of Philosophy in Nursing (PhD Program)

Hampton University School of Nursing enrolled its inaugural class of six PhD nursing students into its doctoral program in 1999, making its program the first of its kind at an HBCU. This program builds upon Hampton's commitment to prepare nursing leaders with a high-quality, value-added education. Further, Hampton received tremendous commitment from other HBCUs to support the PhD nursing program.

The doctoral program builds upon a master's program begun in 1976 and gives Hampton the designation of having the oldest graduate nursing program among HBCUs. The program is eight full-time semesters with a minimum of 60 semester credits: 48 hours of course credits hours beyond the master's degree and 12 dissertation credits. The core courses are quite similar to those that are hallmarks in other research-focused doctoral programs. Courses such as statistics and research-focused content (qualitative and quantitative) are core requirements. Hampton's program, like other PhD nursing programs, provides courses in nursing theory as a basis for developing the groundwork for a dissertation. In Hampton's case, the dissertation is focused on family or family-related research.

As of September 2008, there were 26 students enrolled in the PhD program: 17 (65 percent) African American, one (4 percent) Asian, one (4 percent) Pacific Islander, and seven (27 percent) white. There have been a total of 23 graduates from the program since its inception: 16 (70 percent) African American, six (26 percent) white, and one (4 percent) Asian. The average time needed to graduate from the Hampton program is 3.5 years, and the school's graduates are succeeding in their endeavors as researchers, scholars, and educators. Two graduates have completed postdoctoral studies at Johns Hopkins and the University of Pennsylvania; three graduates are determining their options for postdoctoral studies; two graduates are pursuing postdoctoral studies at the University of Iowa and National Eye Institute, National Institutes of Health; eighteen are teaching in schools of nursing; two are employed in primary care; one has secured a position in government; and three have received competitive funding. The graduates have been actively involved in the evaluation of the Hampton University School of Nursing doctoral program, published in peer-reviewed journals or completed manuscripts, presented dissertation research, and contributed to health disparities literature.

The Hampton University faculty conducted feasibility studies in the planning stages of the doctoral program and noted that potential students' most frequent barriers to enrolling in doctoral education as: inability to leave family and/or geographical location, unable to afford the investment in a higher degree, and unable to afford to leave due to family responsibilities. The PhD program was designed to increase the number of doctorally prepared minority nurses while reducing barriers to obtaining a doctoral degree for those nurses who are unable to earn the doctoral degree due to professional and personal circumstances. Therefore, all of the required courses in the curriculum are offered using distance learning strategies. Students in the program hail from Alabama, Florida, Georgia, Louisiana, Maryland, New York, North Carolina, South Carolina, Virginia, Texas, and Washington, DC. Hampton is committed to continuing to find innovative ways to reduce barriers while educating a diverse nursing workforce.

Hampton's Nursing Research Agenda

Hampton's nursing faculty has long accepted the family as the primary unit of society in need of health promotion, illness prevention, and intervention strategies. The faculty selected family and family-related research as the focus of the PhD program so that graduates would have an understanding of the role of family to the health of a community and, thus, to the health of a nation. Therefore, the study of the family forms the basis for Hampton faculty and graduates to build a research agenda that will help eliminate health disparities. In addition, nursing faculty determined that the focus was narrow enough to be in line with their previous research experience studying African Americans and other minorities. Hampton's experience includes the establishment of a Black Family Institute, an Annual Conference on the Black Family, a Behavioral Sciences Research Center, National Institute of Mental Health funding of three research projects focusing on African American families with nursing faculty as principal investigators, and the establishment of the Center for Minority Family Health.

Nursing faculty members have been recognized nationally for their research and grantsmanship skills. Two nursing faculty members were appointed by the Secretary of Health and Human Services to serve on national advisory boards where research and grant review are a major part of their responsibilities: the National Advisory Council on Minority Health and Health Disparities and the National Committee on Rural Health and Human Services. Two faculty members were appointed by the National Institutes of Health Director as scientific leaders to serve as liaisons between local scientific communities and the Peer Review Working Group of the Advisory Committee to the Director. As such, they gather information from the external community and recommend possible pilot experiments and policy changes affecting the National Institutes of Health.

The School of Nursing's Center for Minority Family Health is a focal point for research about people of color and serves as the research arm of the School of Nursing. The Center is a repository for information on families and places an emphasis on ethnic minority families. Consultations regarding research opportunities and funding mechanisms are provided, as appropriate, to both faculty and students. An annual doctoral residency program is sponsored by the Center for Minority Family Health to disseminate information about research projects on the state of minority health. Through this Center, faculty were funded by the National Center on Minority Health and Health Disparities for the Hampton University Health Disparities Reduction Project, which focused on increasing the numbers of minority faculty and students in health disparities research through a pilot/feasibility funding mechanism.

In 1994, Hampton University School of Nursing and the University of Pennsylvania School of Nursing became research and diversity partners and formed the Hampton-Penn Initiative (Davis, Jemmott, & Hammond, 2005; Hammond, 1998; Hammond & Davis, 2005). This relationship was initiated to meet mutual goals at each school. Hampton saw an association with Penn, a research-intense university, as one way to increase research productivity among its faculty and students. Penn saw an association with Hampton, an HBCU with a history of excellence, as one way to increase the diversity among its faculty and students.

The Teagle Foundation funded the Hampton-Penn Initiative to contribute to faculty development in research at Hampton and to increase the minority presence at Penn. Through this funding, Hampton's nursing faculty was provided opportunities for postdoctoral research study, opportunities to attend an annual Summer Research Institute, and opportunities to collaborate with research mentors. Faculty and selected graduate students from Hampton University and the University of Pennsylvania participated in annual research symposiums held at Hampton University. Penn's faculty served as consultants during the establishment of the PhD program at Hampton. Two African American faculty members and one African American PhD graduate completed postdoctoral education at Penn.

Since its inception, the purpose of the Hampton-Penn Initiative has expanded to include the study of health disparities through joint funding by the National Institute for Nursing Research and the National Center on Minority Health and Health Disparities. The establishment of the Hampton-Penn Center to Reduce Health Disparities has resulted in increased partnered research between the two faculties with undergraduate and graduate students participating in projects that include investigations on HIV prevention, preterm labor, sexual risk behaviors, genetics, obesity, diabetes, and relational aggression. The nursing faculty at Hampton University continues to work with the University of Pennsylvania's nursing faculty through joint research projects and publication activities.

The dissertations completed in the Hampton PhD program are specific to the health of families, particularly minority families, and are geared toward the elimination of health disparities in ethnic and minority communities. The dates, titles, and names of the researchers are listed in Appendix B.

Hampton University pioneered an outstanding doctoral program in a historically black university that rivals other programs of similar size. The Hampton Model has increased the number of minority nurses who have, through their dissertations, conducted independent research projects focusing on family and family-related research and who are serving as nurse educators, administrators, and researchers since graduation. The Model consists of five phases: assess, plan, collaborate, plan, and implement (Hammond & Davis, 2005). A deliberate planning phase to promote and sustain a viable program is a focus of the Model. Faculty members are encouraged to develop position papers on program emphasis and fiscal and human resources development and maintenance. A Doctoral Task Force was established at Hampton to review proposed plans and consultation was obtained from a multidisciplinary group of faculty members. One of the position papers resulted in funding of an educators track within the PhD program. The PhD program was funded by the Department of Health and Human Services, Health Resources and Services Administration, Bureau of Health Professions, Division of Nursing for seven years and can be replicated by other nursing schools using the Hampton Model. Highlights of the Model are listed below and are illustrated in Figure 9-1.

1. Assess support among faculty, administrators, alumni, other allies, and competitors

2. Feasibility studies to determine the need for the program

3. Plan to obtain the "buy-in" of faculty before proceeding by developing a committe structure to support the establishment of the program

4. Determine faculty strengths and weaknesses in the areas of research and grantsmanship

5. Collaborate through the use of consultants, as appropriate

6. Plan to increase the resource base: fiscal and human

7. Implement a manageable program

8. Reevaluate the program annually to insure quality

The Hampton University's School of Nursing's legacy is a blend of trends and traditions. The School of Nursing has been on the cutting edge of higher education and has prepared outstanding leaders for over 118 years. The PhD program at Hampton will continue this legacy.

SOUTHERN UNIVERSITY AND A&M COLLEGE (SOUTHERN)

Overview

Southern University was chartered in April 1880 and was recognized as a land grant college in 1890. In 1914, it was relocated from New Orleans to Baton Rouge, Louisiana. Southern is a publicly supported, coeducational, land-grant, historically black, comprehensive institution that prepares students to compete globally in their respective professions and to engage in advanced study in graduate and professional schools. There are two other campuses, one in Shreveport and one in New Orleans. The University offers 44 bachelor's degrees, one associate degree, 20 masters', and five doctoral degrees. The doctoral programs include the PhD in nursing as well as PhD programs in environmental toxicology, public policy, science/mathematics education, and special education. The enrollment on the Baton Rouge campus averages 9,000 students annually.

The School of Nursing was established in 1985 and admitted a class of 36 undergraduate students in 1986. The bachelor of science in nursing program (BSN) was initially accredited by the National League for Nursing (NLN) in 1991. In 1992, Southern University's master of science in nursing (MSN) program, with a concentration in family nursing, was established. The master's program received initial NLN accreditation in October 1996. The program is approved by the Louisiana State Board of Nursing. Both programs are fully accredited by the National League for Nursing Accrediting Commission and the Commission on Collegiate Nursing Education.

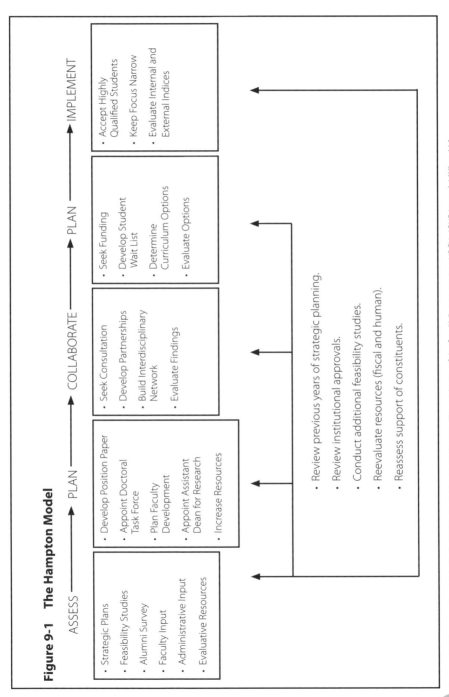

Figure 9-1 The Hampton Model

ASSESS → PLAN → COLLABORATE → PLAN → IMPLEMENT

ASSESS
- Strategic Plans
- Feasibility Studies
- Alumni Survey
- Faculty Input
- Administrative Input
- Evaluative Resources

PLAN
- Develop Position Paper
- Appoint Doctoral Task Force
- Plan Faculty Development
- Appoint Assistant Dean for Research
- Increase Resources

COLLABORATE
- Seek Consultation
- Develop Partnerships
- Build Interdisciplinary Network
- Evaluate Findings

PLAN
- Seek Funding
- Develop Student Wait List
- Determine Curriculum Options
- Evaluate Options

IMPLEMENT
- Accept Highly Qualified Students
- Keep Focus Narrow
- Evaluate Internal and External Indices

- Review previous years of strategic planning.
- Review institutional approvals.
- Conduct additional feasibility studies.
- Reevaluate resources (fiscal and human).
- Reassess support of constituents.

Source. P. V. Hammond and B. L. Davis, (2005). From idea to graduation: The evolution of the first PhD program in a HBCU. *ABNF Journal, 16*(6), p. 116. Copyright 2005 by Tucker Publications, Inc. Reprinted with permission.

The Doctor of Philosophy in Nursing (PhD Program)

Recognizing the need for a PhD program, the administration of the School of Nursing documented the requirements and prepared a strategic plan for the development and implementation of a program. The plan included strengths of the School of Nursing, a needs assessment and a feasibility study, the proposed emphasis of the program, potential students, career paths of the graduates, and attention to the quality indicators of doctoral programs in nursing. The plan also included attention to faculty development, resources needed (library, technology, and support services), potential funding sources, potential community partnerships, and a collaborative agreement with Pennington Biomedical Research Center of Louisiana State University (PBRC), which is nationally recognized for its work in nutrition research and obesity research and education. Plans included facilitation during proposal preparation by an expert consultant in doctoral nursing education. The proposed program was presented to the Louisiana Board of Regents, and in October 2000 the school responded to the recommendations of the Board of Regents. The PhD in nursing program was approved, and in spring 2001 the School of Nursing continued its preparations for program implementation. Southern's nursing program was the first PhD program established in a publicly funded HBCU. However, the environment at Southern is multicultural, multiethnic, and multiracial.

The PhD program builds on the BSN program that has achieved national recognition for educating minority nurses, the MSN in family health nursing, the nurse practitioner program, the nurse-managed center, and the mobile health unit that provides direct access to professional nursing services in non-institutional settings. The program requires completion of 60 credit hours beyond the master's degree and can be completed in three years of full-time study. The curriculum is divided into four content areas (core, focus of study courses, research courses, and cognates) and the dissertation. The program of study includes a practicum in health policy and a required research practicum at PBRC.

The first five students were admitted to the PhD program in fall 2001. The goal of the program is to admit five new students each year. Although most students are from Louisiana, some have come from Texas, Ohio, Mississippi, and Florida. The program has had 16 graduates: 12 (75 percent) African American, four (25 percent) white. Five African American students are at dissertation stage.

Southern's Nursing Research Agenda

The PhD in nursing is a research-oriented doctorate that focuses on the health of vulnerable women and children and issues related to public policy. Though Southern's nursing faculty is keenly aware of the disproportionate representation of minorities among the vulnerable (i.e., those most susceptible to an untoward health state), and sees women and children as a priority, faculty may extend their interests to the vulnerable of other gender, age, racial or ethnic groups. The program prepares scientists whose research in nursing will extend the knowledge base that informs nursing education, nursing practice, and nursing leadership. The School of Nursing's vision is to have a nationally recognized program with an emerging center for nursing research. Included in its goal statements and competencies are the following:

- To provide for an effective research infrastructure to enhance faculty and student scholarship, research, and other creative pursuits
- To place strong emphasis on providing an organizational structure and resources to enhance attainment of educational, research, and public service goals

The competencies of the graduate include the ability to conduct independent research (and to communicate the results of that research) that advances the body of scientific knowledge, and to integrate in-depth knowledge of theory and research into a substantive field of study.

In order to contribute to these goals and competencies, an Office for Nursing Research was established and a director of that office and the graduate nursing program was appointed. The director brought a two-year funded research grant entitled, "Efficacy of a Culturally Sensitive Health Promotion Program to Improve Exercise and Dietary Behaviors in African American Elders with Hypertension." Southern had major responsibility for the first year of the project, which provided necessary funding to help select faculty and students develop the requisite research skills that were used in the study of vulnerable populations. The participating elders, male and female, were experiencing an illness that is one of the leading health problems among African Americans. Such elders require a significant contribution from the family's schedule of time to facilitate an exercise routine and from the family's budget to meet medical and dietary requirements. The co-principal investigator, who was director of the doctoral program in social work at Jackson State University, had major responsibility for the second year of the project.

The dean of the school led an interdisciplinary Adolescent Pregnancy Prevention Research Project that was conducted in collaboration with faculty from Southern's School of Business and School of Public Policy. The School of Nursing received funding for ARM (Access to care - know your Risk - get a Mammogram) and REACH 2010: At the Heart of New Orleans. The current evaluation research project is for "Technology Enhanced Curriculum for Nursing (TECHNE)" and it focuses on the impact of computer-based learning activities and simulated clinical learning experiences on undergraduate nursing students' skill acquisition, overall clinical performance, and critical thinking skills.

Since 2001, the Office of Nursing Research (ONR) has sponsored an annual research symposium that appeals to a national audience. For the past two years, the ONR and Tau Pi Chapter of Sigma Theta Tau International, Honor Society of Nursing® have collaborated in this research event. Each year, students are encouraged to prepare poster presentations and otherwise participate in the implementation of the research symposium agenda. Posters have included content on cancer, tobacco use, substance abuse, responsible sexual behavior, injury and violence, environmental quality, immunizations, and access to health care.

Faculty and students are encouraged to attend research conferences sponsored by regional or national organizations. In addition, students must complete a required research practicum at PBRC. One faculty member studied as a postdoctoral research fellow at PBRC and also completed postdoctoral study at the University of Tennessee at Memphis. Another faculty member is participating in a research emphasis at University of Pittsburgh School of Nursing Center for Research and Chronic Disorders.

Dissertation research at Southern has been on vulnerable women and children, including research that addresses physical activity, overweight and obesity, and mental health, which are three of the leading health indicators that are determinants of the public's health (DHHS, 2000). Other subject areas include social resources, self-care, health promotion, and hypertension, problems common across race, age, and gender. A majority of research participants have been African American. The dissertation titles are listed in Appendix C, along with the year and names of the researchers.

Graduates

Nine of the graduates are educators in colleges or universities (two are in leadership roles). Four of these graduates are in positions at HBCUs. One graduate is in a staff development position in a hospital and teaches a research course in a college as a part-time faculty member. Another graduate is in a leadership role in a health care organization with responsibility in strategic development and empowered decision making, and still another graduate is continuing in the practitioner role with research involvement. In terms of other activities, one graduate has presented her dissertation research on obesity at two conferences. The National Institute of Nursing Research selected one of the graduates to be a fellow in 2007, and this graduate began postdoctoral study in clinical genetics at the University of Iowa in January 2008. Another graduate has been accepted as a fellow in the National Institutes of Health 2008 summer program for research on aging and received an institutional research grant from the American Cancer Society to study colorectal cancer in African American men. All of the graduates have participated in program evaluation, and faculty members have embraced their observations. Clearly, at Southern there is an interest in conducting research on the leading health indicators in the United States and the leading causes of death, especially as they relate to the issue of health disparities. Continuing research in these areas will provide information to direct education, practice, and research that will ultimately contribute to eliminating health disparities.

CONCLUSION

The PhD programs in nursing at Hampton University and Southern University and A&M College have the potential to be replicated by other schools of nursing seeking to build specific research agendas. These programs are built upon philosophies and objectives that undergird existing graduate-level nursing programs. Hampton and Southern's doctoral programs were developed in accord with degree requirements for accrediting/approval agencies in higher education, AACN *Indicators of Quality in Research-Focused Doctoral Programs in Nursing*, and the NLN *Excellence in Nursing Education Model*. The two programs are designed to be supported by core and cognate courses with an interdisciplinary focus and their methodology can be used as a map for beginning a PhD nursing program. Each of the graduates has demonstrated the ability to conduct independent research on families, vulnerable populations, or public policy.

To further develop their programs, Hampton and Southern plan campaigns to increase research in nursing through the funding of endowed chairs, university-sponsored incentives for junior faculty to continue their research careers, and institutional grants for faculty members who want to expand their research agendas or for those who need to change direction. Funding is allocated for faculty travel to present research findings and for an editor to assist in the development of manuscripts for dissemination of research results. Available funds also include monies to bring researchers to both campuses to insure that as many individuals as possible are able to benefit from hearing presentations.

The doctoral programs at Hampton University and Southern University have, at times, operated with a lack of human and fiscal resources: insufficient availability of qualified faculty and lack of financial incentives for students and junior faculty to begin and/or continue their programs of research. What makes these two institutions different is that both have a long history of collaborating with others to make the most of their limited resources. Faculties at Hampton and Southern anticipated these challenges when they sought and received permission to develop PhD programs. These institutions knew that they would have to work harder by carrying an extra load, continually seeking funding, and including part-time and adjunct faculty in their community of scholars, but they took on the challenge with pride. Together, both institutions have produced 39 new doctorally prepared nurses and although the percentages change with each graduating class, both universities have maintained greater than 70 percent African Americans among their graduates. These new graduates have joined the nursing workforce and serve as educators, researchers, and administrators. Historically black colleges and universities were created to fill a niche - Hampton University and Southern University and A&M College are definitely carrying on this longstanding tradition.

REFERENCES

American Association of Colleges of Nursing. (2001). [Position statement]. *Indicators of quality in research-focused doctoral programs in nursing.* Washington, DC: Author.

Baldwin, D. M. (2003, January 31). Disparities in health and health care:Focusing efforts to eliminate unequal burdens. *The Online Journal of Issues in Nursing, 8*(1), Manuscript 1. Retrieved from http://cms.nursingworld.org/MainMenuCategoriesANA MarketplaceANAPeriodicalsOJINTableofContents/Volume82003No1Jan2003Disparitiesin HealthandHealthCare.aspx?css=print

Bessent, H. (1997) Survey of select universities regarding recruitment, enrollment, retention, and graduation of minorities in nursing. In H. Bessent (Ed.), *Strategies for recruitment, retention, and graduation of minority nurses in colleges of nursing* (pp. 19-25). Washington, DC: American Nurses Publishing.

Carter-Pokras, O., & Baquet, C. (2002). What is a health disparity? *Public Health Reports, 117,* 426-434.

Centers for Disease Control. (2006). *Women and heart disease fact sheet.* Retrieved May 15, 2008, from http://www.cdc.gov/DHDSP/library/fs_women_heart.htm

Cooper, L. A., Hill, M. N., & Powe, N. R. (2002). Designing and evaluating interventions to eliminate racial and ethnic disparities in health care. *Journal of General Internal Medicine, 17,* 477-486.

Davis, B. L., Sweet-Jemmott, L., & Hammond, P.V. (2005, Summer). Anatomy of collaboration: Sustaining support for leadership in scholarship. *NBNA News,* 25-26.

Fang, D., Htut, A., & Bednash, G. D. (2008). *2007-2008 enrollment and graduations in baccalaureate and graduate programs in nursing.* Washington, DC: American Association of Colleges of Nursing.

Fleming, J. W. (1997). Ensuring ethnic and racial diversity in nursing. In H. Bessent (Ed.), *Strategies for recruitment, retention, and graduation of minority nurses in colleges of nursing* (pp. 19-25). Washington, DC: American Nurses Publishing.

Hammond, P. V. (1998, Spring). Increasing the number of doctorally prepared African American nurses. *NLN Research and Policy: PRISM, 1,* 10.

Hammond, P. V., & Davis, B. L. (2005). From idea to graduation: The evolution of the first PhD program in a HBCU. *ABNF Journal, 16*(6), 112-117.

Health Resources and Services Administration. (2003). *Changing demographics: Implications for physicians, nurses, and other health workers.* Rockville, MD: Author.

Health Resources and Services Administration. (2006). *The registered nurse population. Findings from the March 2004 National Sample Survey of Registered Nurses.* Rockville, MD: Author.

Institute of Medicine. (1999). *Leading health indicators for healthy people 2010: Final report.* Washington, DC: National Academies Press.

Institute of Medicine. (2006). *Examining the health disparities research plan of the National Institutes of Health: Unfinished business.* Washington, DC: National Academies Press.

National Center for Health Statistics (2002). *Health, United States, 2002: With chartbook on trends in the health of Americans.* Hyattsville, MD: Author.

National Center for Health Statistics (2007). *Health, United States, 2007: With chartbook on trends in the health of Americans.* Hyattsville, MD: Author.

National Center for Health Statistics. (2008). *Fast stats: A to Z.* Retrieved May 15, 2008, from http://www.cdc.gov/nchs/fastats/Default.htm

National League for Nursing. (2006). *Excellence in nursing education model.* New York: Author.

Saha, S., Arbelaez, J. J., & Cooper, L. A. (2003). Patient-physician relationships and health disparities in the quality of health care. *American Journal of Public Health, 93*(10), 1713-1719.

Sullivan Commission (2004). *Missing persons: Minorities in the health professions.* Retrieved from http://www.aacn.nche.edu/Media/pdf/SullivanReport.pdf

U.S. Department of Health and Human Services. (2000). *Healthy people 2010: Understanding and improving health* (2nd ed.). Washington, DC: U.S. Government Printing Office.

van Ryn, M., & Fu, S. S. (2003). Paved with good intentions: Do public health and human service providers contribute to racial/ethnic disparities in health? *American Journal of Public Health, 93*(2), 248-255.

Virginia Department of Health. (2006). *Chronic disease in Virginia: A comprehensive data report.* Richmond, VA: Division of Chronic Disease Prevention and Control.

ACKNOWLEDGMENTS

The Hampton University PhD nursing program was supported by funds from the Division of Nursing, Bureau of Health Professions, Health Resources and Services Administration, Department of Health and Human Services under grant number D09HP00247, Advanced Nursing Education for $1,669,745. The authors also acknowledge the W. K. Kellogg Foundation, the Delta Sigma Theta Sorority, Inc., and Dr. William R. Harvey, president of Hampton University, for their support in making the first PhD in nursing program at an HBCU a reality.

APPENDIX A
AUTHOR PROFILES

PAMELA V. HAMMOND, PhD, RN, FAAN, ANEF

Dr. Hammond is Provost at Hampton University in Hampton, Virginia. She is the immediate past Dean of the School of Nursing at Hampton University. Dr. Hammond has held a variety of leadership positions and dedicated herself to promoting the education and well-being of students and the health and welfare of underserved, abused, and neglected individuals. Her most notable appointments have been to the National Advisory Council on Minority Health and Health Disparities, National Library of Medicine Environmental Health Information Partnership, Virginia Board of Nursing, and the Advisory Council on the Future of Nursing in Virginia. She has authored and co-authored articles and chapters on a variety of topics, including doctoral education, recruitment and retention of minority students, and child abuse and neglect. Dr. Hammond is a program evaluator for the National League for Nursing Accrediting Commission. Through Dr. Hammond's efforts, Hampton University implemented the first PhD program in nursing at a historically black college or university in 1999, resulting in an increase in the numbers of doctorally prepared racial and ethnic minority nurses.

SPENCER R. BAKER, PhD, CCFC

Dr. Baker is Professor and Coordinator of the Graduate Program in Counseling at Hampton University in Hampton, Virginia. A research scientist with the Behavioral Science Research Center, College of Education and Continuing Studies, Hampton University, Dr. Baker's primary research interests include adolescent cognitive development; adolescent behavior problems, including development of psychopathologies; and the antecedents of adult personality. His research focuses on the individual in a social context and requires using advanced statistical procedures of multilevel analyses with covariance structure modeling. He has presented at national and international conferences and serves on review panels for the National Institute of Mental Health, National External Advisory Committee for the Hampton-Penn Center to Reduce Health Disparities, and Hampton University Health Disparities Reduction Project.

RICHARDEAN BENJAMIN, PhD, PMHCNS-BC, MPH, ANEF

Dr. Benjamin is Assocaite Dean, College of Health Sciences at Old Dominion University in Norfolk, Virginia. She is the immediate past Chair of the School of Nursing at Old Dominion University. Dr. Benjamin has been a nurse educator for over 27 years and taught courses in psychiatric-mental health nursing, community health nursing, and epidemiology. She is a former American Nurse Association Minority Fellow, Kellogg Project LEAD Fellow, and participant in the Salzburg Seminar on Cultural Diversity held in Salzburg, Austria. She has served as principal investigator of funded grants and programs, presented at numerous professional conferences in the United States and abroad, and authored and co-authored journal articles and book chapters on distance education and the use of simulation to enhance cultural competency of nurses. Dr. Benjamin completed a postdoctoral fellowship in psychiatric epidemiology at the Western Psychiatric Institute and Clinic at the University of Pittsburgh.

JANICE GILYARD BREWINGTON, PhD, RN, FAAN

Dr. Brewington is Chief Program Officer for the National League for Nursing in New York. Dr. Brewington has served as provost and vice chancellor for academic affairs, assistant dean and interim dean in the School of Nursing and associate vice chancellor for academic affairs/institutional planning, assessment, and research at North Carolina Agricultural and Technical State University. She has received many professional honors and awards; been involved with national and international research activities; led numerous grant and special funding projects; and published in refereed journals, books, and other publications. Her global activities have included outreach programs in Egypt, women in leadership and health care projects in Thailand, and women's health issues in Africa.

BERTHA L. DAVIS, PhD, RN, FAAN, ANEF

Dr. Davis is Professor of Nursing and Director of the Hampton-Penn Center to Reduce Health Disparities at Hampton University School of Nursing in Hampton, Virginia. Dr. Davis' research focusing on reducing health disparities among racial and ethnic minorities was funded by the National Institute of Nursing Research and National Center on Minority Health and Health Disparities. She was funded by the National Institute of Mental Health for research relating to African American families coping with stress, the role of ethnicity in eating disorders, and training grants for psychiatric-mental health nursing. She received the Isabelle Stewart Award for Excellence in the Teaching of Nursing from the National League for Nursing, E. L. Hamm Sr. Teaching Award, B. C. Powders Teaching Award, a commendation from the Virginia Senate for excellence in nursing education, and earned the rank of lieutenant colonel (retired) in the U.S. Army Reserve Nurse Corps. Dr. Davis has also served on the Human Resources Advisory Committee and Board of Medical Assistance Services for the Commonwealth of Virginia.

MARY H. HILL, DSN, RN

Dr. Hill is Associate Dean and Professor, Division of Nursing, College of Pharmacy, Nursing and Allied Health Sciences at Howard University in Washington, DC. Formerly dean and professor of the School of Nursing at Alcorn State University, Natchez, Mississippi, Dr. Hill's publications have focused on diversity in organizations and major health problems experienced by African Americans. Dr. Hill received a HUD grant in response to Hurricaine Katrina, Building Healthy Communities Through Partnerships, and a Teacher of the Year Award. She has served on the Southern Regional Education Board Council on Collegiate Education for Nursing, National Network for Nurse Managed Centers, and Southwest Mississippi Area Health Education Center. Dr. Hill also served as a member of the American Association of Colleges of Nursing Patient Safety Task Force that developed *Hallmark of Quality and Patient Safety: Recommended Baccalaureate Competencies and Curricular Guidelines to Assure High Quality and Safe Patient Care*. In addition, she has served as a Malcolm Baldrige National Quality Award Examiner, National League for Nursing Accrediting Commission (NLNAC) Program Evaluator and a member of NLNAC Evaluation Review Panel for Baccalaureate and Master's Programs.

DELROY M. LOUDEN, PhD, FRSH

Dr. Louden is Professor and Principal Investigator, Office of Research, Development, Planning and Coordination at Lincoln University of the Commonwealth of Pennsylvania in Lincoln University, Pennsylvania. Dr. Louden has over 25 years of experience working in international academic settings and the nonprofit community. A former Fulbright Scholar, he has held academic appointments in Nigeria, the Caribbean, England, Canada, and the United States. Dr. Louden has served as a consultant to the Ministry of Health, Government of Anguilla, West Indies, and has provided consultations to the Substance Abuse and Mental Health Administration for Project Integration of HIV/AIDS, Substance Abuse, Mental Health, and Hepatitis. He serves as a grant reviewer for SAMHSA, HRSA, and OMH Bilingual/Bicultural Service Demonstration Program and developed chart review instruments for CBOs providing services to HIV/AIDS clients in Washington, DC.

BEVERLY MALONE, PhD, RN, FAAN

Dr. Malone is Chief Executive Officer for the National League for Nursing in New York. Dr. Malone's career has combined policy, education, administration, and clinical practice. In 1996, she was elected for two terms to serve as president of the American Nurses Association. In 2000, she became deputy assistant secretary for health within the US Department of Health and Human Services, the highest position so far held by any nurse in the United States government. From June 2001 to January 2007, Dr. Malone served as general secretary of the Royal College of Nursing (RCN), the United Kingdom's largest professional union of nurses. She represented the RCN at the pan-European nursing body, the European Federation of Nurses Associations; Commonwealth Nurses Federation; and International Council of Nurses with the RCN president. Dr. Malone is lending her professional stature to the latest phase of the renowned Harvard Nurses' Health Study, joining the initiative's select Advisory Committee by special invitation.

EARLENE B. MERRILL, EdD, RN, CNE

Dr. Merrill is Professor of Nursing and Director of Kinship Care at Coppin State University in Baltimore, Maryland. Dr. Merrill specializes in community health and has had experience in nursing education, administration, and research. She developed a mentoring program for students by coordinating the efforts of nursing alumni and has received gubernatorial appointments to committees and boards. Dr. Merrill is a member of the Maryland Board of Nursing and has served on the Faculty Issues Sub-Committee of the Maryland Commission on the Crisis in Nursing. Dr. Merrill has also served as an evaluator for the National League for Nursing Accrediting Commission. She has published articles and book reviews in addition to serving on several editorial boards and actively participating in professional organizations. Dr. Merrill has been successful in obtaining funds for projects focusing on grandparent families and HIV/AIDS.

JANET SIMMONS RAMI, PhD, RN

Dr. Rami is Dean and Professor at the School of Nursing, Southern University and A & M College in Baton Rouge, Louisiana. Dr. Rami has served as dean of the School of Nursing at Southern University at Baton Rouge since its inauguration in 1986. She has led the school in the development of BSN and MSN programs and the first PhD in nursing program in the state of Louisiana. She is nationally recognized for her success in educating minority students and providing access to health services for underserved populations through the school's mobile health clinics. Dean Rami's publications address educating minority students for the health professions and helping the underserved gain access to health care. She has served on the Board of Directors of the Louisiana State Nurses Association and currently serves on the National Advisory Council on Nurse Education and Practice and the Louisiana Health Works Commission. NurseWeek magazine named her one of its "Nurse Heroes for 2007" for her leadership in aiding Katrina evacuees.

MAURICE C. TAYLOR, PhD, JD

Dr. Taylor is Vice President for University Operations at Morgan State University in Baltimore, Maryland. Dr. Taylor is the immediate past dean for the School of Graduate Studies at Morgan State University. He has also served as the secretary of the Conference of Southern Graduate Schools, and former president of the Council of Historically Black Graduate Schools. Dr. Taylor is chair of the Graduate Record Examination Board and a member of the Executive Committee of the Board of Trustees at Juniata College. He has served as an attorney in the law firm of Gordon, Feinblatt, Rothman, Hoffberger & Hollander in Baltimore, Maryland. He received continuing professional training through Harvard University's Institute for Educational Management and as a Fellow in the NAFEO Kellogg Leadership Program for Minority Serving Institutions. Dr. Taylor has conducted research and published on a variety of topics focusing on historically black and minority serving institutions, community engagement and partnerships, board relationships, and graduate education.

SANDRA MILLON UNDERWOOD PhD, RN, CHN, FAAN

Dr. Underwood is American Cancer Society Oncology Nursing Professor, Northwestern Mutual Life Research Scholar, and Professor at the University of Wisconsin Milwaukee, College of Nursing in Milwaukee, Wisconsin. Dr. Underwood's research is focused on cancer education, cancer prevention and control, and management of risks that affect many at-risk and underserved populations. She has received awards to support her research from the National Cancer Institute, American Cancer Society, Susan G. Komen Foundation for the Cure, Sigma Theta Tau International®, UWM Center on Race and Ethnicity, and UWM Urban Research Center. Dr. Underwood is the founding director of the UWM House of Peace Community Nursing Center. She has authored and co-authored papers focused on cancer prevention and control among minority, underserved, and at-risk populations. Dr. Underwood has had distinguished appointments to the National Institutes of Health Council of Councils, National Cancer Advisory Board, National Institute of Nursing Research Advisory Council, National Cancer Policy Board, Department of Defense Prostate Cancer Integration Panel, and National Advisory Board of the American Cancer Society.

WILLAR F. WHITE-PARSON, PhD, APRN, BC, FAAN

Dr. White-Parson is a Nursing Consultant and former Professor and Chair of Nursing at Norfolk State University in Norfolk, Virginia. Dr. White-Parson has been a nurse educator for more than 32 years. Dr. White-Parson has been an advocate for faculty mentoring and developed mentoring programs for faculty in both urban and rural institutions of higher education. Her leadership experience is in program development, curriculum development, teaching-learning strategies, and the accreditation process at both the departmental and university levels. Her research focuses on underrepresented populations including minority students, faculty, communities, women, children, and youth. She has more than 21 invited papers, presentations, and publications in referred journals and a vast amount of expertise in grantsmanship due to her experience writing and serving as a peer reviewer for the US Department of Health and Human Services and other agencies. Dr. White-Parson is also a nurse psychotherapist in private practice and is the CEO and president of Behavioral Health Care Resources in Norfolk, Virginia.

APPENDIX B

PhD DISSERTATIONS:
HAMPTON UNIVERSITY SCHOOL
OF NURSING, 2002 - 2009

Year	Student
2009	Figueroa, Lydia. Spiritual perspectives and comfort levels of African American families and mental health nurses within the context of depression.
2009	Barker, Melinda. Hope, self-care and quality of life in selected clients diagnosed with chronic hepatitis C.
2008	Ramsey, Carolyn P. Advance directives: Young adult African American family members' perception, knowledge, attitudes, and utilization.
2008	Cody-Conner, Crystal. Perceptions of elder abuse among African American elders and African American family members.
2008	Barron, Michelle S. Relationship of depression and stress to social support among family caregivers of adults with hepatitis C genotype 1.
2008	Eaton, Phyllis M. Coping strategies of family members of hospitalized psychiatric patients.
2008	Nicholson-Gillis, Shelita. Lived experiences of selected African American grandmothers raising their grandchildren.
2008	Nance, Kimya Du Ewa. Psychosocial adjustment and maternal role activities among mothers receiving hemodialysis for end-stage renal disease.
2007	Johnson, Lowanda, D. Self-care practices and dependent care activities of African American single mothers.
2007	Roberts, Dionne, S. A nurse-client interaction on adherence to a hypertensive regimen.
2007	Saligan, Leorey, N. Living with ocular sarcoidosis: A Roy adaptation model-based study.
2007	Daniels, Lawrence, W. An investigation of the child passenger safety knowledge of selected caregivers.
2007	Gibbons, Mary, E. The relationship between hope and self-efficacy to health promoting behaviors among adults with selected chronic illness.
2007	Johnson-Spruill, Ida. The relationships among health beliefs, quality of care, and health outcomes in Gullah families with type 2 diabetes.
2007	Gomes, Melissa, M. Peer relational aggression victimization experienced by African American adolescent females.
2006	Allen, Deborah, C. Coping experiences of parents with chronically ill children.

2005   Tillerson-Lane, Crystal. Evaluating the efficacy of a behavior modification program in overweight African-American adolescents.

2005   Gipson-Jones, Trina, L. The relationship between work-family conflict, job satisfaction, and psychological well-being.

2004   Hurst, Charlotte. The relationship between social support and self-care agency and self-care practices of African American women who are HIV-positive.

2004   Swann, Edith. Improving the functional status of minority mothers with human immunodeficiency virus (HIV) infection through a comprehensive medication adherence program.

2003   Orton, Charmaine, C. The relationship of hope and self-care in single low income African American mothers.

2003   Cannon, Sheila, J. Caregiving of African American daughters: Applying   the Neuman's systems model.

2002   Henderson, Phyllis. African American women coping with breast cancer: A qualitative analysis.

APPENDIX C

PhD Dissertations:
Southern University and
A&M College School of Nursing,
2004 - 2009

APPENDIX C

Year	Student
2009	Jefferson, Lenetra. Exploring effects of therapeutic massage and patient teaching in diaphragmatic breathing on blood pressure, stress and anxiety in hypertensive African American women: An intervention study.
2009	Wells, Janie. Self-Efficacy, Social support, hemodialysis knowledge and medical adherence in African Americans diagnosed with end stage renal disease.
2008	Simmonds, Gwenneth C. Sexual refusal/negotiation skills, educational aspirations, and intent to be sexually active: Is there a difference between Southern and Midwestern adolescents?
2008	Smith, Charlene Brown. Evaluating the effectiveness of a culturally sensitive educational program in increasing breast cancer knowledge and screening practices among African American women.
2008	Bennett, Betty Clavijo. Correlational study of minority women's symptom experience with perimenopause and myocardial infarction.
2007	Anderson, Stacie. Knowledge, spirituality, and cancer fatalism as predictors of breast cancer screening practices for African American and Caucasian women.
2006	Cady, Faye W. Perceived caregiver burden and coping strategies used by informal caregivers of adults with developmental disabilities.
2006	Brannagan, Kim B. The role of event related stress, perceived exertion, exercise self-efficacy, and demographic factors in predicting physical activity among college freshmen: Path analysis.
2005	Lewis Trabeaux, Shirleen. The effects of age, physical health, and social resources on self-care capacity among community dwelling older women.
2005	Godley, Linda H. Perceived health status, perceived self-efficacy, and health-promoting practices related to nutrition and physical activity among overweight and obese rural African American women.
2005	Powell-Young, Yolanda. Obesity, self-perception, and health promoting behaviors among African-American adolescent females: A prediction equation.
2005	Baker, Janelle R. The relationship between acculturation and health conception on health promoting behaviors among older African-American women.
2004	Bienemy, Cynthia T. Examining relationships between chronic stress, clinical depression, and blood pressure in clinically diagnosed hypertensive African American women.

2004   Ellis, Joan A. The effects of an 8-week school based intervention on obesity, cardiovascular fitness, and nutritional knowledge in fourth grade students.

2004   Ferdinand, Daphne P. Obesity, psychological factors, and the metabolic syndrome in African American women: A correlational study.

2004   Webb, Shelia J. Development and exploration of culturally-enhanced breast health measures and the relationship of selected cultural attributes to knowledge, beliefs, and behaviors for early breast cancer detection among African American women.